C. H. (Charles Haddon) Spurgeon

Autobiography of Charles H. Spurgeon

Vol. II

C. H. (Charles Haddon) Spurgeon

Autobiography of Charles H. Spurgeon
Vol. II

ISBN/EAN: 9783337042011

Printed in Europe, USA, Canada, Australia, Japan

Cover: Foto ©ninafisch / pixelio.de

More available books at **www.hansebooks.com**

THE AUTOBIOGRAPHY

OF

CHARLES H. SPURGEON

COMPILED FROM
HIS DIARY, LETTERS, AND RECORDS

BY
HIS WIFE
AND
HIS PRIVATE SECRETARY

"The law of truth was in his mouth, and iniquity was not found in his lips; he walked with Me in peace and equity, and did turn many away from iniquity."—MALACHI II. 6

VOL. II.   1854-1860

CURTS & JENNINGS
CINCINNATI   CHICAGO   ST. LOUIS
1899

CONTENTS OF VOL. II.

C. H. SPURGEON'S AUTOBIOGRAPHY.

CHAPTER XXXIV.

Love, Courtship, and Marriage.

By Mrs. C. H Spurgeon.

HEN I came to deal with the sacred and delicate task of writing the following chapters, to record the events of the years 1854 and '1855, two courses only seemed to open before me ;—the one, to conceal, as gracefully as possible, under conventional phraseology and common-place details, the tender truth and sweetness of our mutual love-story :—the other, to write out of the fulness of my very soul, and suffer my pen to describe the fair visions of the past as, one by one, they grew again before my eyes into living and loving realities. I chose the latter alternative, I felt *compelled* to do so. My hand has but obeyed the dictates of my heart, and, I trust also, the guidance of the unerring Spirit.

It may be an unusual thing thus to reveal the dearest secrets of one's past life ; but I think, in this case, I am justified in the course I have taken. My husband once said, " You may write my life across the sky, I have nothing to conceal ;" and I cannot withhold the precious testimony which these hitherto sealed pages of his history bear to his singularly holy and blameless character.

So, I have unlocked my heart, and poured out its choicest memories. Some people may blame my prodigality ; but I am convinced that the majority of readers will gather up, with reverent hands, the treasures I have thus scattered, and find themselves greatly enriched by their possession.

It has cost me sighs, and multiplied sorrows, as I have mourned over my vanished joys ; but, on the other hand, it has drawn me very near to " the God of all consolation," and taught me to bless Him again and again for having ever given me the priceless privilege of such a husband's love.

A

Many years ago, I read a most pathetic story, which is constantly recalled to mind as the duties of this compilation compel me to read the records of past years, and re-peruse the long-closed letters of my beloved, and live over again the happy days when we were all-in-all to each other. I do not remember all the details of the incident which so impressed me, but the chief facts were these. A married couple were crossing one of the great glaciers of Alpine regions, when a fatal accident occurred. The husband fell down one of the huge crevasses which abound on all glaciers,—the rope broke, and the depth of the chasm was so great that no help could be rendered, nor could the body be recovered. Over the wife's anguish at her loss, we must draw the veil of silence.

Forty years afterwards saw her, with the guide who had accompanied them at the time of the accident, staying at the nearest hotel to the foot of the glacier, waiting for the sea of ice to give up its dead ; for, by the well-known law of glacier-progression, the form of her long-lost husband might be expected to appear, expelled from the mouth of the torrent, about that date. Patiently, and with unfailing constancy, they watched and waited, and their hopes were at last rewarded. One day, the body was released from its prison in the ice, and the wife looked again on the features of him who had been so long parted from her!

But the pathos of the story lay in the fact that she was then an old woman, while the newly-rescued body was that of quite a young and robust man, so faithfully had the crystal casket preserved the jewel which it held so long. The forty years had left no wrinkles on that marble brow, Time's withering fingers could not touch him in *that* tomb ; and so, for a few brief moments, the aged lady saw the husband of her youth, *as he was in the days which were gone for ever !*

Somewhat similar has been my experience while preparing these chapters. I have stood, as it were, at the foot of the great glacier of Time, and looked with unspeakable tenderness on my beloved as I knew him in the days of his strength, when the dew of his youth was upon him, and the Lord had made him a mighty man among men. True, the cases are not altogether parallel, for I had my beloved with me all the forty years, and we grew old together ; but his seven years in glory seem like half a century to me ; and now, with the burden of declining years upon me, I am watching and waiting to see my loved one again,—not as he was forty years or even seven years ago, but as he will be when I am called to rejoin him through the avenue of the grave, or at the coming of our Lord Jesus Christ with all His saints. So I am waiting, and "looking for that blessed hope, and the glorious appearing of the great God and our Saviour Jesus Christ."

The first time I saw my future husband, he occupied the pulpit of New Park Street Chapel on the memorable Sunday when he preached his first sermons there. I was no stranger to the place. Many a discourse had I there listened to from Pastor James Smith (afterwards of Cheltenham),—a quaint and rugged preacher, but one well versed in the blessed art of bringing souls to Christ. Often had I seen him administer the ordinance of baptism to the

PASTOR JAMES SMITH.

candidates, wondering with a tearful longing whether I should ever be able thus to confess my faith in the Lord Jesus.

I can recall the old-fashioned, dapper figure of the senior deacon, of whom I stood very much in awe. He was a lawyer, and wore the silk stockings and knee-breeches dear to a former generation. When the time came to give out the hymns, he mounted an open desk immediately beneath the pulpit; and from where I sat, I had a side view of him. To the best of my remembrance, he was a short, stout man, and his rotund body, perched on his undraped legs, and clothed in a long-tailed coat, gave him an unmistakable resemblance to a gigantic robin; and when he chirped out the verses of the hymn in a piping, twittering voice, I thought the likeness was complete!

Well also did I know the curious pulpit without any stairs; it looked like a magnified swallow's-nest, and was entered from behind through a door in the wall. My childish imagination was always excited by the silent and "creepy" manner in which the minister made his appearance therein. One moment the big box would be empty,—the next, if I had but glanced down at Bible or hymn-book, and raised my eyes again,—there was the preacher, comfortably seated, or standing ready to commence the service! I found it very interesting, and though I knew there was a matter-of-fact *door*, through which the good man stepped into his rostrum, this knowledge was not allowed to interfere with, or even explain, the fanciful notions I loved to indulge in concerning that mysterious entrance and exit. It was certainly somewhat singular that, in the very pulpit which had exercised such a charm over me, I should have my first glimpse of the one who was to be the love of my heart, and the light of my earthly life. After Mr. Smith left, there came, with the passing years, a sad time of barrenness and desolation upon the church at New Park Street; the cause languished, and almost died; and none even dreamed of the overwhelming blessing which the Lord had in store for the remnant of faithful people worshipping there.

From my childhood, I had been a greatly-privileged favourite with Mr. and Mrs. Olney, Senr. ("Father Olney" and his wife), and I was a constant visitor at their homes, both in the Borough and West Croydon, and it was by reason of this mutual love that I found myself in their pew at the dear old chapel on that Sabbath evening, December 18th, 1853. There had been much excitement and anxiety concerning the invitation given to the country lad from Waterbeach to come and preach in the honoured, but almost empty sanctuary; it was a risky experiment, so some thought; but I believe that, from the very first sermon he heard him preach, dear old "Father Olney's" heart was fixed in its faith that God was going to do great things by this young David.

When the family returned from the morning service, varied emotions filled their souls. They had never before heard just such preaching; they were bewildered, and amazed, but they had been fed with royal dainties. They were, however, in much concern for the young preacher himself, who was greatly discouraged by the sight of so many empty pews, and manifestly wished himself back again with his loving people, in his crowded chapel in Cambridgeshire.

"What can be done?" good Deacon Olney said; "we *must* get him a better congregation to-night, or we shall lose him!" So, all that Sabbath afternoon, there ensued a determined looking-up of friends and acquaintances, who, by some means or other, were coaxed into giving a promise that they would be at Park Street in the evening to hear the wonderful boy preacher. "And little Susie must come, too," dear old Mrs. Olney pleaded. I do not think that "little Susie" particularly cared about being present; her ideas of the dignity and propriety of the ministry were rather shocked and upset by the reports which the morning worshippers had brought back concerning the young man's unconventional outward appearance! However, to please my dear friends, I went with them, and thus was present at the second sermon which my precious husband preached in London.

Ah! how little I then thought that my eyes looked on him who was to be my life's beloved; how little I dreamed of the honour God was preparing for me in the near future! It is a mercy that our lives are not left for us to plan, but that our Father chooses for us; else might we sometimes turn away from our best blessings, and put from us the choicest and loveliest gifts of His providence. For, if the whole truth be told, I was not at all fascinated by the young orator's eloquence, while his countrified manner and speech excited more regret than reverence. Alas, for my vain and foolish heart! I was not spiritually-minded enough to understand his earnest presentation of the gospel, and his powerful pleading with sinners;—but the huge black satin stock, the long, badly-trimmed hair, and the blue pocket-handkerchief with white spots, which he himself has so graphically described,—these attracted most of my attention, and, I fear, awakened some feelings of amusement. There was only one sentence of the whole sermon which I carried away with me, and that solely on account of its quaintness, for it seemed to me an extraordinary thing for the preacher to speak of the "living stones in the Heavenly Temple perfectly joined together with the vermilion cement of Christ's blood."

I do not recollect my first introduction to him; it is probable that he spoke to me, as to many others, on that same Sabbath evening; but when the final arrangement was made for him to occupy New Park Street pulpit, with a view to the permanent pastorate, I used to meet him occasionally at the house of our mutual friends, Mr. and Mrs. Olney, and I sometimes went to hear him preach.

I had not at that time made any open profession of religion, though I was brought to see my need of a Saviour under the ministry of the Rev. S. B. Bergne, of the Poultry Chapel, about a year before Mr. Spurgeon came to London. He preached, one Sunday evening, from the text, "The word is nigh thee, even in thy mouth, and in thy heart" (Romans x. 8), and from that service I date the dawning of the true light in my soul. The Lord said to me, through His servant, "Give Me thine heart," and, constrained by His love, that night witnessed my solemn resolution of entire surrender to Himself. But I had since become cold and indifferent to the things of God; seasons of darkness, despondency, and doubt, had passed over me, but I had kept all my religious experiences carefully concealed in my own breast, and perhaps this guilty hesitancy and reserve had much to do with the sickly and sleepy condition of my soul when I was first brought under the ministry of my beloved. None could have more needed the quickening and awakening which I received from the earnest pleadings and warnings of that voice,—soon to be the sweetest in all the world to me.

Gradually I became alarmed at my backsliding state, and then, by a great effort, I sought spiritual help and guidance from Mr. William Olney ("Father

MR. WILLIAM P. OLNEY.

Olney's" second son, and my cousin by marriage), who was an active worker in the Sunday-school at New Park Street, and a true Mr. Greatheart, and comforter of young pilgrims. He may have told the new Pastor about me,—I cannot say;—but, one day, I was greatly surprised to receive from Mr. Spurgeon an illustrated copy of *The Pilgrim's Progress*, in which he had written the inscription which is reproduced in *facsimile* on the following page :—

Miss Thompson
with desires for her progress
in the blessed pilgrimage
from
C. H. Spurgeon
Ap 20. 1854

I do not think my beloved had, at that time, any other thought concerning me than to help a struggling soul Heavenward; but I was greatly impressed by his concern for me, and the book became very precious as well as helpful. By degrees, though with much trembling, I told him of my state before God; and he gently led me, by his preaching, and by his conversations, through the power of the Holy Spirit, to the cross of Christ for the peace, and pardon my weary soul was longing for.

Thus things went quietly on for a little while; our friendship steadily grew, and I was happier than I had been since the days at the Poultry Chapel; but no bright dream of the future flashed distinctly before my eyes till the day of the opening of the Crystal Palace at Sydenham, on June 10, 1854. A large party of our friends, including Mr. Spurgeon, were present at the inauguration, and we occupied some raised seats at the end of the Palace where the great clock is now fixed. As we sat there talking, laughing, and amusing ourselves as best we could, while waiting for the procession to pass by, Mr. Spurgeon handed me a book, into which he had been occasionally dipping, and, pointing to some particular lines, said, "What do you think of the poet's suggestion in those verses?" The volume was Martin Tupper's *Proverbial Philosophy*, then recently published, and already beginning to feel the stir of the breezes of adverse criticism, which afterwards gathered into a howling tempest of disparagement and scathing sarcasm. No thought had I for authors and their woes at that moment. The pointing finger guided my eyes to the chapter on "Marriage," of which the opening sentences ran thus,—

> "Seek a good wife of thy God, for she is the best gift of His providence;
> Yet ask not in bold confidence that which He hath not promised:
> Thou knowest not His good will; be thy prayer then submissive thereunto,
> And leave thy petition to His mercy, assured that He will deal well with thee.
> If thou art to have a wife of thy youth, she is now living on the earth;
> Therefore think of her, and pray for her weal."

" Do you pray for him who is to be your husband ? " said a soft low voice in my ear,—so soft that no one else heard the whisper.

I do not remember that the question received any vocal answer ; but my fast-beating heart, which sent a tell-tale flush to my cheeks, and my downcast eyes, which feared to reveal the light which at once dawned in them, may have spoken a language which love understood. From that moment, a very quiet and subdued little maiden sat by the young Pastor's side, and while the brilliant procession passed round the Palace, I do not think she took so much note of the glittering pageant defiling before her, as of the crowd of newly-awakened emotions which were palpitating within her heart. Neither the book nor its theories were again alluded to, but when the formalities of the opening were over, and the visitors were allowed to leave their seats, the same low voice whispered again, " Will you come and walk round the Palace with me ? " How we obtained leave of absence from the rest of the party, I know not ; but we wandered together, for a long time, not only in the wonderful building itself, but in the gardens, and even down to the lake, beside which the colossal forms of extinct monsters were being cunningly modelled. During that walk, on that memorable day in June, I believe God Himself united our hearts in indissoluble bonds of true affection, and, though we knew it not, gave us to each other for ever. From that time our friendship grew apace, and quickly ripened into deepest love,—a love which lives in my heart to-day as truly, aye, and more solemnly and strongly than it did in those early days ; for, though God has seen fit to call my beloved up to higher service, He has left me the consolation of still loving him with all my heart, and believing that our love shall be perfected when we meet in that blessed land where Love reigns supreme and eternal.

It was not very long (August 2, 1854,) before the sweet secret between us was openly revealed. Loving looks, and tender tones, and clasping hands had all told " the old, old story," and yet, when the verbal confession of it came, how wonderful it was ! Was there ever quite such bliss on earth before ? I can see the place where the marvel was wrought, as plainly, at this distance of over forty years, as I saw it then. It was in a little, old-fashioned garden (my grandfather's), which had high brick walls on three sides, and was laid out with straight, formal gravel paths, and a small lawn, in the midst of which flourished a large and very fruitful pear tree,—the pride of old grandad's heart. Rather a dreary and unromantic place, one would imagine, for a declaration of love ; but people are not particularly careful as to the selection of their surroundings at such a moment, and do not often take pains to secure a delightful background to the picture which will for ever be photo-graphed on their hearts. To this day, I think of that old garden as a sacred place, a paradise of happiness, since there my beloved sought me for his very own, and told me how much he loved me. Though I thought I knew this already, it was a very different matter to hear him say it, and I trembled and was silent for very joy and gladness. The sweet ceremony of betrothal needs no description; every loving and true heart can fill up the details either from experience or anticipation. To me, it was a time as *solemn* as it was sweet; and, with a great awe in my heart, I left my beloved, and hastening to the house, and to an upper room, I knelt before God, and praised and thanked Him, with happy tears, for His great mercy in giving me the love of so good a man. If I had known, then, *how* good he was, and how great he would become, I should have been overwhelmed, not so much with the happiness of being his, as with the responsibility which such a position would entail. But, thank God, throughout all my blessed married life, the perfect love which drew us together never slackened or faltered; and, though I can now see how undeserving I was to be the life companion of so eminent a servant of God, I know *he* did not think this, but looked upon his wife as God's best earthly gift to him.

FACSIMILES OF LOVERS' KEEPSAKES.

In the diary I then kept, I find this brief but joyful entry:—"August 2, 1854.—It is impossible to write down all that occurred this morning. I can only adore in silence the mercy of my God, and praise Him for all His benefits."

After our engagement, we met pretty constantly; I attended the services at New Park Street Chapel as often as possible, and on February 1, 1855, I was baptized there by my beloved, upon my profession of repentance towards God, and faith in our Lord Jesus Christ. When I had to "come before the church," he endeavoured to keep the matter as quiet as possible, lest inconvenient curiosity should be aroused; but the fact must have found some small leakage, for we were amused to hear afterwards of the following little incident. An old man, named Johnny Dear, preceded me in the list of candidates; and when he had given in his experience, and been questioned and dismissed, two maiden ladies, sitting at the back of the room, were overheard to say, "What was that man's name?" "Johnny Dear." "Oh, well; I suppose it will be 'sister dear' next!" And I am thankful to say her surmise was correct, and that I happily passed through the somewhat severe ordeal.

Mr. Spurgeon had expressed a wish that I should write out my confession of repentance and faith, which I accordingly did. I do not know whether it was read to the officers of the church, or retained solely for his own perusal; but it is preserved among his papers, and in the following words he gave me assurance of his satisfaction with my testimony:—

"75, Dover Road,
"January 11, 1855.

"My Dearest,

"The letter is all I can desire. Oh! I could weep for joy (as I certainly am doing now) to think that my beloved can so well testify to a work of grace in her soul. I knew you were *really* a child of God, but I did not think you had been led in such a path. I see my Master has been ploughing deep, and it is the deep-sown seed, struggling with the clods, which now makes your bosom heave with distress. If I know anything of spiritual symptoms, I think I know a cure for you. Your position is not the sphere for earnest labour for Christ. You have done all you could in more ways than one; but you are not brought into actual contact either with the saints, or with the sinful, sick, or miserable, whom you could serve. Active service brings with it warmth, and this tends to remove doubting, for our works thus become evidences of our calling and election.

"I flatter no one, but allow me to say, honestly, that few cases which have come under my notice are so satisfactory as yours. Mark, I write not now as your *admiring friend*, but impartially as your Pastor. If the Lord had intended your destruction, He would not have told you such things as these, nor would He enable you so unreservedly to cast yourself upon His faithful promise. As I hope to stand at the bar of God, clear of the blood of all men, it would ill become me to flatter; and as I love you with the deepest and purest affection, far be it from me to trifle with your immortal interests; but I will say again that my gratitude to God ought to be great, as well on my own behalf as yours, that you have been so deeply schooled in the lessons of the heart, and have so frequently looked into the charnel-house of your own corruption. There are other lessons to come, that you may be thoroughly furnished ; but, oh ! my dear one, how good to learn the first lesson well ! I loved you once, but feared you might not be an heir of Heaven ;—God in His mercy showed me that you were indeed *elect*. I then thought I might without sin reveal my affection to you,—but up to the time I saw your note, I could not imagine that you had seen such great sights, and were so thoroughly versed in soul-knowledge. God is good, very good, infinitely good. Oh, how I prize this last gift, because I now know, more than ever, that the Giver loves the gift, and so I may love it, too, but only in subservience to Him. Dear purchase of a Saviour's blood, you are to me a Saviour's gift, and my heart is full to overflowing with the thought of such continued goodness. I do not wonder at His goodness, for it is just like Him ; but I cannot but lift up the voice of joy at His manifold mercies.

"Whatever befall us, trouble and adversity, sickness or death, we need not fear a final separation, either from each other, or our God. I am glad you are not here just at this moment, for I feel so deeply that I could only throw my arms around you and weep. May the choicest favours be thine, may the Angel of the Covenant be thy companion, may thy supplications be answered, and may thy conversation be with Jesus in Heaven ! Farewell ; unto my God and my father's God I commend you.

"Yours, with pure and holy affection, as well as terrestrial love,

"C. H. SPURGEON."

My dear husband used often to write his name and a brief comment in any of his books which he specially valued. His first volume of Calvin's *Commentaries* contains an inscription which is such a direct confirmation of what I have written on page 9, that it makes a most fitting conclusion to the present chapter :—

The volumes making up a complete set of Calvin were a gift to me from my own most dear, & tender wife! Blessed may she be among women. How much of comfort & strength she has ministered unto me it is not in my power to estimate, she has been to me God's best earthly gift, & not a little even of heavenly treasure has come to me by her means, She has often been as an angel of God unto me.

C. H. Spurgeon

CHAPTER XXXV.

Love, Courtship, and Marriage *(Continued)*.

OUR TRYSTING-PLACE.

T this time, the Crystal Palace was a favourite resort with us. It possessed great attractions of its own, and perhaps the associations of the opening day gave it an added grace in our eyes. In common with many of our friends, we had season tickets ; and we used them to good purpose, as my beloved found that an hour or two of rest and relaxation in those lovely gardens, and that pure air, braced him for the constant toil of preaching to crowded congregations, and relieved him somewhat from the ill effects of London's smoky atmosphere. It was so easy for him to run down to Sydenham from London Bridge that, as often as once a week, if possible, we arranged to meet there for a quiet walk and talk. After the close of the Thursday evening service, there would be a whispered word to me in the aisle, "Three o'clock to-morrow," which meant that, if I would be at the Palace by that hour, "somebody" would meet me at the Crystal Fountain. I was then living

at 7, St. Ann's Terrace, Brixton Road, in the house which my parents, Mr. and Mrs. R. B. Thompson, shared with my uncle, H. Kilvington, Esq., and the long walk from there to Sydenham was a pleasant task to me, with such a meeting in view, and such delightful companionship as a reward. We wandered amid the many Courts, which were then chiefly instructive and educational in character; we gazed with almost solemn awe at the reproductions of Egypt, Assyria, and Pompeii, and I think we learned many things beside the tenderness of our own hearts towards each other, as the bright blissful hours sped by.

MY BRIXTON HOME.

The young minister had not much time to spare from his duties, but he usually came to see me on a Monday, bringing his sermon with him to revise for the press; and I learned to be quiet, and mind my own business, while this important work was going on. It was good discipline for the Pastor's intended wife, who needed no inconsiderable amount of training to fit her in any measure for the post she was ordained to occupy. I remember, however, that there was one instance of preparation for future duty, which was by no means agreeable to my feelings, and which, I regret to say, I resented. As a chronicler must be truthful, I tell the story, and to show how, from the very beginning of his public life, my dear husband's devotion to his sacred work dominated and even absorbed every other passion and purpose of his heart. He was a "called, and chosen, and faithful" servant of Christ in the very highest degree ; and during all his life he put God's service first, and all earthly things second. I have known him to be so abstracted, on a Sabbath morning at the Tabernacle, just before preaching, that if I left his vestry for a few moments, he would, on my return, rise and greet me with a handshake, and a grave " How are you ?" as if I were a strange visitor ; then, noting the amused look on my face, he would discover his mistake, and laughingly say, " Never mind, wifey dear, I was thinking about my hymns." This happened not once only, but several times, and when the service was over, and we were driving home, he would make very merry over it.

But I must tell the promised story of the earlier days, though it is not at all to my own credit ; yet, even as I write it, I smile at the remembrance of his enjoyment of the tale in later years. If I wanted to amuse him much, or chase some gloom from his dear face, I would remind him of the time when he took his sweetheart to a certain service, and there was so preoccupied with the discourse he was about to deliver, that he forgot all about her, and left her to take care of herself as best she could. As I recalled the incident, which really was to me a very serious one at the time, and might have had an untoward ending, he would laugh at the ludicrous side of it till the tears ran down his cheeks, and then he would lovingly kiss me, and say how glad he was that I had borne with his ill manners, and how much I must have loved him.

This is the story. He was to preach at the large hall of "The Horns," Kennington, which was not very far from where we then resided. He asked me to accompany him, and dined with us at St. Ann's Terrace, the service being in the afternoon. We went together, happily enough, in a cab ; and I well remember trying to keep close by his side as we mingled with the mass of people thronging up the staircase. But, by the time we had reached the landing, he had forgotten my existence ; the burden of the message he had to proclaim to that crowd of immortal souls was upon him, and he turned into the small side door where the officials were awaiting him, without for a moment realizing that I was left to struggle as best I could with the rough and eager throng around me. At first, I was utterly bewildered, and then, I am sorry to have to confess, I was *angry*. I at once returned home, and told my grief to my gentle mother, who tried to soothe my ruffled spirit, and bring me to a better frame of mind. She wisely reasoned that my chosen husband was no ordinary man, that his whole life was absolutely dedicated to God and His service, and that I must never, *never* hinder him by trying to put myself first in his heart. Presently, after much good and loving counsel, my heart grew soft, and I saw I had been very foolish and wilful ; and then a cab drew up at the door, and dear

Mr. Spurgeon came running into the house, in great excitement, calling, " Where's Susie? I have been searching for her everywhere, and cannot find her ; has she come back by herself?" My dear mother went to him, took him aside, and told him all the truth : and I think, when he realized the state of things, she had to soothe him also, for he was so innocent at heart of having offended me in any way, that he must have felt I had done him an injustice in thus doubting him. At last, mother came to fetch me to him, and I went downstairs. Quietly he let me tell him how indignant I had felt, and then he repeated mother's little lesson, assuring me of his deep affection for me, but pointing out that, before all things, he was *God's servant*, and I must be prepared to yield my claims to His.

I never forgot the teaching of that day ; I had learned my hard lesson *by heart*, for I do not recollect ever again seeking to assert my right to his time and attention when any service for God demanded them. It was ever the settled purpose of my married life that I should never hinder him in his work for the Lord, never try to keep him from fulfilling his engagements, never plead my own ill-health as a reason why he should remain at home with me. I thank God, now, that He enabled me to carry out this determination, and rejoice that I have no cause to reproach myself with being a drag on the swift wheels of his consecrated life. I do not take any credit to myself for this ; it was the Lord's will concerning me, and He saw to it that I received the necessary training whereby, in after years, I could cheerfully surrender His chosen servant to the incessant demands of his ministry, his literary work, and the multiplied labours of his exceptionally busy life. And now I can bless God for what happened on that memorable afternoon when my beloved preached at " The Horns," Kennington. What a delightfully cosy tea we three had together that evening, and how sweet was the calm in our hearts after the storm, and how much we both loved and honoured mother for her wise counsels and her tender diplomacy !

Some little time afterwards, when Mr. Spurgeon had an engagement at Windsor, I was asked to accompany him, and in forwarding the invitation, he referred to the above incident thus :—" My Own Darling,—What do you say to this? As you wish me to express my desire, I will say, 'Go ;' but I should have left it to your own choice if I did not know that my wishes always please you. Possibly, I may be again inattentive to you if you do go ; but this will be nice for us both,—that 'Charles' may have space for mending, and that 'Susie' may exhibit her growth in know-ledge of his character, by patiently enduring his failings." So the end of this little "rift in the lute" was no patched-up peace between us, but a deepening of our confidence in each other, and an increase of that fervent love which can look a misunderstanding in the face till it melts away and vanishes, as a morning cloud before the ardent glances of the sun.

Two tender little notes, written by my husband sixteen years later (1871), will show what an abundant reward of loving approval was bestowed on me for merely doing what it was my duty to do :—

"My Own Dear One,—None know how grateful I am to God for you. In all I have ever done for Him, you have a large share, for in making me so happy you have fitted me for service. Not an ounce of power has ever been lost to the good cause through you. I have served the Lord far more, and never less, for your sweet companionship. The Lord God Almighty bless you now and for ever!"

"I have been thinking over my strange history, and musing on eternal love's great river-head from which such streams of mercy have flowed to me. I dwell devoutly on many points ;—the building of the Tabernacle,—what a business it was, and how little it seems now! Do you remember a Miss Thompson who collected for the enlargement of New Park Street Chapel as much as £100? Bless her dear heart! Think of the love which gave me that dear lady for a wife, and made her such a wife ; to me, the ideal wife, and, as I believe, without exaggeration or love-flourishing, the precise form in which God would make a woman for such a man as I am, if He designed her to be the greatest of all earthly blessings to him ; and in some sense a spiritual blessing, too, for in that also am I richly profited by you, though you would not believe it. I will leave this 'good matter' ere the paper is covered ; but not till I have sent you as many kisses as there are waves on the sea."

It was our mutual desire to pay a visit to Colchester, that I might be introduced to Mr. Spurgeon's parents as their future daughter-in-law ; and, after some trouble and disappointment, my father's consent was obtained, and we set off on our first important journey together, with very keen and vivid perceptions of the delightful novelty of our experience. It is not to be wondered at that my memories of the visit are somewhat hazy, although intensely happy. I was welcomed, petted, and entertained most affectionately by all the family, and I remember being taken to see every place and object of interest in and around Colchester ; but *what* I saw, I know not ; the joy of being all the day long with my beloved, and this for three or four days together, was enough to fill my heart with gladness, and render me oblivious of any other pleasure. I think we must have returned on the Friday of our week's holiday, for, according to our custom, we exchanged letters on the Saturday as usual, and this is what we said to each other : –

"75, Dover Road,

"April, '55.

"My Own Doubly-dear Susie,

"How much we have enjoyed in each other's society! It seems almost impossible that I could either have conferred or received so much happiness. I feel now, like you, very low in spirits ; but a sweet promise in Ezekiel cheers me, ' I will give thee the opening of the mouth in the midst of them.' (This was in reference to the preparation of sermons for the Sabbath.—S. S.) Surely my God has not forgotten me. Pray for me, my love ; and may our united petitions win a blessing through the Saviour's merit ! Let us take heed of putting ourselves too prominently in our own hearts, but let us commit our way unto the Lord. ' What I have in my own hand, I usually lose,' said Luther ; ' but what I put into God's hand, is still, and ever will be, in my possession.' I need not send my love to you, for, though absent in body, my heart is with you still, and I am, your much-loved, and ardently-loving, C. H. S."

"P.S.—The devil has barked again in *The Essex Standard*. It contains another letter. Never mind ; when Satan opens his mouth, he gives me an opportunity of ramming my sword down his throat."

(MY REPLY.)

" St. Ann's Terrace,
" April, '55.

My Dearest,

"I thank you with warm and hearty thanks for the note just received. It is useless for me to attempt to tell you how much happiness I have had during the past week. Words are but cold dishes on which to serve up thoughts and feelings which come warm and glowing from the heart. I should like to express my appreciation of all the tenderness and care you have shown towards me during this happy week ; but I fear to pain you by thanks for what I know was a pleasure to you. I expect your thoughts have been busy to-day about ' the crown jewels.' (He had talked of preaching on this subject.—S. S.) The gems may differ in size, colour, richness, and beauty, but even the smallest are ' precious stones ', are they not ?

"That *Standard* certainly does not bear ' Excelsior ' as its motto ; nor can ' Good will to men ' be the device of its floating pennon, but it matters not ; *we know* that all is under the control of One of whom Asaph said, ' Surely the wrath of man shall praise Thee ; the remainder of wrath shalt Thou restrain.' May His blessing rest in an especial manner on you to-night, my dearly-beloved ; and on the approaching Sabbath, when you stand before the great congregation, may you be ' filled with all the fulness of God ' ! Good-night. Fondly and faithfully yours,—SUSIE."

The mention of *The Essex Standard*, in the foregoing letters, points to the fact that, even thus early in his ministerial career, the strife of tongues had commenced against God's servant, and the cruel arrows of the wicked had sorely wounded him. He had also begun to learn that some of his severest critics were the very men who ought to have been his heartiest friends and warmest sympathizers. The first reference to this persecution is in a letter to me, written January 1, 1855, where he says :—" I find much stir has been made by ' Job's letter ', and hosts of unknown persons have risen up on my behalf. It seems very likely that King James (James Wells) will shake his own throne by lifting his hand against one of the Lord's little ones." Then, in May, in one of the Saturday letters, there occur these sentences :—" I am down in the valley, partly because of two desperate attacks in *The Sheffield Independent*, and *The Empire*, and partly because I cannot find a subject. Yet faith fails not. I know and believe the promise, and am not afraid to rest upon it. All the scars I receive, are scars of honour ; so, faint heart, on to the battle ! My love, were you here, how you would comfort me ; but since you are not, I shall do what is better still, go upstairs alone, and pour out my griefs into my Saviour's ear. ' Jesus, *Lover* of *my soul*, I *can* to Thy bosom fly !' "

These were only the first few drops of the terrible storm of detraction, calumny, and malice, which afterward burst upon him with unexampled fury ; but which, blessed be God, he lived through, and lived down. I do not say more concerning these slanders, as they will be described in detail in later chapters.

When my parents removed to a house in Falcon Square, City, we met much more frequently, and grew to know each other better, while our hearts were knit closer and closer in purest love. A little more "training" also took place, for one day my beloved brought with him an ancient, rusty-looking book, and, to my amazement, said, "Now, darling, I want you to go carefully through this volume, marking all those paragraphs and sentences that strike you as being particularly sweet, or quaint, or instructive ; will you do this for me ?" Of course, I at once complied ; but he did not know with what a trembling sense of my own inability the promise was given, nor how disqualified I then was to appreciate the spiritual beauty of his favourite Puritan writers. It was the simplest kind of literary work which he asked me to do, but I was such an utter stranger to such service, that it seemed a most important and difficult task to discover in that " dry " old book the bright diamonds and red gold which he evidently reckoned were therein enshrined. Love, however, is a matchless teacher, and I was a willing pupil ; and so, with help and suggestion from so dear a tutor, the work went on from day to day till, in due time, a small volume made its appearance, which he called, *Smooth Stones taken from Ancient Brooks*. This title was a pleasant and Puritanic play upon the author's name, and I think the compilers were well pleased with the results of their happy work together. I believe the little book is out of print now, and copies are very rarely to be met with ; but those who possess them may feel an added interest in their perusal, now that they know the sweet love-story which hides between their pages.

As the days went by, my beloved's preaching engagements multiplied exceedingly, yet he found time to make me very happy by his loving visits and letters ; and, on Sunday mornings, I was nearly always allowed by my parents to enjoy his ministry. Yet this pleasure was mingled with much of pain ; for, during the early part of the year 1855, he was preaching in Exeter Hall to vast crowds of people, and the strain on his physical power was terrible. Sometimes his voice would almost break and fail as he pleaded with sinners to come to Christ, or magnified the Lord in His sovereignty and righteousness. A glass of Chili vinegar always stood on a shelf under the desk before him, and I knew what to expect when he had recourse to that remedy. Oh, how my heart ached for him ! What self-control I had to exercise to appear calm and collected, and keep quietly in my seat up in that little side gallery ! How I longed to have the *right* to go and comfort and cheer him when the service was over ! But I had to walk away, as other people did,—I, who belonged to him, and was closer to his heart than anyone there ! It was severe discipline for a young and loving spirit. I remember, with strange vividness at this long distance of time, the Sunday evening when he preached from the text, " His Name shall endure for ever." It was a subject in which he revelled, it was his chief delight to exalt his glorious Saviour, and he seemed in that discourse to be pouring out his very soul and life in homage and adoration before his gracious King. But I really thought he would have died there, in face of all those people ! At the end of the sermon, he made a mighty effort to recover his voice ; but utterance wellnigh failed, and only in broken accents could the pathetic peroration be heard,— " Let my name perish, but let Christ's Name last for ever ! Jesus ! *Jesus !* JESUS ! Crown Him Lord of all ! You will not hear me say anything else. These are my last words in Exeter Hall for this time. Jesus ! *Jesus !* JESUS ! Crown *Him* Lord of all ! " and then he fell back almost fainting in the chair behind him.

In after days, when the Lord had fully perfected for him that silver-toned voice which ravished men's ears, while it melted their hearts, there was seldom any recurrence of the painful scene I have attempted to describe. On the contrary, he spoke with the utmost ease, in the largest buildings, to assembled thousands, and, as a master musician playing on a priceless instrument, he could at will either charm his audience with notes of dulcet sweetness, or ring forth the clarion tones of warning and alarm.

He used to say, playfully, that his throat had been macadamised ; but, as a matter of fact, I believe that the constant and natural use of his voice, in the delivery of so many sermons and addresses, was the secret of his entire freedom from the serious malady generally known as " clergyman's sore throat." During this first visit to Exeter Hall, New Park Street Chapel was enlarged, and when this improvement was completed, he returned to his own pulpit, the services at the hall ceased, and for a short time, at least, my fears for him were silenced.

But his work went on increasing almost daily, and his popularity grew with rapid strides. Many notable services in the open-air were held about this time, and my letters give a glimpse of two of these occasions. On June 2, 1855, he writes :— " Last evening, about 500 persons came to the field, and afterwards adjourned to the chapel kindly lent by Mr. Eldridge. My Master gave me power and liberty. I am persuaded souls were saved ; and, as for myself, I preached like the chief of sinners, to those who, like me, were chief sinners, too. Many were the tears, and not a few the smiles."

Then, on the 23rd of the same month, I had a jubilant letter, which commenced thus :—" Yesterday, I climbed to the summit of a minister's glory. My congregation was enormous, I think 10,000 (this was in a field at Hackney) ; but certainly twice as many as at Exeter Hall. The Lord was with me, and the profoundest silence was observed ; but, oh, the close,—never did mortal man receive a more enthusiastic ovation ! I wonder I am alive ! After the service, five or six gentlemen endeavoured to clear a passage, but I was borne along, amid cheers, and prayers, and shouts, for about a quarter of an hour,—it really seemed more like a week ! I was hurried round and round the field without hope of escape until, suddenly seeing a nice open carriage, with two occupants, standing near, I sprang in, and begged them to drive away. This they most kindly did, and I stood up, waving my hat, and crying, ' The blessing of God be with you !' while, from thousands of heads the hats were lifted, and cheer after cheer was given. Surely, amid these plaudits I can hear the low rumblings of an advancing storm of reproaches ; but even this I can bear for the Master's sake."

This was a true prophecy, for the time did come when the hatred of men to the truths he preached rose to such a height, that no scorn seemed too bitter, no sneer too contemptuous, to fling at the preacher who boldly declared the gospel of the grace of God, as he had himself learned it at the cross of Christ ; but, thank God, he lived to be honoured above most men for his uprightness and fidelity, and never, to the last moment of his life, did he change one jot or tittle of his belief, or vary an iota of his whole-hearted testimony to the divinity of the doctrines of free grace.

CHAPTER XXXVI.

Lobe, Courtship, and Marriage *(Concluded)*.

N July of this year (1855), my dear one went to Scotland, intending to combine a holiday with the fulfilment of many preaching engagements ;—a very bad plan this, as he afterwards found, for an overtaxed mind needs absolute repose during resting times, and sermons and spirits both suffer if this reasonable rule be broken. His letters to me during this journey are not altogether joyful ones ; I give a few extracts from them, which will serve to outline his first experiences in a form of service into which he so fully entered in after years. On this occasion, he was not happy, or " at home," and was constantly longing to return. This was, too, his *first* long journey by rail, and it is curious to note what physical pain the inexperienced traveller endured. In those days, there were no Pullman cars, or luxurious saloon carriages, fitted up with all the comforts and appliances of a first-class hotel, so our poor voyager fared badly. He writes a note from Carlisle, just to assure me of his safety, and then, on reaching Glasgow, he gives this account of his ride :—" At Watford, I went with the guard, and enjoyed some conversation with him, which I hope God will bless to his good. At 10.45, I went inside,—people asleep. I could not manage a wink, but felt very queer. At morning-light, went into a second-class carriage with another guard, and rejoiced in the splendid view as well as my uncomfortable sensations would allow. Arrived here tired, begrimed with dust, sleepy, not over high in spirits, and with a dreadful cold in my head. Last night, I slept twelve hours without waking, but I still feel as tired as before I slept. I will, I think, never travel so far at once again. I certainly shall not come home in one day ; for if I do, my trip will have been an injury instead of a benefit. I am so glad you did not have my *horrid* ride ; but if I could spirit you here, I would soon do it. Pray for me, my love."

The next epistle I will give at length. I have been trying in these pages to leave the "love" out of the letters as much as possible, lest my precious things should appear but platitudes to my readers, but it is a difficult task ; for little rills of tenderness run between all the sentences, like the singing, dancing waters among the boulders of a brook, and I cannot still the music altogether. To the end of his beautiful life it was the same, his letters were always those of a devoted lover, as well as of a tender husband; not only did the brook never dry up, but the stream grew deeper and broader, and the rhythm of its song waxed sweeter and stronger.

"Aberfeldy,
" July 17th, 1855.

"My Precious Love,

"Your dearly-prized note came safely to hand, and verily it did excel all I have ever read, even from your own loving pen. Well, I am all right now. Last Sabbath, I preached twice; and to sum up all in a word, the services were 'glorious.' In the morning, Dr. Patterson's place was crammed; and in the evening, Dr. Wardlaw's Chapel was crowded to suffocation by more than 2,500 people, while persons outside declared that quite as many went away. My reception was enthusiastic; never was greater honour given to mortal man. They were just as delighted as are the people at Park Street. To-day, I have had a fine drive with my host and his daughter. To-morrow, I am to preach *here*. It is quite impossible for me to be left in quiet. Already, letters come in, begging me to go here, there, and everywhere. Unless I go to the North Pole, I never can get away from my holy labour.

"Now to return to you again, I have had day-dreams of you while driving along, I thought you were very near me. It is not long, dearest, before I shall again enjoy your sweet society, if the providence of God permit. I knew I loved you very much before, but now I feel how necessary you are to me; and you will not lose much by my absence, if you find me, on my return, more attentive to your feelings, as well as equally affectionate. I can now thoroughly sympathize with your tears, because I feel in no little degree that pang of absence which my constant engagements prevented me from noticing when in London. How then must you, with so much leisure, have felt my absence from you, even though you well knew that it was unavoidable on my part! My darling, accept love of the deepest and purest kind from one who is not prone to exaggerate, but who feels that here there is no room for hyperbole. Think not that I weary myself by writing; for, dearest, it is my delight to please you, and solace an absence which must be even more dreary to you than to me, since travelling and preaching lead me to forget it. My eyes ache for sleep, but they shall keep open till I have invoked the blessings from above—mercies temporal and eternal—to rest on the head of one whose name is sweet to me, and who equally loves the name of her own, her much-loved, C. H. S."

The dear traveller seems to have had his Scotch visit interrupted by the necessity of a journey to fulfil preaching engagements at Bradford and Stockton. On his way to these towns, he stayed to see the beauties of Windermere, and sought to enjoy a little relaxation and rest ; but he writes very sadly of these experiences. " This is a bad way of spending time," he says, " I had rather be preaching five times a day than be here. Idleness is my *labour.* I long for the traces again, and want to be in the shafts, pulling the old coach. Oh, for the quiet of my own closet ! I think, if I have one reason for wishing to return, more cogent than even my vehement desire to see you, it is that I may see *my Lord,* so as I have seen Him in my retirement."

Of the services at Bradford, he gives this brief record :—" Last Sabbath was a day of even greater triumph than at Glasgow. The hall, which holds more people than Exeter Hall, was crammed to excess at both services, and in the evening the crowds outside who went away were immense, and would have furnished another hall with an audience. At Stockton, I had a full house, and my Master's smile ; I left there this morning at 8 o'clock."

Returning to Glasgow, *via* Edinburgh, he preached in that city, and I afterwards had a doleful little note, in which he wrote bitter things against himself,— perhaps without reason. His words, however, show with what tenderness of conscience he served his God, how quick he was to discover in himself anything which might displease his Master, and how worthless was the applause of the people if the face of his Lord were hidden. He says :—" I preached in Edinburgh, and returned here, full of anguish at my ill-success. Ah ! my darling, your beloved behaved like Jonah, and half wished never more to testify against Nineveh. Though it rained, the hall was crowded, and there was I,—*without my God !* It was a sad failure on my part ; nevertheless, God can bless my words to poor souls." (A further reference to this incident will be found in the chapters in which Mr. Spurgeon describes his Scotch tour in fuller detail than I have given.)

A hurried excursion to the Highlands,—a day's sight-seeing in Glasgow.— another Sabbath of services, when enormous crowds were disappointed,—20,000 people being turned away, because admittance was impossible,—and then the Scotch journey—the forerunner of so many similar events,—was a thing of the past, and work at home was recommenced with earnestness and vigour.

Even at this early period of my beloved's ministry, while he was still so youthful that none need have wondered had he been puffed up by his popularity and success, there was in his heart a deep and sweet humility, which kept him low at the Master's feet, and fitted him to bear the ever-increasing burden of celebrity and fame. This is manifest in so many of these letters of 1855, that I have felt constrained to refer to it, since even now some dare to speak of him as self-confident and arrogant, when, had they known him as his dearest friends knew him, they would have marvelled at his lowliness, and borne witness—as these have often done, —that "the meekness and gentleness of Christ" was one of the many charms of his radiant character. His dear son in the faith, Pastor Hugh D. Brown, of Dublin, speaks truly when he says of him, in a lately-published eulogy, "So wonderful a man, and yet so simple,—with a great child-heart ;—or rather, so simple because so great, needing no scaffoldings of pompous mannerism to buttress up an uncertain reputation ; but universally esteemed, because he cared nought for human opinion, but only for what was upright, open-hearted, and transparent, both in ministry and life :—we never knew a public man who had less of self about him, for over and above aught else, his sole ambition seemed to be, ' How can I most extol my Lord ? ' " These thoughtful, discriminating words would have been applicable to him if they had been written in the long-past days, when his marvellous career had but just commenced, and his glorious life-work lay all before him.

The following letter reveals his inmost heart, and it costs me a pang to give it publicity ; but it should silence for ever the untrue charges of egotism and self-conceit which have been brought against him by those who ought to have known better :—" I shall feel deeply indebted to you, if you will pray very earnestly for me. I fear I am not so full of love to God as I used to be. I lament my sad decline in spiritual things. You and others may not have observed it, but I am now conscious of it, and a sense thereof has put bitterness in my cup of joy. Oh ! what is it to be popular, to be successful, to have abundance, even to have love so sweet as yours,—if I should be left of God to fall, and to depart from His ways ? I tremble at the giddy height on which I stand, and could wish myself unknown, for indeed I am unworthy of all my honours and my fame. I trust I shall now commence anew, and wear no longer the linsey-woolsey garment ; but I beseech you, blend your hearty prayers with mine, that two of us may be agreed, and thus will you promote the usefulness, and holiness, and happiness of one whom you love."

Then, some months later, he wrote :—" *The Patriot* has a glowing account of me, which will tend to make me more popular than ever. MAY GOD PRESERVE ME ! I believe all my little troubles have just kept me right. I should have been upset by flattery, had it not been for this long balancing rod."

Let any impartial reader decide whether these are the words of a vain and self-complacent man !

The year 1855 was now drawing to a close, and we were looking forward, with unutterable joy, to having a home of our own, and being united by the holy ties of a marriage "made in Heaven." My beloved went to spend Christmas with his parents in Colchester ; and after a personal "Good-bye," wrote again thus :—"Sweet One,— How I love you! I long to see you ; and yet it is but half-an-hour since I left you. Comfort yourself in my absence by the thought that my heart is with you. My own gracious God bless you in all things,—in heart, in feeling, in life, in death, in Heaven! May your virtues be perfected, your prospects realized, your zeal continued, your love to Him increased, and your knowledge of Him rendered deeper, higher, broader,— in fact, may more than even *my heart* can wish, or *my* hope anticipate, be yours for ever! May we be mutual blessings ;—wherein I shall err, you will pardon ; and wherein you may mistake, I will more than overlook. Yours, till Heaven, *and then,*—C. H. S."

Ah! my husband, the blessed earthly ties which we welcomed so rapturously are dissolved now, and death has hidden thee from my mortal eyes ; but not even death can divide thee from me, or sever the love which united our hearts so closely. I feel it living and growing still, and I believe it will find its full and spiritual development only when we shall meet in the glory-land, and worship " together before the throne."

There is just one relic of this memorable time. On my desk, as I write this chapter, there is a book bearing the title of *The Pulpit Library ;* it is the *first* published volume of my beloved's sermons, and its fly-leaf has the following inscription :—

The wedding-day was fixed for January 8th, 1856; and I think, till it came, and passed, I lived in a dreamland of excitement and emotion, the atmosphere of which was unfriendly to the remembrance of any definite incidents. Our feet were on the threshold of the gate which stands at the entry of the new and untrodden pathway of married life; but it was with a deep and tender gladness that the travellers clasped each other's hand, and then placed them both in that of the Master, and thus set out on their journey, assured that He would be their Guide, " *even unto death*."

I have been trying to recall in detail the events of the—to me—notable day on which I became the loved and loving wife of the best man on God's earth; but most of its hours are veiled in a golden mist, through which they look luminous, but indistinct;—only a few things stand out clearly in my memory.

I see a young girl kneeling by her bedside in the early morning; she is awed and deeply moved by a sense of the responsibilities to be taken up that day, yet happy beyond expression that the Lord has so favoured her; and there alone with Him she earnestly seeks strength, and blessing, and guidance through the new life opening before her. The tiny upper chamber in Falcon Square was a very sacred place that morning.

Anon, I see a very simply-dressed damsel, sitting by her father's side, and driving through the City streets to New Park Street Chapel,—vaguely wondering, as the passers-by cast astonished glances at the wedding equipage, whether they all knew what a wonderful bridegroom she was going to meet!

As we neared our destination, it was evident that many hundreds of people *did* know and care about the man who had chosen her to be his bride, for the building was full to overflowing, and crowds of the young preacher's admirers thronged the streets around the chapel. I do not remember much more. Within the densely-packed place, I can dimly see a large wedding party in the table-pew, dear old Dr. Alexander Fletcher beaming benignly on the bride and bridegroom before him, and the deacons endeavouring to calm and satisfy the excited and eager onlookers.

Then followed the service, which made " us twain most truly one," and with a solemn joy in our hearts we stood hand in hand, and spake the few brief words which legally bound us to each other in blessed bonds while life lasted. But the golden circlet then placed on my finger, though worn and thin now, speaks of love beyond the grave, and is the cherished pledge of a spiritual union which shall last throughout eternity.

It would not have been possible for me to describe the marriage ceremony, or recollect the prayers and counsels then offered on our behalf; but, as reporters were present, and I have preserved their notes, I am able to record (in a much-condensed form) some of the Doctor's kind and earnest words on the memorable occasion. The service was commenced by the congregation singing the hymn,—

"Salvation, O the joyful sound!"

Dr. Fletcher then read the 100th Psalm, and offered the following prayer:— "Father of mercies, our God and Father in Christ Jesus, we approach Thy throne in the Name of our great Surety, our Intercessor, now pleading for us before Thy face! Glory to God in the highest, that salvation is provided for our ruined race! May it be the happiness of all here, constituting this immense assembly, to be interested in that salvation! Oh, that each individual now present on this joyful occasion may be enabled to say, in the language of appropriating faith, 'Salvation, and pardon, and acceptance are mine; Jesus is mine, and I am His!' Lord, look upon us in mercy in this place! Give us Thy presence, give us Thy countenance and smile! Multitudes of prayers have ascended to Thy throne on behalf of our beloved young friends, now about to be united by the most sacred union existing under the heavens. Oh, let Thy Spirit descend upon them! May they feel that they are now enjoying the light of Thy countenance, and that this important event in their history is under Thy blessed sanction, by Thy blessed direction, and shall be crowned with Thy blessing while they live, to be followed by blessings lasting as eternity, when they are called to their Heavenly home! Thou, Lord Jesus, who wast present at the marriage in Cana of Galilee, be tenderly with us at this time, and fill this house with Thy glory! These, our feeble supplications, we present before Thy mercy-seat in the Name of our exalted Advocate, and to the Father, Son, and Holy Spirit, be ascribed the kingdom, the power, and the glory, for ever and ever. Amen."

ADDRESS.

"Allow me, my respected friends, to address you only for a few moments, previous to that most important event which we have met to celebrate. Marriage is not the invention of man, it is the institution of God. It originated in God's wisdom and mercy; and, if necessary for man while in a state of innocence, it is much more indispensable for us in our fallen condition. It bears the impress of the Deity, and so important is it that it is presented to us in the Scripture as a figure of the union that is formed betwixt Christ and His chosen people,—that marriage union which is never to end. Christ has honoured this institution by comparing Himself to the Husband of the Church, and by designating the Church as His bride. 'I have espoused you,' says the apostle Paul, when writing to the believing Corinthians, 'I have espoused you to one Husband, that I may present you as a chaste virgin to Christ.' Look at the advantages marriage confers upon individuals, and families ; on communities, on nations, and on the Church of Christ. The founding of families is an epitome of the organization of nations, without which they could never be properly consolidated. Marriage is the foundation of all those distinguished privileges which are enjoyed by us in this island of the sea. I have referred before to the presence of Christ at the marriage at Cana ; what a lovely sight it must have been to see the blessed Jesus in the midst of that little assembly ! He blessed the bridegroom, and He blessed the bride ; He diffused joy through the hearts of all around. Your beloved Pastor has many times, in his preaching, alluded to Christ's smiles ; and if He smiled upon little children, whom He took up in His arms and blessed, He must surely have smiled upon the bride and bridegroom whose marriage feast was graced by His presence. Lord Jesus, Thou art here ! Thy humanity is in Heaven, but Thy Deity pervades the universe. With the eyes of our faith we can see Jesus in the midst of us, ready to bless both bride and bridegroom. He has blessed them already, and He has more blessings in reserve for their enjoyment, felicity, and usefulness ; and we trust He will crown them, through life, and through all eternity, with lovingkindness and tender mercy."

[The ceremony was then performed in the usual manner.]

A portion of Scripture was read, the congregation joined in singing " the Wedding Hymn," and Dr. Fletcher again engaged in prayer :—

" Look down, O Lord, with great kindness, complacency, and grace on our beloved young friends who have now entered into this sacred covenant with each other ! We praise Thee for that grace which Thou hast given them, an inheritance infinitely more precious than the wealth of empires. We praise Thee for the love to Jesus which Thou hast enkindled in their hearts, and for that mutual affection which they cherish, and by which they are united in the most endearing and sacred ties. Lord, bless them ! Bless them with increasing usefulness, increasing happiness, increasing enjoyment of Thy fellowship ! Long preserve them ! May they live to a good old age, like Zacharias and Elizabeth, walking in all the commandments and ordinances of the Lord blameless ! May this most interesting relationship be accompanied with innumerable mercies, especially to Thy dear ministering servant, engaged in the most honourable of all employments, and placed by the great Head of the Church in a sphere of usefulness seldom, if ever, equalled in this land of our nativity ! Lord, this is Thy doing ; Thou hast provided for him the sphere, and Thou hast fitted him by Thy providence and grace to fill it. May he be preserved in bodily vigour, as well as mental and spiritual strength, to prosecute that glorious work in which he has embarked ; and may he long continue to serve Thee, and be as useful at the close of life as he is at the commencement of his career! We now commit him and the beloved partner of his days to Thine everlasting arms; we lay them in the bosom of Thy love. Lord, bless all here present! Vast is the multitude, but it is nothing compared with the plenitude of Thy mercy, or the abundance of Thy grace. We thank Thee for presiding over the assembly, and that no accident has happened to this large concourse of people. All we ask is in the name of Jesus Christ our Lord. Amen.

"May the grace of the Lord Jesus Christ, and the love of God the Father, and the fellowship of the Holy Ghost, be with us all, now and for ever! Amen."

A London newspaper, of January 9th, 1856, contained the following notice of our wedding :—

"Yesterday morning, a curious scene was witnessed in the neighbourhood of New Park Street Chapel, Southwark, a large building belonging to the Baptist body of Dissenters, at the rear of the Borough Market. Of this place of worship the minister is the Rev. C. H. Spurgeon, a very young man, who, some months since, produced an extraordinary degree of excitement at Exeter Hall, where he preached during the time his chapel was in course of enlargement. Yesterday morning, the popular young preacher was married; and although the persons who evinced an interest in the proceedings were not quite of the aristocratic character of those who usually attend West End weddings, in point of numbers and enthusiasm they far outstripped any display which the West End is in the habit of witnessing. Shortly after eight o'clock, although the morning was dark, damp, and cold, as many as five hundred ladies, in light and gay attire, besieged the doors of the chapel, accompanied by many gentlemen, members of the congregation, and personal friends. From that hour, the crowd increased so rapidly, that the thoroughfare was blocked up by vehicles and pedestrians, and a body of the M division of police had to be sent for to prevent accidents. When the chapel doors were opened, there was a terrific rush, and in less than half-an-hour the doors were closed upon many of the eager visitors, who, like the earlier and more fortunate comers, were favoured with tickets of admission. The bride was Miss Susannah Thompson, only daughter of Mr. Thompson, of Falcon Square, London; and the ceremony was performed by the Rev. Dr. Alexander Fletcher, of Finsbury Chapel. At the close of the ceremony, the congratulations of the congregation were tendered to the newly-married pair with heartiest goodwill."

Mr. Spurgeon's own inscription in our family Bible, recording the marriage, and adding a loving comment eleven years afterwards, is reproduced in *facsimile* on the following page.

THE FAMILY REGISTER

Charles Haddon Spurgeon and
Susannah Thompson were by
the precious arrangement of
Divine Providence, most happily
married at New Park Street Chapel
by Dr Alexander Fletcher on
Tuesday, January 8th 1856.
"And as year rolls after year
"Each to other still more dear

EXCEPT THE LORD BUILD THE HOUSE.

THEY LABOR IN VAIN THAT BUILD IT.

CHAPTER XXXVII

Early Criticisms and Slanders.

In these days, there is a growing hatred of the pulpit. The pulpit has maintained its ground full many a year, but partially by its becoming inefficient, it is losing its high position. Through a timid abuse of it, instead of a strong stiff use of the pulpit, the world has come to despise it; and now most certainly we are not a priest-ridden people one-half so much as we are a press-ridden people. By the press we are ridden indeed. *Mercuries, Despatches, Journals, Gazettes,* and *Magazines* are now the judges of pulpit eloquence and style. They thrust themselves into the censor's seat, and censure those whose office it should rather be to censure them. For my own part, I cheerfully accord to all men the liberty of abusing me; but I must protest against the conduct of at least one Editor, who has misquoted in order to pervert my meaning, and who has done even more than that; he has manufactured a "quotation" from his own head, which never did occur in my works or words.—C. H. S., *in sermon preached at the Music Hall, Royal Surrey Gardens, January 25, 1857.*

WHILE reading again the letters referred to in the preceding chapters, Mrs. Spurgeon has been reminded that, before her marriage, she made a collection of newspaper cuttings relating to her beloved. As the different articles appeared, Mr. Spurgeon sent them on to her, usually saying with regard to each one, "Here's another contribution for your museum." It would not be difficult to fill a volume with reprints of the notices—favourable and otherwise,—of the young preacher's first years in London; but it is not likely that any useful purpose would be thereby served. It will probably suffice if a selection is given from the contents of this first scrap-book, especially as the papers it contains were published in various parts of the kingdom at considerable intervals during the years 1855 and 1856. They are therefore fairly representative of the press notices of the period, and they will be of greater interest to many readers because they were gathered by the dear preacher himself. The book in which the extracts are preserved bears upon its title-page, in his handwriting, the following inscription :—

Facts, Fiction, and Facetiæ.

The last word might have been Falsehood, for there is much that is untrue, and very little that can be regarded as facetious in the whole series. Some of the paragraphs are too abusive or too blasphemous to be inserted in this work; and one

C

cannot read them without wondering how any man could have written in such a cruel fashion concerning so young and so earnest a servant of the Lord Jesus Christ, who was labouring with all his might to bring sinners to the Saviour. At that early stage of his ministry, he had not become so accustomed as he was in later years to attacks from all quarters, and his letters show that he felt very keenly the aspersions and slanders to which he was subjected. Occasionally, also, he alluded from the pulpit to this form of fiery trial. In a sermon, preached March 15, 1857, he said :—" I shall never forget the circumstance, when, after I thought I had made a full consecration to Christ, a slanderous report against my character came to my ears, and my heart was broken in agony because I should have to lose that, in preaching Christ's gospel. I fell on my knees, and said, ' Master, I will not keep back even my character for Thee. If I must lose that, too, then let it go ; it is the dearest thing I have ; but it shall go, if, like my Master, they shall say I have a devil, and am mad ; or, like Him, I am a drunken man and a wine-bibber." In after years, he was less affected by the notices which appeared. Perhaps this was all the easier as the tone adopted by most of the writers very greatly improved, while the friendly articles and paragraphs were so much more numerous than the unfavourable ones that they obliterated the memory of any that might have caused sorrow and pain. The habit of preserving newspaper and other records of his career was continued by Mr. Spurgeon to the last ; and as each caricature, criticism, or commendation came to hand, he would say, " That is one more for my collection," while the praise or blame it contained would be of less importance in his esteem than his concern to have a conscience void of offence toward God and men. Preaching in the Tabernacle, in 1884, he thus referred to his early experience, and to the change the intervening period had witnessed :—

" ' They compassed me about like bees,' says David ;. that is to say, they were very many, and very furious When bees are excited, they are among the most terrible of assailants ; sharp are their stings, and they inject a venom which sets the blood on fire. I read, the other day, of a traveller in Africa, who learned this by experience. Certain negroes were pulling his boat up the river, and as the rope trailed along it disturbed a bees' nest, and in a moment the bees were upon him in his cabin. He said that he was stung in the face, the hands, and the eyes. He was all over a mass of fire, and to escape from his assailants he plunged into the river, but they persecuted him still, attacking his head whenever it emerged from the water. After what he suffered from them, he said he would sooner meet two lions at once, or a whole herd of buffaloes, than ever be attacked by bees again ; so that the simile which David gives is a very striking one A company of mean-spirited, wicked men, who are no bigger than bees, mentally or spiritually, can get together, and sting a good man in a thousand places, till he is well-nigh maddened by their scorn, their ridicule, their slander, and their misrepresentation. Their very littleness gives them the power to wound with impunity. Such has been the experience of some of us, especially in days now happily past. For one, I can say, I grew inured to falsehood and spite. The stings at last caused me no more pain than if I had been made of iron ; but at first they were galling enough. Do not be surprised, dear friends, if you have the same experience ; and if it comes, count it no strange thing, for in this way the saints have been treated in all time. Thank God, the wounds are not fatal, nor of long continuance ! Time brings ease, and use creates hardihood. No real harm has come to any of us who have run the gauntlet of abuse ; not even a bruise remains."

According to chronological order, the first serious attack resulted from the publication, by Rev. Charles Waters Banks, in *The Earthen Vessel*, December, 1854, of an article, the opening paragraphs of which appear on the next page.

"THE PASTORS OF OUR CHURCHES; THE PREACHERS OF OUR DAY.

"A BRIEF AND IMPARTIAL REVIEW OF MR. SPURGEON'S MINISTRY.

["As we have nearly come to the close of another year, we are striking out a new line of mental labour,—it is a glance at ministers as they are. It is not an easy task; but, then, we go to this work with a two-fold determination,—first, knowing that there is some good thing in all good men, we will try to find out, and to show, how that good thing is developed in different ways in different men. Secondly, knowing that there are imperfections in all men, we are determined, by help Divine, to have no hand in exhibiting them: 'We can do nothing against the truth, but for the truth.']

"Mr. C. H. Spurgeon is the present Pastor of New Park Street Chapel, in the Borough of Southwark. He is a young man of very considerable ministerial talent, and his labours have been amazingly successful in raising up the before drooping cause at Park Street to a state of prosperity almost unequalled. We know of no Baptist minister in all the metropolis—with the exception of our highly-favoured and long-tried brother, James Wells, of the Surrey Tabernacle,—who has such crowded auditories, and continued overflowing congregations, as Mr. Spurgeon has. But, then, very solemn questions arise. 'WHAT IS HE DOING?' 'WHOSE SERVANT IS HE?' '*What proof does he give that, instrumentally, his is a heart-searching, a Christ-exalting, a truth-unfolding, a sinner-converting, a church-feeding, a soul-saving ministry?*' This is the point at issue with many whom we know,—a point which we should rejoice to see clearly settled—in the best sense—and demonstrated beyond a doubt in the confidence of all the true churches of Christ in Christendom. In introducing this subject to the notice of our readers, we have no object in view further than a desire to furnish all the material which has been thrown into our hands,—a careful and discriminating examination of which may, to some extent, be edifying and profitable. We wish our present remarks to be considered merely *introductory*, not *conclusive;* but seeing that the minds of so many are aroused to *enquiry* as to what may be considered the *real position* of this young Samuel in the *professing* church, we are disposed to search the records now before us, and from thence fetch out all the evidence we can find expressive of a real work of grace in the soul, and a Divine call to publish the tidings of salvation, the mysteries of the cross, and the work of the Holy Spirit, in the hearts of the living in Jerusalem"

The article contained a kindly reference to Mr. Spurgeon's spiritual experience, and included the friendly testimony of a recent hearer, whose judgment carried weight with Mr. Banks, though his name was not given, but most of the space was devoted to extracts from the young preacher's published discourses. In *The*

Earthen Vessel for the following month (January, 1855), a long communication was inserted, bearing the signature, "Job." Mr. Spurgeon believed that the writer was the redoubtable James Wells ("King James," see page 19).

REV. JAMES WELLS.

The following extracts will show how the veteran wrote concerning the stripling who was destined far to surpass his critic in fame and usefulness :—

"I have no personal antipathy to Mr. Spurgeon; nor should I have written concerning him, but for your review of his ministry. His ministry is a public matter, and therefore open to public opinion; and as you assure us that the sermon on 1 Cor. i. 6,—'The Testimony of Christ Confirmed in You,'—by Mr. Spurgeon, is *by far* the best, I will, by your permission, lay before you my opinion of the same. But I will first make a few remarks concerning Mr. Spurgeon, to which remarks I think he is entitled.

"It is, then, in the first place, clear that he has been, from his childhood, a very industrious and ardent reader of books, especially those of a theological kind ; and that he has united with his theological researches books of classic and of scientific caste, and has thus possessed himself of every kind of information which, by the law of association, he can deal out at pleasure ; and these acquirements, by reading, are united, in Mr. Spurgeon, with good speaking gifts. The laws of oratory have been well studied, and he suits the action to his words. This mode of public speaking was, in the theatres of ancient Greece, carried to such an extent that one person had to speak the words, and another had to perform the gestures, and suit, with every variety of face and form, the movement to the subject in hand. Mr. Spurgeon has caught the idea, only with this difference, that he performs both parts himself. Mr. Spurgeon is too well acquainted with Elisha Coles not to see in the Bible the sovereignty of God ; and too well acquainted with the writings of Toplady and Tucker not to see in the Bible the doctrine of predestination, and an overruling providence ; and too well versed in the subtleties of the late Dr. Chalmers not to philosophize upon rolling planets, and methodically-moving particles of earth and water, each particle having its ordained sphere.

"But, in addition to this, he appears to be a well-disposed person,—kind, benevolent, courteous, full of goodwill to his fellow-creatures,—endearing in his manners, social,—a kind of person whom it would seem almost a cruelty to dislike. The same may be, with equal truth, said both of Dr. Pusey and of Cardinal Wiseman. But, then, it becomes us to be aware, not only of the rough garment of a mock and 'arrogant humility', but also of Amalekite-measured and delicate steps ; and also of the soft raiment of refined and studied courtesy (Matt. xi. 8), and fascinating smile with, ' Surely the bitterness of death is past' (1 Sam. xv. 32). But Samuel had too much honesty about him to be thus deceived. We must, then, beware of words that are smoother than butter, and softer than oil (Psalm lv. 21). Not one of the Reformers appears to have been of this *amiable* caste ; but these creature-refinements pass with thousands for religion ; and tens of thousands are deluded thereby. It was by great, very great *politeness* that the serpent beguiled Eve ; and, unhappily, her posterity love to have it so ;—so true is it that Satan is not only a prince of darkness, but transformed also as ' an angel of light,' to deceive, if it were possible, even the very elect.

"And yet further than all this, Mr. Spurgeon was, so says the *Vessel*, brought to know the Lord when he was only fifteen years old. Heaven grant it may prove to be so,—for the young man's sake, and for that of others also ! But I have—*most solemnly have—my doubts* as to the Divine reality of his conversion. I do not say— it is not for me to say—that he is not a regenerated man ; but this I do know, that there are conversions which are not of God ; and whatever convictions a man may have, whatever may be the agonies of his mind as to the possibility of his salvation, whatever terror anyone may experience, and however sincere they may be, and whatever deliverance they may have by dreams or visions, or by natural conscience, or the letter or even apparent power of the Word, yet, if they cannot stand, in their spirit and ministry, the test of the law of truth, and the testimony of God, there is no *true* light in them ; for a person may be intellectually enlightened, he may taste of the Heavenly gift, and be made partaker of the Holy Ghost, *professionally*, and taste of the good Word of God (Hebrews vi.), and yet not be regenerated, and therefore not beyond the danger of falling away, even from that portion of truth which such do hold. Such are never thoroughly convinced of what they are by nature ; Psalm xxxviii. and Romans vii. show a path to which they make some approaches, and of which they may eloquently talk, but at the same time give certain proofs that they are not truly walking therein. Mr. Spurgeon tells us, in his sermon on the Ministry of Angels, that he has more angelology about him than most people. Well, perhaps he has ; but then, if a *real* angel from Heaven were to preach another gospel, he is not to be received. . . .

"Concerning Mr. Spurgeon's ministry, I believe the following things :—

"1st. That it is most awfully deceptive ; that it passes by the essentials of the work of the Holy Ghost, and sets people by shoals down for Christians who are not Christians by the quickening and indwelling power of the Holy Ghost. Hence, free-willers, *intellectual* Calvinists, high and low, are delighted with him, together with the philosophic and classic-taste Christian ! This is simply deceiving others with the deception wherewith he himself is deceived.

"2nd. That, as he speaks some truth, convictions will in some cases take place under his ministry ; such will go into real concern for their salvation ; and will, after a time, leave his ministry, for a ministry that can accompany them in their rugged paths of wilderness experience.

"3rd Though I do not attach the moral worth to such a ministry as I should to the true ministry of the Spirit, yet it may be morally and socially beneficial to some people, who perhaps would care to hear only such an intellectually, or rather rhetori-cally-gifted man as is Mr. Spurgeon ; but then they have this advantage at the cost of being *fatally deluded*.

"4th. My opinion is, and my argument is, and my conclusion is, that no man who knows his own heart, who knows what the daily cross means, and who knows the difference between the form and the power, the name and the life itself, the semblance and the substance, the difference between the sounding brass or the tinkling cymbal and the voice of the turtle, pouring the plaintive, but healing notes of Calvary into the solitary and weary soul ;—he who walks in this path, could not hear with profit the ministry of Mr. Spurgeon.

"5th. I believe that Mr. Spurgeon could not have fallen into a line of things more adapted to popularity : his ministry pays its address courteously to all ; hence, in this sermon, he graciously receives us all,—such a reception as it is,—he who preaches all doctrine, and he who preaches no doctrine ; he who preaches all experience, and he who preaches no experience ; and, hence, *intellectually* High Calvinists of *easy virtue* receive such a ministry into their pulpits, at once showing that the man of sin, the spirit of apostacy, is lurking in their midst. Low Calvinists also receive him, showing that there is enough of their spirit about him to make him their *dear brother ;* only his Hyperism does sometimes get a little in their way, but they hope *experience* will soon take away this Calvinistic taint, and so make things more agreeable. But in this I believe they will be disappointed ; he has chosen his sphere, his orbit may seem to be eccentric, but he will go *intellectually* shining on, throwing out his cometary attractions, crossing the orbits of all the others, seeming friendly with all, yet belonging to none.

"His originality lies not in the materials he uses, but in ranging them into an order that suits his own turn of mind ; at this he industriously labours. (In this he is a reproof to some ministers of our own denomination who are not industrious, nor studious, nor diligent, but sluggish, slothful, negligent, empty-headed, and in the pulpit as well as in the parlour, empty-handed. Preaching then is like sowing the wind, and reaping the whirlwind ; and many on this account leave our ministers, and prefer a half-way gospel, ingenuously and enthusiastically preached, to a whole gospel, not half preached, or preached without variety, life, or power. May the Lord stir up His own servants, that they may work while it is day !)

" But, in conclusion, I say,—I would make every allowance for his youth ; but while I make this allowance, I am, nevertheless, thoroughly disposed to believe that we have a fair sample of what he will be even unto the end."

This letter was followed by editorial comments, and a long correspondence, *pro* and *con.* "JOB" wrote again, explaining one expression he had previously used, but making even more definite his assertion concerning what he supposed to be Mr. Spurgeon's lack of true spiritual life :—

" Dear Mr. Editor,—In one part of my review of Mr. Spurgeon's sermon, I have said of him, as a *minister,* ' I am thoroughly (it should have been *strongly*) *disposed to believe that we have a fair sample of what he will be to the end.*' It is to be regretted that some persons have tried to make the above mean that, as Mr. Spurgeon is in a state of nature now, he will so continue even unto the end ; whereas, I neither did, *nor do I mean,* any such thing : all I mean is, that his *ministry,* as it now is, is I am strongly disposed to believe a fair sample of what *it* will be even unto the end. I do not here refer to his personal destiny at all,—though no doubt many would have been glad to have seen me commit myself, by rushing in 'where angels fear to tread.' . . .

"I am, Mr. Editor, credibly informed that Mr. Spurgeon *himself* intends taking no notice of what I have written; and if I am to be counted an enemy because I have spoken what I believe to be the truth (Gal. iv. 16), I am perfectly willing to bear the reproach thereof; and most happy should I be to have just cause to think differently of his ministry; but I am at present (instead of being shaken,) more than ever *confirmed* in what I have written. I beg therefore to say that anything said upon the subject by Mr. Spurgeon's friends will be to me as straws thrown against a stone wall (Jeremiah i. 18), and of which I shall take no notice. Only let them beware lest a voice from Him, by whom *actions* are weighed, say unto them, 'Ye have not spoken of Me the thing that is right, as My servant Job hath' (Job xlii. 7.)"

Mr. Wells long continued his spirit of opposition to Mr. Spurgeon, even refusing to fulfil an engagement to preach because his brother-minister was to take one of the services on the same day; but many of his strict Baptist brethren did not sympathize with him in his action, and cordially welcomed the young preacher who held so many truths that were dear also to them

The Editor of *The Earthen Vessel* (Mr. Banks) published, in later numbers of his Magazine for 1855, three articles from his own pen, in the course of which, reviewing Mr. Spurgeon's life and ministry up to that time, he wrote :—

"It was a nice word of Richard Sibbes when he said, '*The office of a minister is to be a wooer, to make up the marriage between Christ and Christian souls :*' and we will plainly speak our minds ;—we have hoped that C. H. Spurgeon's work, in the hands of the Holy Ghost, is to woo and to win souls over unto Jesus Christ ; and we have an impression, should his life be spared, that, through his instrumentality, all our churches will, by-and-by, be increased. God Almighty grant that we may be true prophets ; and then, to all our cruel correspondents we will say, 'Fire away ; cut up, cast out, and condemn *The Earthen Vessel* as much as ye may, ye will do us no harm.' . . . We have no ground for suspecting the genuineness of Mr. Spurgeon's motives, nor the honesty of his heart. We are bound to believe that his statements respecting his own experience are just and true. We are bound to believe that, in prosecuting his ministry, he is sincerely aiming at three things,—THE GLORY OF CHRIST,—*the good of immortal souls,*—and *the well-being of Zion,*—and that, in all this, the love of Christ constrains him. If, in thoroughly weighing the sermons before us, proof to the contrary appeared, we would not hide it up ; but we sincerely trust no evidence of that kind can be produced. . . . In the course of Mr. Spurgeon's ministry, there are frequently to be found such gushings forth of love to God, of ravishing delights in Christ, of the powerful anointings of the Holy Ghost, as compel us to believe that God is in him of a truth. We must confess that is the deep-wrought conviction of our spirit; and we dare not conceal it. Why should we? We may be condemned by many; but, whatever it may cast upon us,—whoever may discard us,—we must acknowledge that, while in these sermons we have met with sentences that perplex us, and with what some might consider contradiction, still, we have found those things which have been powerful demonstrations of the indwelling of THE LIFE AND THE LOVE OF THE TRIUNE GOD in the preacher's heart.

"In thus giving, without reserve, *an unbiassed verdict* respecting the main drift of the sermons contained in *The New Park Street Pulpit*, we do not endorse every sentence, nor justify every mode of expression; our first work has been to search for that which, in *every new work* that comes to hand, we always search for,— that which we search for in every candidate for church-membership,—that is, LIFE: and if we have not found evidences of a Divine life in the ministry at New Park Street Chapel, we are deceived; yea, we are blind; and the powers of spiritual discernment are not with us. . . . We beseech all Christian people, who long for a revival in the midst of our churches, to pray for this young man, *whom we do earnestly hope* THE LORD HAS SENT AMONGST US. Let us not be found fighting against him, lest unhappily we be found fighting against God. Let us remember, he has not made himself, he has not qualified himself, he has not sent himself; all that he has, which is good, Godlike, and gracious, the Lord has given him;—all that he is doing, that is of real benefit to immortal souls, the Lord is doing by him."

CHAPTER XXXVIII.

Early Criticisms and Slanders *(Continued)*

There are some of us who come in for a very large share of slander. It is seldom that the slander market is much below par; it usually runs up at a rapid rate; and there are persons who will take shares to any amount. If men could dispose of railway stock as they can of slander, those who happen to have any scrip would be rich enough by to-morrow at twelve o'clock. There are some who have a superabundance of that matter; they are continually hearing rumours of this, that, and the other; and there is one fool or another who has not brains enough to write sense, nor honesty sufficient to keep him to the truth, who, therefore, writes the most infamous libels upon some of God's servants, compared with whom he himself is nothing, and whom for very envy he chooses to depreciate. Well, what matters it? . . . Young men, are you striving to do good, and do others impute wrong motives to you? Do not be particular about answering them; just go straight on, and your life will be the best refutation of the calumny. David's brother said that, in his pride and the naughtiness of his heart, he had come to see the battle. "Ah!" thought David, "I will answer you by-and-by." Off he went across the valley to fight Goliath; he cut off his head, and then came back to his brother with a glorious answer in his conquering hand. If any man desires to reply to the false assertions of his enemies, he need not say a word; let him go and do good, that will be his answer. I am the subject of detraction, but I can point to hundreds of souls that have been saved by my feeble instrumentality, and my reply to all my enemies is this, "You may say what you like; you may find fault with the matter and manner of my preaching, but God saves souls by it, and I will hold up that fact, like giant Goliath's head, to show you that, although my preaching is only like David's sling and stone, God has thereby gotten the victory."—*C. H. S., in sermon preached at Exeter Hall, June 15, 1856.*

I do not expect to see so many conversions in this place as I had a year ago, when I had far fewer hearers. Do you ask why? Why, a year ago, I was abused by everybody; to mention my name, was to mention the name of the most abominable buffoon that ever lived. The mere utterance of it brought forth oaths and curses; with many men it was the name of contempt, kicked about the street as a football; but then God gave me souls by hundreds, who were added to my church, and in one year it was my happiness personally to see not less than a thousand who had then been converted. I do not expect that now. My name is somewhat esteemed, and the great ones of the earth think it no dishonour to sit at my feet; but this makes me fear lest my God should forsake me while the world esteems me. I would rather be despised and slandered than aught else. This assembly, that you think so grand and fine, I would readily part with, if by such a loss I could gain a greater blessing. . . . It is for us to recollect, in all times of popularity, that "Crucify Him! Crucify Him!" follows fast upon the heels of "Hosanna!" and that the crowd of to-day, if dealt with faithfully, may turn into the handful of to-morrow; for men love not plain speaking. We should learn to be despised, learn to be contemned, learn to be slandered, and then we shall learn to be made useful by God. Down on my knees have I often fallen, with the hot sweat rising from my brow, under some fresh slander poured upon me; in an agony of grief, my heart has been well-nigh broken; till at last I learned the art of bearing all, and caring for none. And now my grief runneth in another line, it is just the opposite; I fear lest God should forsake me, to prove that He is the Author of salvation, that it is not in the preacher, that it is not in the crowd, that it is not in the attention I can attract, but in God, and in God alone. This I hope I can say from my heart,—if to be made as the mire of the streets again, if to be the laughing-stock of fools and the song of the drunkard once more will make me more serviceable to my Master, and more useful to His cause, I will prefer it to all this multitude, or to all the applause that man could give.— *C. H. S., in sermon preached at the Music Hall, Royal Surrey Gardens, May 10, 1857.*

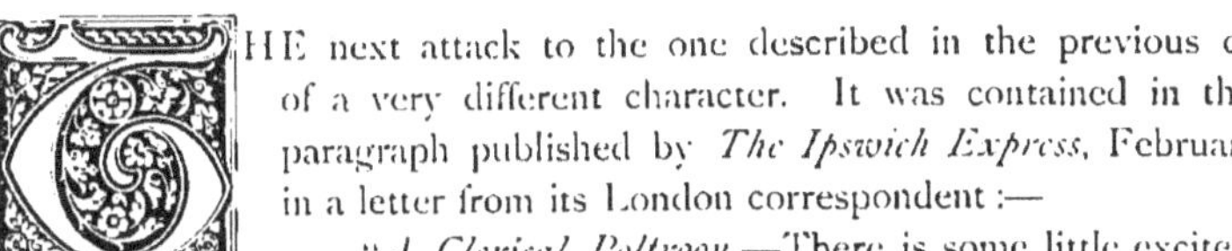

HE next attack to the one described in the previous chapter was of a very different character. It was contained in the following paragraph published by *The Ipswich Express*, February 27, 1855, in a letter from its London correspondent :—

"*A Clerical Poltroon.*—There is some little excitement in the religious world, created by a young man, a Baptist minister, and whose father, I am told, is an Independent minister of the name of Spurgeon, in

Colchester. This youth is fluent, and the consequences are most distressing. As his own chapel is under repair, he preaches in Exeter Hall every Sunday, and the place is crammed to suffocation. All his discourses are redolent of bad taste, are vulgar and theatrical, and yet he is so run after that, unless you go half-an-hour before the time, you will not be able to get in at all. I am told, one leading minister of the Independent denomination, after hearing this precocious youth, said that the exhibition was 'an insult to God and man.' Actually, I hear, the other Sunday, the gifted divine had the impudence, before preaching, to say, as there were many young ladies present, that he was engaged,—that his heart it was another's, he wished them clearly to understand that,—that he might have no presents sent him, no attentions paid him, no worsted slippers worked for him by the young ladies present. I suppose the dear divine has been rendered uncomfortable by the fondness of his female auditors ; at any rate, such is the impression he wishes to leave. The only impression, however, he seems to have produced upon the judicious few is one of intense sorrow and regret that such things should be, and that such a man should draw."

Mr. Spurgeon's feeling about the matter can be judged by the following letter to his father :—

"75, Dover Road,

"4th March, 1855.

"Dear Father,

"Do not be grieved at the slanderous libel in this week's *Express*. . . .

"Of course, it is *all a lie*, without an atom of foundation ; and while the whole of London is talking of me, and thousands are unable to get near the door, the opinion of a penny-a-liner is of little consequence.

"I beseech you not to write ; but if you can see Mr. Harvey, or some official, it might do good. A full reply on all points will appear next week.

"I only fear for you ; I do not like you to be grieved. For myself, I WILL REJOICE ; the devil is roused, the Church is awakening, and I am now counted worthy to suffer for Christ's sake. . . . Good ballast, father, good ballast ; but, oh ! remember what I have said before, and do not check me.

"Last night, I could not sleep till morning light, but now my Master has cheered me ; and I 'hail reproach, and welcome shame.'

"Love to you all, especially to my dearest mother. I mean to come home April 16th. So, amen.

"Your affectionate son,

"C. H. SPURGEON."

On March 6, *The Ipswich Express* contained the following paragraphs :—
"THE REV. C. H. SPURGEON.

"A gentleman of good position in London complains, as 'a friend of the Rev. C. H. Spurgeon,' of the statements respecting that gentleman, last week, in the letter of our London correspondent, which are, he assures us, 'a tissue of falsehoods.' That being the case, we lose no time in contradicting them, and at the same time expressing our regret that they should have appeared in our columns. Of Mr. Spurgeon we know nothing personally, and, of course, can have no desire to say anything which should cause pain to him or his friends. It has been, and will still be, our constant desire in criticising public men to avoid anything like personalities. We much regret that our London correspondent should have reported mere hearsay (which we are now informed was incorrect) respecting Mr. Spurgeon, and also that we did not give his letter that revision before its appearance in print which all letters for the press should receive, but which Editors, in the hurry of the day of publication, are too apt to neglect.

"A London publisher also sends us a sermon delivered by Mr. Spurgeon on the 11th ult., at Exeter Hall, stating that we ought to read and review it, in justice to the rev. gentleman. We have received, from an anonymous correspondent in London, another sermon delivered by Mr. Spurgeon last November, accompanied by a like request. It is not our habit to review sermons ; but, under the circumstances, we admit the justice of these demands, and shall comply with them. Our correspondent having criticised Mr. Spurgeon's preaching (harshly, as the friends of the preacher think), we shall consider ourselves bound to take an opportunity of reviewing these discourses. In so doing, the friends of Mr. Spurgeon may be assured we shall bring to the task the best of our ability, and a perfectly unbiassed judgment ; we shall 'nothing extenuate, nor set down aught in malice.' "

The Editor published several letters from those who wrote in Mr. Spurgeon's defence, as well as from others who attacked him, and on April 24 he commenced his promised review of the sermons, as follows :—

"Some are born great, some achieve greatness, and some have greatness thrust upon them. We have had, in a measure, the reviewal of Mr. Spurgeon's sermons thrust upon us, and in the fulfilment of our task we may, perhaps, assist our readers to judge whether that gentleman has achieved any real, permanent greatness, or whether he has had a factitious, fleeting greatness thrust upon him by his ignorant admirers.

"The *Express* of February 27th contained, as usual, a letter from our London correspondent, a gentleman favourably known as a writer on politics and general literature. This letter contained some rather severe criticism on Mr. Spurgeon's style of preaching, and a line or two respecting a rumour, heard by our correspondent, of some absurd remarks said to have been made on a certain occasion by Mr. Spurgeon previous to preaching. We did not read the letter until it appeared in print. . . . As soon as we saw the paragraph, we blamed ourselves for publishing, as well as our correspondent for forwarding, anything of *mere hearsay* which could possibly give annoyance to the preacher in question or his friends. And we have since learned, on the undoubted authority of his own published effusions, that Mr. Spurgeon really does run into so many extravagancies that to attribute to him any which he has never perpetrated would not only be a wrong, but a 'wasteful and ridiculous excess.'

"However, in a day or two, we received from several of Mr. Spurgeon's acquaintances (some of them his intimate friends) a flat contradiction of the absurd story of 'the slippers.' For the credit of the ministry we were glad to have it thus authoritatively denied, and lost no time in stating our sincere regret that we had, through an inadvertence, given publicity to an incorrect report. More than this, we published several of the longest letters out of the many we received from Mr. Spurgeon's friends,—stuffed full of the most glowing eulogiums of that gentleman as a minister and a man,—and in compliance with the wishes of some very ardent in his cause, we promised to review Mr. Spurgeon's sermons. We printed about twenty times as much in his praise as had appeared in his dispraise,—we courteously carried on for some time a considerable correspondence with the London Spurgeonites,— and although we think theology is out of place in a newspaper, we agreed, for once, rather than the least injustice should be committed, to step out of our usual course, and criticise sermons. Could we do more? Indeed, the line we took showed so clearly the absence of any ill-feeling on our part to Mr. Spurgeon, that the gentleman who first (rather angrily) called our attention to the obnoxious paragraph, finished a lengthy correspondence with us by saying, 'I am perfectly satisfied with your explanation, and think it does you honour.'"

The "review" was continued on May 1st, and concluded on May 29th. The tone of it may be judged from the closing paragraphs :—"There is enough foolishness in London to keep up, in flourishing style, Tom Thumb, Charles Kean, the Living Skeleton, C. H. Spurgeon, and many other delusions all at once, and yet to allow a vast mass of sober-minded citizens to go 'the even tenor of their way,' quite unaffected by such transient turmoils. Our decided opinion is, that in no other place but London could Mr. Spurgeon have caused the *furor* that he has excited. It must not be forgotten that in London, or anywhere else, a religious delusion is, of all others, the most easy to inaugurate and carry on. When a man obtains possession of a pulpit, he has credit for meaning well, at any rate, and expressions are thenceforward often listened to from him, without hostile criticism, which would not be tolerated, if enunciated from any other position.

"Mr. Spurgeon's career is suggestive of various interesting questions. If such a man can obtain, in a short time, the position he now certainly occupies, does that fact say much for the condition of a great portion of the religious world? If Mr. S. be, as is stated, the very best among a large section of preachers, what sort of a man is the very worst of that section? Does the pulpit, upon the whole, keep pace with the age, or does it lag behind? Will not the immense success of such as Spurgeon go far to account for that aversion of men of taste to the public profession of Evangelical Religion complained of long ago by John Foster?"

Although the falsehood published in *The Ipswich Express* was promptly contradicted, it was widely copied into other papers. *The Empire* (London), and *The Christian News* (Glasgow), published the paragraph in full, while portions of it were incorporated into articles that appeared in various parts of the kingdom, and the story of "the slippers" was repeated so often that probably many people were foolish enough to believe it, and others were wicked enough to say that they heard Mr. Spurgeon make the statement!

The Essex Standard, April 18, 1855 (see Mr. Spurgeon's remarks on page 18), contained a long letter, signed "Iconoclast," describing a Sunday evening service at Exeter Hall. The writer said:—"The mighty gathering and the 'religious *furor*' made me think of Demosthenes haranguing the Athenians, Cicero before the Roman senate, Peter the Hermit preaching the Crusade, Wesley on his father's tomb at Epworth, and Whitefield stirring the breasts of the thousands in Hyde Park; and therefore I scanned somewhat curiously both 'orator' and auditors. A young man, in his 21st year, but looking much older, short in stature and thick set, with a broad massive face, a low forehead, an expressionless eye, a wide and sensual mouth, a voice strong but not musical,—suggestive of *Stentor* rather than *Nestor*,—the very reverse of a *beau idéal* of an orator: without the eye of fire, where was the heart of flame? Orpheus without his lyre (*flute*, Mr. Spurgeon says), what was the potent charm that was to change the 'swine of the metropolis' into men, and convert sinners into saints? We must wait for the thoughts that breathe, and the words that burn. The hymn was sung right lustily, and the preacher proceeded to read and expound the 3rd of Philippians. . . . It was evident that *exposition* was not his forte. Then followed what his audience called prayer. It was an apostrophe to the Invisible, containing certain petitions first for himself, then for the elect saints, and then for the outer-court worshippers. It was such an utterance as indicated low views of Deity, and exalted views of self. Indeed, self is never out of sight, and is presented to the listener as a 'little child', a 'babbler', a 'baby', a 'battering ram', '*little* David,' 'this despised young man,' 'this ranting fellow,' and 'an empty ram's horn.' If reverence is the greatest mark of respect to an earthly parent, how much more is it due to the Supreme Father of all! . . . When the painful effect of this most arrogant dictation to Deity allowed me to think, I could not but rejoice in that 'form of sound words' by which the devotions of the Church are sustained from Sabbath to Sabbath, and by which,

THE SLOW COACH.

also, such outrageous violations of decorum are rendered impossible. The discourse was from Philippians iii. 10: '*That I may know Him.*' The various objects of human pursuit being designated and discussed, we had put before us the object, nature, and effects of Paul's knowledge. . . . Speaking of his study, Mr. Spurgeon said it was his '*dukedom*', where he could talk to Milton and Locke as *slaves*, and say, 'Come down here.' Mr. Spurgeon loves controversy, but with the modesty peculiar to himself told us that, nowadays, 'he found no foeman worthy of *his* steel.' His favourite action is that of washing his hands, and then rubbing them dry. He belongs to the peripatetic, or Walker school, perpetually walking up and down as an actor treading the boards of a theatre. His style is that of the vulgar colloquial, varied by rant. . . . All the most solemn mysteries of our holy religion are by him rudely, roughly, and impiously handled. Mystery is vulgarised, sanctity profaned,

THE FAST TRAIN.

common sense outraged, and decency disgusted. . . . His rantings are interspersed with coarse anecdotes that split the ears of the groundlings; and this is popularity! and this is the 'religious *furor*' of London! and this young divine it is that throws Wesley and Whitefield in the shade! and this is the preaching, and this the theology, that five thousand persons from Sabbath to Sabbath hear, receive, and approve, and—profit by it!"

The next issue of *The Essex Standard* contained another communication in a similar strain :—

"Mr. Editor,—The letter of 'Iconoclast' in your Wednesday's impression is a faithful delineation of the young preacher who is making so great a stir just now. Had we seen it previously, we should have been kept from taking the trouble to go to Earl's Colne yesterday, to hear what extremely disgusted us,—a young man of 21 years assuming airs, and adopting a language, which would be scarcely tolerated in the man of grey hairs. In common with many others, though obliged to smile during his performances, we felt more inclined to weep over such a prostitution of the pulpit and hours devoted to professedly religious worship. His prayer, to us, appeared most profanely familiar ; and never were we impressed more with the contrast between this effusion and the beautifully-simple, reverential, and devout language of the Church of England Liturgy, and said, within our hearts, 'Would that Dissenters would bind down their ministers to use those forms of sound words, rather than allow of these rhapsodies, which, to all persons of taste and true devotion, must have been very offensive !' It is a matter of deep regret to many that one of the best Dissenting chapels in London should be occupied by a youth of Mr. Spurgeon's caste and doctrinal sentiments ; and they very properly shrink from recognizing him among the regular ministers of the Baptist denomination ; and we heard it regretted more than once yesterday that he should have been chosen to represent a Society so respectable as the Baptist Home Missionary Society. If gain were their object, they certainly obtained it, as we understand the collections were large ; but we submit no such motive can be tolerated at the cost of so much propriety. I exceedingly regret to write thus of one who, until I heard him yesterday, I thought probably was raised up for usefulness ; but a sense of duty to the public leads me to express my opinions and sentiments in this plain, unflinching manner.

"I am, Mr. Editor,

"Halstead,   "Yours respectfully,
    "April 18th, 1855."   "A LOVER OF PROPRIETY."

The following week, a letter of quite another kind was published in the same paper :—

"Sir,—Your readers have had the opinions of two supporters of the Established Church on the preaching of the Rev. C. H. Spurgeon ; and I trust to your well-known fairness to allow a Dissenter an opportunity of expressing the sentiments held by many who have enjoyed the pleasure of listening to the fervid words of that distinguished minister of the gospel.

"Mr. Spurgeon institutes a new era, or more correctly, revives the good old style of Bunyan, Wesley, and Whitefield,—men whose burning eloquence carried conviction to the hearts of their hearers,—men who cared nought for the applause of their fellow-mortals, but did all for God's glory. In the steps of these apostles does Mr. S. follow, and who could desire more noble leaders?

"The pulpit is now too much abused by the mere display of intellect; instead of the indignant burst of a Luther against the iniquities of mankind, we have only the passive disapprobation of the silvery-tongued man of letters. The preachers address their cold, 'packed-in-ice' discourses to the educated portion of their audience; and the majority, the uneducated poor, are unable, in these 'scientific' sermons, to learn the way of holiness, from the simple fact that they are above their comprehension. How unlike these ministers—who appear to consider the gospel so frail that it would lose its power if delivered with unflinching candour,—are to the holy Saviour! His words were always characterized by the greatest simplicity, and by a thorough detestation of those 'blind guides who strain at a gnat, and swallow a camel.'

"Mr. Spurgeon goes to the root of the evil; his discourses are such as a child can understand, and yet filled with the most elevating philosophy and sound religious instruction. Taking the Word as his only guide, and casting aside the writings—however antiquated—of fallible men, he appeals to the *heart*, not to the *head*; puts the living truth forcibly before the mind, gains the attention, and then, as he himself says, fastens in the bow the messenger shaft, which, by the blessing and direction of the Almighty, strikes home to the heart of the sinner.

"He holds that irreligion is to be fought against, not to be handled with 'fingers of down,' and hence Exeter Hall is crammed. It is objected that these are the lowest of the London poor. What of that? They, above all, need religious training. I suppose there are few advocates in this country for the opinion that the aristocracy of the land *alone* have souls; Jehovah has breathed His spirit into the democracy, and Mr. S. is the man for them. In my humble opinion, if there were more C. H. Spurgeons, there would be fewer Sabbath desecrationists, fewer tendencies to the idol-worship of Rome, and fewer disciples of Holyoake and Paine.

"In conclusion, let me suggest that, even if Mr. Spurgeon were guilty of all laid to his charge, would it not be better for Christians to gloss over the failings of a brother-worker (for no one doubts the sincerity of the young man's efforts), than to seek here and there for the dross amongst the pure metal,—making mountains out of molehills, and wantonly refusing the golden ears because mixed with the necessary chaff?

"I am, Sir,

"Your obedient servant,

"Vox Populi."

To the Editor of *The Chelmsford Chronicle*, who had published an article of a more friendly character than those in other East Anglian papers, Mr. Spurgeon wrote :—

"75, Dover Road,

" April 24th, 1855.

" My Dear Sir,

"I am usually careless of the notices of papers concerning myself,—referring all honour to my Master, and believing that dishonourable articles are but advertisements for me, and bring more under the sound of the gospel.   But you, my dear sir (I know not why), have been pleased to speak so favourably of my labours that I think it only right that I should thank you.   If I could have done so personally, I would have availed myself of the pleasure, but the best substitute is by letter.   Amid a constant din of abuse, it is pleasant to poor flesh and blood to hear *one* favourable voice.   I am far from deserving much that you have said in my praise, but as I am equally undeserving of the coarse censure poured on me by *The Essex Standard*, &c., &c., I will set the one against the other.   I am neither eloquent nor learned, but the Head of the Church has given me sympathy with the masses, love to the poor, and the means of winning the attention of the ignorant and unenlightened.   I never sought popularity, and I cannot tell how it is so many come to hear me ; but shall I now change?   To please the polite critic, shall I leave ' *the people* ', who so much require a simple and stirring style?   I am, perhaps, ' vulgar ', and so on, but it is not intentional, save that I *must* and *will* make the people listen.   My firm conviction is, that we have quite enough *polite* preachers, and that ' the many ' require a change.   God has owned me to the most degraded and off-cast ; let others serve their class : these are mine, and to them I must keep. My sole reason for thus troubling you is one of gratitude to a disinterested friend. You may another time have good cause to censure me ;—do so, as I am sure you will, with all heartiness ; but my young heart shall not soon forget ' a friend.'

" Believe me,

" My dear sir,

" Yours very sincerely,

"C. H. SPURGEON."

The Bucks Chronicle, April 28, 1855, published an article signed, " A BRITON," of which the following portion sufficiently indicates the character of the whole :—

"THE POPULAR MINISTER.

(" *From our London correspondent.*)

" Scarcity produces dearness ; rarity, curiosity.   Great preachers are as scarce as Queen Anne's farthings.   The market is glutted with mediocrity ;—a star is looked upon, in the theological world, as a prize equally with green peas in Covent Garden Market at Christmas. We have been inundated with the slang phrases of the profession until they have acquired the sameness of our milkman's cry, when he places his pails upon the ground, and, as he gives the bell-handle a spasmodic twitch, utters his well-known 'M-i-l-k.'

"We had thought the day for dogmatic, theologic dramatising, was past,—that we should never more see the massive congregation listening to outrageous manifestations of insanity,—no more hear the fanatical effervescence of ginger-pop sermonising, or be called upon to wipe away the froth, that the people might see the colour of the stuff. In this we were mistaken. A star has appeared in the misty plain of orthodoxy; and such a star that, were it not for the badge which encircles that part of it called neck, we should, for the more distinguishing characteristic, write comet. It has made its appearance in Exeter Hall; and is to be seen on the first day of the week, by putting a few 'browns' into a basket. The star is a Spurgeon, —not a carp, but much resembling a pike. Thousands flock weekly to see it; and it shines grandiloquently. It is a parson.—a young parson. Merciful goodness! such a parson seldom talks. It is a railway speed of joining sentences, conflabergasticated into a discourse. It is now near eleven o'clock a.m. He rises to read; and, as if the Book of Inspiration was not fine enough in its composition, enters into explanations of his own as apt as a coal-heaver would give of Thucydydes (sic). Never mind! the great gun of starology in theology has a mission. Not to convert the doggerelisms of Timbuctoo into rationalisms,—not to demonstrate the loving-kindness of the great Fatherhood,—not to teach the forgiveness of Jehovah Jirah (sic) in His great heart of mercy,—not to proclaim the extension of the kingdom of the Master of assemblies. No! but to teach that, if Jack Scroggins was put down in the black book, before the great curtain of events was unfolded, that the said Jack Scroggins, in spite of all he may do or say, will and must tumble into the limbo of a brimstone hell, to be punished and roasted, without any prospect of cessation, or shrinking into a dried cinder; because Jack Scroggins had done what Jack Scroggins could not help doing. . . . It is not pleasant to be frightened into the portal of bliss by the hissing bubbles of the seething cauldron. It is not Christian-like to say, 'God must wash brains in the Hyper-Calvinism a Spurgeon teaches before man can enter Heaven.' It does not harmonize with the quiet majesty of the Nazarene. It does not fall like manna for hungry souls; but is like the gush of the pouring rain in a thunderstorm, which makes the flowers to hang their heads, looking up afterwards as if nothing had happened. When the Exeter Hall stripling talks of Deity, let him remember that He is superior to profanity, and that blasphemy from a parson is as great a crime as when the lowest grade of humanity utters the brutal oath at which the virtuous stand aghast."

In one of Mr. Spurgeon's discourses delivered in the year 1855, there is the following remarkable paragraph, which shows that the foregoing article entirely misrepresented the usual style of his preaching; careful readers will note that he protested against some of the very expressions that he was charged with uttering :—

" Enthusiastic divines have thought that men were to be brought to virtue by the hissings of the boiling cauldron ; they have imagined that, by beating a hell-drum in the ears of men, they should make them believe the gospel ; that, by the terrific sights and sounds of Sinai's mountain, they should drive men to Calvary. They have preached perpetually, ' Do this, and thou art damned.' In their preaching, there preponderates a voice horrible and terrifying ; if you listened to them, you might think you sat near the mouth of the pit, and heard the ' dismal groans and sullen moans,' and all the shrieks of the tortured ones in perdition. Men think that by these means sinners will be brought to the Saviour. They, however, in my opinion, think wrongly : men are frightened into hell, but not into Heaven. Men are sometimes driven to Sinai by powerful preaching. Far be it from us to condemn the use of the law, for ' the law was our schoolmaster to bring us unto Christ ;' but if you want to get a man to Christ, the best way is to bring Christ to the man. It is not by preaching law and terrors that men are made to love God.

"' Law and terrors do but harden,
All the while they work alone ;
But a sense of blood-bought pardon,
Soon dissolves a heart of stone.'

" I sometimes preach ' the terror of the Lord,' as Paul did when he said, ' Knowing therefore the terror of the Lord, we persuade men ;' but I do it as did the apostle, to bring them to a sense of their sins. The way to bring men to Jesus, to give them peace, to give them joy, to give them salvation through Christ, is, by God the Spirit's assistance, to preach Christ,—to preach a full, free, perfect pardon. Oh, how little there is of preaching Jesus Christ ! We do not preach enough about His glorious Name. Some preach dry doctrines ; but there is not the unction of the Holy One revealing the fulness and preciousness of the Lord Jesus. There is plenty of ' Do this, and live,' but not enough of ' Believe on the Lord Jesus Christ, and thou shalt be saved.'"

The Sheffield and Rotherham Independent, April 28, 1855, to which Mr. Spurgeon alludes on page 19, had an article somewhat similar to the one in the Buckinghamshire paper of the same date :—

" Just now, the great lion, star, meteor, or whatever else he may be called, of the Baptists, is the Rev. M. (*sic*) Spurgeon, minister of Park Street Chapel,

Southwark.   He has created a perfect *furor* in the religious world.   Every Sunday, crowds throng to Exeter Hall—where for some weeks past he has been preaching during the enlargement of his own chapel,—as to some great dramatic entertainment. The huge hall is crowded to overflowing, morning and evening, with an excited auditory, whose good fortune in obtaining admission is often envied by the hundreds outside who throng the closed doors.   For a parallel to such popularity, we must go back to Dr. Chalmers, Edward Irving, or the earlier days of James Parsons.   But I will not dishonour such men by comparison with the Exeter Hall religious demagogue.*   They preached the gospel with all the fervour of earnest natures. Mr. Spurgeon preaches *himself.*   He is nothing unless he is an actor,—unless exhibiting that matchless impudence which is his great characteristic, indulging in coarse familiarity with holy things, declaiming in a ranting and colloquial style, strutting up and down the platform as though he were at the Surrey Theatre, and boasting of his own intimacy with Heaven with nauseating frequency.   His fluency, self-possession, oratorical tricks, and daring utterances, seem to fascinate his less-thoughtful hearers, who love excitement more than devotion. . . . I have glanced at one or two of Mr. Spurgeon's published sermons, and turned away in disgust from the coarse sentiments, the scholastical expressions, and clap-trap style I have discovered   It would seem that the poor young man's brain is turned by the notoriety he has acquired and the incense offered at his shrine.   From the very pulpit he boasts of the crowds that flock to listen to his rodomontade.   Only lately, he told his fair friends to send him no more slippers, as he was already engaged ; and on another occasion gloried in the belief that, by the end of the year, not less than 200,000 of his published trashy sermons would be scattered over the length and breadth of the land.   This is but a mild picture of the great religious lion of the metropolis.   To their credit be it spoken, Mr. Spurgeon receives no countenance or encouragement from the ornaments of his denomination.   I don't think he has been invited to take part in any of their meetings.   Nor, indeed, does he seek such fellowship.   He glories in his position of lofty isolation, and is intoxicated by the draughts of popularity that have fired his feverish brain.   He is a nine days' wonder,—a comet that has suddenly shot across the religious atmosphere.   He has gone up like a rocket, and ere long will come down like a stick.   The most melancholy consideration in the case is the diseased craving for excitement which this running after Mr. Spurgeon by the 'religious world' indicates.   I would charitably conclude that the greater part of the multitude that weekly crowd to his theatrical exhibitions consists of people who are not in the habit of frequenting a place of worship."

---

* It is worthy of note that the paper which, in 1855, thus described Mr. Spurgeon, in 1898, in reviewing Vol. I. of his *Autobiography*, spoke of him as " this noble Puritan preacher and saintly Christian."

What higher compliment than this could the slanderer have paid the dear young preacher! Mr. Spurgeon's own testimony, concerning many of his first London hearers, was that they had not been accustomed to attend any house of prayer until they came to New Park Street Chapel, Exeter Hall, or the Surrey Gardens Music Hall. Best of all, many of them became truly converted, and so helped to build up the great church which afterwards worshipped in the Metropolitan Tabernacle. In one of his earliest sermons at the Music Hall, Mr. Spurgeon said :—

"I have many a time had doubts and fears, as most of you have had ; and where is the strong believer who has not sometimes wavered ? I have said, within myself, 'Is this religion true, which, day after day, I incessantly preach to the people ? Is it correct that this gospel has an influence upon mankind ?' And I will tell you how I have reassured myself. I have looked upon the hundreds, nay, upon the thousands whom I have around me, who were once the vilest of the vile,—drunkards, swearers, and such like,—and I now see them 'clothed, and in their right mind,' walking in holiness and in the fear of God ; and I have said within myself, 'This must be the truth, then, because I see its marvellous effects. It is true, because it is efficient for purposes which error never could accomplish. It exerts an influence among the lowest order of mortals, and over the most abominable of our race.' . . . I could a tale unfold, of some who have plunged head-first into the blackest gulfs of sin ; it would horrify both you and me, if we could allow them to recount their guilt. I could tell you how they have come into God's house with their teeth set against the minister, determined that, say what he would, they might listen, but it would be only to scoff. They stayed a moment ; some word arrested their attention ; they thought within themselves, 'We will hear that sentence.' It was some pointed, terse saying, that entered into their souls. They knew not how it was, but they were spell-bound, and stood to listen a little longer ; and, by-and-by, unconsciously to themselves, the tears began to fall, and when they went away, they had a strange, mysterious feeling about them that led them to their chambers. Down they fell on their knees ; the story of their life was all told before God ; He gave them peace through the blood of the Lamb, and they came again to His house, many of them, to say, 'Come, all ye that fear the Lord, and hear what He hath done for our souls.'"

The Lambeth Gazette was a paper published so near to the scene of Mr. Spurgeon's ministry that it would have been easy for the Editor to ascertain *facts* concerning his life and work ; yet its issue for September 1, 1855, contained an article from which the following is an extract :—

"The fact cannot be concealed, mountebankism is, to a certain class of minds, quite as attractive in the pulpit as in the fields of a country town. The Rev. C. H. Spurgeon is now the star of Southwark. Mr. Wells (commonly known by the curious *sobriquet* of 'Wheelbarrow Wells'), of the Borough Road, has, for some years past, had the run in this line ; but he has, at last, got a rival well up in his 'tip', and likely to prove the favourite for a long time.   He is a very young man, too, and the young 'sisters' are dancing mad after him.   He has received slippers enough from these lowly-minded damsels to open a shoe shop ; and were it not that he recently advertised them that he was 'engaged', he would very soon have been able to open a fancy bazaar with the nicknacks that were pouring in upon him.   No doubt he is a very good young man, with the best of intentions ; but will not this man-worship spoil him?   Between the parts of the service, his mannerism in the pulpit is suggestive of affectation and vanity ;—it might' be only an overpowering sense of responsibility ; yet it would do for either state of feeling.   Who can wonder at it? . . .

"Let it not be supposed that the writer has any wish to cripple the usefulness of the young minister.   On the contrary, he would be happy to hear of 'much good being done.'   What he laments over is the spiritual poverty and want of taste indicated by the crowds who are so eager to feed upon the very 'husks' of a discarded style of preaching.   Doubtless, the young minister will be the means of breaking up much fallow ground,—would that it were then passed over to a more skilful husbandman !—but it is painful to hear of old Christians turning again to such 'beggarly elements', instead of allowing themselves to be 'built up and established in the faith.'   May prosperity attend you, Mr. Spurgeon ; but try, do try, to instruct as well as amuse your congregation,   Do not be satisfied with the ripple that passes over the face of the waters ; but stir them, if you can, to their lowest depths."

The Bristol Advertiser, April 12, 1856, thus introduced its report of a sermon by Mr. Spurgeon in that city :—

"It is very easy for public opinion to mistake the signs of greatness ; and for individuals to mistake the signs of public opinion.   For a time, weakness may command notoriety,—it never can hold fame.   We are not among those, therefore, who accept the hasty verdicts of the crowd.   We have often seen that audacity, eccentricity, or even stolidity itself can secure the homage which is always paid to genius ; but rash and ignorant devotees discover their mistake very soon ; and, though their quondam hero continue to make a noise, they, from sheer indifference, cease to notice him.   Indeed, there are quackeries in public as well as in professional life ; Dr. Holloways among the vendors of religious doctrine as well as among the vendors of patent medicines.   They work wonderful cures.   They get advertised everywhere.   They have agents all about the country, ready and willing to assist them in pushing the trade.   And, unfortunately, there is a world of superstitious, curious, and idle people who provide a profitable market for the spurious article.

But quacks are always short-lived ; and though a Morrison may find a successor, he himself quickly gets bowed out of society.

" Now, what is there in Mr. Spurgeon to account for the extraordinary sensation he makes everywhere ? It is not the doctrine he preaches ; for that is 'orthodox'; that is, it is preached by a thousand other clergymen. It is not his personal appearance, for that is but ordinary : his forehead is low ; his eye is small, and though capable of vivid flashes of self-appreciation, not radiant with those 'heavenly' rays by which sentimental ladies are usually fascinated ; his figure is broad and stumpy ; his manners are rude and awkward. In short, we can find no genuine qualities in this gentleman sufficient to explain the unrivalled notoriety he has acquired. If he were simple in his pretensions, and had the serene and sacred dignity of religious earnestness to support him, his destitution of refinement, his evident ignorance, his positive vulgarities of expression and of manner might be forgiven. We should feel that he was doing good in an important direction, and that to follow him with criticism or contempt would be, in a sort, profane. Or if he possessed unusual powers of mind, imagination, or speech, we could understand how many would seek to hear him. But his intellect not only lacks culture, it is evidently of meagre grasp. He has fancy, but all his larger illustrations failed, either in fitness or in development. He is fluent ; he talks on without stopping ; he has certain theatrical attitudes of which he knows how to make the most ; his voice is powerful ; and his enunciation clear ; and thus many of the *mechanical* effects of oratory are under his sway. But his thoughts are commonplace, and his figures false, though striking. He says good things smartly ; but his best things are his tritest, and his most striking are his most audacious sentences. . . . Solemnly do we express our regret that insolence so unblushing, intellect so feeble, flippancy so ostentatious, and manners so rude should, in the name of religion, and in connection with the church, receive the acknowledgment of even a momentary popularity. To our minds, it speaks sad things as to the state of intelligence, and calm, respectful, and dignified piety among a mass of people who call themselves the disciples of Jesus. Where curiosity is stronger than faith, and astonishment easier to excite than reverence to edify, religious life must either be at a very low ebb, or associated with some other deleterious elements."

The Daily News, a paper from which something better might have been expected, had, in its issue of September 9, 1856, a long article on " Popular Preachers,—The Rev. Mr. Spurgeon," in which it said :—" We are accustomed to look grave when the old mysteries and miracle-plays are mentioned. We pity the ignorance of those ancestors of ours who could find food for amusement or helps to devotion in the representation of doggerel dramas, where God the Father, our

Saviour, the Holy Spirit, the devil, Adam and Eve, and, in short, all the principal personages, human or supernatural, mentioned in Scripture, were brought on the stage. We are liable to entertain shrewd doubts as to the piety of the writers of these horrible travesties of the sacred narratives, and to lament over the crassness of the intellect of those who could find entertainment in them. We can see nothing more instructive than in the awful contest between the devil and the baker, which was generally the concluding scene of the 'galantee show' performances with which the Christmas of our childhood was enlivened. In Protestant countries in general, and in England in particular, we shrink from undue familiarity with holy words and things. We have just as much aversion to see a church turned into a theatre as to see a theatre turned into a church. We hold an opinion, grounded as much on the principles of good taste as of religion, that it is almost as offensive to see a clergyman perform in his pulpit as to hear actors invoke Heaven in a theatre. This opinion, however, is not quite universally entertained. Let any person who wishes to convince himself of the truth of this, take his station opposite to Exeter Hall on Sunday evening at about a few minutes before six o'clock. We say opposite, because, unless he arrives some time before the hour mentioned, there will be no standing-room on the pavement from which the entrance to the hall ascends. At six, the doors open, and a dense mass of human beings pours in. There is no interruption now to the continuous stream until half-past six o'clock, when the whole of the vast hall, with its galleries and platform, will be filled with the closely-packed crowd.

"If the spectator has not taken care to enter before this time, he will have but small chance of finding even standing-room. Suppose him to have entered early enough to have found a seat, he will naturally look around him to scan the features of the scene. They are remarkable enough to excite attention in the minds of the most listless. Stretching far away to the back are thousands of persons evidently eager for the appearance of someone. Towering up the platform, the seats are all crowded. Nearly all the eyes in this multitude are directed to the front of the platform. The breathless suspense is only broken occasionally by the struggle, in the body of the hall, of those who are endeavouring to gain or maintain a position. Suddenly, even this noise is stopped. A short, squarely-built man, with piercing eyes, with thick black hair parted down the middle, with a sallow countenance only redeemed from heaviness by the restlessness of the eyes, advances along the platform towards the seat of honour. A cataract of short coughs, indicative of the relief afforded to the ill-repressed impatience of the assembly, announces to the stranger that the business of the evening has commenced. He will be told with a certain degree of awe by those whom he asks for information, that the person just arrived is the Rev. C. H. Spurgeon. He will perhaps hear, in addition to this, that Mr. Spurgeon is beyond all question the most popular preacher in London ; that he is obliged to leave off preaching in the evening at his chapel in New Park Street, Southwark, on account of the want of room to accommodate more than a mere fraction of the thousands who flock to hear him ; that Exeter Hall has been taken for the purpose of diminishing in a slight degree the disappointment experienced ; but that nothing will be done to afford effectual relief until the new chapel which is in contemplation is built, and which is intended to hold 15,000 persons " (In a later chapter, it will be seen that Mr. Spurgeon corrected this inaccuracy concerning the accommodation to be provided in the Metropolitan Tabernacle ; he never had any intention of building a chapel "to hold 15,000 persons.")

The article concluded thus:—"We might fill columns with specimens of this pulpit buffoonery, but we have given enough to show the nature of Mr. Spurgeon's preaching. We might have brought forward instances of his utter ignorance of any theology except that current among the sect to which he belongs ; and of his ludicrous misinterpretations of Scripture, occasioned by his want of even a moderate acquaintance with Oriental customs and forms of language. . . . A congregation that constantly listens to the spiritual dram-drinking that Mr. Spurgeon encourages, will become not only bigoted, but greedy after stronger doses of excitement. What excited them once, will fall flat upon their palate. The preacher will be obliged to become more and more extravagant as his audience becomes more and more exacting, and the end may be an extensive development of dangerous fanaticism."

The Illustrated Times, October 11, 1856, published a portrait—or rather, a caricature—of Mr. Spurgeon; with a lengthy article containing one of the many prophecies that subsequent events proved to be false. The writer said :—

'Mr. Spurgeon's popularity is unprecedented ; at all events, there has been nothing like it since the days of Wesley and Whitefield. Park Street Chapel cannot hold half the people who pant to hear him, and even Exeter Hall is too small. Indeed, it is reported on good authority that his friends mean to hire the Concert Room at the Surrey Gardens, and firmly believe that he will fill that. Nor is his popularity confined to London ; in Scotland, he was very much followed ; and, lately, we ourselves saw, on a week-day, in a remote agricultural district, long lines of people all converging to one point, and on enquiring of one of the party where they were going, received for answer, ' We're a go'in' to hear *Macster Spudgin*, sir.

" WILL HIS POPULARITY LAST ?

"We more than doubt it. It stands on no firm basis. Thousands who go now to hear him only go through curiosity. Men are very much like sheep ; one goes through a hedge, then another, and another ; at last the stream gathers *crescit eundo*, and the whole flock rushes madly forward. This has been a good deal the case with

Mr. Spurgeon's congregation, but the current will soon turn and leave him ; and as to those who have gone from a slightly different, if not better, motive, it is hardly likely that he will retain them long. He must bid high if he does,—offering them every Sunday a stronger dram than they had the last."

POSTSCRIPT BY MRS. C. H. SPURGEON.

No defence of my beloved is needed now. God has taken him to Himself, and "there the wicked cease from troubling; and there the weary be at rest." The points of these arrows are all blunted,—the stings of these scorpions are all plucked out,—the edge of these sharp swords is rusted away. "And where is the fury of the oppressor?"

A strange serenity has brooded over my spirit as these chapters have recalled the heartless attacks made on God's servant; I have even smiled as I read once again the unjust and cruel words written by his enemies ; for he is so safe now, "with God eternally shut in ;" and I can bless the Lord for the suffering all ended, and the eternity of bliss begun. "For Thou hast made him most blessed for ever : Thou hast made him exceeding glad with Thy countenance."

But, at the time of their publication, what a grievous affliction these slanders were to me ! My heart alternately sorrowed over him, and flamed with indignation against his detractors. For a long time, I wondered how I could set continual comfort before his eyes, till, at last, I hit upon the expedient of having the following verses printed in large Old English type, and enclosed in a pretty Oxford frame. (This was before the days of the illuminated mottoes which at present are so conspicuous in our homes, and so often silently speak a message from God to us.)

> "Blessed are ye, when men shall revile you, and
> persecute you, and shall say all manner of evil
> against you falsely, for My sake. Rejoice, and be
> exceeding glad : for great is your reward in Heaven :
> for so persecuted they the prophets which were before
> you."—*Matthew* v. 11, 12.

The text was hung up in our own room, and was read over by the dear preacher every morning,—fulfilling its purpose most blessedly, for it strengthened his heart, and enabled him to buckle on the invisible armour, whereby he could calmly walk among men, unruffled by their calumnies, and concerned only for their best and highest interests

CHAPTER XXXIX.

First Literary Friends.

I was reading, some time ago, an article in a newspaper, very much in my praise. It always makes me sad,—so sad that I could cry, if ever I see anything praising me; it breaks my heart, I feel I do not deserve it; and then I say, " Now I must try and be better, so that I may deserve it." If the world abuses me, I am a match for that; I begin to like it. It may fire all its big guns at me, I will not return a solitary shot, but just store them up, and grow rich upon the old iron. All the abuse it likes to heap upon me, I can stand; but when a man praises me, I feel it is a poor thing I have done, and that he commends what does not deserve commendation. This crushes me down, and I say to myself, " I must set to work and deserve this; I must preach better, I must be more earnest, and more diligent in my Master's service."—C. H. S.

LTHOUGH many assailed Mr. Spurgeon through the press in the first years of his ministry in London, there were always loyal and true hearts ready to come to his help, and write in his defence. This chapter and the next contain the principal favourable articles published during 1855 and 1856 ; they furnish a marked contrast to the slanders and calumnies which the young preacher had to endure at that time.

One of the earliest encouraging notices appeared appropriately in *The Friend*, and was supplied by a member of the Society of Friends. The writer said :—

"An extraordinary sensation has recently been produced in London by the preaching of a young Baptist minister named C. H. Spurgeon. The crowds which have been drawn to hear him, the interest excited by his ministry, and the conflicting opinions expressed in reference to his qualifications and usefulness, have been altogether without parallel in modern times. What renders the present case remarkable is, the juvenility of the preacher,—his hold on the public being established before he had attained his twentieth year ; and his first appearance in London being that of a country youth, without any of the supposed advantages of a College education or ordinary ministerial training. Early in 1854, he undertook the charge of the congregation assembling in New Park Street Chapel, Southwark. It was a remarkable sight to see this round-faced country youth thus placed in a position of such solemn and arduous responsibility, yet addressing himself to the fulfilment of its onerous duties with a gravity, self-possession, and vigour, that proved him well fitted to the task he had assumed. In a few weeks, the pews, which had been so long tenantless, were crowded, every sitting in the chapel was let, and ere many months had elapsed, the eagerness to hear him had become so great, that every standing-place within the chapel walls was occupied on each succeeding Sabbath, and it became evident that increased accommodation must be provided for the wants of the congregation. It was about this period, in the autumn of 1854, that we first heard C. H. Spurgeon, on the occasion of his preaching to the Young Men's Christian Association. The preliminary portions of the service were conducted in a manner at once to impress the hearer with a sense of the earnest reverence which the young Pastor felt in his work. He read a portion of Scripture, accompanying it with a few forcible and pointed remarks,—these expository efforts being of peculiar value to the class of hearers of which his congregations are mostly composed. His sermon was a deeply-impressive one. He spoke as a young man to young men,—sympathizing in their tastes, their trials, their temptations, and their wants. He unfolded the plan of salvation, and urged the importance of a manly and decided profession of Christianity."

One of the first and one of the ablest of Mr. Spurgeon's champions among literary men was Mr. James Grant, the Editor of *The Morning Advertiser*, which, under his management, a contemporary writer testifies, was raised " to the position of a first-class morning paper, second only to *The Times*, either in circulation or influence." In its columns, on February 19, 1855, he published an article, the tenor of which may be judged by the following extracts :—

"THE REV. MR. SPURGEON.

" A young man, in the twenty-first year of his age, has just appeared, under this name, among our metropolitan preachers, and is creating a great sensation in the religious world. He had only been a few weeks settled as minister of Park Street Chapel, Southwark, before that commodious place was filled to overflowing, while hundreds at each service went away who were unable to effect an entrance. The result was, that it was agreed to enlarge the chapel, and that the youthful minister should preach in the large room of Exeter Hall for eight Sundays, until the re-opening of his own place of worship. It will easily be believed how great must be the popularity of this almost boyish preacher, when we mention that, yesterday, both morning and evening, the large hall, capable of containing from 4,000 to 5,000 persons, was filled in every part. Mr. Spurgeon belongs to the Baptist denomination. . . . He is short in stature, and somewhat thickly built, which, with an exceedingly broad, massive face, gives him the appearance of a man twenty-six or twenty-seven years of age instead of twenty-one. His doctines are of the Hyper-Calvinist school. He is a young man, we are told, of extensive information, especially on theological subjects, and of a highly cultivated mind. There can be no doubt that he possesses superior talents, while, in some of his happier flights, he rises to a high order of pulpit oratory. It is in pathos that he excels, though he does not himself seem to be aware of the fact. But for some sad drawbacks in the young divine, we should anticipate great usefulness from him, because he not only possesses qualities peculiarly adapted to attract and rivet the attention of the masses, but he makes faithful and powerful appeals to the consciences of the unconverted. In the spirit of sincere friendship, we would advise him to study to exhibit an aspect of greater gravity and seriousness. Let us also impress upon him the indispensable

necessity of relinquishing those theatrical—we had almost said melo-dramatic attitudes into which he is in the habit of throwing himself. In Exeter Hall, yesterday, instead of confining himself to the little spot converted into a sort of pulpit for him, he walked about on the platform just as if he had been treading the boards of Drury

Lane Theatre, while performing some exciting tragedy. Altogether, he seems to want the reverence of manner which is essential to the success of a minister of the gospel.* We hope, however, that in these respects he will improve. It is with that view we give him our friendly counsels. He is quite an original preacher, and therefore will always draw large congregations, and, consequently, may be eminently made the means of doing great good to classes of persons who might never otherwise be brought within the sound of a faithfully-preached gospel. He has evidently made George Whitefield his model; and, like that unparalleled preacher, that prince of pulpit orators, is very fond of striking apostrophes. Like him, too, he has a powerful voice, which would, at times, be more pleasing, and not less impressive, were it not raised to so high a pitch."

Mr. Spurgeon's own testimony confirms Mr. Grant's assertion that he had "evidently made George Whitefield his model." He wrote, in 1879 :—"There is no end to the interest which attaches to such a man as George Whitefield. Often as I have read his life, I am conscious of distinct quickening whenever I turn to it. *He lived.* Other men seem to be only half-alive ; but Whitefield was all life, fire, wing, force. My own model, if I may have such a thing in due subordination to my Lord, is George Whitefield ; but with unequal footsteps must I follow in his glorious track."

Mr. Grant's article was reprinted in the March number of *The Baptist Messenger*, which was originated, and, until his death, edited, by Rev. Jonathan Whittemore, of Eynsford, who had, in the autumn of 1854, availed himself of Mr. Spurgeon's literary assistance, and so commenced a connection with the Magazine which has continued to the present day. In the meantime, the correspondence referred to in the previous chapter was being published, and consequently the April issue of the *Messenger*, as it was usually termed, contained several of the most friendly letters, together with the following article on "Mr. Spurgeon and his Detractors" :—

"It is not at all a matter of surprise that the extraordinary popularity of this estimable young minister should have evoked censure and commendation of all kinds and degrees. The pulpit and the forum alike invite attention, and challenge criticism ; and so long as this test is legitimately and truthfully applied, no public character, if right-hearted, will shrink from its decisions. But if the criticism be made the vehicle of calumny, and if the censors of the press—instead of employing

---

* In the *Autobiography*, Vol. I., page 353, a quotation is given from the reminiscences of Professor Everett, who had been Mr. Spurgeon's fellow-tutor at Newmarket. Soon after the young Pastor's settlement at New Park Street Chapel, he invited his former colleague to pay him a visit. During their conversation, Mr. Everett referred to this supposed irreverence ; and recalling the interview, in 1892, he wrote :—"I remember suggesting to him, in this connection, that a man ought to feel and show some sense of awe in the presence of his Maker, and his reply was to the effect that awe was foreign to his nature,—that he felt perfectly at home with his Heavenly Father."

their pens in commending excellences, or in censuring and correcting faults, however severely, if fairly done,—seek by detraction and falsehood to damage the reputation and lessen the usefulness of those whose efforts they decry, then do they degrade an otherwise honourable occupation into that of a dirty and despicable slanderer. Several of Mr. Spurgeon's critics, we regret to say, have thus disgraced themselves. If they have not originated, they have given a wide circulation to fabrications as grossly absurd as they are totally false. By Mr. S., however, these falsehoods are treated with no other feelings than those of pity for the individuals from whom they emanated. It was thus, a century ago, with the seraph-tongued Whitefield, to whom, by some of his more friendly critics, Mr. Spurgeon has been compared.

"We have been induced to make this reference to those attacks upon Mr. Spurgeon, not more from the circumstance that we are favoured monthly with his valuable contributions to our pages, than from the high and honourable position in which it has pleased the great Head of the Church to place him, in which it should be the aim of all who love Zion to uphold and encourage this youthful and gifted brother ; and also because we have had put into our hands, by a party altogether disinterested, the following correspondence, a portion of which is addressed to a provincial paper, which had been made the medium of circulating slanderous reports concerning Mr. S., to whom it is but fair to state, the Editor of the paper referred to has made most ample and satisfactory apology."

In the June number of *The Baptist Messenger*, the Editor wrote :—"Several articles and extracts from provincial papers, condemnatory of the Rev. C. H. Spurgeon, have been forwarded for insertion in the *Messenger*. This, however, we must decline doing It is, indeed, most pitiful that this excellent and useful servant of Christ cannot go about his Master's business quietly and unobtrusively— for his popularity is altogether unsought by him,—without exciting unkind and envious remarks."

In the quotation from Mr. Spurgeon's letter, given on page 26, there is an allusion to a glowing account of his life and work which had been published in *The Patriot*, on September 21, 1855. The following are some of the writer's kind expressions concerning the young preacher :—

"Although the name of the Rev. C. H. Spurgeon has been frequently mentioned in the columns of this Journal, we have not introduced him to our readers by any formal description of his preaching. Such, however, is its effect, that curiosity cannot but have been awakened by intelligence of the immense crowds collected to hear him while occupying Exeter Hall from Sunday to Sunday, and also when he returned to his own enlarged chapel in New Park Street, over Southwark Bridge. There must surely be something extraordinary in a mere youth who could command an attendance of from ten to twelve thousand persons in the open field, and who, on visiting the North, though received with cold suspicion at first, soon compelled the fixed and admiring attention of the reluctant Scotch ; though, he says, 'they seemed to be all made of lumps of ice fetched from Wenham Lake.' Those who go to hear Mr. Spurgeon, enquiring, 'What will this babbler say?' are not long left in doubt as to either the manner or the matter of his discourses. . . . We have ourselves heard Mr. Spurgeon but once ; and, on that occasion, not having succeeded in gaining an entrance to the chapel, we squeezed ourselves into a side vestry, from which the speaker could be heard, but not seen. We found him neither extravagant nor extraordinary. His voice is clear and musical ; his language is plain ; his style flowing, yet terse ; his method lucid and orderly ; his matter sound and suitable ; his tone and spirit cordial ; his remarks always pithy and pungent, sometimes familiar and colloquial, yet never light or coarse, much less profane. Judging from this single sermon, we supposed that he would become a plain, faithful, forcible, and affectionate preacher of the gospel in the form called Calvinistic ; and our judgment was the more favourable because, while there was a solidity beyond his years, we detected little of the wild luxuriance naturally characteristic of very young preachers.

" Our opinion of Mr. Spurgeon as a preacher has been somewhat modified by a perusal of his published discourses, which, issued in a cheap form, appear to be bought up with great eagerness. These show him to be a more extraordinary person than we supposed, and not to be quite so far from extravagance as at first we thought him. But it is more for the sake of information than with a view to criticism that we refer to the subject. From whatsoever cause it springs, whether from force of native character, or from a vigour superinduced upon that basis by the grace of God, there is that in Mr. Spurgeon's reported sermons which marks him a superior man.

" Models of different styles of preaching are so numerous, that originality must be of rare occurrence ; but he appears to be an original genius. To the pith of Jay, and the plainness of Rowland Hill, he adds much of the familiarity, not to say the coarseness, of the Huntingtonian order of ultra-Calvinistic preachers. 'It has been my privilege,' he says, 'to give more prominence in the religious world to those old doctrines of the gospel.' But the traits referred to present themselves in shapes and with accompaniments which forbid the notion of imitation, and favour the opinion of a peculiar bent. Neither in the style and structure, nor in handling, is there appearance of art, study, or elaboration. Yet, each discourse has a beginning, a middle, and an end : and the subject is duly introduced and stated, divided and discussed, enforced and applied. But all is done without effort, with the ease and freedom of common conversation, and with the artlessness, but also with the force, of spontaneous expression.

"Mr. Spurgeon waits for nothing which requires what we understand by composition, and he rejects nothing by which attention may be arrested, interest sustained, and impression made permanent. The vehicle of his thoughts is constructed of well-seasoned Saxon speech ; and they are conveyed to the hearer's mind in terms highly pictorial and often vividly dramatic. Great governing principles are freely personified ; and religious experience, past, present, and future, appears in life-like action upon the scene. Tried by such tests as the unities, Mr. Spurgeon might sometimes be found wanting ; but it is enough for him that, as face answers to face in the glass, so do his words elicit a response in the hearts of those who hear him. This end secured, what cares he for a mixed metaphor or a rhetorical anachronism ? Were it his aim to rival the Melvilles and Harrises of the day, he lacks neither the talent nor the taste ; and, with these, he has the faculty of gathering what is to be learned from men or from books, and of turning all to account. But his single aim is to preach the gospel ; and he depends for success, not upon the enticing words of man's wisdom, but upon the influence of the Spirit of God, and, with a view to that, the prayers of his people.

"Mr. Spurgeon evinces much aptitude in borrowing illustrations, not only from the pages of antiquity, and from modern life and literature, but also from the most familiar incidents, as well as from public events. Thus, the war suggests to him the idea that even the believer 'carries within him a bomb-shell, ready to burst at the slightest spark of temptation.' In like manner, the fatal exposure of the officers to the sharp-shooting of the enemy, furnishes him with a comparison by which to illustrate the peculiar liability of Christian ministers to hostile attack, though with a great difference in the result. 'Some of us,' he says, 'are the officers of God's regiments ; and we are the mark of all the riflemen of the enemy. Standing forward, we have to bear all the shots. What a mercy it is, that not one of God's officers ever falls in battle! God always keeps them.'

"His sermons abound with aphoristic and pointed sayings, which often afford a striking proof of his genius. . . . Many instances might easily be given of a force and beauty of language indicative of a high degree of eloquence. 'Bright-eyed cheerfulness and airy-footed love,' are fine phrases. Winter is described as not killing the flowers, but as 'coating them with the ermine of its snows.' Again, the sun is not quenched, but is behind the clouds, 'brewing up summer ; and, when he cometh forth again, he will have made those clouds fit to drop in April showers, all of them mothers of the sweet May flowers.' God 'puts our prayers, like rose-leaves, between the pages of His book of remembrance ; and when the volume is opened at last, there shall be a precious fragrance springing up therefrom.' 'There is one thing,' the sinner is told, 'that doth outstrip the telegraph : " Before they call, I will answer : and while they are yet speaking, I will hear."' The memory, infected by the Fall, is described as 'suffering the glorious timbers from the forest of Lebanon to swim down the stream of oblivion; but she stoppeth all the draff that floateth from the foul city of Sodom.' With quaintness, yet with force and truth, the caste feeling of society is hit off: 'In England, a sovereign will not speak to a shilling, a shilling will not notice a sixpence, and a sixpence will sneer at a penny.' A singular quaintness and vigour may be remarked in Mr. Spurgeon's diction; as when he speaks of the lightning 'splitting the clouds, and rending the heavens;' of 'the mighty hand wherein the callow comets are brooded by the sun;' and of 'the very spheres stopping their music while God speaks with His wondrous bass voice.'

"The manly tone of Mr. Spurgeon's mind might be illustrated from the admirable thoughts which he expresses on the connection between the diffusion of the gospel and the increase of civil liberty. His graphic skill in delineating character might be demonstrated from his life-like pictures of the prejudiced Jew and the scoffing Greek of modern times; his unsparing fidelity, from the sarcastic severity with which he rebukes the neglect of the Bible by modern professors; his powers of personification and dramatic presentation, from the scene which he paints between the dying Christian and Death, or between Jesus and Justice and the justified sinner; his refined skill in the treatment of a delicate subject, in the veiled yet impressive description of the trial of Joseph; the use that he can make of a single metaphor by his powerful comparison of the sinner to 'Mazeppa bound on the wild horse of his lust, galloping on with hell's wolves behind him,' till stopped and liberated by a mighty hand. The sermon entitled, 'The People's Christ,' contains a very striking description of the resurrection of our Lord. In that on 'The Eternal Home,' the contrast between the dying thief before and after his conversion, is powerfully drawn. The rage of Satan, on the rescue of a sinner from his grasp, forms a picture of terrific grandeur. In the sermon on 'The Bible,' the respective characteristics of the holy penmen are sketched with a masterly comprehension of their peculiarities and command of words. . . . The beautiful sermon on the words, 'So He giveth His beloved sleep,' exhibits a variety and force which stamp the master."

CHAPTER XL.

First Literary Friends (*Continued*).

I have striven, with all my might, to attain the position of complete independence of all men. I have found, at times, if I have been much praised, and if my heart has given way a little, and I have taken notice of it, and felt pleased, that the next time I was censured and abused I felt the censure and abuse very keenly, for the very fact that I accepted the commendation, rendered me more sensitive to the censure. So that I have tried, especially of late, to take no more notice of man's praise than of his blame, but to rest simply upon this truth,—I know that I have a pure motive in what I attempt to do, I am conscious that I endeavour to serve God with a single eye to His glory, and therefore it is not for me to take either praise or censure from man, but to stand independently upon the solid rock of right doing.—C. H. S.

O N February 18, 1856, just a year after his first article, Mr. James Grant wrote as follows in *The Morning Advertiser* :—"When Mr. Spurgeon was preaching in Exeter Hall to the most densely-crowded audiences that ever assembled within the walls of that spacious place, we called especial attention to his qualities as a preacher and as a theologian. We pointed out freely, but in the spirit of sincere friendship, what we conceived to be his faults both in matter and manner, and expressed not only a hope but a belief that, as he was so young a man,—not having then reached his majority,—he would, with the lapse of time, which generally matures the judgment, as well as mellows the mind, get rid, in a great measure, if not wholly, of what we then specified as defects. It gives us great gratification to say that, having heard him recently in his own chapel, in New Park Street, Southwark, we discern a decided improvement both as regards his matter and manner.

"Not that there is any change in Mr. Spurgeon's doctrinal views, or in his mode of illustrating, enforcing, and applying them, but that there is less of the pugnacious quality about him when grappling with the views of those from whom he differs. He does not speak so often with asperity of other preachers of the gospel, whom he conceives—and we must say, in the main, rightly,—to be unfaithful to their high calling. There is, too, a marked and gratifying improvement in Mr. Spurgeon as regards the manner of his pulpit appearances. He was always profoundly earnest in his appeals to the consciences of the unconverted ; and spoke with an emphasis which showed how deeply he felt, when dwelling on the joys and sorrows, the hopes and the fears of believers. And yet, strange to say, there was at times associated with this a seeming irreverence which, we know, frequently caused much pain to some of his greatest friends and admirers. In this respect also, we are happy to say, we can discern a decided amendment. . . .

"Never, since the days of George Whitefield, has any minister of religion acquired so great a reputation as this Baptist preacher, in so short a time. Here is a mere youth,—a perfect stripling, only twenty-one years of age,—incomparably the most popular preacher of the day. There is no man within her Majesty's dominions who could draw such immense audiences ; and none who, in his happier efforts, can so completely enthral the attention, and delight the minds of his hearers. Some of his appeals to the conscience, some of his remonstrances with the careless, constitute specimens of a very high order of oratorical power. . . . When this able and eloquent preacher first made his appearance in the horizon of the religious world, and dazzled the masses in the metropolis by his brilliancy, we were afraid that he might either get intoxicated by the large draughts of popularity which he had daily to drink, or that he would not be able, owing to a want of variety, to sustain the reputation he had so suddenly acquired. Neither result has happened. Whatever may be his defects, either as a man or as a preacher of the gospel, it is due to him to state that he has not been spoiled by popular applause. Constitutionally he has in him no small amount of self-esteem, but so far from its growing with his daily-extending fame, he appears to be more humble and more subdued than when he first burst on our astonished gaze. With regard again to our other fear, that his excellence as a preacher would not be sustained, the event has, we rejoice to say, no less agreeably proved the groundlessness of our apprehensions. There is no falling off whatever. On the contrary, he is, in some respects, improving with the lapse of time. We fancy we can see his striking originality to greater advantage than at first."

As a specimen of the early friendly notices in the provincial press, the following may be given from *The Western Times*, February 23, 1856 :—

"ANOTHER EXTRAORDINARY PREACHER.

"It is a remarkable fact that, in the Baptist denomination of Christians in this country, there have sprung up, from time to time, ministers of extraordinary Biblical and other learning, and of great talent and pulpit eloquence. We may refer to Dr. Carey, Dr. Gill, Dr. Rippon, the distinguished Robert Hall, of Bristol (whose discourses Brougham and Canning were glad to listen to), and many others, in proof of this peculiarity. It seems that another light has now sprung up among the Baptists, which bids fair to rival, if not to eclipse, the departed luminaries : we mean, the Rev. C. H. Spurgeon, who, although but just arrived at twenty-one years of age, seems in the pulpit and the press to have astonished the religious world. This young Baptist minister's preaching created a great sensation in Bristol, a short time since, and his visits to other places have excited intense interest. In Glasgow and other parts of Scotland, this gifted young minister has also, with marvellous effect, carried home to the hearts of crowded audiences the saving truths of 'the everlasting gospel.' There is a singularity also about Mr. Spurgeon, for he is emphatically 'one of the people ;' and, by the gifts and graces with which he is endowed, he shows to the world that the great Head of the Church of Christ, as He called His apostles from the class of humble fishermen, when He 'tabernacled on earth in the flesh,' so now that He is in Heaven, He continues to call labourers into His vineyard from the working-men of polished society."

It was not easy to decide whether the following paragraphs, from *The Freeman,* February 27, 1856, should be inserted here or be included in Chapter XXXVIII. ; readers may be able to settle that point to their own satisfaction .—

"Mr. Spurgeon is unquestionably a phenomenon ; a star, a meteor, or at all events something strange and dazzling in the horizon of the 'religious world.' The old lights have gone down, and since Irving, and Hall, and Chalmers 'fell asleep,' there has been no preacher who has created a 'sensation' at all to be compared with the young minister of New Park Street Chapel. But do not let our readers imagine that they have found here a luminary of the same class with those we have just named. Whatever Mr. Spurgeon's merits may be,—and he has some rare ones,— they are of a very different order from those which distinguished the mighty preachers of the last generation. *They* were all men of gigantic reasoning powers, of refined taste, of profound scholarship, and of vast theological learning. Of all these qualities, Mr. Spurgeon has little enough ; nor, to do him justice, does he pretend to any of them, except perhaps in some unlucky moments to the last. But it will probably be agreed, by all competent judges, that neither Irving, nor Hall, nor even Chalmers, was so well fitted to carry the gospel to the poor and ignorant, as is this modern orator of the pulpit. Their writings will last for many generations, and will be as fresh to the latest as they are to-day ; Mr. Spurgeon's sermons will perhaps * soon be forgotten for ever, but they go to the hearts of the multitude ; and as he has the good sense to know the direction in which his talent lies, he promises to be incomparably useful in a class of society which preachers too often complain is utterly beyond their reach.

"A lively imagination, sometimes rising to the region of poetry, but more frequently delighting in homely and familiar figures of speech ; a free, colloquial manner of address, that goes directly to the understanding of the simplest ; and an

---

* That " perhaps " just saves the prophet's reputation. Over a hundred millions of Mr. Spurgeon's sermons have been already issued, and they are prized beyond measure by an ever-increasing circle of readers. Can this be said of " the old lights, —Irving, and Hall, and Chalmers " ?

enthusiastic ardour, that must prove catching to all his hearers, unless they are more than usually insensible, are the chief legitimate attractions of Mr. Spurgeon's style ; and they are qualities so rare in their combination, and are in him so strongly developed, as to stamp him, in our judgment, with the decided impress of genius. We should suppose that it must be impossible to hear him without acquiring for him a sentiment of respect ; for if offended by his extravagances, as the thoughtful certainly will be, the offence is so immediately atoned for by some genuine outburst of feeling, that you remember that his extravagances are but the errors of a youth, and that the material on which these excrescences appear is that out of which apostles and martyrs have in every age been fashioned. You pardon his follies, for they are nothing else, for the sake of his unquestionable sincerity and impassioned zeal. You wish it had been possible that a mind so gifted might have received more culture before it was called into its present dangerous position ; but finding it as it is, you accept it with gratitude, and pray God, the All-wise, to be its Guide and Protector. . . . We see in Mr. Spurgeon a soul-loving preacher of Christ's gospel. Few have his peculiar gifts for arresting the attention of the thoughtless, or inspiring the cold with fervour. These are high endowments ; high, but awfully responsible. Of that responsibility we believe, too, that Mr. Spurgeon has no mean sense. And therefore, we hope, not without confidence, that his usefulness will continually augment, and that whatever detracts from it will gradually disappear."

A more favourable notice appeared in *The Christian Weekly News*, March 4, 1856 :—" Great orators, whether pulpit, platform, or senatorial, make many friends and many foes. This is inevitable ; but it is not our purpose, just now, to investigate or set forth the reasons for this result. The fact being granted, we are at no loss to account for the applause and contumely which have been heaped upon the young minister whose sermons are before us. His appearance and labours in this metropolis have excited in all religious circles, and even beyond them, attention and surprise, if not admiration. Scarcely more than a youth in years, comparatively untutored, and without a name, he enters the greatest city in the world, and almost simultaneously commands audiences larger than have usually listened to her most favoured preachers. Almost daily has he occupied pulpits in various parts of town and country, and everywhere been greeted by overflowing congregations. As might be expected, many who have listened to him have gone away to speak ill of his name ; while others, and by far the larger number, have been stimulated by his earnestness, instructed by his arguments, and melted by his appeals. We have seen, among his hearers, ministers of mark of nearly every section of the Christian Church ; laymen well known in all circles as the supporters of the benevolent and Evangelical institutions of the day ; and citizens of renown, from the chief magistrate down to the parish beadle. That the man who causes such a *furor* must possess some power not commonly found in men of his profession, will only be doubted by his detractors. Whether that power be physical, intellectual, or moral, or a happy blending of them all, is, perhaps, a question not yet fully decided even in the minds of many of his warmest admirers. The sermons before us would, we think, if carefully examined, help them to a decision. . . . Among the reasons to which, in our opinion, may be attributed the unbounded popularity of our author, we would name his youth, his devotedness, his earnestness, but especially that thrilling eloquence which can at once open the floodgates of the soul of the thousands forming a Sabbath morning audience within the walls of Exeter Hall. May the Lord continue to hold him as a star in His right hand, and through his instrumentality bring many souls to bow to the sceptre of His love and mercy ! "

The list of " first literary friends " would not be complete unless it included Rev. Edwin Paxton Hood. His volume, *The Lamps of the Temple*, published in 1856, contained a long and appreciative article on Mr. Spurgeon, in the course of which the writer said :—

"It is not too much to say that this mere lad—this boy preacher—is the most remarkable pulpit celebrity of his day; it must be admitted that, amidst all the popularities, there is no popularity like his. . . . Among things—remarkable or not remarkable according to the reader's ideas,—is the treatment of the young preacher by his brethren—shall we say, brethren?—in the ministry. We understand they have pretty generally agreed to regard him as a black sheep. His character is good, —unexceptionable ;—his doctrines have no dangerous heresy in them ;—still, he is tabooed. The other day, a very eminent minister, whose portrait we have attemped to sketch in this volume, and whom we certainly regarded as incapable of so much meanness when we were sketching it,—perhaps the most eminent of the London Dissenting ministers,—was invited to open a chapel in the country,—at any rate, to take the evening service; but he found that Spurgeon was to take the morning, and he smartly refused to mix in the affair: it was pitiable, and we discharged ourselves, as in duty bound, of an immense quantity of pity upon the head of the poor jealous man, who dreaded lest the shadow of a rival should fall prematurely over his pulpit. No; usually the ministers have not admired this advent ; the tens of thousands of persons, who flock to hear the youth preach his strong nervous gospel, do not at all conciliate them,—perhaps rather exasperate them. It would be easy to pick up a thousand criticisms on the preacher ; many, not to say most of them, very severe. He is flattered by a hurricane of acrimonious remark and abuse, and perhaps owes his popularity in no small degree to this sweeping condemnation. One thing is certain.—Spurgeon's back is broad, and his skin is thick ; he can, we fancy, bear a good deal, and bear a good deal without wincing. Little more than twenty-one years of age, he is the topic and theme of remark now in every part of England ; and severe as some of his castigators are, he returns their castigation frequently with a careless, downright, hearty goodwill. Beyond a doubt, the lad is impudent, very impudent ;—were he not, he could not, at such an age, be where he is, or what he is. . . .

"A characteristic mark of the fulness of Mr. Spurgeon's mind, and his entire abandonment to his subject, is his plunging at once into it from the first paragraph of his sermon. He does not often beat about with prepared exordiums, and yet his exordium is frequently not only very beautiful, but perhaps the most beautiful portion of his discourse. Is it not a rule with the rhetoricians, with Dr. Whately and others, that the exordium should be prepared nearly at the close of the oration, when all the powers of the mind and heart are alive with the subject, so that the auditors may have their attention arrested by those passages which will represent the orator's most inflamed and pathetic state of feeling ? We can very well acquit our speaker of any slavish following of this rule; possibly, probably, he may be ignorant of it, but he is the subject of it. Wrapt and possessed by his topics of thought and feeling, he frequently seems to cast over the people the state of mind induced in him by the last impressions of his text. His words often are more calm, beautiful, suggestive, and subduing in his opening than in any of his following remarks. . . . We hear that Mr. Spurgeon has models upon which he forms his mind and style. We think it very doubtful; but, at any rate, he does not follow them slavishly; he has in his speech true mental and moral independence. Robert Hall was charged with imitating Robert Robinson, of Cambridge;—in fact, there was not the slightest resemblance between those two minds. Spurgeon is said to imitate Robert Hall and William Jay. No doubt he has read them both, but his style is wholly unlike theirs; he, perhaps, has something of William Jay's plan and method, and that is all; but to Robert Hall there is not the most remote resemblance. He has not the purity, power, nor speed of that inimitable master; he is not at all qualified to shine in the brilliant intellectual firmament in which he held his place. We should give to him a very different location. He has the unbridled and undisciplined fancy of Hervey, without his elegance; but, instead of that, the drollery of Berridge and the ubiquitous earnestness of Rowland Hill, in his best days. But it is probable that many of us walk far too gingerly in our estimate of public speech. He who determines never to use a word that shall grate harshly on the ears of a refined taste, may be certain that he will never be very extensively useful; the people love the man who will condescend to their idiom, and the greatest preachers—those who have been the great apostles of a nation,—have always condescended to this. Bossuet, Massillon, Hall, Chalmers, McAll, were the doctors of the pulpit; at their feet sat the refinement, the scholarship, the politeness of their times; but such men as Luther and Latimer, St. Clara and Knox, Whitefield and Christmas Evans—such men have always seized on the prevailing dialect, and made it tell with immense power on their auditors.

"A question repeatedly asked by many persons, when they have either heard, or heard of, this young man is, 'Will he last, will he wear?' To which we have always replied, 'Why not?' There is, apparently, no strain in the production of these discourses; they bear every appearance of being, on the whole, spontaneous talkings. The preacher speaks from the full and overflowing spring within him, and speaks, as we have said, many times during the week. Some of his sermons are characterized by great mental poverty; some, and most, by a great mental wealth; so is it with all preachers, even those who consume the midnight oil, and make it their boast that they can only produce one sermon a week. . . . Our preacher's fulness and readiness is, to our mind, a guarantee that he will wear, and not wear out. His present amazing popularity will of course subside, but he will still be amazingly followed; and what he is now, we prophesy, he will on the whole remain : for polished diction, we shall not look to him ; for the long and stately argument, we shall not look to him ; for the original and profound thought, we shall not look to him ; for the clear and lucid criticism, we shall not look to him ;—but for bold and convincing statements of Evangelical truth, for a faithful grappling with convictions, for happy and pertinent illustrations, for graphic description, and for searching common sense, we shall look, and we believe we shall seldom look in vain.   In a word, he preaches,—not to metaphysicians or logicians,—neither to poets nor to *savans*,—to masters of erudition or masters of rhetoric ; he preaches to men.'

This chapter may be fitly closed with extracts from a pamphlet entitled, "*Why so Popular?   An Hour with Rev. C. H. Spurgeon.*   By a Doctor of Divinity."   It caused a great stir in the religious world when it appeared, and there is a special appropriateness in the poetical conclusion now that the beloved preacher, as a star, has melted into the light of Heaven.   The writer, addressing his remarks personally to Mr. Spurgeon, says :—

"Your ministry has attained the dignity of a moral phenomenon ; you stand on an eminence which, since the days of Whitefield, no minister—with a single exception, if indeed, there be one,—of any church in this realm has attained.   You have access to a larger audience than the magic of any other name can gather ; you have raised a church from obscurity to eminence,—perhaps I might add (rumour is my authority) from spiritual indigence to affluence.   You entered on a sphere, where—to use the mildest word,—languor 'held unbroken Sabbath ;' and in less than three short years you have, instrumentally, gathered a large, united, zealous, energetic church, second, in numbers, in burning zeal, and in active effort, to no other church in the metropolis. . . .

"Nor has God given you favour with your own people alone.   Blessed with a vigorous mind, and with great physical energy,—*mens sana in corpore sano*,—you have consecrated all to your Master's service, and hence you have become an untiring evangelist.   East, West, North, South,—in England, Wales, and Scotland, your preaching is appreciated by the people, and has been blessed of God.   No place has been large enough to receive the crowds who flocked to hear 'the young Whitefield'; and, on many occasions, you have preached the glorious gospel, the sward of the green earth being the floor on which, and the vault of the blue heaven the canopy under which, you announced, to uncounted thousands, 'all the words of this life.'   Your name has thus become 'familiar as a household word' in most of the churches and many of the families of our land ; and the young Pastor of Southwark has taken his place among the celebrities of our land,—and, among the ecclesiastical portion of these, he is 'higher than the highest.'

"On another, and much higher ground, I would offer my congratulations. Usefulness is the law of the moral universe. This, in relation to the Christian ministry, means the moral renovation, the saving conversion of human souls. Nothing short of this can satisfy the desires of any 'godly minister of Christ's gospel,' and, therefore, all such will estimate the amount of their success by the number of well-sustained instances of conversion, which are the fruit, under God's blessing, of their ministerial labours. Subjected to this test, the ministry of him to whom my congratulations are now presented, is placed above all the ministries with which I have any acquaintance, or of which I possess any authentic information. He states—so I am informed,—that more than one thousand souls have been hopefully converted to God, during the past year, by the instrumentality of his ministry ; and that, as the result of his metropolitan and provincial labours, during the period of his short but successful pastorate, several thousands, who had erred from the truth, or never known it, have been raised or restored to holiness, happiness, and God. 'This is the Lord's doing ; it is marvellous in our eyes.' I know something of the state of religion in our British churches, and I do not hesitate to avow my belief that, among the thousands—and, happily, their name is legion—who now proclaim the fundamental verities of the Christian revelation, there is not one who can truthfully say, as you can, that, during three short years, thousands—as the fruit of his ministry—have been added to the fellowship of his own church, and of other churches. . . .

"I am fully aware that, if I asked yourself the question, 'Why so popular, and why so useful?' you would reply, in a self-humbling, God-exalting spirit, 'I am nothing : God is all ; and to His sovereignty I ascribe all my popularity and all my success.' While admiring the spirit of this declaration, I decline to accept it as an answer to my question. God *is* a Sovereign ; and in His sovereignty—essential to his Godhead,—He has a right to give His Spirit when, where, to whom, and in what proportion He pleases ; but He has no caprice, no senseless, reasonless arbitrariness in His administration. He never acts without reason, though, in His sovereign right, He often withholds from His creature, man, the reasons which influence the Divine mind. This, and not caprice, is God's sovereignty.

"If I cannot discover the secret of your popularity in *what* you preach, can I find it in any peculiarity in your mode of preaching ? Here is, in my judgment, the explanation of the secret. *You have strong faith, and, as the result,* INTENSE EARNESTNESS. *In this lies,* as in the hair of Samson, *the secret of your power.* Go on, my brother, and may God give you a still larger amount of ministerial success ! 'Preach the Word,' the old theology, that 'glorious gospel of the blessed God' for which apostles laboured and martyrs died. In all your teachings, continue to exhibit the cross of Christ as occupying, in the Christian revelation, like the sun in our planetary system, the very centre, and imparting to all their lignt and heat. Tell the people that every doctrine, duty, or promise of the Scriptures stands intimately connected with the cross, and from that connection derives its meaning and value to us. Thus exhibiting the whole system of Divine Truth in its harmony and symmetry,—judging even by your own antecedents,—what a glorious prospect of honour, happiness, and usefulness presents itself to your view! A star in the churches,—a star of no mean magnitude, of no ordinary brilliancy,—you may be honoured to diffuse, very luminously, the derived glories you possess, and, having run your appointed course, ultimately set—but far distant be the day!—as sets the morning star,—

> "'Which falls not down behind the darkened West,
> Nor hides obscured amid the tempests of the sky,
> *But melts away into the light of Heaven!'*"

(N.B.—Mr. Spurgeon's autobiographical narrative is resumed in the following chapter.)

CHAPTER XLI.

"In Labours More Abundant."

If Christ should leave the upper world, and come into the midst of this hall, this morning, what answer could you give, if, after showing you His wounded hands and feet, and His rent side, He should put this question, "I have suffered thus for thee, what hast thou done for Me?" Let me put that question for Him, and in His behalf. You have known His love, some of you fifty years, some of you thirty, twenty, ten, three, one. For you He gave His precious life, and died upon the cross, in agonies most exquisite. What have you done for Him? Turn over your diary. Can you remember the contributions you have given out of your wealth? What do they amount to? Add them up. Think of what you have done for Jesus, how much of your time you have spent in His service. Add that up, turn over another leaf, and then observe how much time you have spent in praying for the progress of His Kingdom. What have you done there? Add that up. I will do so for myself; and I can say, without a boast, that I have zealously served my God, and have been "in labours more abundant;" but when I come to add all up, and set what I have done side by side with what I owe to Christ, it is less than nothing and vanity; I pour contempt upon it all, it is but dust of vanity. And though, from this day forward, I should preach every hour in the day; though I should spend myself and be spent for Christ; though by night I should know no rest, and by day I should never cease from toil, and year should succeed to year till this hair was hoary and this frame exhausted; when I come to render up my account, He might say, "Well done;" but I should not feel it was so, but should rather say, "I am still an unprofitable servant; I have not done that which it was even my bare duty to do, much less have I done all I would to show the love I owe." Now, as you think what you have done, dear brother and sister, surely your account must fall short equally with mine.—C. H. S., *in sermon preached at the Music Hall, Royal Surrey Gardens, June 26, 1859.*

BEFORE I came to London, I usually preached three times on the Lord's-day, and five nights every week; and after I became Pastor at New Park Street Chapel, that average was fully maintained. Within two or three years, it was considerably exceeded, for it was no uncommon experience for me to preach twelve or thirteen times a week, and to travel hundreds of miles by road or rail. Requests to take services in all parts of the metropolis and the provinces poured in upon me, and being in the full vigour of early manhood, I gladly availed myself of every opportunity of preaching the gospel which had been so greatly blessed to my own soul. In after years, when weakness and pain prevented me from doing all that I would willingly have done for my dear Lord, I often comforted myself with the thought that I did serve Him with all my might while I could, though even then I always felt that I could never do enough for Him who had loved me, and given Himself for me. Some of my ministerial brethren used to mourn over the heavy burden that rested upon them because they had to deliver their Master's message twice on the Sabbath, and once on a week-night; but I could not sympathize with them in their complaints, for the more often I preached, the more joy I found in the happy service. I was also specially sustained under the strain of

F

such constant labour by continual tokens of the Lord's approval. I find that, preaching to my own people at New Park Street, on the last Sabbath of 1855, from Deuteronomy xi. 10—12,—" For the land, whither thou goest in to possess it, is not as the land of Egypt, from whence ye came out, where thou sowedst thy seed, and wateredst it with thy foot, as a garden of herbs: but the land, whither ye go to possess it, is a land of hills and valleys, and drinketh water of the rain of heaven: a land which the Lord thy God careth for: the eyes of the Lord thy God are always upon it, from the beginning of the year even unto the end of the year;"—I was able to bear this testimony to the Divine power that had accompanied the Word :—

" Beloved friends, I can say that, as a minister of the gospel, the eyes of the Lord have been specially upon me all this year. It has been my privilege very frequently to preach His Word; I think, during the past twelve months, I have stood in the pulpit to testify His truth more than four hundred times, and blessed be His Name, whether it has been in the North, in the South, in the East, or in the West, I have never lacked a congregation; nor have I ever gone again to any of the places where I have preached, without hearing of souls converted. I cannot remember a single village, or town, that I have visited a second time, without meeting with some who praised the Lord that they heard the Word of truth there from my lips. When I went to Bradford last time, I stated in the pulpit that I had never heard of a soul being converted through my preaching there; and the good pew-opener came to Brother Dowson, and said, ' Why didn't you tell Mr. Spurgeon that So-and-so joined the church through hearing him?' and instantly that dear man of God told me the cheering news."

It would not be possible for me to make more than a very incomplete list of my multitudinous engagements during those early years; and, indeed, there is no occasion for me to attempt to do so, for the record of them is on high; yet certain circumstances impressed a few of the services so powerfully upon my mind that I can distinctly recall them even after this long interval.

I had promised to give some of my " Personal Reminiscences " at the annual meeting of the Pastors' College held in the Tabernacle on December 1, 1880; and while I sat in my study, that morning, with my two secretaries, Mr. Keys and Mr. Harrald, I said to the former :—" I recollect an incident, which occurred during my first year in London, in which you were concerned." This is the story. Old Mr. Thomas Olney—" Father Olney," as he was affectionately called by our Park Street friends,—was very anxious that I should go and preach at Tring, the little Hertfordshire town where he was born, and where his father, Mr. Daniel Olney, was for many years a deacon in one of the three Baptist churches. He found it was not a very easy matter to arrange, for the people had heard either so much or so little about me that I could not be allowed to appear in one of the chapels because I was too high in doctrine for the good folk who worshipped there, and permission could not be obtained for the use of another chapel because I was too low in doctrine for the dear Hyper-Calvinist friends who met there, and sang, with a meaning good Dr. Watts never intended,—

> "We are a garden wall'd around,
> Chosen and made peculiar ground;
> A little spot, enclosed by grace
> Out of the world's wide wilderness."

But there was a third place,—the West End Chapel,—the minister of which was a Mr. William Skelton, who thought that I was all right in doctrine, so Mr. Olney obtained consent for me to preach there. If I remember rightly, the worthy man's stipend only amounted to about fifteen shillings a week. He had invited us to tea at his house; but while we sat in his humble home, my conscience rather smote me because my good deacon and I were consuming some of his scanty store of provisions, and I began to think of some plan by which we could repay him for his kindness. I noticed that our friend was wearing an alpaca coat, which was very shiny, and in places was so worn that I could see through it. We went to the chapel, and the service proceeded, and all the while I was pondering in my mind what could be done for the worthy man who had lent us his chapel, and entertained us so generously. During the singing of one of the hymns, Mr. Keys came up to the pulpit, and said to me, "The pastor of this church is a very poor man, the people are able to give him very little; it would be a great kindness, sir, if you could have a collection for him, and get him a new coat." That was just what I had been thinking, so at the close of the service I said to the congregation :—" Now, dear friends, I have preached to you as well as I could, and you know that our Saviour said to His disciples, 'Freely ye have received, freely give.' I don't want anything from you for myself, but the minister of this chapel looks to me as though he would not object to a new suit of clothes." I pointed down to my worthy deacon, and said, "Father Olney, down there, I am sure will start the collection with half a sovereign (he at once nodded his head to confirm my statement); I will gladly give the same amount; and if you will all help as much as you can, our brother will soon have a new suit, and a good one, too."

The collection was made, it realized a very fair sum, and the minister was in due time provided with suitable garments. I apologised to him, after the service, for my rudeness in calling public attention to his worn coat; but he heartily thanked me for what I had done, and then added, "Ever since I have been in the service of the Lord Jesus Christ, my Master has always found me my livery. I have often wondered where the next suit would come from, and I really was wanting a new one very badly; but now you have provided it for me, and I am very grateful both to the Lord and also to you." I don't remember doing quite the same thing on any other occasion, though I may have helped some of the Lord's poor servants in a different way.

As far as I can remember, this is a true account of what happened at Tring in August, 1854; and I have often related the story. Someone else, however, evidently thought that it was not sufficiently sensational, so it was very considerably altered, and ultimately found its way into *The Glasgow Examiner*, in May, 1861, as a communication from the London correspondent of that paper. It is worth while to compare the "authorized" and "revised" versions of the incident, for the discrepancies in the latter are fairly typical of the inaccuracies in hundreds of other "stories" that have been told of me during my ministry in London. This is what the London correspondent wrote :—

"Rev. C. H. Spurgeon and the Farmers.

"Apropos of Mr. Spurgeon, I have to chronicle a circumstance which displays the characteristic benevolence of the rev. gentleman in a most amiable light. I had the anecdote from an eye-witness, and hence can vouchsafe *(sic)* for its authenticity. A short time ago, Mr. Spurgeon, while temporarily resident at Tring, received a requisition, signed by the principal inhabitants of that rural locality, begging him to address them. The rev. gentleman having courteously assented, the good people of Tring began to look about them for a building suitable to the occasion. A Nonconformist minister was first applied to for the loan of his chapel, but returned an indignant refusal. An application to the vicar for the use of the parish church met with a similar response. An open-air meeting, in the existing state of the weather, was out of the question ; and, there being no room in the village sufficiently large to accommodate a quarter of the expected audience, it began to be feared that the whole affair would drop through, more especially as Mr. Spurgeon had to leave for town by an early train on the following morning.

"In this dilemma, a small farmer in the neighbourhood offered the use of a large barn, which was gladly accepted. An extemporaneous pulpit was hastily constructed, and long before the hour appointed every corner of the place was crowded with expectant listeners. On entering the pulpit, Mr. Spurgeon informed his congregation that, although he had only been asked to give one sermon, it was his intention to deliver two. After a long and brilliant discourse in his own peculiarly forcible and impressive style, he paused for a few minutes, and then proceeded :— 'And now for sermon number two,—a plain, practical sermon. Our friend who gave us the use of this building is a poor man. When I saw him, this morning, he wore a coat all in tatters ; his shirt absolutely grinned at me through the holes. Let us show our appreciation of his kindness by buying him a new suit of clothes.' The suggestion was immediately adopted, and in the course of a few minutes some £10 or £12 was collected. On his return to London, Mr. Spurgeon related the circumstance to some of his congregation, who testified their appreciation of the respect paid to their Pastor by subscribing a further sum of £20 for the benefit of the Hertfordshire farmer."

I believe the friends at Tring were pleased with the service, for, not long afterwards, I was invited to go there again, to preach the Sunday-school anniversary sermons. This was, I think, at one of the other Baptist chapels in the town. I addressed the children in the afternoon, and preached to the adults in the evening. At the close of the afternoon service, some of the Hyper-Calvinist friends, who had been present, found fault with what they called my unsound teaching. The Holy Spirit had very graciously helped me in speaking to the many young people who were gathered together, and I believe that some of them were brought to the Saviour ; but, among other things, I had said to them that God had answered my prayers while I was a child, and before I was converted. That was certainly true, for, on many occasions, long before I knew the Lord, I had gone to Him with my childish petitions, and He had given me what I had asked of Him. I told the children that this fact had greatly impressed me while I was a boy, and it led me to believe more firmly in God's overruling power, and in the efficacy of prayer, and I urged them also to pray to Him. This gave great offence to my critics, so five or six of those grave old men gathered round me, and tried to set me right in their peculiar fashion. Did I not know that the Scripture declared that "the prayer of a sinner is abomination unto the Lord " ? That is a sentence which I have never been able to find in my Bible, and I told them so. Then they asked, " How can a dead man pray ? " I could not tell, but I knew that *I* prayed even while I was "dead in trespasses and sins." They said that it was impossible ; but I was equally positive that it could be done, for I had done it. They still maintained that it was not sound doctrine, and that God did not hear the prayers of sinners. There was quite a little ring formed around me, and I did my best to answer the objections ; but, after all, the victory was won, not by Barak, but by Deborah. A very old woman, in a red cloak, managed to squeeze herself into the circle, and turning to my accusers, she said, " What are you battling about with this young man ? You say that God does not hear the prayers of unconverted people, that He hears no cry but that of His own children. What do you know about the Scriptures ? Your precious passage is not in the Bible at all, but the psalmist did say, ' He giveth to the beast his food, and to the young ravens which cry ' (Psalm cxlvii. 9). Is there any grace in *them* ? If God hears the cry of the ravens, don't you think He will hear the prayers of those who are made in His own image ? You don't know anything at all about the matter, so leave the young man alone, and let him go on with his Master's work." After that vigorous speech, my opponents quickly vanished, and I walked away in happy conversation with the dear old soul who had so wisely delivered me from the cavillers.

I had quite a different experience on the occasion when I went to preach at Haverhill, in Suffolk. The congregation that day had the somewhat unusual privilege, or affliction, of listening to two preachers discoursing by turns upon the same text! The passage was that grand declaration of the apostle Paul, "For by grace are ye saved through faith ; and that not of yourselves : it is the gift of God " (Ephesians ii. 8). It does not often happen to me to be late for service, for I feel that punctuality is one of those little virtues which may prevent great sins. But we have no control over railways and breakdowns ; and so it happened that I reached the appointed place considerably behind time. Like sensible people, they had begun their worship, and had proceeded as far as the sermon. As I neared the chapel, I perceived that someone was in the pulpit preaching, and who should the preacher be but my dear and venerable grandfather! He saw me as I came in at the front door, and made my way up the aisle, and at once he said, "Here comes my grandson! He may preach the gospel better than I can, but he cannot preach a better gospel ; can you, Charles?" As I pressed through the throng, I answered, "You can preach better than I can. Pray go on." But he would not agree to *that*. I must take the sermon, and so I did, going on with the subject there and then, just where he left off. " There," said he, " I was preaching on 'For by grace are ye saved.' I have been setting forth the source and fountain-head of salvation ; and I am now showing them the channel of it, 'through faith.' Now, you take it up, and go on."

I am so much at home with these glorious truths, that I could not feel any difficulty in taking from my grandfather the thread of his discourse, and joining my thread to it, so as to continue without a break. Our agreement in the things of God made it easy for us to be joint-preachers of the same discourse. I went on with " through faith," and then I proceeded to the next point, " and that not of yourselves." Upon this, I was explaining the weakness and inability of human nature, and the certainty that salvation could not be of ourselves, when I had my coat-tail pulled, and my well-beloved grandsire took his turn again. When I spoke of our depraved human nature, the good old man said, " I know most about that, dear friends ; " so he took up the parable, and for the next five minutes set forth a solemn and humbling description of our lost estate, the depravity of our nature, and the spiritual death under which we were found. When he had said his say in a very gracious manner, his grandson was allowed to go on again, to the dear old man's great delight ; for now and then he would say, in a gentle tone, "Good! Good!" Once he said, "Tell them that again, Charles,' and of course I did tell them *that* again. It was a happy exercise to me to take my share in bearing witness to truths of such vital importance, which are so deeply impressed upon my heart. Whenever I read this text, I seem to hear that dear voice, which has been so long lost to earth, saying to me, "TELL THEM THAT AGAIN." I am not contradicting the testimony of forefathers who are now with God. If my grandfather could return to earth, he would find me where he left me, steadfast in the faith, and true to that form of doctrine which was once for all delivered to the saints. I preach the doctrines of grace because I believe them to be true; because I see them in the Scriptures; because my experience endears them to me; and because I see the holy result of them in the lives of believers. I confess they are none the less dear to me because the advanced school despises them: their censures are to me a commendation. I confess also that I should never think the better of a doctrine because it was said to be "new." Those truths which have enlightened so many ages appear to me to be ordained to remain throughout eternity. The doctrine which I preach is that of the Puritans: it is the doctrine of Calvin, the doctrine of Augustine, the doctrine of Paul, the doctrine of the Holy Ghost. The Author and Finisher of our faith Himself taught most blessed truth which well agreed with Paul's declaration, "By grace are ye saved." The doctrine of grace is the substance of the testimony of Jesus.

Some of the special services it was my privilege to conduct in London, in those long-past days, remain in my memory with great vividness. The first time I was asked to preach at one of the representative gatherings of the denomination was on January 10, 1855, when the annual meetings of the London Association of Baptist Churches were held at New Park Street Chapel, which was crowded both afternoon and evening, to the manifest astonishment of the grave and venerable ministers and delegates who had usually met on such occasions in much smaller numbers. My subject was, "The Holy War," the text being 2 Cor. x. 4: "For the weapons of our warfare are not carnal, but mighty through God to the pulling down of strong holds." Rev. Thomas Binney, of the Weigh House Chapel, near the Monument, was in the congregation that afternoon, and as he walked away, one of our friends heard him say, concerning the service, "It is an insult to God and man; I never heard such things in my life before." Our brother was so indignant that he turned to him, and said, "The man who can speak like that of a young minister of Jesus Christ is one of whom I shall be ashamed as long as I live, unless he repents having uttered such unkind remarks." I know this story is true, for I had it from the lips of the good man himself. Many years afterwards, he was again in Mr. Binney's company, so he reminded him of the incident; and our friend told me that no one could have spoken of me with more intense and hearty esteem than did the venerable man at that time. "But," he added, "you know, my dear sir, that your minister has greatly improved since those early days.   I very soon found out my mistake, and you may depend upon it that my sentiments with regard to Mr. Spurgeon are completely changed.   I did not at all blame you for rebuking me as you did ; I only wish I had as many friends to stick to me, and speak up for me, as your minister has always had.   If I ever said anything against him, I might just as well have pulled down a skep of bees about my head ; but now I have no feeling towards him but that of the utmost regard and affection."   I also know that, long before this confession,

REV. THOMAS BINNEY, LL.D.

Mr. Binney, while addressing the students of one of the Congregational Colleges, had said, in reply to some disparaging remarks concerning me which he had over-heard :—" I have enjoyed some amount of popularity, I have always been able to draw together a congregation ; but, in the person of Mr. Spurgeon, we see a young man, be he who he may, and come whence he will, who at twenty-four hours' notice can command a congregation of twenty thousand people.   Now, I have never been able to do that, and I never knew of anyone else who could do it."

The *Freeman* thus reported the meetings of the day :—

" LONDON BAPTIST ASSOCIATION.—Whatever reason may be assigned for the fact, it is certain that an Association meeting in London is very different from one in the country.   Perhaps the ministers and members of the several churches meet so often that an annual gathering is no novelty ; perhaps the walk through London streets, or the jolt in an omnibus or cab, has fewer attractions than the Whitsuntide jaunt by railroad or pleasant country lane ; or perhaps the thing has escaped due attention amid the throng of metropolitan claims ;—but certain it is, that the London Particular Baptist Association, holding, as it does, from a sense of duty, a meeting every year, has only given generally the impression of being a somewhat dull affair. Indeed, it is not enlivening either to preacher or hearer to find one's self in New Park Street Chapel with a congregation of seventy people, on a January week-day afternoon !

"This year, we are bound to say, all was different. The popularity of the Rev. C. H. Spurgeon, the recently-settled Pastor at New Park Street, attracted a crowded audience on the afternoon of the 10th instant. The metropolitan churches of the denomination appeared for the most part well represented, the only noticeable exception being the absence of several leading ministers, owing, as was explained, to the Quarterly Mission Committee being holden, by some mischance which will probably not occur again, upon the same day. The preacher treated with much earnestness on the 'strongholds' of the evil one that we are called to subdue, and on 'the weapons of our warfare,' which are 'mighty through God' to the task. The vigour and originality of the sermon, we cannot forbear remarking, sufficiently accounted to us for the popularity of the youthful preacher, and indicated powers which, with due culture, may by the Divine blessing greatly and usefully serve the Church in days to come. A very large company remained in the chapel to tea, and in the evening the place was thronged to overflowing for the public meeting,—which, however, was not distinguished by any feature worthy of remark, save the delivery of two or three brief, simple, Evangelical addresses. It appears that many churches in London are not connected with the Association, and of those which are, several sent no reports No complete statistics, therefore, could be presented. Of those churches from which letters were read, most seemed stationary,—some were prosperous. The accounts, perhaps, on the whole, were quite equal to the average."

C. H. SPURGEON PREACHING AT EXETER HALL, FEBRUARY, 1855.

CHAPTER XLII.

"In Labours More Abundant" *(Continued)*.

UR first sojourn at Exeter Hall, from February 11 to May 27, 1855, like the later assemblies in that historic building, was one long series of "special" services, which gave the church at New Park Street a position it had not previously attained. The simple record in our church-book scarcely conveys an adequate idea of the importance of the "forward movement" that was about to be inaugurated :—

"Our Pastor announced from the pulpit that our place of worship would be closed for enlargement for the eight following Lord's-days, during which period the church and congregation would worship in the large room at Exeter Hall, Strand, on Lord's-days, morning and evening, and that accommodation had also been provided for the usual week-evening services to be held at Maze Pond Chapel."

The following paragraph, published in *The Globe*, March 22, was extensively copied into other papers ; and the comments upon it, both favourable and otherwise, helped still further to attract public attention to our services :—

"The circumstances under which the Rev. C. H. Spurgeon has recently come before the public are curious, and demand a passing notice. Some months since, he became minister of New Park Street Chapel ; and it was soon found that the building, capacious as it was, was far too small to accommodate the crowds of persons who flocked to hear the young and eloquent divine. In this state of affairs, there was no alternative but to enlarge the chapel ; and while this process was going on, Exeter Hall was engaged for him. For some weeks past, he has been preaching there every Sunday morning and evening ; but he has filled the great hall, just as easily as he filled New Park Street Chapel. A traveller along the Strand, about six o'clock on a Sunday evening, would wonder what could be the meaning of a crowd which literally stopped the progress of public vehicles, and sent unhappy pedestrians round the by-streets, in utter hopelessness of getting along the wider thoroughfare. Since the days of Wesley and Whitefield,—whose honoured names seem to be in danger of being thrown into the shade by this new candidate for public honours,— so thorough a religious *furor* has never existed. Mr. Spurgeon is likely to become a great preacher ; at present, his fervid and impassioned eloquence sometimes leads him a little astray, and sometimes there is a want of solemnity, which mars the beauty of his singularly happy style."

Before we had completed the two months for which we had engaged Exeter Hall, we found that it was advisable to continue there for eight more Sabbaths (making sixteen in all). Our return to our own chapel is thus recorded in the church-book :—

"The meeting-house in New Park Street was re-opened, after the enlargement, on Thursday, May 31st, 1855, when two sermons were preached, that in the forenoon by the Rev. James Sherman, of Blackheath, and that in the evening by our Pastor."

It was a very wet day, and, although I am not a believer in omens, I told the people that I regarded it as a prognostication of the "showers of blessing" we hoped to receive in the enlarged building ; and that, as it had rained literally at the re-opening services, I prayed that we might have the rain spiritually as long as we worshipped there. To the glory of God, I am grateful to testify that it was so. I also quoted to the crowded congregation Malachi iii. 10,—" Bring ye all the tithes into the storehouse, that there may be meat in Mine house, and prove Me now herewith, saith the Lord of hosts, if I will not open you the windows of heaven, and pour you out a blessing, that there shall not be room enough to receive it ;"—and reminded the friends that, if they wished to have the promised blessing, they must comply with the condition attached to it. This they were quite ready to do, and from the time of our return to our much-loved sanctuary until the day when we finally left it, we never had " room enough to receive" the blessings which the Lord so copiously poured out for us.

There were two evenings—June 22, and September 4, 1855,—when I preached in the open air in a field in King Edward's Road, Hackney. On the first occasion,* I had the largest congregation I had ever addressed up to that time, but at the next service the crowd was still greater.† By careful calculation, it was estimated that

---

* This was the service which is referred to in Mr. Spurgeon's letter on page 21. Readers may be interested in knowing that the discourse then delivered is published by Messrs. Passmore & Alabaster in their series of " Rare Jewels from Spurgeon." It is untitled, " Christ is All." *The Clerkenwell News*, in an appreciative account of the service and the preacher, said :—" His discourse, which was bold, imaginative, and abounding in felicitous and appropriate metaphors, was listened to with the most profound attention,—a distinction rarely shown to open-air preaching."

† The text on the second occasion was Matthew viii. 11, 12 ; and the sermon was printed in *The New Park Street Pulpit* (Nos. 39-40), under the title, " Heaven and Hell." Translations were published in various languages, including Russian and French. Copies of the Russian version reached Mr. Spurgeon from time to time, each one bearing on its front cover the " Alpha and Omega " in the centre of the official stamp certifying that it might be read and circulated by faithful members of the Greek Church; on the back, was a list of nine more of the sermons issued by the same publisher. As soon as the permission of the censor had been obtained, the gentleman who had sought it ordered a million copies of the sermons to be printed, and scattered over the Russian Empire. " That day " alone will reveal how many souls have been saved through this method of spreading the truth in that dark region. A copy of the French translation was recently received by Mrs. Spurgeon, from M. Robert Dubarry, one of the French students in the Pastors' College, who found it a few years ago in a Parisian hospital, where it had been left by a former patient, who had evidently been greatly benefited by reading it. The margin is almost covered with a most elaborate system of marks, and the discourse itself is underlined as though every word had been read and pondered again and again. At the end is written, in French : —" A Souvenir for my children ! Sunday, 3rd June, 1860. Lord, grant that this worthy and true sermon may become to them a salutary and precious blessing, and that it may remind them of their mother ! " The beloved preacher had many similar testimonies to the usefulness of his words when translated into foreign tongues, although he was not spared to see this one, which would have greatly interested him.

from twelve to fourteen thousand persons were present. I think I shall never forget the impression I received when, before we separated, that vast multitude joined in singing—

"Praise God from whom all blessings flow."

That night, I could understand better than ever before why the apostle John, in the Revelation, compared the " new song " in Heaven to " the voice of many waters." In that glorious hallelujah, the mighty waves of praise seemed to roll up towards the sky, in majestic grandeur, even as the billows of old ocean break upon the beach.

Among the notable gatherings in various provincial towns, my visit to Trowbridge has a special interest because of the singularity of an extra service that was crowded into my programme. I had promised to preach in one place of worship in the afternoon and evening of Monday, April 7, 1856, and in another chapel the following morning. At both the services on the Monday, the building was densely packed, and hundreds had to go away, unable to gain admission, so I offered to preach again at ten o'clock at night if the friends could make it known, and bring in a fresh congregation. Many remained after the first evening service, and before the appointed hour others came in such numbers that the place was again crowded.

That was a memorable night, but it was quite eclipsed by another, which I spent in a meeting-house not far from the place which was the scene of the terrible explosion in the Risca colliery in December, 1860. That charming spot in South Wales has frequently yielded me a quiet and delightful retreat. Beautiful for situation, surrounded by lofty mountains, pierced by romantic valleys, the breathing of its air refreshes the body, and the sight of the eyes makes glad the heart. I have climbed its hills, I have seen the ever-widening landscape, the mountains of Wales, the plains of England, and the sea sparkling afar. I have mingled with its godly men and women, and worshipped God in their assemblies. I have been fired with the glorious enthusiasm of the people when they have listened to the Word; but that night I shall never forget in time or in eternity, when, crowded together in the place of worship, hearty Welsh miners responded to every word I uttered, with their "Gogoniants" encouraging me to preach the gospel, and crying "Glory to God!" while the message was proclaimed. They kept me well-nigh to midnight, preaching three sermons, one after another, almost without a break, for they loved to listen to the gospel. God was present with us, and many a time has the baptismal pool been stirred since then by the fruit of that night's labour.

Nor shall I ever forget when, standing in the open air beneath God's blue sky, I addressed a mighty gathering within a short distance of that same place, when the Spirit of God was poured upon us, and men and women were swayed to and fro under the Heavenly message, as the corn is moved in waves by the summer winds. Great was our joy that day when the people met together in thousands, and with songs and praises separated to their homes, talking of what they had heard.

I must mention the visit I paid to Stambourne, on May 27, 1856, when I preached, at my dear grandfather's request, in commemoration of his ministerial jubilee. He had then been Pastor of the Congregational Church at Stambourne for forty-six years, and he had previously been minister at Clare, in Suffolk, for four years. I suppose such a service is almost unique ; certainly, I have no recollection of any other instance in which a grandson has had the privilege of preaching for his grandfather under similar circumstances, and I bless God that this was my happy lot. On the previous Sabbath morning, at New Park Street Chapel, I delivered substantially the same discourse from Isaiah xlvi. 4, and it was published under the title, "The God of the Aged" (Nos. 81-2). Some fifteen hundred or two thousand persons assembled at Stambourne for the celebration ; and to accommodate them, a large covered space was extemporized by the use of a barn, and tents, and tarpaulins. The proceedings were, naturally, full of interest. My venerable friend, Rev. Benjamin Beddow, who assisted me in the compilation of *Memories of Stambourne*, has recorded the following incident which, otherwise, I might have forgotten :—

"In the afternoon, Mr. C. H. Spurgeon made some allusions to Thomas Binney's volume, *How to make the best of both worlds*, and expressed his opinion that no man could serve two masters, or live for more than one world. The ardent spirit of a Congregationalist minister was aroused, and he interrupted the speaker. This was a mistake ; but though it raised discussion, it produced no result upon the evening congregation, which was as thronged and as enthusiastic as that which preceded it. We only refer to it for the sake of the sequel to the anecdote. Years after, the gentleman who interrupted had such an opinion of C. H. Spurgeon that, in a very kind and genial letter, he reminded him of the incident, and asking for a sermon from him, pressed the request by quoting the old saying about Cranmer, ' If you do my Lord of Canterbury an ill turn, he will be your friend all the days of your life.' At that time it was not in the power of C. H. Spurgeon to grant the request, for the season had long been promised to others ; but he felt that he would right gladly have done so had it been within the region of the possible.

"Great were the crowds of that day : very busy were all the ladies of the region in making tea, and very liberal were the gifts. The venerable old man, whose ministerial jubilee was thus celebrated, seemed to feel rather the weight of the years than any special exhilaration because of their having reached to fifty. Within himself he held a quiet jubilee of rest, which the world could neither give nor take away."

My experiences in those early years were very varied, and some of them were so singular that I cannot easily forget them. At one place, I was preaching to a great crowd of people, and during the sermon many in the congregation were visibly affected. I felt that the power of the Lord was working there very manifestly; one poor creature absolutely shrieked out because of the wrath of God against sin.

On another occasion, I had scarcely finished my discourse, when a Christian woman, who had been listening to it, dropped dead in her pew. That was at a village in Kent. Not very long afterwards, I went to Tollesbury, in Essex, to preach on a week-day afternoon on behalf of the Sunday-school at my father's chapel. There was a large assembly of friends from the surrounding district; and at the close of the service, tea was provided for them in a tent. Before they had finished, the wife of one of the deacons was seized with a fit, and died in a few minutes. I had not arranged to preach in the evening; but, under the circumstances, I did so, taking for my text Paul's words, " For to me to live is Christ, and to die is gain."

An old countryman once came to me, after a service, and said, " Ah! young man, you have had too deep a text; you handled it well enough, but that is an old man's text, and I felt afraid to hear you announce it." I replied, " Is God's truth dependent on age? If the thing is true, it is just as well to hear it from me as from anyone else; but if you can hear it better anywhere else, you have the opportunity."

I recollect one hearer that I had of quite a different sort. Preaching about in the country, I had often noticed, in a certain county, a man in a smock frock who was a regular follower. He seemed to be amazingly attentive to the service, and thinking that he looked an extremely poor man, I one day gave him five shillings. When I preached twenty miles off, there he was again, and I gave him some more help, fancying that he was a tried child of God. When I was preaching in another place in the same county, there he was again; and the thought suddenly occurred to me, "That man finds something more attractive in the palms of my hands than in the words of my lips,"—so I gave him no more. The next time I saw him, he put himself in my way, but I avoided him; and then, at last, being again in the same county, he came up, and asked me to give him something. " No," I said, "you will have no more from me; I see why you have come; you have followed me, pretending to delight in the Word, and to be profited by it, whereas it is profit you get out of me, not profit from the gospel."

In another part of the country, I was preaching once to people who kept continually looking round, and I adopted the expedient of saying, " Now, friends, as it is so very interesting to you to know who comes in, and it disturbs me so very much for you to look round, I will, if you like, describe each one as he comes in, so that you may sit and look at me, and keep up at least a show of decency." I described one gentleman who came in, who happened to be a friend whom I could depict without offence, as "a very respectable gentleman who had just taken his hat off," and so on ; and after that one attempt I found it was not necessary to describe any more, because they felt shocked at what I was doing, and I assured them that I was much more shocked that they should render it necessary for me to reduce their conduct to such an absurdity. It cured them for the time being, and I hope for ever, much to their pastor's joy.

On one of my many early journeys by the Eastern Counties Railway,—as the G.E.R. was then called,—I had a singular adventure, upon which I have often looked back with pleasurable recollections. I had been into the country to preach, and was returning to London. All at once, I discovered that my ticket was gone ; and a gentleman—the only other occupant of the compartment,—noticing that I was fumbling about in my pockets as though in search of something I could not find, said to me, " I hope you have not lost anything, sir ? " I thanked him, and told him that it was my ticket that was missing, and that, by a remarkable coincidence, I had neither watch nor money with me. I seldom wear a watch, and probably the brother whom I had gone to help had seemed to me in need of any coin that I might have had in my possession before I started on my homeward journey. " But," I added, " I am not at all troubled, for I have been on my Master's business, and I am quite sure all will be well. I have had so many interpositions of Divine providence, in small matters as well as great ones, that I feel as if, whatever happens to me, I am bound to fall on my feet, like the man on the Manx penny." The gentleman seemed interested, and said that no doubt it would be all right, and we had a very pleasant, and, I hope, profitable conversation until the train had nearly reached Bishopsgate Station, and the collectors came for the tickets. As the official opened the door of our compartment, he touched his hat to my travelling companion, who simply said, " All right, William ! " whereupon the man again saluted, and retired. After he had gone, I said to the gentleman, " It is very strange that the collector did not ask for my ticket." " No, Mr. Spurgeon," he replied,—calling me by my name for the first time,—" it is only another illustration of what you told me about the providence of God watching over you even in little things ; I am the General Manager of this line, and it was no doubt Divinely arranged that I should happen to be your companion just when I could be of service to you. I knew you were all right, and it has been a great pleasure to meet you under such happy circumstances."

A somewhat similar instance of the presence of " a friend in need " occurred at a later period of my life, but it follows so appropriately upon the previous one that it may as well be related here. I was going to preach somewhere in the North of London ; and to reach my destination, I had to pass through the City. When I was in Princes Street, near the Bank, my horse fell, some of the harness gave way, and one of the shafts of the carriage was broken.   Almost at the instant that the accident happened, a hand was thrust in at the window, and the owner of it gave me his card, and said, " I know where you are going, Mr. Spurgeon ; you have no time to lose in getting to the chapel.   Take a cab, and go on about your Master's business ; I'll stay with the coachman, and see what can be done with the horse and carriage."   I did as the gentleman suggested, and after I had preached, and was ready to return, there was the carriage at the chapel door, ready for me, and the coachman gave me the message that there was " nothing to pay."   I wrote to thank the generous friend for his timely and welcome help and gift, and in his reply he said, " I only hope that, next time your horse goes down, I may be close at hand, or that somebody else may be there who will feel it as great a pleasure to be of service to you as I have done. You do not know me, but I am well acquainted with one of your deacons, and through him I have heard a good deal about you."   So he took care of me for my deacon's sake, and still more for my Lord's sake ; and many and many a time have I had kindnesses shown to me by those who, until then, had been complete strangers to me.   Other people may not think much of such incidents ; but to me they are intensely interesting, and they fill me with adoring gratitude to God.

(The following letters, written by Mr. Spurgeon to his very intimate friend, Mr. J. S. Watts, Regent Street, Cambridge,—to whom reference was made in Vol. I., Chapter XXII., of the *Autobiography*.—have been most kindly placed at Mrs. Spurgeon's disposal by Miss Watts ; they record the young Pastor's experiences during the period now under review, and throw a vivid light on many of the notable incidents which occurred in 1854—1856 :—)

" 75, Dover Road,
" August 25, 1854.

" My Very Dear Friend,

" I am astonished to find that fame has become so inveterate a fabricator of untruths, for I assure you that I had no more idea of coming to Cambridge on Wednesday than of being dead last week.

" I have been, this week, to Tring, in Hertfordshire, on the border of Bucks. I have climbed the goodly hills, and seen the fair vale of Aylesbury below.   In the morning, I startled the hare from her form, and at eve talked with the countless stars. I love the glades and dells, the hills and vales, and I have had my fill of them.   The week before, I was preaching at Ramsgate, and then tarried awhile at Margate, and came home by boat.   Kent is indeed made to rejoice in her God, for in the parts I traversed the harvest was luxuriant, and all seemed thankful.

G

"The Crystal Palace is likewise a favourite haunt of mine ; I shall rejoice to take your arm one day, and survey its beauties with you.

" Now for the cause at New Park Street. We are getting on too fast. Our harvest is too rich for the barn. We have had one meeting to consider an enlargement,—quite unanimous ;—meet again on Wednesday, and then a committee will be chosen immediately to provide larger accommodation. On Thursday evenings, people can scarcely find a vacant seat,—I should think not a dozen in the whole chapel. On Sabbath days, the crowd is immense, and seat-holders cannot get into their seats ; half-an-hour before time, the aisles are a solid block, and many stand through the whole service, wedged in by their fellows, and prevented from escaping by the crowd outside, who seal up the doors, and fill the yard in front, and stand in throngs as far as the sound can reach. I refer mainly to the evening, although the morning is nearly the same.

" Souls are being saved. I have more enquirers than I can attend to. From six to seven o'clock on Monday and Thursday evenings, I spend in my vestry ; I give but brief interviews then, and have to send many away without being able to see them. The Lord is wondrous in praises. A friend has, in a letter, expressed his hope that my initials may be prophetic,—

" C. H. S.

" COMFORT. HAPPINESS. SATISFACTION.

" I can truly say they are, for I have *comfort* in my soul, *happiness* in my work, and *satisfaction* with my glorious Lord. I am deeply in debt for your offer of hospitality ; many thanks to you. My kindest regards to all my friends, and yours, especially your sons and daughters. I am sure it gives me delight to be remembered by them, and I hope it will not be long before I run down to see them. Hoping you will be *blessed* in going out, and coming in,

" I am,
" Yours truly,
" C. H. SPURGEON."

" 75, Dover Road,
" Saturday [Oct. or Nov., 1854].

" My Dear Friend,

" I do not think I can by any means manage to see you. There is just a bare possibility that I may be down by the half-past-one train on Monday morning ; but do not prepare for me, or expect me. I can only write very briefly to-day, as it is Saturday. Congregations as crowded as ever. Twenty-five added to the church last month ; twelve proposed this month. Enlargement of chapel to be commenced speedily. £1,000 required. Only one meeting held, last Friday evening, £700 or £800 already raised; we shall have more than enough. I gave £100 myself to start the people off. Friends firm. Enemies alarmed. Devil angry. Sinners saved. Christ exalted. Self not well. Enlargement to comprise 300 seats to let, and 300 free sittings; 200 more to be decided on. I have received anonymously in one month for distribution, £18 5s., and have given it to poor Christians and sick persons.

"Love to you all. Excuse haste. Forgot to say,—Prayer-meeting, 500 in regular attendance. Glory to the Master!

"Yours in Jesus,
"C. H. SPURGEON."

"75, Dover Road,
"March 23, 1855.

"My Dear Friend and Brother,

"Often have I looked for a note from you, but I have not reproached you, for I, too, have been negligent. Really, I never seem to have an hour to call my own. I am always at it, and the people are teasing me almost to death to get me to let them hear my voice. It is strange that such a power should be in one small body to crowd Exeter Hall to suffocation, and block up the Strand, so that pedestrians have to turn down by-ways, and all other traffic is at a standstill.

"*The Globe*, of last evening, says that, never since the days of Whitefield was there such a religious *furor*, and that the glories of Wesley and Whitefield seem in danger of being thrown into the shade. Well, the press has *kicked* me quite long enough, now they are beginning to *lick* me; but one is as good as the other so long as it helps to fill our place of worship. I believe I could secure a crowded audience at dead of night in a deep snow.

"On Fast-day, all Falcon Square was full,—police active, women shrieking,— and at the sight of me the rush was fearful. . . . Strange to say, nine-tenths of my hearers are *men*; but one reason is, that *women* cannot endure the awful pressure, the rending of clothes, &c., &c. I have heard of parties coming to the hall, from ten or twelve miles distance, being there half-an-hour before time, and then never getting so much as near the door.

"Dear me, how little satisfies the crowd! What on earth are other preachers up to, when, with ten times the talent, they are snoring along with prosy sermons, and sending the world away? The reason is, I believe, they do not know what *the gospel* is; they are afraid of *real gospel Calvinism*, and therefore the Lord does not own them.

"And now for spiritual matters. I have had knocking about enough to kill a dozen, but the Lord has kept me. Somewhere in *nubibus* there lies a vast mass of *nebulæ* made of advice given to me by friends,—most of it about humility. Now, my Master is the only one who can humble me. My pride is so infernal that there is not a man on earth who can hold it in, and all their silly attempts are futile ; but then my Master can do it, and He will. Sometimes, I get such a view of my own insignificance that I call myself all the fools in the world for even letting pride pass my door without frowning at him. I am now, as ever, able to join with Paul in saying, 'Having nothing, and yet possessing all things.'

"Souls are being converted, and flying like doves to their windows. The saints are more zealous, and more earnest in prayer.

"Many of the man-made parsons are mad, and revile me ; but many others are putting the steam on, for this is not the time to sleep in.

"The Lord is abroad. The enemy trembles. Mark how the devil roars ;—see *Era*, last week, a theatrical paper, where you can read about 'EXETER HALL THEATRE' linked with Drury Lane, Princess's, &c. Read the slander in *Ipswich Express* and the London *Empire*. The two latter have made an apology.

"What a fool the devil is ! If he had not vilified me, I should not have had so many precious souls as my hearers.

"I long to come and throw one of my *bombs* into Cambridge ; you are a sleepy set, and want an explosion to wake you. (Here omit a gentleman whose initials are J. S. W.) I am coming on Good Friday ; is your house still the Bishop's Hostel ? Of course it is. Now, no write me ; I love you as much as ever, and owe you a vast debt. Why not come and see me ? I know you pray for me.

"With Christian love to you, and kind remembrances to all your family,

"I am,

"Yours ever truly,

"C. H. SPURGEON."

"75, Dover Road,

"Tuesday [April, 1855].

"Dear Friend and Brother,

"(D.V.) Thursday, I shall be with you at 1.30 by the mail train. I shall be glad to preach in St. Andrew's Street Chapel, but shall disappoint you all. The people are silly to follow me so much. It now gets worse. *Crowds awful* on Sunday last. Collected £90 morning and evening at the hall. At Shoreditch, on Tuesday, there were eight or nine hundred where only six hundred should have been admitted ; upon *personally* appealing to the throng outside, disappointed at not getting in, most of them dispersed, and allowed the rest of us to worship as well as we could with windows open to let those hear who remained outside.

"Joseph is still shot at by the archers, and sorely grieved; (see *Baptist Reporter, United Presbyterian Magazine, Critic, Christian News,* &c., with a lot of small fry ;) but his bow abides in strength, neither does he tremble. Oh, my dear brother, envy has vexed me sorely ;—scarcely a Baptist minister of standing will own me ! I am sick of *man ;* but when I find a good one, I love him all the better because of the contrast to others.

"I have just received a handsome silver inkstand, bearing this inscription :— 'Presented to Mr. C. H. Spurgeon by J. and S. Alldis, as a token of sincere gratitude to him as the instrument, under Almighty God, of turning them from darkness to light, March 30, 1855.' The devil may look at *that* as often as he pleases ; it will afford him sorry comfort.

"And now, farewell. Christian love to you and yours, from—

"Yours deeply in debt,

"C. H. SPURGEON."

"New Kent Road,
"Southwark,
"Feb. 23, 1856.

"My Dear Brother,

"A wearied soldier finds one moment of leisure to write a despatch to his brother in arms. Eleven times this week have I gone forth to battle, and at least thirteen services are announced for next week. Additions to the church, last year, 282 ; received this year, in three months, more than 80 :—30 more proposed for next month,—hundreds, who are equally sincere, are asking for admission ; but time will not allow us to take in more. Congregation more than immense,—even *The Times* has noticed it. Everywhere, at all hours, places are crammed to the doors. The devil is wide awake, but so, too, is the Master.

"The Lord Mayor, though a Jew, has been to our chapel ; he came up to my vestry to thank me. I am to go and see him at the Mansion House. The Chief Commissioner of Police also came, and paid me a visit in the vestry ; but, better still, some thieves, thimbleriggers, harlots, &c., have come, and some are now in the church, as also a right honourable hot-potato man, who is prominently known as 'a hot Spurgeonite.'

"The sale of sermons is going up,—some have sold 15,000. *Wife*, first-rate ; beloved by all my people, we have good reason mutually to rejoice.

"I write mere heads, for you can fill up details.

"I have been this week to Leighton Buzzard, Foots Cray, and Chatham; everywhere, no room for the crowd.   Next week, I am to be thus occupied :—

"*Sabbath*, Morning and evening, New Park Street.
Afternoon, to address the schools.

Monday, Morning, at Howard Hinton's Chapel.
Afternoon, New Park Street.
Evening, „   „

Tuesday, Afternoon,
Evening, } Leighton.

Wednesday, Morning,
Evening, } Zion Chapel, Whitechapel.

Thursday, Morning, Dalston.
Evening, New Park Street.

Friday, Morning, Dr. Fletcher's Chapel.
Evening, Mr. Rogers' Chapel, Brixton.

"With best love,

"Yours in haste,

"C. H. SPURGEON."

CHAPTER XLIII.

First Visit to Scotland.

(At one of the services in Glasgow, during the tour described in the following chapter, Mr. Spurgeon referred to some ministers "who apologize for not preaching so often or so vigorously as they once did, because they are now fifty-seven years of age;" and then added, "Fifty-seven! only fifty-seven! What a happiness to preach till one is fifty-seven! *I wish I could preach till I was fifty-seven;* how many souls I might be the means of converting by that time!" Mr. Spurgeon *did* preach till he was fifty-seven; and only the Lord knows how many souls had been up to that date brought to the Saviour through his ministry, nor how great will be the ultimate number saved through his printed sermons and other works.)

MY first visit to Scotland was paid in July, 1855, and for many reasons it left lasting impressions on my memory. It began with some discomfort, for I journeyed from London to Glasgow by night, and travelling at that time was accomplished under conditions very different from those of the present day. On my arrival in the morning, I found my esteemed friend, Mr. John Anderson, ready to receive me, and to conduct me to his hospitable mansion. (This good brother must not be confounded with his namesake, Rev. John Anderson, of Helensburgh, whose acquaintance I did not make until several months later, but who, from our first meeting, became my life-long champion and friend.) On the Sabbath, July 15, I preached in the morning at Hope Street Baptist Chapel (Dr. Patterson's), and in the evening in West George Street Chapel, where the eminent Dr. Wardlaw had formerly ministered with great acceptance. It was a glorious sight to see the people crowding both places of worship, but it also increased my own sense of responsibility. I believe that we had the presence of God at each of the services, and that much good was done. Various newspapers gave reports, characterized by more or less truthfulness and kindly feeling; but in the case of one, the contrast to its contemporaries, was all the more marked from the fact that it bore in its title the sacred name of *Christian*, while others were looked upon as secular papers.

The Daily Bulletin, July 16, contained the following article :—

"VISIT TO GLASGOW OF THE REV. MR. SPURGEON, OF LONDON.

"The visit to Glasgow of this gentleman, when announced a few days ago, was looked forward to with great pleasure by those who knew anything of his extraordinary gifts and powers. He preached twice yesterday; in the forenoon, in

Hope Street Baptist Chapel ; in the evening, in West George Street Church. There was, on the first occasion, a full audience ; on the second, many hundreds had to turn away, while every available inch within the church, and without it as far as the speaker's magnificent voice could reach, was occupied. Mr. Spurgeon owes his celebrity to the possession of first-class oratorical gifts, which seem to have attained maturity of development at a very early age, so that he has established a reputation at a period of life earlier than that at which ordinary men enter upon a profession. His appearance indicates him somewhat beyond his actual age ; and like his great model, Whitefield, he seems blessed with 'no constitution,' that is, he is endowed with a voice strong, clear, bell-like, which could be heard by an audience of very many thousands ; and with a physical frame equal to a vast amount of hard work. In contour of face, he reminds us somewhat of the Rev. John Caird, and his eye has the lustrous light of genius in it. You cannot listen for a few minutes to the bright-eyed boy, whether he be preaching, or pleading in prayer, without feeling that no mere clap-trap rhetorician is before you. There is a force and massiveness about his thoughts and language, a touching, compelling sincerity, which give us the best idea we have ever had of the great early preachers. Like some of these, or like Rowland Hill or Whitefield, of later times, he descends to a homeliness of illustration, to anecdotage, even to mimicry,—a dangerous style, for great taste must be always exercised along with it ; but in the ability to pass from the homely or the grotesque to the dizzy heights of imagination, the real power of the orator is seen. The impression is too vivid to permit of our entering on any critical review of the discourses of yesterday ;—the subject of the one was, 'The Saviour on the Tree ;' and of the other, 'The Lamb upon the Throne.' Suffice it to say that, as most brilliant and thrilling pulpit appeals, we have rarely heard them equalled ; certainly, in some points of effect, never surpassed."

The Glasgow Examiner, which had previously displayed a very friendly feeling, thus reported, in its issue of July 21, the first Sabbath's services :—

"THE REV. C. H. SPURGEON.

" It having been for some time generally understood that this distinguished divine, for and against whom so much has been written and said, would visit Glasgow, the curiosity of the church-going people was thoroughly roused. So many and varied were the opinions of his critics that we believe many of the crowd assembled in Hope Street Baptist Chapel, last Sunday morning, expected to see a nondescript who, instead of elevating their thoughts to the throne of the Most High, would merely endeavour to excite laughter. But when the first tones of the speaker's clear, full voice fell upon their ears, invoking, in language most sublime and beautiful, the presence and blessing of God, they must indeed have felt that truth had been said when he was compared to George Whitefield, the prince of preachers. After singing, he read a chapter in the New Testament, expounding as he went along,—a method which it is to be regretted our ministers do not more often adopt, as it affords such an excellent opportunity of dispelling the difficulties which so often arise in reading the Scriptures. The subject of discourse was from Matthew xxvii. 36: 'And sitting down, they watched Him there.' Seldom has a discourse, so thrillingly eloquent, been delivered in Glasgow. The arrangement was exceedingly neat, the ideas original, while the whole breathed a spirit of most genuine piety. One thing in particular we noticed, Mr. Spurgeon follows the example of the great Teacher of Christianity in illustrating his meaning from external objects,—a mode which cannot be too highly recommended, it so much aids the retention of the discourse upon the memory.

"In the evening, West George Street Chapel was filled in every part, and, long before the appointed hour, many were unable to gain admittance. The text was from Rev. xiv. 1. Many parts of the sermon were distinguished by exceeding pathos and strength of imagination, and the preacher's allusions to the Covenant and martyrs of Scotland showed that he had discovered the nearest way to the strong brave hearts of the Scottish people. One incident proved that he had completely thawed their hearts. On coming out of the chapel, every one, to whom it was possible, rushed forward to shake hands with him, so that it was with considerable difficulty he entered the carriage which stood in waiting.

"When Mr S. again preaches in Glasgow, we hope that it will be in a larger chapel, as doubtless many more will wish to hear him from the report carried away by those who had that privilege yesterday."

The Christian News, July 21, published an article in quite another strain :—

"C. H. SPURGEON.

"Heralded by certain paragraphs, for which those who know how to 'sound a trumpet before them' are able, by some occult influences, to find a place in not a few of the newspapers (albeit they are occasionally extinguished by the *avant-coureur,* 'Advertisement,' or snubbed by the dogged and dogging 'Communicated'), the Rev. C. H. Spurgeon made his *début* in this city on Sunday last. In the morning, he amused, or disgusted, a respectable audience in Hope Street Baptist Chapel ; and in the evening, he flung out platitudes and stale anti-Arminianisms to a large audience in West George Street Chapel, where was *(sic)* wont to be heard the silver tones of the classic Wardlaw. We did not form part of the morning audience ; but, from credible reports, we have not ceased, since till now, congratulating ourselves that we neither witnessed the buffoonery of that exhibition, nor listened to the commonplace denunciation of bigotry (repeated, by the way, in the evening) which Mr. S. *consistently* hedged round by doctrines or dogmas of the most rampant exclusiveness. The evening's exhibition was, we are informed, a little quieter than the morning one. Perhaps the preacher had heard, in the interval, that Scotland is not so thoroughly Calvinistic as he in his dreams had fancied ; and it may have been hinted to him that the pulpit in which, by some unaccountable oversight, we may not say manœuvring, he was to be permitted to stand, had been consecrated to the *intelligent* proclamation of doctrines certainly, even in their deficiencies, more heart and mind satisfying than the mire and dirt with which he has himself become muddled, and by casting forth which he seeks to muddle the minds of others. . . . We must also remind those who play lacquey to Mr. S., that their strength or weakness is apt to be known from the company *they* keep, so that, striking hands with bigots and buffoons, they may be suspected of a fellowship therewith, notwithstanding any half-hearted disclaimers they may put forth. If you can't alone fight Arminianism, do engage one for the contest who knows what Arminianism is, and do not bring disgrace upon yourselves and your creed by endeavouring to screen both behind the mask of the clown. In compassion, too, upon the boy who has fallen into your hands, remember the mischief you may bring upon him, if it be not already brought, and against which Paul guards in 1 Tim. iii. 6. There may be occasion to deal a blow to the mask ;—if so, let the masker look to himself."

As I had gone to the North partly for a holiday, during the week I journeyed on to the Highlands, where I revelled in the grand scenery of the country of which Sir Walter Scott wrote :—

> "Caledonia! stern and wild,
> Meet nurse for a poetic child!
> Land of brown heath and shaggy wood ;
> Land of the mountain and the flood."

There was one place where my friend Anderson was particularly anxious for me to preach ; that was Aberfeldy, an obscure and curious village. There was an Independent Chapel there, and the usual kirk, but nobody appeared even to have heard the name of Spurgeon, so there was some difficulty in knowing how to draw the people together to hear the Word. However, early in the morning, Mr. Anderson knocked at my door, and said, " I have thought of a plan for getting you a congregation to-night." I answered, " I am not very particular about the plan, so you try it if you think it will succeed." He sent round the crier at nine, and twelve, and three o'clock, with a notice to this effect :—" Your auld acquaintance, Johnny Anderson, who used to live here in Aberfeldy, has arrived, and has brought with him his adopted son Timothy, who is going to preach to-night." Then followed an account of my labours and successes in London, and an earnest invitation to all to be present.

As the appointed hour drew nigh, the "brither Scots" began to assemble, and by the time for beginning the service, the chapel was well filled. The good minister gave out one of the Psalms, which was sung in a very devout style, but not with that heartiness to which I had been accustomed among my own warm-hearted friends. I then read and expounded a portion of Scripture, and was much pleased to see nearly every one following me most attentively, and very devoutly listening to the simple exposition which it is my custom to offer. After prayer and singing I began to preach; but there were no eyes of fire, and no beaming countenances, to cheer me while proclaiming the gospel message. The greater part of the congregation sat in apparent indifference; they seemed made of lumps of ice fetched from Wenham Lake. I tried all means to move them, but in vain. At one time, a racy remark provoked a smile from two or three; but the rest, deeming it profane to laugh, sat like those two eminent Egyptian gentlemen in the Crystal Palace, looking at me with majestic, but affected solemnity. Then I advanced to more pathetic themes, and although I myself wept, not a tear came from the eyes of my audience, with but one or two exceptions. I felt like the Welshman who could make Welshmen jump, but could not move the English. I thought within myself, "Surely your blood is very cold here, for everywhere else I should have seen signs of emotion while preaching Christ and Him crucified." Certainly, some did appear impressed; but, on the whole, I never saw so cold an assembly in my life. The sermon over, and the concluding prayer offered, a rush was made for the door; and before I could descend the pulpit stairs, the chapel was deserted, and the whole flock scattered abroad. Never did I see so hasty an evacuation, and I am certain that, if the village were ever threatened by the Russians, the inhabitants would be able to escape "over the hills and far away" at an hour's notice, if they used the same expedition.

Feeling rather sad at our singular service, I went into the street, and was delighted to find that, although cold as marble in the building, they were now hearty and full of feeling. I will not limit the Holy One of Israel. I trust some secret work was done: the earnest thanks for my trouble, and the eager request that I would come again, showed that there had been some appreciation of the service, despite that formality which their training had engendered. I retired to rest with the conviction that the last day would prove that the seed was not lost; and I confidently expect to see in glory some soul plucked from the burning by the arm of the Holy Spirit, through the message delivered by me to the people of Aberfeldy.

On my way back to Glasgow, I had an adventure which was somewhat un-pleasant, and which might have had more serious consequences. The accounts of it were considerably exaggerated; my friends in London were told that I had been thrown into the water, and dragged out by the hair of my head. It was not so, though there certainly was some danger, as my letter, published in the *North British Daily Mail*, July 20, plainly shows :—

"NARROW ESCAPE AT GOVAN FERRY.

"To the Editor of the *North British Daily Mail*,

  "Sir,

      "The value of the press as the corrector of abuses is incalculable. Will you allow me to avail myself of your columns to expose an individual who ought to suffer some more severe penalty for his folly? On returning, on Wednesday evening, from a tour in the Highlands, I requested to be set on shore at Govan Ferry. A boat was brought alongside, into which I entered, and was not a little distressed to find that strong drink had been doing mischief with the brains of the boatman. We were propelled, much to the dismay of the ladies on board, upon the track which a steamer then approaching was certain to take. The boat was, however, after some remonstrance, guided safely to the side of the other steamer, and then the manager of the boat, who was 'as drunk as a lord,' filled it until we stood so thickly together that we could not move, and the slightest motion must have sent us all to the bottom.

      "Now, sir, I have not the honour to be a Scotchman, but I may ask,— Are there no authorities who can prevent boats from being overcrowded, and call a man to account who was so drunk as to be incapable of anything except the lowest abuse and swearing? Should an important ferry be in the hands of a man who has not sufficient respect for himself to avoid drunkenness, and is so careless of the lives of others that he can so foolishly expose them? We were safely landed, but not until one gentleman had been over his knees in the water; but should another time be less propitious, some life must be lost. I have written, not for myself, but for the other four-and-twenty who were placed in so perilous a situation.

                                    "Yours, &c.,

                                    "C. H. SPURGEON."

      (The following letter, written by Mr. Spurgeon to his father, at this date, has been preserved : he had it copied, and laid aside with other material for his *Autobiography* :—)

                                    "Fairfield.

                                      "Near Glasgow,

                                        "July 19, 1855.

  "My Dear Father,

      "During the past week, I have been among the noble mountains in the Highlands ; and you will rejoice to hear how much better I feel. Last Sabbath, I preached twice in Glasgow to immense crowds.

"There is as much stir about me here as there is in London, and I hope souls are really being saved. I am sure you will excuse my being brief, since I have so many letters to answer, and I do not want to keep indoors, but to have all the air I can.

"Oh, what must God be, if such are His works! I suppose Mother is back; kiss her for me, and give my love to all. I am happy, but had rather be home again ;—you will guess the reason. I only want that one person to make the trip a very fine one ;—but patience, Charles.

"Best love to you, my very dear Father,

"From your affectionate son,

"CHARLES."

I had promised to preach at Bradford, the following Sabbath (July 22) ; and on my way to Yorkshire, I made a short stay at Lake Windermere, round which I sailed, and greatly enjoyed the beauties of its scenery. On reaching Bradford, I found that the friends had engaged the Music Hall, which, they said, held a thousand persons more than Exeter Hall ; but it was not large enough to contain the crowds that came. On the Sunday morning, almost as many had to go away as were accommodated in the building ; in the evening, the streets presented a solid block of living men and women. The place was crammed to excess, and I had scarcely room to move about to deliver what I had to say to the people. At the end of the day, I was delighted to find that, not only had thousands of persons heard the Word, but they had given £144 towards the Sabbath-schools in connection with which the services had been held. From Bradford, I went to Stockton-on-Tees, and there again I preached to a very large congregation.

Journeying back again to Scotland, I conducted a service in Queen Street Hall, Edinburgh, on Wednesday evening, July 25. Notwithstanding pouring rain, a great crowd of people again assembled. I was very delighted, after the sermon, to meet with a military officer who grasped my hand, and said, "For twenty years I have served her Majesty, yet never had I heard the Word of God to my soul's profit until I stepped into Dr. Wardlaw's Chapel, at Glasgow, a week ago last Sabbath. But now I am enlisted in the army of the King of kings. The Lord God of hosts bless you! The King of kings be with you! The God of Jacob help you everywhere!" I blessed the dear man, and retired to rest, conscious that, if I had done nothing else, yet, through my instrumentality, one of the heroes of the Crimea, who had not turned his back in the day of battle, was found numbered among the good soldiers of Jesus Christ.

The Christian News, July 28, thus described this service :—

"THE REV. C. H. SPURGEON IN EDINBURGH.

" According to announcement in the newspapers and by placards, this reverend gentleman, whose appearances have created such an interest in Exeter Hall, London, preached a sermon in Queen Street Hall, Edinburgh, on Wednesday evening, 25th inst. Favoured with a seat which commanded an admirable prospect of the platform, we waited for three-quarters of an hour, in company with a multitude of sight-seers, who had been drawn together by the fame or notoriety of the preacher, and, as the sequel proved, were but rather sparingly rewarded for our pains. . . . Mr. Spurgeon's oratory was unequal and clumsy in the extreme,—the Spirit having deserted him, according to his own confession. Might not this be a punishment for his non-preparation? for he glories that he never prepares, which in our ears, particularly from a minister, sounds very much like glorying in his shame, though he informed his audience that, at times, his eloquence is like the mountain torrent, and rolls along like a winged chariot. We were sorry for Mr. Spurgeon, more sorry for his friends, and most sorry for the audience, many of whom were competent persons, and had evidently come to listen to something extraordinary in the use of the pulpit. That Mr. Spurgeon should have become an idol in London, we do not wonder, for we remember Mr. Jay, of Bath, saying 'that the London public is the most gullible public on the face of the earth, and that any man who should vociferate standing on his head would gather immense congregations around him, whatever his vulgarity and insolence.' Mr. S., in our estimation, is just a spoiled boy, with abilities not more than mediocre, and will for certain, if he do not retrace his steps, share the fate of the 'early gooseberry' or the 'monster cucumber', that appear almost annually in the columns of the newspapers,—sink into obscurity, leaving only the memorial of his career, that he was, and that he has descended to that nihility from which, by puffing and blustering, he originally and unworthily sprang."

The reference, in the above paragraph, to desertion by the Spirit of God was a gross perversion of fact, for I had not neglected preparation for the service. The incident was very vividly impressed upon my mind and heart, but I think the true lesson to be learned from it was the one I tried to teach my own people after I returned to London. I said to them :—" Once, while preaching in Scotland, the Spirit of God was pleased to desert me ; I could not speak as usually I have done. I was obliged to tell the people that the chariot wheels were taken off, and that the chariot dragged along very heavily. I have felt the benefit of that experience ever since. It humbled me bitterly ; and if I could, I would have hidden myself in any obscure corner of the earth. I felt as if I should speak no more in the Name of the Lord ; and then the thought came, 'Oh, thou art an ungrateful creature! Hath not God spoken by thee hundreds of times? And this once, when He would not do so, wilt thou upbraid Him for it? Nay, rather thank Him that He hath so long stood by thee; and if once He hath forsaken thee, admire His goodness, that thus He would keep thee humble.' Some may imagine that want of study brought me into that condition, but I can honestly affirm that it was not so. I think that I am bound to give myself unto reading, and not to tempt the Spirit by unthought-of effusions. I always deem it a duty to seek my sermons from my Master, and implore Him to impress them on my mind; but, on that occasion, I think I had prepared even more carefully than I ordinarily do, so that unpreparedness was not the reason for the lack of force I then mourned. The simple fact is this, 'The wind bloweth where it listeth;' and, sometimes, the winds themselves are still. Therefore, if I rest on the Spirit, I cannot expect that I should always feel His power alike. What could I do without His celestial influence? To that, I owe everything. Other servants of the Lord have had experiences similar to mine. In the Life of Whitefield we read that, sometimes, under one of his sermons, two thousand persons would profess to be saved, and many of them were really so; at other times, he preached just as powerfully, and no conversions were recorded. Why was that? Simply, because, in the one case, the Holy Spirit went with the Word; and in the other case, He did not. All the Heavenly result of preaching is owing to the Divine Spirit sent from above."

On the next Sabbath (July 29), I preached twice more in Glasgow. The morning service was at West Nile Street Chapel (Rev. A. Fraser's), and there again I found the necessity for a much larger building to hold all the people who wanted to be present. In the evening, I preached in Greyfriars' Church (Dr. King's), and that spacious house of prayer was crowded to its utmost capacity, while I was afterwards assured by the Editor of one of the papers that 20,000 persons went away, unable to obtain admission. Once more I received the help of my gracious Master as I proclaimed His truth to the eager crowd that came to hear it.

John Smith, Esq., M.A., the Editor of *The Glasgow Examiner*, inserted in his paper an account of these two services, with a lengthy critique upon my ministry, commencing thus:—"The way moth-eaten routine generally settles off anyone who dares to break away from its old, time-worn tracks is, by pronouncing him an empiric. Galileo, Columbus, Luther, Knox, the apostle Paul, and even the Author of Christianity Himself, were, by the accredited orthodoxy of their day, stigmatized as empirics; and so will it be with anyone who ventures to do or say otherwise than according to the existing modes and fashions. . . . Routine in religious services is extremely liable to beget a listless, lukewarm compliance with its prescribed forms, while the spirit or *animus* gradually subsides. The preacher speaks his usual time;

the people sit patiently enough, perhaps; a few may even listen; the usual number of verses is sung, and the business of the day is over; there is generally no more about it. No one can deny that this is more or less than a simple statement of the real state of matters in the majority of our churches at the present day. Should the minister during his discourse sharpen his intellects with a sprinkling of snuff, let fall his handkerchief on the Psalm-book, or give one thump louder than usual with the fist ecclesiastic, that will be noted, remembered, and commented on, while there is all but total oblivion of the subject and the nature of the discussion. To break up this deadening process, to shake the dry bones and make them live, ought to be the great aim of the preacher at the present day; but it is not everyone who can do it. Affectation of manner or style won't do it; talent—we may say, genius—of a peculiar nature is required; and we have no hesitation in saying that Mr. Spurgeon possesses the requisites in an unusual degree. No doubt many respectable and sensible men, when hearing of the odd, and to them, uncanonical expressions of this young preacher, would be very apt to find the word 'empiric' or 'quack' upon their tongue's end.

"We must ourselves plead guilty to some such expression when we first heard of his youth, unsystematic training, and official boldness. We, in common with our fellow-citizens, had seen and heard so much of boy-preaching, lay-preaching, and bold preaching, that there was nothing uncharitable in entertaining some doubts of his intrinsic excellence; still, that large London audiences daily waited on his ministry, was a fact that could not be stifled with a sneer. It could not be any novelty in the theme itself, as there were thousands of preachers, and millions of books and tracts, dilating on it before Mr Spurgeon made his appearance; it could not be any new doctrine, for this was the same as John Calvin preached centuries ago, and circumstantially the same as that preached by the Evangelical denominations around him; neither could it be his youth, as there are in the churches of Britain scores of preachers as young as he is; neither could it be the few *outré* sentences that were scattered through his discourses, for there are many in London who say stranger and odder things than any that he has yet uttered. But what was the character of these crowds that went to hear him? Were they the profane, the ignorant and illiterate, the light-hearted and frivolous young people of the metropolis? There might have been some of these among the many; but, as far as we can learn, they were fair examples of the respectable church-going community, perfectly capable of judging rationally on all subjects that engross public attention. We maintain that no man could have sustained such excitement, and kept together such crowds of people for two or three years, unless he was possessed of more than ordinary gifts. But we do not now require to judge him by the effects of his preaching upon a metropolitan crowd. He has appeared amongst us, and the

London verdict has been fully confirmed by immense audiences, that have been equally spell-bound by his oratory. According to reports, he indulged somewhat freely in the out-of-the-way expressions on the first Sabbath of his sojourn in this city; but such was not the case last Sabbath, and his discourses on that occasion were still more fascinating and attractive. In the first place, there is about him that hearty, open, English frankness, which has no hesitation in giving full and free utterance to its opinions, loves, and dislikes. Then there is the ready, acute perception which never fails to bring out fresh and striking illustrations from any text on which the attention is directed. Again, there is an extensive acquaintance with literature, which, by the aid of a retentive memory, can at a moment's notice furnish the speaker with choice and appropriate material. And lastly, there is a power of voice, and volubility of utterance, which enable him to speak with great ease, and at the same time to give powerful effect to his sentiments. We may have heard many preachers who could reason more correctly and profoundly, who displayed more classical elegance and polish, but we have not heard one who can more powerfully arrest the attention and carry the sympathies of an audience along with him. . . .

"Though it has been extensively circulated that his prayers are irreverent, presumptuous, and blasphemous, there was nothing in them on Sabbath last which could with truth be so characterized. On the contrary, they were correct, appropriate, and beautiful. He certainly has not followed the usual pulpit style, but has opened his eyes on the state of society in all its forms and phases, and adapted his confessions, and petitions, and thanksgivings. He confesses the peculiar sins of the times, as well as the inherent and changeless depravity of man's nature ; the sins of the parlour, the counting-house, and the public assembly ; the sins of individuals, families, and nations. He offers petitions for various classes of characters,—for the profligate and careless, for the old, the young, and for little children ; petitions for churches, for nations, for the world, all in a somewhat novel manner. While he gives thanks for special blessings, and employs language which none but the genuine believer can appropriate, and which even *he* must sometimes acknowledge with hesitancy, he forgets not the common benefits which all share, and the common blessings with which all are crowned. We have heard much of undue familiarities and daring impieties, but we witnessed none of them. There was an earnestness, an unction, a fluency, and an urgency, which are but too seldom imitated. His reading and exposition of the Word of God, we reckon exceedingly good. Every word receives its proper emphasis and tone, and his remarks are generally terse, original, and instructive.

On the following Thursday, my kind host, Mr. Anderson, invited about a hundred friends to meet me at his mansion, that I might bid them farewell. I gave them an account of the way the Lord had led me into the ministry, and of the blessing He had already bestowed upon my service ; and, at their urgent request, I promised to go and see them once a year, if possible. I told them that they had treated me far better than I deserved,—surely, it was for my Master's sake. I don't know how it is that people are so good to me,—I have never sought the applause of men,—however, if God has given me any favour in the eyes of the people, it is for me to use that favour to His glory ; not to be exalted by it, but to thank Him for it, and to employ it all in His service.

REV. JOHN ANDERSON, HELENSBURGH.

Though it belongs to the following year, part of the letter from Rev. John Anderson, of Helensburgh, which was published in *The Scottish Guardian*, April 18, 1856, may be appropriately inserted here :—

"Sir,—When Mr. Spurgeon was in Glasgow, last summer, the fame of his eloquence had reached me in my seclusion here, by the shores of the sounding sea, the noise of whose waves delights me more than the 'din of cities' or the tumult of the people. I had heard him 'spoken against' by some, but spoken of by others as a preacher of remarkable, and, since the days of Whitefield himself, of unprecedented popularity. But being one of those who judge for themselves in the matter of preaching, and whose opinions as to what constitutes good preaching are somewhat peculiar, I did not attach much, I may almost say, any, importance whatever to what I heard of Mr. Spurgeon and his popularity in Glasgow. One of his printed sermons, however, having fallen in my way, I had no sooner read a few paragraphs of it than I said, ' Here at last is a preacher to my mind,—one whom not only I, but whom Paul himself, I am persuaded, were he on earth, would hear, approve, and own.' I forget what was the subject of the discourse ; but I remember well saying to myself, ' I would rather have been the author of that sermon than of all the sermons, or volumes of sermons, published in my day.' I had lately before this been reading Guthrie and Caird, but here was something entirely different, and, to my mind, in all that constitutes a genuine and a good gospel sermon, infinitely superior.

" For some time after this, I heard little, and thought little, about Mr. Spurgeon. Having been, however, in London, on the last Sabbath of March, and having been unexpectedly released from an engagement to preach, I thought I could not do better than go and hear for myself the preacher of whom I had heard so much in my own country. . . . Though, from the crowd which choked the doors and passages, we did not see the preacher very well, we—and this was what we wanted,—heard him distinctly. When we entered, he was expounding, as is his custom, a portion of the Scriptures. The passage expounded was Exodus, 14th chapter, which contains an account of the Israelites at the Red Sea,—a passage of Scripture peculiarly interesting to me, having stood on its shore, and sailed on the very spot where the waters were so wondrously divided. The remarks of the preacher on each of the verses were very much in the style of Henry, and were rich and racy. His text was from the 106th Psalm, and the subject of the discourse was the same with that of the chapter he had just expounded,— ' The Israelites at the Red Sea.' . . .

" Such was the method of one of the richest and ripest sermons, as regards Christian experience, I ever heard,—all the more wonderful as being the sermon of so young a man. It was a sermon far in advance of the experience of many of his hearers ; and the preacher evidently felt this. But, notwithstanding this, such was the simplicity of his style, the richness and quaintness of his illustrations, his intense earnestness, and the absolute and admirable naturalness of his delivery, it told upon his audience generally, and told powerfully. Many, indeed most of them, were of ' the common people,' and when I looked on their plebeian faces, their hands brown with labour, and, in many cases, their faded attire, I could not help remembering Him of whom it is said, ' the common people heard Him gladly.' Yes, Mr. Spurgeon is the minister of ' the common people ; ' I am told he considers himself to be such, and well he may. Happy London people, if they but knew their happiness, to have such a minister ! . . . Mr. Spurgeon is equally great in the tender and the terrible. Nor is he without humour. Here, many will refuse him their sympathy, and think him censurable.   I scarcely think he is.   Others will think, and do think differently. His taste, according to others, is bad.   It is, I admit, often so.   But then, think of the immaturity of his years.   I was told he was conceited.   I saw no proofs of it ; and if I had, was I on that account to think less of his sermons ?   I do not say I will not eat good bread, because the maker of it is conceited.   His conceit may be a bad thing for himself ;—his bread is very good for me.   I am far from thinking Mr. Spurgeon perfect.   In this respect he is not like Whitefield, who from the first was as perfect as an orator as he was at the last.   In respect of his power over an audience, and a London one in. particular, I should say he is not inferior to Whitefield himself.   Mr. Spurgeon is a Calvinist, which few of the Dissenting ministers in London now are.   He preaches salvation, not of man's *free will*, but of the Lord's *good will*, which few in London, it is to be feared, now do.   On all these accounts, we hail the appearance of Mr. Spurgeon with no ordinary delight, and anticipate for him a career of no ordinary usefulness.   ' Happy are they which stand continually before him, and hear his words of wisdom.'   As for myself, I shall long remember with delight the day on which I stood among them, and recommend such of my countrymen as may have a Lord's-day to spend in London, to spend it, as I did, in New Park Street Chapel, in hearing Mr. Spurgeon."

CHAPTER XLIV.

Marbellous Increase.—Facts and Figures.

Any man, who has his eyes open to the world at large, will acknowledge that there are many clouds brooding over England, and over the world. I received lately a letter from a gentleman at Hull, in which he tells me that he sympathizes with my views concerning the condition of the Church at large. I do not know whether Christendom was ever worse off than it is now. At any rate, I pray God it never may be. Read the account of the condition of the Suffolk churches, where the gospel is somewhat flourishing, and you will be surprised to learn that they have had hardly any increase at all in the year. So you may go from church to church, and find scarcely any that are growing. Here and there, a chapel is filled with people; here and there, you see an earnest minister; here and there, an increasing church; here and there, a good prayer-meeting; but these are only like green spots in a great desert. Wherever I have gone through England, I have always been grieved to see how the Church of Christ is under a cloud, - how " the precious sons of Zion, comparable to fine gold, are esteemed as earthen pitchers, the work of the hands of the potter." It is not for me to set myself up as universal censor of the Church; but I must be honest, and say that spiritual life, and fire, and zeal, and piety seem to be absent in ten thousand instances. We have abundance of agencies, we have good mechanism, but the Church, nowadays, is very much like a large steam engine without any fire, and, therefore, without any steam. There is everything but steam, everything but life. England is veiled in clouds;—not clouds of infidelity; I care not one fig for all the infidels in England, and I do not think it is worth Mr. Grant's trouble to go after them. Nor am I afraid of Popery for old England; I do not think she will go back to that, nay, I am sure she never will; but I *am* afraid of this deadness, this sloth, this indifference, that has come over our churches. The Church wants shaking, like the man on the mountain-top does when the cold benumbs him into a deadly slumber. The churches are gone to sleep for want of zeal, for want of fire. Even those that hold sound doctrine are beginning to slumber. Oh, may God stir the Church up! One great black cloud, only broken here and there by a few rays of sunlight, seems to be hanging over the entire area of this our happy island. But, beloved, there is this comfort, "the clouds are the dust of His feet." God can scatter them in a moment. He can raise up His chosen servants, who have only to put their mouth to the trumpet, and one blast shall awake the sleeping sentinels, and startle the slumbering camp. God has only to send out again some earnest evangelist, like Wesley or Whitefield, and the churches shall start up once more; and she, who has been clothed in sackcloth, shall doff her robes of mourning, and put on the garment of praise. The day is coming, I hope, when Zion shall sit, not without her diadem; but, with her crown on her head, she shall grasp her banner, take her shield, and, like that heroic maiden of old who roused a whole nation, shall go forth conquering and to conquer.—C. H. S., *in sermon preached at New Park Street Chapel, August 19, 1855.*

HATEVER may be the present condition of the Church of Christ in general, and of the Baptist denomination in particular, it is certain that, at the time Mr. Spurgeon began his ministry in London, the state of affairs was far from satisfactory. Mr. Horace Mann's report on the attendance at places set apart for public worship proved that, even in the mere external observances of religion, there was at that period much to be desired; he wrote :—"Comparing the number of actual attendants with the number of persons *able* to attend, we find that, of 10,398,013 (58 per cent. of the whole population) who would be at liberty to worship at one period of the day, there were actually worshipping but 4,647,482 in the morning, 3,184,135 in the afternoon, and 3,064,449 in the evening. So that, taking any one service of the day, there were actually attending public worship less than half the number who, as far as physical impediments prevented, *might* have been attending. In the morning there were absent, without physical hindrance, 5,750,531 ; in the afternoon, 7,213,878 ; in the evening, 7,333,564. There exist no data for determining how many persons attended twice, and how many three times, on the Sunday, nor, consequently, for deciding how many attended altogether on *some* service of the day ; but if we suppose that half of those attending service in the afternoon had not been present in the morning, and that a third of those attending service in the evening had not been present at either of the previous services, we should obtain a total of 7,261,032 separate persons, who attended service either once or oftener upon the Census Sunday. But, as the number who would be able to attend at *some* time of the day is more than 58 per cent. (which is the estimated number able to be present *at one and the same time*), probably reaching 70 per cent., it is with this latter number (12,549,326) that this 7,261,032 must be compared ; and the result of such comparison would lead to the conclusion that, upon the Census Sunday, 5,288,294 persons, able to attend religious worship once at least, neglected to do so."

This was sufficiently sad ; but to those who looked below the surface, to see the true spiritual condition of the people, the revelation was still more depressing. At the re-opening of New Park Street Chapel, after the enlargement, good Mr. Sherman said, in the course of his sermon :—"It is only here and there that God is pouring out His Spirit ; but most of the churches are lying like barges at Blackfriars Bridge when the tide is down,—right in the mud,—and all the king's horses and all the king's men cannot pull them off ; they need the tide to turn, and the water to flow, and set them all afloat."

Our own denomination was not at all in a flourishing condition. At the Baptist Union session, in 1854, the following resolution was passed :—"That the Union learn, with unfeigned regret, that the rate of increase in the churches, as shown by the Association Returns of 1853, is smaller than in preceding years, and smaller than it has been in any year since 1834,—the limit of the Union records,—it being only at an average of 1⅓ per church per annum ;—that, while the impression made by this numerical statement might be somewhat modified by a regard to the temporary causes—such as emigration, for example,—which have operated to the diminution of the churches (and the statement cannot alone be taken as a satisfactory basis on which to form an estimate of the spiritual state of the churches), in the judgment of the Union it presents at once an occasion for humiliation and a loud call to united activity and prayer ; the former in every department of the work of the Lord, the latter for the gracious outpouring of His Holy Spirit."

In London, the interest in denominational affairs had sunk so low that *The Baptist Messenger*, in reporting the meeting of the London Association of Baptist Churches, held at the Mission House, October 17, 1855, said that "the number in attendance, representing thirty-three metropolitan churches, consisted of NINE PERSONS,—six ministers, and three lay-brethren. Alas! 'how is the gold become dim!' Who can wonder at the low state of the churches, when the princes among the people are thus negligent and supine?"

Three months later, the same Magazine was able to give a somewhat more cheering account of the proceedings in connection with the Association :—

"The annual meetings were held on January 9. In the afternoon, the Rev. James Harcourt, of Regent Street, Lambeth, preached from Acts i. 8. In the evening, a public meeting was held, at which letters from the churches were read, and addresses delivered by the chairman, the Rev. C. Stovel, the Rev. Joshua Russell, and the Rev. Jonathan George. The letters, which were encouraging, reported a clear increase, during the year, of 207 members, principally owing to the extraordinary success attending the labours of the Rev. C. H. Spurgeon."

The truth of the last sentence is confirmed by the remarks of the young Pastor when preaching at New Park Street Chapel on the last Lord's-day morning in 1855 ; he said :—" Ought we to let this year pass without rehearsing the works of the Lord? Hath He not been with us, and prospered us exceeding abundantly? . . . We shall not soon forget our sojourn in Exeter Hall,—shall we? During those months, the Lord brought in many of His own elect, and multitudes, who had been up to that time unsaved, were called by Divine mercy, and brought into the fold. How God protected us there! What peace and prosperity hath He given to us! How hath He enlarged our borders, and multiplied our numbers, so that we are not few ; and increased us, so that we are not weak! I do think we were not thankful enough for the goodness of the Lord which carried us there, and gave us so many who have now become useful to us in our church, . . . Some old writer has said, ' Every hour that a Christian remains a Christian, is an hour of miracle.' It is true ; and every year that the church is kept a united church, is a year of miracle. This has been a year of miracles. Tell it to the wide, wide world ; tell it everywhere : ' The eyes of the Lord ' have been upon us, ' from the beginning of the year even unto the end of the year.' Two hundred and ten persons [*] have this year united with us in church-fellowship ;—about enough to have formed a church. One half the churches in London cannot number so many in their entire body ; yet the Lord has brought so many into our midst. And still they come ; whenever I have an opportunity of

---

[*] It appears, from the New Park Street church-book, that the number was even larger than this. At the end of 1854, there were 313 names on the roll ; during 1855, there was a net increase of 282 ; and the following year the net increase was 265 ; making the total membership 800.

seeing those who are converted to God, they come in such numbers that many have to be sent away; and I am well assured that I have as many still in this congregation who will, during the next year, come forward to put on the Lord Jesus Christ."

(N.B.—In the next paragraph, the autobiographical narrative is resumed.)

Great numbers of the converts of those early days came as the direct result of the slanders with which I was so mercilessly assailed. My name was so often reviled in the public press that it became the common talk of the street, and many a man, going by the door of our house of prayer, has said, "I'll go in, and hear old Spurgeon." He came in to make merriment of the preacher (and very little that troubled *him*); but the man stood there until the Word went home to his heart, and he who was wont to beat his wife, and to make his home a hell, has before long been to see me, and has given me a grip of the hand, and said, "God Almighty bless you, sir; there is something in true religion!" "Well, let me hear your tale." I have heard it, and very delightful has it been in hundreds of instances. I have said to the man, "Send your wife to me, that I may hear what she says about you." The woman has come, and I have asked her, "What do you think of your husband now, ma'am?" "Oh, sir, such a change I never saw in my life! He is so kind to us; he is like an angel now, and he seemed like a fiend before. Oh, that cursed drink, sir! Everything went to the public-house; and then, if I came up to the house of God, he did nothing but abuse me. Oh! to think that now he comes with me on Sunday; and the shop is shut up, sir; and the children, who used to be running about without a bit of shoe or stocking, he takes them on his knee, and prays with them so sweetly. Oh, there is such a change!"

One Sabbath evening, two brothers were brought to the Lord at New Park Street Chapel the very first time they met with us. These were the circumstances of the case. A widowed mother had two sons, who had nearly come to man's estate. They had been excellent children in their boyhood, but they began to be headstrong, as too many young people are prone to be, and they would not brook maternal control; they would spend their Sunday as they pleased, and sometimes in places where they should not have been seen. Their mother determined that she would never give up praying for them, and one night she thought she would stop at home from the house of God, shut herself up in her room, and pray for her sons' conversion.

The very night she had thus set apart for prayer on their behalf, the elder son said to her, "I am going to hear the minister that preaches down Southwark way; I am told he is an odd man, and I want to hear him preach." The mother herself did not think much of that minister, but she was so glad that her boy was going anywhere within the sound of the Word, that she said, " Go, my son." He added, " My brother is going with me." Those two young men came to the house of God, and that odd minister was blessed to the conversion of both of them.

C. H. SPURGEON IN THE PULPIT AT NEW PARK STREET CHAPEL.

When the mother opened the door, on their return home, the elder son fell upon her neck, weeping as if his heart would break. " Mother," he said, " I have found the Saviour ; I am a believer in the Lord Jesus Christ." She looked at him a moment, and then said, " I knew it, my son ; to-night I have had power in prayer, and I felt that I had prevailed." " But," said the younger brother, " oh, mother ! I, too, have been cut to the heart, and I also have given myself to the Lord Jesus Christ." Happy was that mother, and I was happy, too, when she came to me, and said, " You have been the means of the conversion of my two sons ; I have never thought of baptism before, but I see it now to be the Lord's own ordinance, so I will be baptized with my children." It was my great joy to lead the whole three down into the water, and to baptize them "into the Name of the Father, and of the Son, and of the Holy Ghost."

Not only were many converted who had been indifferent or careless about their souls, but I had peculiar joy in receiving not a few, who had themselves been numbered amongst the slanderers and blasphemers who seemed as if they could not say anything cruel and wicked enough concerning me, even though they had never been to hear me. Many a man has come to me, when he was about to be added to the church, and his first speech has been, " Will you ever forgive me, sir ? "   I have said, " Forgive you for what ? "   " Why, because," he has answered, "there was no word in the English language that was bad enough for me to say of you ; and yet I had never seen you in my life, and I had no reason for speaking like that.   I have cursed God's people, and said all manner of evil of them ; will you forgive me ? " My reply has been, " I have nothing to forgive ; if you have sinned against the Lord's people, I am heartily glad that you are ready to confess the sin to God ; but as far as I was concerned, there was no offence given, and none taken."   How glad I have been when the man has said that his heart was broken, that he had repented of his sins, that Christ had put away all his iniquities, and that he wished to follow the Lord, and make confession of his faith !   I think there is only one joy I have had greater than this ; that has been when those converted through my instrumentality have been the means of the conversion of others.   Constantly has this happened during my ministry, until I have not only been surrounded by those who look upon me as their father in Christ, but I have had quite a numerous company of spiritual grand-children, whom my sons and daughters in the faith have led to the Saviour.

The love that exists between a pastor and his converts is of a very special character, and I am sure that mine was so from the very beginning of my ministry.   The bond that united me to the members at New Park Street was probably all the stronger because of the opposition and calumny that, for a time at least, they had to share with me.   The attacks of our adversaries only united us more closely to one another ; and, with whole-hearted devotion, the people willingly followed wherever I led them.   I have never brought any project before them, or asked them to aid me in any holy enterprise, but they have been ready to respond to the call, no matter what amount of self-sacrifice might be required.   Truly I may say, without the slightest flattery, that I never met with any people, on the face of the earth, who lived more truly up to this doctrine—that, chosen of God, and loved by Him with special love, they should do extraordinary things for Him,—than those among whom it has been my privilege to minister.   I have often gone on my knees before God to thank Him for the wondrous deeds I have seen done by some of the Christians with whom I have been so long and so happily associated.   In service, they have gone beyond anything I could have asked.   I should think they would have considered me unreasonable if I had requested it ; but they have done it without request.   At the risk of everything, they have served their Master, and not only spent all that they could spare, but have even spared what they could ill afford to devote to the service of Jesus.   Often have I brushed the tears from my eyes when I have received from some of them offerings for the Lord's work which utterly surpassed all my ideas of giving.   The consecration of their substance has been truly apostolic.   I have known some who have, even in their poverty, given all that they had ; and when I have even hinted at their exceeding the bounds of prudence, they have seemed hurt, and pressed the gift again for some other work of the Master whom they love. A man once said to me, " If you want a subscription from me, sir, you must get at my heart, and then you will get at my purse." " Yes," I answered, " I have no doubt I shall, for I believe that is where your purse lies." But that was not the case with the great bulk of my dear friends at New Park Street ; their hearts were in the Lord's work, and therefore they generously gave of their substance for the advancement of their Saviour's Kingdom.

(Perhaps the consecration and liberality of the members can be accounted for, at least in part, by the example set before them from the very first by their young minister. At the great meeting, held in the Metropolitan Tabernacle, on Tuesday evening, May 20, 1879, to commemorate the completion of Mr. Spurgeon's twenty-fifth year as Pastor of the church, Mr. William Olney, in presenting the testimonial of £6,233, said, among many other kind things :—"After the very able paper of Mr. Carr, it will not be necessary for me to say much about our Pastor. But one point demands most explicit utterance to-night,—a point upon which he has been greatly misunderstood. The generosity of our Pastor, his self-abnegation, and his self-denial, I will speak of from a deacon's point of view. I should like it to be clearly understood,—for I know the words I utter will be heard beyond this place, and beyond the audience now listening,—I should like it to be understood that, after twenty-five years' intimate fellowship with him on money matters, I can testify to this one thing,—whilst the world says, concerning him, that he has made a good thing of it by becoming the minister of this Tabernacle, I can say it is *we* that have made a good thing of it, and *not he*. The interests of this church have always been first with him, and personal interests have always been second. Now, facts are stubborn things. Let me give you a few of them. When he first came, at the invitation of the church, we were a few feeble folk ; the sittings at Park Street had for some years gone a-begging ; the minister's salary was exceedingly small, and the difficulty we had in keeping the doors open was very great. Incidental and other expenses of one sort and another were a heavy burden upon the people. When Mr. Spurgeon came, the arrangement between him and the deacons was that, whatever the seat-rents produced, should be his. Those seat-rents had been supplemented in the case of all former pastorates by a great number of collections, and the hat had to go round frequently, a few having to give at the end of the year to keep matters straight. When Mr. Spurgeon came, the seats went begging no longer. The seat-rents, as they came in, all belonged to him. Did he keep them? No! The first thing he did, at the close of three months, was to say, ' Now we will have no more collections for incidental expenses. I will pay for the cleaning and lighting myself ;'

124 C. H. SPURGEON'S AUTOBIOGRAPHY.

and from that time till now he has done so. There has never been a collection for the current incidental expenses in this Tabernacle, and I believe there never will be as long as he lives ;—I hope not until the end of time. Now for another important fact. There was what we might fairly call an interregnum between the time that this church was worshipping in New Park Street, and its removal here. During those three years, we were wandering, in some senses of the word. At one part of the time, we worshipped in Exeter Hall, and also in the Surrey Music Hall. During the whole of that time, the crowds collected to hear our Pastor were so great that certain charges were made for admission to the several buildings. Tickets, called preference tickets, were issued in large numbers for the privilege of early admission to hear Mr. Spurgeon, and the whole of the proceeds legitimately belonged to him. Did he take them? Not one farthing. I speak from the book, mind; and such facts ought to be made known on such nights as these. During those three years, Mr. Spurgeon paid over to the treasury of this church, for the building of this Tabernacle, just upon £5,000, all of which belonged to himself, for he was fairly and clearly entitled to it.* That is what we have received at the hand of our Pastor.

" Now listen again. Our Pastor says, ' That will do ;' but it will not do for me, and I do not believe that it will do for you. I want this to be heard outside this Tabernacle. The report of this great meeting will be in the newspapers, and be read by many who do not understand Mr. Spurgeon, and who do not understand us ; and I wish all the world, reporters and everybody else, clearly to know that I am speaking facts which can be demonstrated and proved. For many years, the most generous helper of all the institutions connected with this place of worship has been Mr. Spurgeon. He has set us an example of giving. He has not stood to preach to us here for what he has got by preaching, but he has set an example to every one of us, to show that every institution here must be maintained in full vigour and strength. The repairs in connection with this place of worship, the maintenance of it, the management of all its institutions, and of everything connected with the building, and the property, and everything else,—all has been under his fostering care.

* Readers of Vol. I. of the *Autobiography* may remember that the total income of the New Park Street Church for the year 1853 was less than £300. The following figures prove the truth of Mr. William Olney's statement, and also show how rapid and how great was the growth of the finances after Mr. Spurgeon's pastorate commenced in April, 1854 :—

Year.	Church Receipts.			Ordinance Poor Fund.			Receipts for other purposes.			Separate Services Account.			Building and Enlargement Account.		
	£	s.	d.	£	s.	d.	£	s.	d	£	s.	d.	£	s.	d.
1854	515	5	5	...			57	14	4	...			...		
1855	834	7	9	104	17	6	74	17	3	...			1,359	18	6
1856	868	0	9	140	0	1	125	10	9	479	2	3	229	11	6
1857	1,146	8	8	165	9	10	255	18	2	3,211	4	0	6,100	0	0†
1858	1,090	2	5	216	12	1	213	6	10	1,956	5	9	9,639	3	10†
1859	1,104	16	2	222	16	5	307	3	5	1,298	9	4	16,868	6	2†

† These figures represent the amounts in hand, at the end of each year, towards the cost of the new Tabernacle, and they include a large proportion of the sums received on the Separate Services Account.

Not only so, but the proceeds to which he was fully entitled have never been taken by him from the first day until now, and he does not take them at the present moment. But, instead of that, I will tell you what he does. He told you, at our public meeting, and if he had not told it then, it deserves to be told a dozen times over, he has expended upon the Lord's work so much of what he has received for preaching in the Tabernacle that he has, during some of the years, returned as much as he received. This does not represent all we owe to him, and it is putting our obligation to him on a very low scale indeed. What we owe to him, as a church, God only knows. Why, sir, there are hearts here that love you with an intense affection, —an affection which only eternity will fully reveal to you. We shall have to tell you, when time is no more, of the benefits and blessings conferred on our souls within these walls, and conferred on us as a church and congregation, for words are wanting to express such obligations as these.

" I have now to perform an exceedingly pleasant duty, and I will do it without troubling you any more, though this is a theme on which one might go on for a long time yet. But I will turn at once away from this matter which you will read a great deal more about, I daresay, in the paper that is to be published ; and I will, as your representative, speak to our Pastor, and beg, in your name, that he will accept the testimonial which it has been our privilege and pleasure to raise for him, and to put at his absolute disposal, to commemorate the very happy event which has gathered us together in this Tabernacle to-night. Let it go forth to the world,—I know that I am anticipating what Mr. Spurgeon himself is going to say, but I cannot help it,— he told us last night, and it is too good to let him speak of it alone ; in the matter of this testimonial, he says, ' Not one farthing for me : you may give it to me for myself, if you like, but I will not keep it. It shall all be the Lord's, and all shall belong to the Lord's cause.' Many of you know how it is going to be appropriated, or our Pastor will tell you presently as to that point ; but, still, it has been raised by you as an expression of your love for him, and I have to hand it over to him, in the name of the deacons, and in the name of the committee, to be at his absolute disposal, as a gift without conditions, and as an expression of our great attachment to him and love for him."

As intimated by Mr. William Olney, the Pastor had stated, on the previous evening, that he would not accept any part of the testimonial for himself ; on that occasion, Mr. Spurgeon said :—" I shall simply make a remark about the testimonial. My dear brethren, the deacons, said from the very first that there ought to be a testimonial to ME *personally* ; I mean, for my own use. But I said that it was God who had wrought so graciously with us, and therefore I would have nothing to do with a testimonial to me unless it could be used in His service. We thought of the almswomen, whose support has drawn so heavily upon our funds, and I felt that it would be of the utmost service to the church if we could raise an endowment for the support of our poor sisters. We have built rooms, but have not provided the weekly pensions, and I thought that it would be a good thing to put this matter out of hand. £5,000 was suggested as the amount, and to this object £5,000 will go. But you have contributed £6,200, and I have been considerably scolded by several friends, who have declared that they would have given much more if some personal benefit had accrued to me. I am, however, obstinate in this matter, and it shall be even as I said at the first, that the whole of your generous offering shall go to the carrying on of the work of the Lord among you. It is to God that the honour belongs, and to God shall the whole of your offerings go,—with this exception, that I wish to raise a memorial in the Almshouses to Dr. Rippon, the founder, and to add to it the record of the way in which the Almshouses were extended and endowed : and, in addition, there is this much for myself, I said that I should like to have in my house a piece of bronze, which should be a memorial of your abiding love. This clock, with candelabra as side ornaments, will stand in my home, and will gladden me, as it calls you to remembrance. This I shall greatly treasure, and I do not doubt that one or other of my sons will treasure it after me : they are so nearly of an age, and so equal in all respects, that either of them is worthy to be heir to his father's valuables.

"The rest of the money shall be devoted to various purposes, some of which I shall name to-morrow ; but I shall leave the amount in the hands of Mr. Thomas Olney and Mr. Greenwood, who are the treasurers, and they will see that it is so used ; so that all may know and be assured that not a penny comes to me, but I shall draw it from them for the different objects as it is wanted. I shall have the credit of having received this large sum, and I shall have a corresponding number of begging letters to get it out of me, and that will be my personal gain. I daresay you have all heard that 'Spurgeon makes a good thing of this Tabernacle.' Well, whenever anybody hints that to you, you may on my authority assure them that I do. I should not like anybody to think that my Master does not pay His servants well. He loadeth us with benefits, and I am perfectly satisfied with His wages : but if any persons assert that, by my preaching in this place, I have made a purse for myself, I can refer them to those who know me, and my way of life among you. 'Ah, but!' they say, 'he has had a testimonial of £6,000 presented to him.' Yes, he has had it, and he thanks everybody for it. Perhaps there are some other persons who would like a similar testimonial, and I wish they may get it, and do the same with it as I have done.

"Legacies left to me and sums subscribed for the Orphanage and College and so on are spoken of as if I had some private interest in them, whereas I have neither a direct nor indirect pecuniary interest in any of these works to the amount of a penny a year. With regard to all things else, from the first day until now, I have acted on no other principle but that of perfect consecration to the work whereunto I am called. I have no riches. I sometimes wish that I had, for I could use money in an abundance of profitable ways. What have I gained of late years in my ministry here? I have received all that I wished by way of salary, but I have for years expended almost all of it in the cause of God, and in some years even more than all. As far as my pastoral office is concerned, the net income for myself, after giving my share to all holy service, is not so much that any man need envy me. Yet this is not your fault, or anyone's fault, it is my joy and delight to have it so. The Lord is a good and a gracious Paymaster; and inasmuch as men say, ' Doth Spurgeon serve God for nought?' Spurgeon replies, ' No, he is paid a thousand times over, and finds it a splendid thing to be in the service of the Lord Jesus.' If anyone will serve the Lord Jesus Christ after the same or a better fashion, he too will make the same splendid thing of it; he shall have splendid opportunities for working from morning till night, and far into the night on many an occasion; splendid openings for giving away as much as he can earn; splendid opportunities of finding happiness in making other people happy, and easing the sorrows of others by entering into hearty sympathy with them.'

After the presentation, Mr. Spurgeon said :—" Dear friends, I thank you very, very, very heartily for this testimonial, and I hope that you will not consider that I do not take it to myself, and use it personally, because I hand it over to works of charity, for my Lord's work is dear to me, and to use it for Him, and for His poor, is the sweetest way of using it for myself. I said, at the very first, that, if a testimonial could be made the means of providing for our aged sisters in the Almshouses, I would be doubly glad to receive it; and when friends urged that they had rather give *to me*, I begged them to let me have my own way, for surely a man may have his way on his silver-wedding day, if at no other time. The matter was commenced on that footing, but I never dreamed that you would give anything like this right royal amount. Our communion fund has been so heavily drawn upon for the support of the almswomen that we have been embarrassed in providing for the very large number of poor persons, who, I am thankful to say, belong to this church. I hope we shall always have a large number of the Lord's poor among us, for thus we are able to show kindness unto our Lord Himself. We erected more almsrooms than we had money for, and I felt it to be wrong to leave the church in future years with these unendowed houses; for times might come when this extra burden could not be borne, since in these days of our strength we find it a load. For such an object, I heartily approved of an endowment. Endowments for the support of ministers are confessedly a great evil, since they enable a man to keep among a people long after his usefulness is over; but no such evil can arise in the present instance. £5,000 was considered by our dear friend Mr. Greenwood, who is my invaluable guide in such matters, to be about sufficient for our object. Therefore £5,000 of this noble testimonial is hereby devoted to that end ; and I have told you that all the rest of the money will be given to the Lord's work.

" Mr. William Olney said more than enough about what I have done in money matters : I will only add that I serve a good Master, and am so sure that He will provide for me that I never thought it worth my while to be scraping and hoarding for myself. When I gave myself up at first to be His minister, I never expected anything beyond food and raiment ; and when my income was £45 a year, I was heartily content, and never thought of a need without having it supplied. It is with me much the same now : ' I have all, and abound.' I have only one grievance, and that is, being asked for loans and gifts of money when I have none to spare. Under the impression that I am a very rich man, many hunt me perpetually ; but I wish these borrowers and beggars to know that I am not rich. They argue that a man must be rich if he gives away large sums ; but, in my case, this is just the reason why I am not rich. When I have a spare £5, the College, or Orphanage, or Colportage, or something else, requires it, and away it goes. I could very comfortably do with much more. Oh, that I could do more for Christ, and more for the poor ! For these, I have turned beggar before now, and shall not be ashamed to beg again. The outside world cannot understand that a man should be moved by any motive except that of personal gain ; but, if they knew the power of love to Jesus, they would understand that, to the lover of the Saviour, greed of wealth is vile as the dust beneath his feet."

On June 19, 1884, when Mr. Spurgeon's Jubilee was celebrated, a further testimonial of £4,500 was presented to him, and he speedily gave this amount to the Lord's work as he had given the previous £6,233.)

In the year 1865, *The Nonconformist* newspaper did good service to all sections of the Christian Church by the issue of a statistical statement as to the religious condition of London. At the census of 1861, the Government did not collect religious statistics in the same fashion as ten years before, so *The Nonconformist* did well in supplying the deficiency. Notwithstanding all that had been done to meet the needs of the ever-increasing population, the destitution of the metropolis was still appalling. There were some cheering signs, and Baptists especially had good cause to take heart, and gird themselves for the battle still before them. I quote with pleasure the annexed tabular statement, and the note appended to it, giving glory to God that, during the greater part of the period referred to, He had enabled us to make some small discernible mark upon the mass of ignorance and sin around us :—

RELIGIOUS DENOMINATION.	1851. SITTINGS.	1865. SITTINGS.	INCREASE SINCE 1851.
Church of England	409,834	512,067	102,233
Congregationalists	100,436	130,611	30,175
Baptists	54,234	87,559	33,325
Wesleyans	44,162	52,454	8,292
United Methodist Free Churches	4,858	13,422	8,564
Methodist New Connexion	984	6 667	5,683
Primitive Methodists	3,380	9,230	5,850
Church of Scotland	3,886	5,116	1,230
English Presbyterians	10,065	12,952	2,887
United Presbyterians	4,280	4,860	580
Roman Catholics	18,230	31,100	12,870

GROUP OF BAPTIST MINISTERS (ABOUT 1856).

"This table speaks for itself, and affords gratifying proof of the Christian activity of the principal Free Churches, though that satisfaction is somewhat diminished by the increase being spread over fourteen years. The large stride taken by the Baptists,—under which designation every section of that denomination is included,—is unquestionably due, in the main, to the Rev. C. H. Spurgeon and his missionary operations in various parts of the metropolis."

Another table gave the statistics for our own district of NEWINGTON, where Dissent had been up to that time singularly strengthened; the Baptists especially, during the fourteen years from 1851 to 1865, having increased far more than all the other denominations put together,—the one place marked in the list as Free Church of England being virtually Baptist, and thus still further increasing our total gain :—

RELIGIOUS DENOMINATION.	1851. POPULATION, 64,816.		1865. ESTIMATED POPULATION, 90,050.		INCREASE OF SITTINGS BETWEEN 1851 AND 1865.	DECREASE OF SITTINGS BETWEEN 1851 AND 1865.
	No. of Places of Worship.	No. of Sittings.	No. of Places of Worship	No. of Sittings.		
Church of England	6	6,878	8	8,680	1,802	...
Free Church of England ...	...	...	1	1,500	1,500	...
Congregationalists	4	2,822	3	2,350	...	472
Baptists ...	7	2,654	8	11,140	8,486	...
Wesleyans	2	1,603	2	876	...	727
U. Methodist Free Churches	...	...	1	400	400	...
Primitive Methodists ..	...	...	1	470	470	
Methodist New Connexion ...	1	582	4	1,500	918	...
Plymouth Brethren	...	...	1	100	100	...
Mixed and undefined ...	2	400	...	...	...	400
Catholic and Apostolic Church	1	400	1	400	...	...
Latter Day Saints ...	1	60	...	...	...	60
Total ...	24	15,399	30	27,416	13,676	1,659

CHAPTER XLV.

Seeking the Souls of Men.

I am occupied, in my small way, as Mr. Great-heart was employed in Bunyan's day. I do not compare myself with that champion, but I am in the same line of business. I am engaged in personally-conducted tours to Heaven; and I have with me, at the present time, dear Old Father Honest : I am glad he is still alive and active. And there is Christiana, and there are her children. It is my business, as best I can, to kill dragons, and cut off giants' heads, and lead on the timid and trembling. I am often afraid of losing some of the weaklings. I have the heart-ache for them; but, by God's grace, and your kind and generous help in looking after one another, I hope we shall all travel safely to the river's edge. Oh, how many have I had to part with there! I have stood on the brink, and I have heard them singing in the midst of the stream, and I have almost seen the shining ones lead them up the hill, and through the gates, into the Celestial City.—C. H. S.

 OFTEN envy those of my brethren who can go up to individuals, and talk to them with freedom about their souls. I do not always find myself able to do so, though, when I have been Divinely aided in such service, I have had a large reward. When a Christian can get hold of a man, and talk thus personally to him, it is like one of the old British men-of-war lying alongside a French ship, and giving her a broadside, making every timber shiver, and at last sending her to the bottom..

How many precious souls have been brought to Christ by the loving personal exhortations of Christian people who have learned this holy art! It is wonderful how God blesses very little efforts to serve Him. One night, many years ago, after preaching, I had been driven home by a cabman, and after I had alighted, and given him the fare, he took a little Testament out of his pocket, and showing it to me, said, "It is about fifteen years since you gave me that, and spoke a word to me about my soul. I have never forgotten your words, and I have not let a day pass since without reading the Book you gave me." I felt glad that, in that instance, the seed had, apparently, fallen into good ground.

Having promised to preach, one evening, at a certain river-side town, I went to the place early in the day, as I thought I should like to have a little time in a boat on the river. So, hailing a waterman, I made arrangements with him to take me, and, whilst sitting in the boat, wishing to talk with him about religious matters, I began the conversation by asking him about his family. He told me that the cholera had visited his home, and that he had lost no less than thirteen of his relatives, one after another, by death.   My question, and the man's answer, prepared the way for a dialogue somewhat in this fashion :—

Spurgeon.—Have you, my friend, a good hope of Heaven if you should die?

Waterman.—Well, sir, I think as how I have.

S.—Pray tell me, then, what your hope is ; for no man need ever be ashamed of a good hope.

W.—Well, sir, I have been on this here river for five-and-twenty or thirty years, and I don't know that anybody ever saw me drunk.

S.—Oh, dear! Oh, dear! Is that all you have to trust to?

W.—Well, sir, when the cholera was about, and my poor neighbours were bad, I went for the doctor for 'em, and was up a good many nights ; and I do think as how I am as good as most folk that I know.

Of course, I told him that I was very glad to hear that he had sympathy for the suffering, and that I considered it far better to be charitable than to be churlish ; but I did not see how his good conduct could carry him to Heaven.   Then he said :—

" Well, sir, perhaps it can't ; but I think, when I get a little older, I shall give up the boat, and take to going to church, and then I hope that all will be right,— won't it, sir?"

" No," I answered, " certainly not ; your going to church won't change your heart, or take away your sins.   Begin to go to church as soon as possible ; but you will not be an inch nearer Heaven if you think that, by attending the sanctuary, you will be saved."

The poor man seemed perfectly astounded, while I went on knocking down his hopes one after another.   So I resumed the dialogue by putting another question to him :—

S.—You have sometimes sinned in your life, have you not?

W.—Yes, sir, that I have, many a time.

S.—On what ground, then, do you think that your sins will be forgiven?

W.—Well, sir, I have been sorry about them, and I think they are all gone ;— they don't trouble me now.

S.—Now, my friend, suppose you were to go and get into debt with the grocer where you deal, and you should say to her, " Look here, missus, you have a long score against me, I am sorry to say that I cannot pay you for all those goods that I have had ; but I'll tell you what I will do, I'll never get into your debt any more." She would very soon tell you that was not her style of doing business ; and do you suppose that is the way in which you can treat the great God? Do you imagine that He is going to strike out your past sins because you say you will not go on sinning against Him?

W.—Well, sir, I should like to know how my sins are to be forgiven. Are you a parson?

S.—I preach the gospel, I hope, but I do not go by the name of a parson; I am only a Dissenting minister.

Then I told him, as plainly as I could, how the Lord Jesus Christ had taken the place of sinners, and how those who trusted in Him, and rested in His blood and righteousness, would find pardon and peace. The man was delighted with the simple story of the cross; he said that he wished he had heard it years before, and then he added, "To tell the truth, master, I did not feel quite easy, after all, when I saw those poor creatures taken away to the graveyard; I did think there was something I wanted, but I did not know what it was."

I cannot say what was the final result of our conversation; but I had the satisfaction of knowing that I had at least set before him God's way of salvation in language that he could easily understand.

Sometimes, I have found it less easy, than it might otherwise have been, to influence certain persons for good, because of the neglect of those who ought to have done the work before me. I was trying to say a word for my Master to a coachman, one day, when he said to me, "Do you know the Rev. Mr. So-and-so?" "Yes," I replied, "I know him very well; what have you to say about him?" "Well," said the man, "he's the sort of minister I like, and I like his religion very much." "What sort of a religion is it?" I asked. "Why!" he answered, "he has ridden on this box-seat every day for six months, and he has never said anything about religion all the while; that is the kind of minister I like." It seemed to me a very doubtful compliment for a man who professed to be a servant of the Lord Jesus Christ.

At other times, the difficulty in dealing with individuals has arisen from their ignorance of the plan of salvation. When I have spoken of my own hope in Christ to two or three people in a railway carriage, I have often found myself telling my listeners perfect novelties. I have seen the look of astonishment upon the face of many an intelligent Englishman when I have explained the doctrine of the substitutionary sacrifice of Christ; I have even met with persons who had attended their parish church from their youth up, yet who were totally ignorant of the simple truth of justification by faith; ay, and some who have been to Dissenting places of worship do not seem to have laid hold of the fundamental truth that no man is saved by his own doings, but that salvation is procured by faith in the blood and righteousness of Jesus Christ. This nation is steeped up to the throat in self-righteousness, and the Protestantism of Martin Luther is very generally unknown. The truth is held by as many as God's grace has called, but the great outlying masses still talk of doing their best, and then hoping in God's mercy, and I know not what besides of legal self-confidence ; while the master-doctrine, that he who believes in Jesus is saved by His finished work, is sneered at as the utterance of misguided enthusiasm, or attacked as leading to licentiousness. Luther talked of beating the heads of the Wittenbergers with the Bible, so as to get the great doctrine of justification by faith into their brains. But beating is of no use ; we must have much patience with those we are trying to teach, and we must be willing to repeat over, and over, and over again the elements of truth. Someone asked a mother once, " Why do you teach your child the same thing twenty times ? " She answered, very wisely, " Because I find that nineteen times are not sufficient ; " and it will often be the same with those who need to be taught the A B C of the gospel.

Though this is a Protestant land, it is beyond all question that there are in it people who are Popish enough to perform great religious acts by way of merit. What a goodly row of almshouses was erected by that miserly old grinder of the poor as an atonement for his hoarding propensities ! What a splendid legacy somebody else left to that hospital ! That was a very proper thing, but the man who left it never gave a farthing to a beggar in his life, and he would not have given anything when he died only he could not take his money with him, so he left it to a charity as an atonement for his sin.

Sometimes, persons are so foolish as to think that the doing of some professedly religious act will take them to Heaven ; attending church prayers twice a day, fasting in Lent, decorating the altar with needlework, putting stained glass in the window, or giving a new organ ; at the suggestion of their priest, they do many such things ; and thus they go on working like blind asses in a mill, from morning to night, and making no more real progress than the poor donkeys do. Many who are nominally Christians appear to me to believe in a sort of sincere-obedience covenant, in which, if a man does as much as he can, Christ will do the rest, and so the sinner will be saved ; but it is not so. God will never accept any composition from the man who is in debt to Divine justice ; there is no Heavenly Court of Bankruptcy where so much in the pound may be accepted, and the debtor then be discharged. It must be all or nothing ; he who would pay his debt must bring all, even to the uttermost farthing ; and that can never be, for God's Word declares that " by the deeds of the law there shall no flesh be justified in His sight." Some people have a notion that going to church and chapel, taking the sacrament, and doing certain good deeds that appertain to a respectable profession of religion, are the way to Heaven. If they are put in the place of Christ, they are rather the way to hell ; although it is strewn with clean gravel, and there be grassy paths on either side, it is not the road to Heaven, but the way to everlasting death.

Strange as it may seem at the first glance, yet the very fact that a person has been brought up in a system of error will, sometimes, by force of contrast, make it all the easier to bring home the truth to the heart and conscience. I can bear personal witness that the simple statement of the gospel has often proved, in God's hand, enough to lead a soul into immediate peace. I once met with a lady who held sentiments of almost undiluted Popery ; and in conversing with her, I was delighted to see how interesting and attractive a thing the gospel was to her. She complained that she enjoyed no peace of mind as the result of her religion, and never seemed to have done enough to bring her any rest of soul. She had a high idea of priestly absolution, but it had evidently been quite unable to yield repose to her spirit. Death was feared, God was terrible, even Christ was an object of awe rather than of love. When I told her that whosoever believeth on Jesus is perfectly forgiven, and that I knew I was forgiven,—that I was as sure of it as of my own existence, that I feared neither to live nor to die, for all would be well with me in either case, because God had given to me eternal life in His Son,—I saw that a new set of thoughts had begun to astonish her mind. She said, " If I could believe as you do, I should be the happiest person in the world." I did not deny the inference, but claimed to have proved its truth, and I have reason to think that the little simple talk we had has not been forgotten, or unprofitable.

One advantage of dealing personally with souls is, that it is not so easy for them to turn aside the message as when they are spoken to in the mass. I have often marvelled when I have been preaching. I have thought that I have exactly described certain people ; I have marked in them special sins, and as Christ's faithful servant, I have not shunned to picture their case in the pulpit, that they might receive a well-deserved rebuke ; but I have wondered when I have spoken to them afterwards, that they have thanked me for what I have said, because they thought it so applicable to another person in the assembly. I had intended it wholly for them, and had, as I thought, made the description so accurate, and brought out all their peculiar points, that it must have been received by them. But, on at least one occasion, a direct word to one of my hearers was not only taken by him in a sense I did not mean, but it was resented in a fashion which I did not anticipate. I felt constrained to say that I hoped the gentleman who was reporting my discourse would not do it as a mere matter of business routine, but that he would take the Word as addressed to himself as well as to the rest of the audience. I certainly did not think there was anything offensive in the remark, and I was astonished to see the reporter fling down his pen in anger, as though resolved not to take down anything more that I might say. Before long, however, his better judgment prevailed, he went on with his work, and the sermon duly appeared in *The New Park Street*

Pulpit,—under the circumstances, of course, with the omission of the personal reference which had unintentionally caused offence.*

Whatever may have been the feelings of my hearers, I can honestly say that scores, and, indeed, hundreds of times I have gone from my pulpit groaning because I could not preach as I wished; but this has been my comfort, "Well, I did desire to glorify Christ; I did try to clear my conscience of the blood of all men; I did seek to tell them the whole truth, whether they liked it or not." It will be an awful thing for any man, who has been professedly a minister of Christ, and yet has not preached the gospel, to go before the bar of God, and to answer for the souls committed to him. That ancient message still needs to be heard: " If the watchman see the sword come, and blow not the trumpet, and the people be not warned; if the sword come, and take any person from among them, he is taken away in his iniquity; but his blood will I require at the watchman's hand." This it is that makes our work so weighty that our knees sometimes knock together when we are thinking of going up to our pulpit again. It is no child's play, if there is to be a judgment, and we are to answer for our faithfulness or unfaithfulness. What must be our account if we are not true to God and to man? I have prayed, many a time, that I might be able, at the end of my ministry, to say what George Fox, the Quaker, said when he was dying, " I am clear, I am clear."

It has often been a marvel to me how some old ministers have continued to labour for twenty, or thirty, or even forty years in one place without gathering any fruit from all their toil. I will not judge them,—to their own Master they stand or fall;—but if I had been in such a position, although I should not have dared to leave the vineyard in which my Lord bade me work while I was yet a youth, I should have concluded that He had need of me in some other part of His field where my efforts might be more productive of blessing. I thank God that I have not had to labour in vain, or to spend my strength for nought. He has given me a long period of happy and successful service, for which, with all my heart, I praise and magnify His holy Name. There has been a greater increase sometimes, or a little diminution now and then; but, for the most part, the unbroken stream of blessing has run on at much the same rate all the while. It has ever been my desire, not to " compass sea and land to make proselytes " from other denominations; but to gather into our ranks those who have not been previously connected with any body of believers, or, indeed, who have attended any house of prayer. Of course,

---

* Mr. Passmore preserved a letter, written to himself by Mr. Spurgeon, in which there was the following allusion to the incident here described:—" You may tell Mr. —— that I was so far from intending to insult him by what I said that I uttered the sentence in the purest love for his soul; and that I dare not be unfaithful to him any more than to anyone else in my congregation. God is my witness, how earnestly I long for the salvation of all my hearers, and I would far rather err by too great personality than by unfaithfulness. At the last great day, none of us will be offended with Christ's ministers for speaking plainly to us. I am sorry that Mr. —— was vexed, and have prayed that the sermon may be blessed to him."

many persons have joined us from other communities, when it has seemed to them a wise and right step; but I should reckon it to be a burning disgrace if it could be truthfully said, "The large church under that man's pastoral care is composed of members whom he has stolen away from other Christian churches;" but I value beyond all price the godless and the careless, who have been brought out from the world into communion with Christ. These are true prizes,—not stealthily removed from friendly shores, but captured at the edge of the sword from the enemy's dominions. We welcome brethren from other churches if, in the providence of God, they are drifted into our midst; but we would never hang out the wrecker's beacon, to dash other churches in pieces in order to enrich ourselves with the wreckage. Far rather would we be busy, looking after perishing souls, than cajoling unstable ones from their present place of worship. To recruit one regiment from another, is no real strengthening of the army; to bring in fresh men, should be the aim of all.

From the very early days of my ministry in London, the Lord gave such an abundant blessing upon the proclamation of His truth that, whenever I was able to appoint a time for seeing converts and enquirers, it was seldom, if ever, that I waited in vain; and, usually, so many came, that I was quite overwhelmed with gratitude and thanksgiving to God. On one occasion, I had a very singular experience, which enabled me to realize the meaning of our Lord's answer to His disciples' question at the well of Sychar, "Hath any man brought Him aught to eat? Jesus saith unto them, My meat is to do the will of Him that sent Me, and to finish His work." Leaving home early in the morning, I went to the chapel, and sat there all day long seeing those who had been brought to Christ through the preaching of the Word. Their stories were so interesting to me that the hours flew by without my noticing how fast they were going. I may have seen some thirty or more persons during the day, one after the other; and I was so delighted with the tales of mercy they had to tell me, and the wonders of grace God had wrought in them, that I did not know anything about how the time passed. At seven o'clock, we had our prayer-meeting; I went in, and prayed with the brethren. After that, came the church-meeting. A little before ten o'clock, I felt faint; and I began to think at what hour I had my dinner, and I then for the first time remembered that I had not had any! I never thought of it, I never even felt hungry, because God had made me so glad, and so satisfied with the Divine manna, the Heavenly food of success in winning souls.

I am not sure that I ever had another day quite like that; but I had much to interest me, and sometimes a good deal to humble me, in the different cases with which I had to deal. I have seen very much of my own stupidity while in conversation with seeking souls. I have been baffled by a poor lad while trying to bring him to the Saviour; I thought I had him fast, but he has eluded me again and again with perverse ingenuity of unbelief.   Sometimes, enquirers, who are really anxious, surprise me with their singular skill in battling against hope; their arguments are endless, and their difficulties countless.   They have put me to a nonplus again and again.   The grace of God has at last enabled me to bring them to the light, but not until I have seen my own inefficiency, and realized that, without the Holy Spirit's aid, I should be utterly powerless to lead them into the liberty of the gospel.   Occasionally, I have met with a poor troubled soul who has refused to be comforted. There was one good Christian man who, through feebleness of mind, had fallen into the deepest despair; I have hardly ever met with a person in such an awful condition as he was, and it puzzled me to give him any sort of comfort; indeed, I fear that I failed to do so after all.   He said, "I'm too big a sinner to be saved."   So I told him that God's Word says, "the blood of Jesus Christ His Son cleanseth us from *all* sin."   "Ay!" he replied, "but you must remember the context, which is, 'If we walk in the light, as He is in the light, we have fellowship one with another, and the blood of Jesus Christ His Son cleanseth us from all sin.'   Now, I do not walk in the light; I walk in the dark, and I have no fellowship with the people of God now, and therefore that passage does not apply to me."   "Well," I rejoined, "but Christ is able to save to the uttermost all them that come unto God by Him." "That is the only text," he admitted, "I never can get over, for it says 'to the uttermost,' and I know I cannot have gone beyond that; yet it does not yield me any comfort."   I said, "But God asks nothing of you but that you will believe Him; and you know, if you have ever so feeble a faith, you are like a child,—the feeble hand of a child can receive, and that is the mark of a Christian: 'of His fulness have all we received,' and if you only receive with your hand, that is enough."   "Ay!" said he, "but I have not the hand of faith."   "Very well," I answered, "but you have the mouth of desire: you can ask with your lips if you cannot receive with your hand." "No," said he, "I do not pray, and I cannot pray; I have not the mouth of desire." "Then," I pleaded, "all that is wanted is an empty place, a vacuum, so that God can put the grace in."   "Ah, sir!" said he, "you have me there; I have a vacuum; I have an aching void; if there was ever an empty sinner in this world, I am one." "Well," I exclaimed, "Christ will fill that vacuum; there is a full Christ for empty sinners," and there I had to leave the matter.

Very often, when enquirers have come to me to relate the story of their spiritual history, they have told their little tale with an air of the greatest possible wonder, and asked me, as soon as they have finished it, whether it is not extremely unusual. One has said, "Do you know, sir, I used to be so happy in the things of the world, but conviction entered into my heart, and I began to seek the Saviour; and for a long time, when I was under concern of soul, I was so miserable that I could not bear myself. Surely, sir, this is a strange thing?" And when I have looked the friend in the face, and said, " No, it is not at all strange ; I have had a dozen people here to-night, and they have all told me the same tale ; that is the way almost all God's people go to Heaven,"—he has stared at me, as if he did not think I would tell an untruth, but as if he thought it the queerest thing in the world that anybody else should have felt as he had done.

" Now, sit down," I say sometimes, when I am seeing an enquirer or a candidate for church-membership, " and I will tell you what were my feelings when I first sought and found the Saviour." " Why, sir!" he exclaims, " that is just how I have felt ; but I did not think anyone else had ever gone over the same path that I have trodden." It is no wonder that, when we have little acquaintance with each other's spiritual experience, our way should seem to be a solitary one ; but he who knows much of the dealings of God with poor seeking sinners, is well aware that their experiences are, in the main, very much alike.

Sometimes, a desperate case requires a desperate remedy. I had once to deal with a man who assented to everything I said. When I talked about the evil of sin, he agreed with me, and said that I was very faithful. When I set before him the way of salvation, he assented to it, but it was evident that his heart was not affected by the truth. I could almost have wished that he had flatly denied what I said, for that would have given me the opportunity of arguing the matter with him, and pressing him to come to a decision. At last, I felt that it was quite hopeless to talk to him any longer, so I said, " The fact is, one of these days you will die, and be damned,"—and I walked away without saying another word. As I expected, it was not very long before he sent for me, and when I went to him, he begged me to tell him why I had said such a dreadful thing to him. I answered, " It seems quite useless for me to talk to you about the salvation of your soul, for you never appear to feel the force of anything that I say I might almost as well pour oil down a slab of marble as expect you to be impressed by the truth that I set before you, and my solid conviction is that you will be damned." He was quite angry with me for speaking so plainly ; and I went away again, leaving him very cross. Before many hours were over, he was in an awful state of mind ; the Holy Spirit had convinced him of his state as a sinner, and he was in an agony of soul. That sharp sentence of mine was like the hook in a fish's gills, but that fish was landed all right. The man was brought to repentance and faith ; he was baptized, joined the church, and a few years ago went home to Heaven.

CHAPTER XLVI.

A New School of the Prophets

At the close of his sermon on 1 Cor. ix. 16, - "For though I preach the gospel, I have nothing to glory of: for necessity is laid upon me; yea, woe is unto me, if I preach not the gospel!"—delivered in New Park Street Chapel, on Lord's-day morning, August 5, 1855, Mr. Spurgeon said:—"Now, my dear hearers, one word with you. There are some persons in this audience who are verily guilty in the sight of God because *they* do not preach the gospel. I cannot think, out of the fifteen hundred or two thousand persons now present within the reach of my voice, there are none beside myself who are qualified to preach the gospel. I have not so bad an opinion of you as to imagine myself to be superior to one-half of you in intellect, or in the power of preaching God's Word; and even supposing I should be, I cannot believe that I have such a congregation that there are not among you many who have gifts and talents that qualify you to preach the Word. . . . I cannot conceive but that there are some here, this morning, who are flowers 'wasting their sweetness on the desert air,' 'gems of purest ray serene' lying in the dark caverns of ocean's oblivion. This is a very serious question. If there be any talent in the church at Park Street, let it be developed. If there are any preachers in my congregation, let them preach. Many ministers make it a point to check young men in this respect. There is my hand, such as it is, to help any one of you if you think you can—

"'Tell to sinners round,
What a dear Saviour you have found.'

I would like to find scores of preachers among you. 'Would God that all the Lord's people were prophets!' There are some here who ought to be prophets, only they are half afraid;—well, we must devise some scheme for getting rid of their bashfulness. I cannot bear to think that, while the devil sets all his servants to work, there should be one servant of Jesus Christ asleep. Young man, go home and examine thyself; see what thy capabilities are, and if thou findest that thou hast ability, then try in some humble room to tell to a dozen poor people what they must do to be saved. You need not aspire to become absolutely and solely dependent upon the ministry; but if it should please God, desire even that high honour. 'If a man desire the office of a bishop, he desireth a good work.' At any rate, seek in some way to proclaim the gospel of God. I have preached this sermon especially because I long to commence a movement from this place which shall reach others. I want to find some in my church, if it be possible, who will preach the gospel. And mark you, if you have talent and power, woe is unto you, if you preach not the gospel!"

IT was most appropriate that the Institution, which was destined to be used by God as a means of training many hundreds of soul-winners, should itself have been brought into existence as the direct result of Mr. Spurgeon's successful effort to win the soul of one young and earnest enquirer. Happily, that early convert,—now Pastor T. W. Medhurst,—after serving in the ministry of the gospel for more than forty years in England, Ireland, Scotland, and Wales, is still spared to labour for the Lord at Hope Baptist Chapel, Canton, Cardiff; and he has kindly written for this work a fuller and more accurate account of the events that led to the founding of the Pastors' College than has ever before appeared in print. Mr. Medhurst says :—

"I first saw and heard dear Mr. Spurgeon before he was really elected to the pastorate of the New Park Street Church ; it was in the early part of 1854, at Maze Pond Chapel, at a Sunday-school anniversary meeting. I was very much struck with the address he delivered on that occasion.* I was, at that time, a seat-holder at the old Surrey Tabernacle, where James Wells was pastor. The first sermon I heard Mr. Spurgeon preach was from Hosea vi. 3 : 'Then shall we know, *if* we follow on to know the Lord.' Well do I remember the opening sentence of the discourse :—'You observe, dear friends, that the "*if*" is in italics ; it is not in the original, so we will substitute " as " in its place. There is no " if " in the matter ; once begin " to know the Lord," and it is certain that you will " follow on " to know Him.' That sermon convinced me of sin.

"I continued to listen to Mr. Spurgeon, and, after a while, in soul-trouble, I wrote to him the following letter :—

" Mr. Porter's Rope Factory,

" Blue Anchor Road,

" Rotherhithe,

" Sunday, July 2nd, 1854.

" Dear Sir,

"Will you be kind enough candidly to inform me whether I have any room for hope that I belong to the elect family of God, whether Jesus Christ His Son has died for me, while my affections are in the world? I try to pray, but cannot. I make resolutions only to break them. I from time to time listen to you when you speak of the glory set apart for the saints, when you describe their joys and their feelings, but I feel myself as having nothing to do with them. O sir, that Sunday morning when you spoke of the hypocrite, I felt that you described me ! I go to chapel to hear the Word preached, I return home, and make resolutions ; I go to work, then out into the world, and forget all until the time for preaching comes again. I read the Bible, but do not feel interested ; it seems no more to me than a book I have before read,—dry and insipid. Christ has said that, of all who come to Him, He will not send any away. How am I to come ? I feel that I cannot come. I would if I could, but I cannot. At times, I think that I will give it all up, that I

* Mr. John Eastty, who had been up to the time of his death, in 1896, the senior deacon at Maze Pond Chapel, sent to Mrs. Spurgeon, in 1893, his personal recollections of her dear husband, in which there was the following reference to this meeting :—" The grandfather of Mr. Archibald G. Brown was in the chair. Mr. William Olney had introduced Mr. Spurgeon to us, knowing that he would help the cause by speaking on behalf of the school. What a stripling he then was ! What an impression he made ! It was then that he related the difficulty he felt, when a child, as to how the apple got through the narrow neck of the bottle (see *Autobiography*, Vol. I., page 15), and made the application, ' So, then, you must put it in while it is a little one ! ' And, again, at about the same period, he preached a sermon in the same chapel, one Sunday afternoon, for one of the societies, when my mother pronounced judgment on him, and said, ' He will be a second Whitefield ! ' The minister of Maze Pond, the Rev. John Aldis, at once foresaw for him a very distinguished career, and was the first amongst the London ministers who took him by the hand ; and Mr. Spurgeon never forgot it, for he was not so generally well received by his brethren. Most of what was said by them, is better forgotten, for nearly all of them came round to him at last ; but, at a devotional meeting where Mr. Spurgeon had been invited to be present, a London pastor prayed for ' our young friend, who has so much to *learn*, and so much to *unlearn*.' The narrator of this told me, however, that it did not at all affect him, nor did he betray the least feeling of annoyance."

will not go to chapel any more ; yet when the time comes, I cannot stay away, but feel compelled to go again once more. Do, dear sir, tell me, how am I to find Jesus ? How am I to know that He died for me, and that I belong to His family ? Dear sir, tell me, am I a hypocrite ?

" I remain,

" Dear sir,

" Yours to serve in anxiety,

"T. W. MEDHURST."

" In reply, I received from Mr. Spurgeon this letter, which greatly helped me at the time, and which I still prize more than I can tell :—

" 75, Dover Road,

" Borough,

" July 14th, 1854.

" Dear Sir,

"I am glad that you have been able to write to me and state your feelings. Though my hands are always full, it will ever give me joy to receive such notes as yours.

"You ask me a very important question, *Are you one of God's elect ?* Now, this is a question neither you nor I can answer at present, and therefore let it drop. I will ask you an easier one, '*Are you a sinner ?*' Can you say, 'YES ? All say, 'Yes'; but then they do not know what the word '*sinner*' means.

" A sinner is a creature who has broken all his Maker's commands, despised His Name, and run into rebellion against the Most High. A sinner deserves hell, yea, the hottest place in hell ; and if he be saved, it must be entirely by unmerited mercy. Now, if you are such a sinner, I am glad to be able to tell you the only way of salvation. ' Believe on the Lord Jesus.'

" I think you have not yet really understood what believing means. You are, I trust, really awakened, but you do not see the door yet. I advise you seriously to be much alone, I mean as much as you can ; let your groans go up if you cannot pray ; attend as many services as possible ; and if you go with an earnest desire for a blessing, it will come very soon. But why not believe now ? You have only to believe that Jesus is able and willing to save, and then trust yourself to Him.

" Harbour not that dark suggestion to forsake the house of God ; remember you turn your back on Heaven, and your face to hell, the moment you do that. I pray God that He will keep you. If the Lord had meant to destroy you, He would not have showed you such things as these. If you are but as smoking flax, there is hope. Touch the hem of His garment ; look to the brazen serpent.

"My dear fellow sinner, slight not this season of awakening. Up, and be in earnest It is your soul, your own soul, your eternal welfare, your Heaven or your hell, that is at stake.

"There is the cross, and a bleeding God-man upon it ; look to Him, and be saved ! There is the Holy Spirit able to give you every grace. Look, in prayer, to the Sacred Three-one God, and then you will be delivered.

"I am,

"Your anxious friend,

"Write again."　　　　　　　　　　　　　　　　　　　　　"C. H. SPURGEON."

"I was set at liberty under a Thursday evening sermon from the text John vi. 37 : 'All that the Father giveth Me shall come to Me ; and him that cometh to Me I will in no wise cast out ;' and then I did 'write again,' telling Mr. Spurgeon of my conversion, and of my desire to be baptized, and to join the church. This was his reply to my letter :—

"75, Dover Road,

"August 7th, 1854.

"My Dear Sir,

"Your letters have given me great joy. I trust I see in you the marks of a son of God, and I earnestly pray that you may have the evidence within that you are born of God.

"There is no reason why you should not be baptized. 'If thou believest with all thine heart, thou mayest.' Think very seriously of it, for it is a solemn matter. Count the cost. You are now about to be buried to the world, and you may well say, 'What manner of persons ought we to be in all holy conversation and godliness.' The friends who were with you in the days of your carnal pleasure will strive to entice you from Christ ; but I pray that the grace of God may be mightily manifest in you, keeping you steadfast, unmovable, always abounding in the work of the Lord.

"I should like to see you on Thursday evening, after six o'clock, in the vestry.

"I am,

"Yours faithfully,

"C. H. SPURGEON.'

(Of this interview, Mr. Spurgeon preserved the following record in the book containing his notes concerning applicants for baptism and church-membership :—

"Thomas William Medhurst.

A very promising young man,—his letters to me evince various degrees of progress in the pilgrims' road. He has been very anxious, but has now, I trust, found refuge in the Rock of ages.")

"On September 28, 1854, the beloved Pastor baptized me at New Park Street Chapel, and in due course I was received into the church. I at once began to preach in the open air and elsewhere, though I had not then any idea of entering the ministry. Two persons, who became members at New Park Street through my preaching, led Mr. Spurgeon to suggest that I should seek to prepare myself for

T. W. MEDHURST.

REV. C. H. HOSKEN.

MILL ROAD COLLEGIATE SCHOOL, BEXLEY HEATH, KENT.

pastoral work. I was just then out of my apprenticeship, and not quite twenty-one years of age, so I gladly consented to the proposal, and arrangements were made, in July, 1855, for me to go to reside with Rev. C. H. Hosken, who was pastor of the Baptist Church at Crayford, but who lived at the Mill Road Collegiate School, Bexley Heath, Kent.

"Once a week, I had the privilege of spending several hours with Mr. Spurgeon at his lodgings in the Dover Road, Southwark, that I might study theology under his direction. A letter that he wrote to me, during that period, shows that he had already anticipated a further addition to the ranks of the ministry after my course of training was completed :—

"London,
"September 22nd, 1855.

"My Dear Brother,

"Since your departure, I have been meditating upon the pleasure of being the means of sending you to so excellent a scene of preparation for the ministry, and in prayer to God I have sought every blessing upon you, for I love you very much. Oh, how I desire to see you a holy and successful minister of Jesus! I need not bid you work at your studies : I am sure you will ; but be sure to live near to God, and hold very much intercourse with Jesus.

"I have been thinking that, when you are gone out into the vineyard, I must find another to be my dearly-beloved Timothy, just as you are.

"Now I find it no easy task to get money, and I have been thinking I must get friends to give me a good set of books, which I shall not *give* you, but keep for those who may come after ; so that, by degrees, I shall get together a good Theological Library for young students in years to come.

"If I were rich, I would give you all ; but, as I have to bear all the brunt of the battle, and am alone responsible, I think I must get the books to be always used in future. Those you will purchase to-day are yours to keep ; Mr. Bagster's books must be mine ; and I have just written to a friend to buy me *Matthew Henry*, which shall soon be at your disposal, and be mine in the same way. You see, I am looking forward.

"Believe me,
"Ever your very loving friend,
"C. H. SPURGEON."

"After Mr. Spurgeon's marriage, I continued regularly to study with him, once a week, in the New Kent Road, and afterwards at Nightingale Lane, Clapham Common. Towards the latter part of 1856, I preached at Kingston-on-Thames, and before long received a unanimous invitation to the pastorate of the Baptist Church there. Acting on Mr. Spurgeon's advice, that invitation was accepted temporarily until two years of study had expired. Mr. Spurgeon himself made arrangements with the church that, in addition to the amount they were giving me for my services, they were to repay him the amount he was expending for my tuition at Bexley Heath. At the expiration of the first quarter, he handed me a cheque, saying,

'That is yours; the deacons would not have given that extra if I had not put it in the way I have done.' On my refusing to accept the cheque, he at once said that, as he had given the money to the Lord for two years, he must take a second student. In that way, *the Pastors' College was commenced.*

REV. GEORGE ROGERS.

"I went to reside with Rev. George Rogers, at Albany Road, Camberwell, on March 21, 1857, and in the course of that year, the second student (Mr. E. J. Silverton) was received."

(Mr. Spurgeon's own account of the origin of the College begins near the point where Mr. Medhurst's narration ends; he does not mention the preliminary period of training at Bexley Heath :—)

When, in early days, God's Holy Spirit had gone forth with my ministry at New Park Street, several zealous young men were brought to a knowledge of the truth; and among them some whose preaching in the street was blessed of God to the conversion of souls. Knowing that these men had capacities for usefulness, but laboured under the serious disadvantage of having no education, and were, moreover, in such circumstances that they would not be likely to obtain admission into any of our Colleges, it entered into my heart to provide them with a course of elementary instruction, which might, at least, correct their inaccuracies of speech, and put them in the way of obtaining further information by reading. One young man, of especial promise, seemed to be thrust in my way by Providence, so that I must commence with him at once, and, not long after, the very man of all others the most suitable to assist in carrying out my design was brought before me. The Rev. George Rogers, of Camberwell, had been waiting and ripening for the office and work of a tutor; and while the idea of educating young men was simmering in my brain, he was on the look-out for some such service. We met, and entered into a fellowship which every succeeding year has strengthened.

With a solitary student, our labour of love commenced. Funds were forthcoming for the support of this one brother; but, at the time, it seemed to me to be a very weighty enterprise and a great responsibility. With a limited income, it was no easy thing for a young minister to guarantee £50 a year. This, however, was a small matter ere long, for other brethren, who required the same aid, and were equally worthy, came forward to ask for similar instruction, and we could not deny them. The single student, in 1856, grew into eight ere long; and then into twenty; and, anon, the number rose to nearly one hundred men. Faith trembled when tried with the weight of the support of one man; but the Lord has strengthened her by exercise, so that she has rejoiced under the load when multiplied a hundred-fold.

The work did not begin with any scheme,—it grew out of necessity. It was no choice with him who first moved in it, he simply acted because he was acted upon by a higher power. He had no idea whereunto the matter would grow, nor did he contemplate the institution of any far-reaching and wide-spread agency. To meet the present need, and follow the immediate movement of Providence, was all that was intended, and no idea of the future presented itself at the commencement. It seems to be God's plan that works of usefulness should develop themselves in obedience to a living force within, rather than by scheme and plan from without.

When the Pastors' College was fairly moulded into shape, we had before us but one object, and that was, the glory of God, by the preaching of the gospel. To preach with acceptance, men, lacking in education, need to be instructed; and therefore our Institution set itself further to instruct *those whom God had evidently called to preach the gospel*, but who laboured under early disadvantages. We never dreamed of making men preachers, but we desired to help those whom God had already called to be such. Hence, we laid down, as a basis, the condition that a man must, during about two years, have been engaged in preaching, and must have had some seals to his ministry, before we could entertain his application. No matter how talented or promising he might appear to be, the College could not act upon mere hopes, but must have evident marks of a Divine call, so far as human judgment can discover them. This became a main point with us, for we wanted, not men whom our tutors could make into scholars, but men whom the Lord had ordained to be preachers.

Firmly fixing this landmark, we proceeded to sweep away every hindrance to the admission of fit men. We determined never to refuse a man on account of absolute poverty, but rather to provide him with needful lodging, board, and raiment, that he might not be hindered on that account. We also placed the literary qualifications of admission so low that even brethren who could not read have been able to enter, and have been among the most useful of our students in after days. A man of real ability as a speaker, of deep piety, and genuine faith, may be, by force of birth and circumstances, deprived of educational advantages, and yet, when helped a little, he may develop into a mighty worker for Christ; it would be a serious loss to the Church to deny such a man instruction because it was his misfortune to miss it in his youth. Our College began by inviting men of God to her bosom, whether they were poor and illiterate, or wealthy and educated. We sought for earnest preachers, not for readers of sermons, or makers of philosophical essays. " Have you won souls for Jesus?" was and is our leading enquiry of all applicants. " If so, come thou with us, and we will do thee good." If the brother has any pecuniary means, we feel that he should bear his own charges, and many have done so; but if he cannot contribute a sixpence, he is equally welcome, and is received upon the same footing in all respects. If we can but find men who love Jesus, and love the people, and will seek to bring Jesus and the people together, the College will receive two hundred of such as readily as one, and trust in God for their food; but if men of learning and wealth should come, the College will not accept them unless they prove their calling by power to deliver the truth, and by the blessing of God upon their labours. Our men seek no Collegiate degrees, or classical honours,—though many of them could readily attain them; but to preach efficiently, to get at the hearts of the masses, to evangelize the poor,—this is the College ambition, this and nothing else.

We endeavour to teach the Scriptures, but, as everybody else claims to do the same, and we wish to be known and read of all men, we say distinctly that the theology of the Pastors' College is Puritanic. We know nothing of the new *ologies*; we stand by the old ways. The improvements brought forth by what is called " modern thought " we regard with suspicion, and believe them to be, at best, dilutions of the truth, and most of them old, rusted heresies, tinkered up again, and sent abroad with a new face put upon them, to repeat the mischief which they wrought in ages past. We are old-fashioned enough to prefer Manton to Maurice, Charnock to Robertson, and Owen to Voysey. Both our experience and our reading of the Scriptures confirm us in the belief of the unfashionable doctrines of grace; and among us, upon those grand fundamentals, there is no uncertain sound. Young minds are not to be cast into one rigid mould, neither can maturity of doctrine be expected of beginners in the ministry; but, as a rule, our men have not only gone out from us clear and sound in the faith; but, with very few exceptions, they have continued so. Some few have ascended into Hyper-Calvinism, and, on the other hand, one or two have wandered into Arminian sentiments; but even these have remained earnestly Evangelical, while the bulk of the brethren abide in the faith in which their Alma Mater nourished them. The general acceptance of our students in Scotland is one remarkable proof that they stand by the old Calvinistic, Evangelical doctrines. The Presbyterian Churches of Rotterdam and Amsterdam, which are frequently supplied by our students, and are resolutely orthodox, have again and again sent us pleasing testimony that our men carry to them the old theology of the Westminster Assembly's Confession. Let wiseacres say what they will, there is more truth in that venerable Confession than could be found in ten thousand volumes of the school of affected culture and pretentious thoughtfulness. Want of knowing what the old theology is, is in most cases the reason for ridiculing it. Believing that the Puritanic school embodied more of gospel truth in it than any other since the days of the apostles, we continue in the same line of things; and, by God's help, hope to have a share in that revival of Evangelical doctrine which is as sure to come as the Lord Himself. Those who think otherwise can go elsewhere; but, for our own part, we shall never consent to leave the doctrinal teaching of the Institution vague and undefined, after the manner of the bigoted liberalism of the present day. This is our College motto :—

We labour to hold forth the cross of Christ with a bold hand among the sons of men, because that cross holds us fast by its attractive power. Our desire is, that every man may hold the truth, and be held by it; especially the truth of Christ crucified.

There were many interesting incidents associated with the earliest days of the Pastors' College, or which occurred even before it was actually in existence. When Mr. Medhurst began to preach in the street, some of the very precise friends, who were at that time members at New Park Street, were greatly shocked at his want of education, so they complained to me about it, and said that I ought to stop him; for, if I did not, disgrace would be brought upon the cause. Accordingly, I had a talk with the earnest young brother; and, while he did not deny that his English was imperfect, and that he might have made mistakes in other respects, yet he said, " I must preach, sir; and I shall preach unless you cut off my head." I went to our friends, and told them what he had said, and they took it in all seriousness. " Oh !" they exclaimed, " you can't cut off Mr. Medhurst's head, so you must let him go on preaching." I quite agreed with them, and I added, " As our young brother is evidently bent on serving the Lord with all his might, I must do what I can to get him an education that will fit him for the ministry."

The next one to come to me in trouble was Mr. Medhurst himself. One day, with a very sad countenance, he said to me, " I have been preaching for three months, and I don't know of a single soul having been converted." Meaning to catch him by guile, and at the same time to teach him a lesson he would never forget, I asked, " Do you expect the Lord to save souls every time you open your mouth?" " Oh, no, sir !" he replied. " Then," I said, " that is just the reason why you have not had conversions : 'According to your faith be it unto you.'"

During the time Mr. Medhurst was studying at Bexley Heath, he used to conduct services in the open air. On one occasion, when I went there to preach, I was much amused, after the service, by overhearing the remarks of two good souls who were manifestly very much attached to the young student. "Well," enquired the first, "how did you like Mr. Spurgeon?" "Oh !" answered her companion, " very well ; but *I should have enjoyed the service more if he hadn't imitated our dear Mr. Medhurst so much.*"

There was another explanation, which did not seem to have occurred to the old lady ; and, in after days, when relating the story to other students, I pointed out how serious the consequences might be if any of them imitated me !

At a later date, when I visited Kingston-on-Thames, after Mr. Medhurst had become pastor of the church there, I wanted to find out what the people thought of him, so I spoke of him with apparent coolness to an estimable lady of his congregation. In a very few moments, she began to speak quite warmly in his favour. She said, " You must not say anything against him, sir ; if you do, it is because you do not know him." " Oh !" I replied, " I knew him long before you did ; he is not much, is he ? " " Well," she answered, " I must speak well of him, for he has been a blessing to my family and servants." I went out into the street, and saw some men and women standing about ; so I said to them, " I must take your minister away." " If you do," they exclaimed, " we will follow you all over the world to get him back ; you surely will not be so unkind as to take away a man who has done so much good to our souls ? " After collecting the testimony of fifteen or sixteen persons, I said, " If the man gets such witnesses as these to the power of his ministry, I will gladly let him go on where he is; for it is clear that the Lord has called him into His service."

Mr. Medhurst himself told me of an incident that occurred to him in connection with one young man whom I had accepted for training, because I could see that he might do good service after proper tuition. So extraordinarily ignorant was he of his Bible that, upon hearing Mr. Medhurst mention the story of Nebuchadnezzar's being driven out from men, until his nails grew like birds' claws, and his hair like eagles' feathers, he said to the preacher, at the close of the sermon, "That was a queer story you told the people, certainly; where did you fish that up?" "Why!" replied our friend, "have you never read your Bible? Can you not find it in the Book of Daniel?" The young man had read a great many other books, but he had never read his Bible through, yet he was going to be a teacher of it! I fear that such ignorance is very current in many persons; they do not know what is in the Bible: they could tell you what is in *The Churchman's Magazine*, or *The Wesleyan Magazine*, or *The Baptist Magazine*, or *The Evangelical Magazine;* but there is one old magazine, a magazine of arms, a magazine of wealth, that they have forgotten to read,—that old-fashioned Book called the Bible. I remember saying, of a later student, that if he had been as well acquainted with his Bible as he was with *The Baptist Handbook*, he would have made a good minister; and he was not the only one to whom such a remark might have been applied.

There was one of the early students, who gave me great cause to fear concerning his future, when he began his petition at the Monday night prayer-meeting thus :—"O Thou that art encinctured with an auriferous zodiac!" This was, of course, a grandiloquent paraphrase of Revelation i. 13. Alas! my fears proved to be only too well founded; after he left the College, he went from the Baptists to the Congregationalists, then became a play-writer and play-actor: and where he is now, I do not know. For many years I had the sad privilege of helping to support his godly wife, whom he had deserted. I thank God that, among so many hundreds of men, so few have caused me such sorrow of heart as he did.

CHAPTER XLVII.

First Printed Works.—Author, Publishers, and Readers.

How many souls may be converted by what some men are privileged to *write and print!* There is, for instance, Dr. Doddridge's *Rise and Progress of Religion in the Soul.* Though I decidedly object to some things in it, I could wish that everybody had read that book, so many have been the conversions it has produced. I think it more honour to have composed Watts's *Psalms and Hymns* than Milton's *Paradise Lost;* and more glory to have written old Thomas Wilcocks' book, *A Choice Drop of Honey from the Rock Christ,* or the booklet that God has used so much, *The Sinner's Friend,* than all the works of Homer. I value books for the good they may do to men's souls. Much as I respect the genius of Pope, or Dryden, or Burns, give me the simple lines of Cowper, that God has owned in bringing souls to Him. Oh, to think that I may write and print books which shall reach poor sinners' hearts! The other day, my soul was gladdened exceedingly by an invitation from a pious woman to go and see her. She told me she had been ten years on her bed, and had not been able to stir from it. "Nine years," she said, "I was dark, and blind, and unthinking; but my husband brought me one of your sermons. I read it, and God blessed it to the opening of my eyes. He converted my soul by it; and now, all glory to Him, I love His Name! Each Sabbath morning," she added, "I wait for your sermon. I live on it all the week, it is marrow and fatness to my spirit." Ah! thought I, there is something to cheer the printers, and all of us who labour in that good work. A country friend wrote to me, this week, "Brother Spurgeon, keep your courage up; you are known in multitudes of the households of England, and you are loved, too; though we cannot hear you, or see your living form, yet throughout our villages your sermons are scattered; and I know of cases of conversion from them, more than I can tell you." Another friend mentioned to me an instance of a clergyman of the Church of England, a canon of a cathedral, who frequently preaches the sermons on the Sabbath,—whether in the cathedral or not, I cannot say, but I hope he does. Oh! who can tell, when these words are printed, what hearts they may reach, or what good they may effect?—C. H. S., *in sermon preached at New Park Street Chapel, October* 7, 1855.

HE first product of my pen which found its way into print was No. 1 of a short series of *Waterbeach Tracts,* which bore upon its front page the announcement, "Published by request of numerous friends." This was issued in 1853, and in the same year I sent to *The Baptist Reporter* an account of the conversation I had with the clergyman at Maidstone which was the means of leading me to search the Scriptures, and to find out the teaching of the New Testament concerning believers' baptism.* My letter was printed, although I only gave, for publication, initials for my name and sphere of labour. Soon after I was settled in London, the Editor of *The Baptist Messenger,* then recently started, asked me to write some articles for his Magazine, so I wrote a brief Exposition of Psalm lxxxiv. 6, which was published in September, 1854, under the title, "The Valley of Weeping." The following month, the next verse furnished me with a sequel, which appeared in the October number under the heading, "Onward and Heavenward." Month by month,

---

* See *Autobiography,* Vol. I., chapter vii.

I continued to contribute short meditations to the pages of the *Messenger* until my other work absorbed all my time and strength, and from then up to the present, one of my sermons has regularly occupied the first page of each issue of the little Magazine.

On August 20, 1854, I preached at New Park Street Chapel from the words in 1 Samuel xii. 17: "Is it not wheat harvest to-day?" The sermon was published by Mr. James Paul, as No. 2,234 in his *Penny Pulpit*, under the title, "Harvest Time," and was, I believe, the first of my discourses to appear in print. Before I ever entered a pulpit, the thought had occurred to me that I should one day preach sermons which would be printed. While reading the penny sermons of Joseph Irons, which were great favourites with me, I conceived in my heart the idea that, some time or other, I should have a "Penny Pulpit" of my own. In due course, the dream became an accomplished fact. There was so good a demand for the discourses as they appeared in the *Penny Pulpit* and *Baptist Messenger*, that the notion of occasional publication was indulged, but with no idea of continuance week by week for a lengthened period; *that* came to pass as a development and a growth. With much fear and trembling, my consent was given to the proposal of my present worthy publishers to commence the regular weekly publication of a sermon. We began with the one preached at New Park Street Chapel, on Lord's-day morning, January 7, 1855, upon the text, "I am the Lord, I change not; therefore ye sons of Jacob are not consumed" (Malachi iii. 6); and now, after all these years, it is a glad thing to be able to say, "Having therefore obtained help of God, I continue unto this day, witnessing both to small and great." How many "Penny Pulpits" have been set up and pulled down in the course of these years, it would be hard to tell; certainly, very many attempts have been made to publish weekly the sermons of most eminent men, and they have all run to their end with more or less rapidity, in some cases through the preacher's ill-health or death, but in several others, to my knowledge, from an insufficient sale. Perhaps the discourses were too good: the public evidently did not think them too interesting. Those who know what dull reading sermons are usually supposed to be, will count that man happy who has for over thirty years* been favoured with a circle of willing supporters, who not only purchase but actually *read* his discourses. I am more astonished at the fact than any other man can possibly be, and I see no other reason for it but this,—the sermons contain the gospel, preached in plain language, and this is precisely what multitudes need beyond anything else. The gospel, ever fresh and ever new, has held my vast congregation together these many long years, and the same power has

---

* As this volume of the *Autobiography* is passing through the press, the *forty-fourth* year's publication of the sermons is proceeding, making from No. 2,550 to No. 2,602, in regular weekly succession; and there are still sufficient unpublished discourses to last for several years longer, while the demand for them is as great as ever.

kept around me a host of readers. A French farmer, when accused of witchcraft by his neighbours, because his crops were so large, exhibited his industrious sons, his laborious ox, his spade, and his plough, as the only witchcraft which he had used; and, under the Divine blessing, I can only ascribe the continued acceptableness of the sermons to the gospel which they contain, and the plainness of the speech in which that gospel is uttered.

When the time arrived for issuing Vol. I. of *The New Park Street Pulpit*, I wrote in the Preface :—" Little can be said in praise of these sermons, and nothing can be said against them more bitter than has been already spoken. Happily, the author has heard abuse exhaust itself; he has seen its vocabulary used up, and its utmost venom entirely spent; and yet, the printed discourses have for that very reason found a readier sale, and more have been led to peruse them with deep attention.

" One thing alone places this book above contempt,—and that accomplishes the deed so triumphantly, that the preacher defies the opinion of man,—it is the fact that, to his certain knowledge, there is scarcely a sermon here which has not been stamped by the hand of the Almighty, by the conversion of a soul. Some single sermons, here brought into the society of their brethren, have been, under God, the means of the salvation of not less than twenty souls; at least, that number has come under the preacher's notice from one sermon only; and, doubtless, more shall be discovered at the last day. This, together with the fact that hundreds of the children of God have been made to leap for joy by their message, makes their author invulnerable either to criticism or abuse.

" The reader will, perhaps, remark considerable progress in some of the sentiments here made public, particularly in the case of the doctrine of the Second Coming of our Lord; but he will remember that he who is learning truth will learn it by degrees, and if he teaches as he learns, it is to be expected that his lessons will become fuller every day.

" There are also many expressions which may provoke a smile; but let it be remembered that every man has his moments when his lighter feelings indulge themselves, and the preacher must be allowed to have the same passions as his fellow-men; and since he lives in the pulpit more than anywhere else, it is but natural that his whole man should be there developed; besides, he is not quite sure about a smile being a sin, and, at any rate, he thinks it less a crime to cause a momentary laughter than a half-hour's profound slumber.

" With all faults, the purchaser has bought this book; and, as it was not warranted to be perfect, if he thinks ill of it, he must make the best of his bargain,— which can be done, either by asking a blessing on its reading to himself, or entreating greater light for his friend the preacher."

The New Park Street Pulpit.

THE IMMUTABILITY OF GOD.

A Sermon

DELIVERED ON SABBATH MORNING, JANUARY 7TH, 1855, BY

REV. C. H. SPURGEON,

AT NEW PARK STREET CHAPEL, SOUTHWARK.

"I am the Lord, I change not: therefore ye sons of Jacob are not consumed."—Malachi. iii. 6.

IT has been said by some one that "the proper study of mankind is man." I will not oppose the idea, but I believe it is equally true that the proper study of God's elect is God; the proper study of a Christian is the Godhead. The highest science, the loftiest speculation, the mightiest philosophy, which can ever engage the attention of a child of God, is the name, the nature, the person, the work, the doings, and the existence of the great God whom he calls his Father. There is something exceedingly improving to the mind in a contemplation of the Divinity. It is a subject so vast, that all our thoughts are lost in its immensity; so deep, that our pride is drowned in its infinity. Other subjects we can compass and grapple with; in them we feel a kind of self-content, and go our way with the thought, "Behold, I am wise." But when we come to this master-science, finding that our plumb-line cannot sound its depth, and that our eagle eye cannot see its height, we turn away with the thought, that vain man would be wise, but he is like a wild ass's colt; and with the solemn exclamation, "I am but of yesterday, and know nothing." No subject of contemplation will tend more to humble the mind, than thoughts of God. We shall be obliged to feel—

> "Great God, how infinite art thou,
> What worthless worms are we!"

But while the subject *humbles* the mind, it also *expands* it. He who often thinks of God, will have a larger mind than the man who simply plods around this narrow globe. He may be a naturalist, boasting of his ability to dissect a beetle, anatomize a fly, or arrange insects and animals in classes with well-nigh unutterable names; he may be a geologist, able to discourse of the megatherium and the plesiosaurus, and all kinds of extinct animals; he may imagine that his science, whatever it is, ennobles and enlarges his mind. I dare say it does; but, after all, the most excellent study for expanding the soul, is the science of Christ, and him crucified, and the knowledge of the Godhead in the glorious Trinity. Nothing will so enlarge the intellect, nothing so magnify the whole soul of man, as a devout, earnest, continued investigation of the great subject of the Deity. And, whilst humbling and expanding, this subject is eminently *consolatory*. Oh, there is, in contemplating Christ, a balm for every wound; in musing on the Father, there is a quietus for every grief; and in the influence of the Holy Ghost, there is a balsam for every sore. Would you lose your sorrows? Would you drown your cares? Then go, plunge yourself in the Godhead's deepest sea; lost in his immensity; and you shall come forth as from a couch of rest, refreshed and invigorated. I know nothing which can so comfort the soul, so calm the swelling billows of grief and sorrow, so speak peace to the winds of trial, as a devout musing upon the subject of the Godhead. It is to that subject that I invite you this morning. We shall present you with one view of it,—that is, *the immutability of the glorious Jehovah.* "I am," says my text, "Jehovah," (for so it should be translated) "I am Jehovah, I change not; therefore ye sons of Jacob are not consumed."

No. I.

SWEET COMFORT FOR FEEBLE SAINTS.

thou art as much justified as Paul, Peter, John the Baptist, or the loftiest saint in heaven. There is no difference in that matter. Oh! take courage and rejoice. *Then one thing more. If you were lost, God's honor would be as much tarnished as if the greatest one were lost.* A queer thing I once read, in an old book, about God's children and people being a part of Christ and in union with him. The writer says,—"A father sitteth in his room, and there cometh in a stranger; the stranger taketh up a child on his knee, and the child hath a sore finger; so he saith, 'My child, you have a sore finger.' 'Yes!' 'Well, let me take it off, and give thee a golden one!' The child looketh at him, and saith, "I will not go to that man any more, for he talks of taking off my finger; I love my own finger, and I will not have a golden one instead of it.'" So the saint saith, "I am one of the members of Christ, but I am like a sore finger, and he will take me off, and put a golden one on." "No," said Christ, "no, no; I cannot have any of my members taken away; if the finger be a sore one, I will bind it up, I will strengthen it." Christ cannot allow a word about cutting his members off. If Christ lose one of his people, he would not be a whole Christ any longer. If the meanest of his children could be cast away, Christ would lack a part of his fulness; yea, Christ would be incomplete without his Church. If one of his children must be lost, it would be better that it should be a great one, than a little one. If a little one were lost, Satan would say, "Ah! you save the great ones, because they had strength and could help themselves; but the little one that had no strength, you could not save him." You know what Satan would say; but God would shut Satan's mouth, by proclaiming, "They are all here, Satan, in spite of thy malice, they are all here; every one is safe, now lie down in thy den for ever, and be bound eternally in chains, and smoke in fire!" So shall he suffer eternal torment, but not one child of God ever shall be lost.

One thought more, and I shall have done with this head. *The salvation of great saints often depends upon the salvation of little ones.* Do you understand that? You know that my salvation, or the salvation of any child of God, looking at second causes, very much depends upon the conversion of some one else. Suppose your mother is the means of your conversion; you would, speaking after the manner of men, say, that your conversion depended upon hers; for her being converted, made her the instrument of bringing you in. Suppose such-and-such a minister to be the means of your calling; then your conversion, in some sense, though not absolutely, depends upon his. So it often happens, that the salvation of God's mightiest servants depends upon the conversion of little ones. There is a poor mother; no one ever knows anything about her; she goes to the house of God, her name is not in the newspapers, or anywhere else; she teaches her child, and brings him up in the fear of God; she prays for that boy; she wrestles with God, and her tears and prayers mingle together. The boy grows up. What is he? A missionary—a William Knibb—a Moffat—a Williams. But you do not hear anything about the mother. Ah! but if the mother had not been saved, where would the boy have been? Let this cheer the little ones; and may you rejoice that he will nourish and cherish you, though you are like bruised reeds and smoking flax.

III. Now, to finish up, there is a CERTAIN VICTORY: "Till he send forth judgment unto victory."

Victory! There is something beautiful in that word. The death of Sir John Moore, in the Peninsular war, was very touching; he fell in the arms of triumph; and sad as was his fate, I doubt not that his eye was lit up with lustre by the shout of victory. So also, I suppose, that Wolfe spoke a truth when he said, "I die happy," having just before heard the shout, "They run, they run." I know victory even in that bad sense—for I look not upon earthly victories as of any value—must have cheered the warrior. But, oh! how cheered the saint when he knows that victory is his! I shall fight during all my life, but I shall write "vici" on my shield. I shall be "more than conqueror through him that loved me." Each feeble saint shall win the day; each man upon his crutches; each lame one; each one full of infirmity, sorrow, sickness, and weakness, shall gain the victory. "They shall come with singing unto Zion; so well the blind, and lame, and halt, and the woman with child, together." So saith the Scripture. Not one shall be left out, but he shall "send forth judgment unto victory." Victory! victory!

The first seven volumes were printed in small type, and each discourse formed only eight pages ; but the abolition of the paper duty enabled the publishers to give a more readable type and twelve pages of matter. This has been better in every way, and marks an epoch in the history of the sermons, for their name was at about the same period changed from *The New Park Street Pulpit* to *The Metropolitan Tabernacle Pulpit*, and their sale was largely increased. Constant habit enables me generally to give the same amount of matter on each occasion, the very slight variation almost surprises myself; from forty to forty-five minutes' speaking exactly fills the available space, and saves the labour of additions, and the still more difficult task of cutting down. The earlier sermons, owing to my constant wanderings abroad, received scarcely any revision, and consequently they abound in colloquialisms, and other offences, very venial in extempore discourse, but scarcely tolerable in print ; the later specimens are more carefully corrected, and the work of revision has been a very useful exercise to me, supplying in great measure that training in correct language which is obtained by those who write their productions before they deliver them. The labour has been far greater than some suppose, and has usually occupied the best hours of Monday, and involved the burning of no inconsiderable portion of midnight oil. Feeling that I had a constituency well deserving my best efforts, I have never grudged the hours, though often the brain has been wearied, and the pleasure has hardened into a task.

I have commenced revising the small-type sermons in preparation for their re-issue in type similar to that used for the rest of the series. There were mistakes in orthography and typography, which needed to be corrected ; but I was happy to find that I had no occasion to alter any of the doctrines which I preached in those early days of my ministry. I might, here and there, slightly modify the expressions used thirty or five-and-thirty years ago ; but, as to the truths themselves, I stand just where I did when the Lord first revealed them to me by His unerring Spirit.

(The *facsimiles* of two pages of the revised sermons, reproduced on pages 156 and 157, will show the kind of corrections made by Mr. Spurgeon One is the first page of the first discourse in Vol. I. of *The New Park Street Pulpit*, and the other has a direct reference to the preacher's confidence that the end of the life-long warfare which he would wage, as a good soldier of Jesus Christ, would be, " Victory ! victory ! ")

Before the first volume of my sermons was completed, Mr. W. H. Collingridge had published for me, under the title of *Smooth Stones taken from Ancient Brooks*, a small volume containing " a collection of sentences, illustrations, and quaint sayings, from the works of that renowned Puritan, Thomas Brooks." (See page 19.) In the same year (1855), Mr. James Paul issued Vol. I. of *The Pulpit Library*, which contained ten of my sermons. (See page 27.) Being printed in clear, leaded type, and bound in cloth, the volume was much appreciated, and had a large sale, although half-a-crown was charged for it.

It contained, amongst other discourses, the one preached the night before I came of age,*—" Pictures of Life, and Birthday Reflections;"—another delivered on the Sabbath following the marriage of Mr. and Mrs. Henry Olney, and in the midst of the terrible visitation of cholera,—" The House of Mourning and the House of Feasting;"—and a third, preached from Isaiah liv. 17, on November 5, 1854 (at the very moment when the battle of Inkermann was being fought), in which I urged the importance of Christians and Protestants remembering the day which had been made memorable in English history by the discovery of the Guy Fawkes' plot on November 5, 1605, and by the landing at Torbay of William III., on November 5, 1688. The title of the discourse was, " The Saints' Heritage and Watchword." The volume also included my first printed sermon,—" Harvest Time;" and another entitled, "A Promise for the Blind," preached at the Baptist Chapel, Church Street, Blackfriars Road, on behalf of the Christian Blind Relief Society, in the course of which I referred to three institutions in the neighbourhood which represented the three classes of blind people :—" The physically blind, the mentally blind, and the spiritually blind. . . . In the London Road, you will find the School for the blind,—the physically blind. Just before you is the Roman Catholic Cathedral,—there you have the spiritually blind. And further on is the Bethlehem Hospital (' Bedlam '), where you have the mentally blind."

In 1855,—partly as an answer to the slanders and calumnies by which I was assailed, and partly that my own people might be furnished with a plain statement of " the faith once for all delivered to the saints,"—Messrs. Alabaster and Passmore brought out, under my direction, a new edition of " *The Baptist Confession of Faith,* with Scripture proofs, adopted by the ministers and messengers of the General Assembly which met in London in July, 1689 ;" amongst whom were such notable men as Hanserd Knollys, William Kiffin, Andrew Gifford, and my own illustrious predecessor, Benjamin Keach.

---

* On March 30, 1884, just after the sudden death of the Duke of Albany, I preached again from the same text: " What is your life?" The sermon was published as No. 1,773 in the *Metropolitan Tabernacle Pulpit,* and during the following week a gentleman, who came to see me at the Tabernacle upon some matter of business, said to me, "I felt quite overwhelmed with emotion a minute ago." I asked him the reason; and he answered, "As I entered this building, I saw an announcement that you had lately preached from the words, ' What is your life?' " " Well," I enquired, " what is there special about that?" " Why!" he replied, "the night before you came of age, you preached from the same text." I told the friend that I had no doubt it was a very different discourse from the one I had just delivered, and then he said, " I have never been able to shake hands with you before to-day; but I have great pleasure in doing so now. When you were twenty-one years old, I was dreadfully depressed in spirit; I was so melancholy that I believe I should have destroyed myself if I had not heard you preach that sermon in celebration of your twenty-first birthday. It encouraged me to keep on in the battle of life; and, what is better, it made such an impression on me that I have never gone back to what I was before. Though I live a long way from here, no one loves you more than I do, for you were the means of bringing me up out of the horrible pit, and out of the miry clay." I was very glad to have that testimony to the usefulness of one of my early sermons.

In two Prefatory Notes, one to Christians in general, and the other to my own people, I wrote as follows :—

"TO ALL THE HOUSEHOLD OF FAITH, WHO REJOICE IN THE GLORIOUS DOCTRINES OF FREE GRACE,—

" Dearly-beloved,

" I have thought it meet to reprint in a cheap form this most excellent list of doctrines, which was subscribed unto by the Baptist ministers in the year 1689.

" We need a banner, because of the truth ; it may be that this small volume may aid the cause of the glorious gospel, by testifying plainly what are its leading doctrines. Known unto many of you by face in the flesh, I trust we are also kindred in spirit, and are striving together for the glory of our Three-one God. May the Lord soon restore unto His Zion a pure language, and may the watchmen see eye to eye !

" He who has preserved this faith among us, will doubtless bless our gospel evermore.

" So prays your brother in the gospel of Jesus,

" C. H. SPURGEON."

"TO THE CHURCH IN NEW PARK STREET, AMONG WHOM IT IS MY DELIGHT TO MINISTER,—

" Dearly-beloved,

" This ancient document is a most excellent epitome of the things most surely believed among us. By the preserving hand of the Triune Jehovah, we have been kept faithful to the great points of our glorious gospel, and we feel more resolved perpetually to abide by them.

" This little volume is not issued as an authoritative rule, or code of faith, whereby you are to be fettered, but as an assistance to you in controversy, a confirmation in faith, and a means of edification in righteousness. Here, the younger members of our church will have a Body of Divinity in small compass, and by means of the Scriptural proofs, will be ready to give a reason for the hope that is in them.

" Be not ashamed of your faith ; remember it is the ancient gospel of martyrs, confessors, Reformers, and saints. Above all, it is *the truth of God*, against which the gates of hell cannot prevail.

" Let your lives adorn your faith, let your example recommend your creed. Above all, live in Christ Jesus, and walk in Him, giving credence to no teaching but that which is manifestly approved of Him, and owned by the Holy Spirit. Cleave fast to the Word of God, which is here mapped out to you. May our Father, who is in Heaven, smile on us as ever! Brethren, pray for—

> "Your affectionate Minister,
>
> "C. H. SPURGEON."

I have never seen any reason to alter what I then wrote, and I would, at the present time, just as earnestly commend to my fellow-Christians the prayerful study of *The Baptist Confession of Faith* as I did in the early years of my ministry in London, for I believe it would greatly tend to the strengthening of their faith.

I have already stated that, as soon as the publication of the sermons was commenced, the Lord set His seal upon them in the conversion of sinners, the restoration of backsliders, and the edification of believers ; and, to His praise, I rejoice to write that, ever since, it has been the same. For many years, seldom has a day passed, and certainly never a week, without letters reaching me from all sorts of places, even at the utmost ends of the earth, telling me of the salvation of souls by means of one or other of the sermons. There are, in the long series, discourses of which I may say, without exaggeration, that the Holy Spirit has blessed them to hundreds of precious souls ; and long after their delivery, fresh instances of their usefulness have come to light. For this, to God be all the glory !

There were certain remarkable cases of blessing through the reading of some of the very earliest of the sermons ; I mention these, not merely because of the interest naturally attaching to them, but because they are representative of many similar miracles of mercy that have been wrought by the Holy Ghost all through the years which have followed. On June 8, 1856, I preached in Exeter Hall from Hebrews vii. 25 : " Wherefore He is able also to save them to the uttermost that come unto God by Him, seeing He ever liveth to make intercession for them." The sermon was published under the title, " Salvation to the Uttermost ;" and, more than thirty years afterwards, I received the joyful tidings that a murderer in South America had been brought to the Saviour through reading it. A friend, living not far from the Tabernacle, had been in the city of Para, in Brazil. There he heard of an Englishman in prison, who had, in a state of drunkenness, committed a murder, for which he was confined for life. Our friend went to see him, and found him deeply penitent, but quietly restful, and happy in the Lord. He had felt the terrible wound of blood-guiltiness in his soul, but it had been healed, and he was enjoying the bliss of pardon.

Here is the story of the poor fellow's conversion as told in his own words :—" A young man, who had just completed his contract at the gas-works, was returning to England ; but, before doing so, he called to see me, and brought with him a

K

parcel of books. When I opened it, I found that they were novels ; but, being able to read, I was thankful for anything. After I had read several of the books, I found one of Mr. Spurgeon's sermons (No. 84), in which he referred to Palmer, who was then lying under sentence of death in Stafford Gaol, and in order to bring home the truth of his text to his hearers, he said that, if Palmer had committed many other murders, if he repented, and sought God's pardoning love in Christ, even he would be forgiven ! I then felt that, if Palmer could be forgiven, so might I. I sought the Saviour, and, blessed be God, I found Him ; and now I am pardoned, I am free ; I am a sinner saved by grace. Though a murderer, I have not yet sinned beyond 'the uttermost,' blessed be His holy Name ! "

It made me very happy when I heard the glad news that a poor condemned murderer had thus been converted, and I am thankful to know that he is not the only one who, although he had committed the awful crime of murder, had, through the Spirit's blessing upon the printed sermons, been brought to repentance, and to faith in our Lord Jesus Christ. There was another man, who had lived a life of drunkenness and unchastity, and who had even shed human blood with his bowie knife and his revolver, yet he, too, found the Saviour, and became a new man ; and when he was dying, he charged someone who was with him to tell me that one of my discourses had brought him to Christ. " I shall never see Mr. Spurgeon on earth," he said, "but I shall tell the Lord Jesus Christ about him when I get to Heaven." It was a sermon, read far away in the backwoods, that, through sovereign grace, was the means of the salvation of this great sinner.

One Saturday morning in November, 1856, when my mind and heart were occupied with preparation for the great congregation I expected to address the next day at the Surrey Gardens Music Hall, I received a long letter from Norwich, from a man who had been one of the leaders of an infidel society in that city. It was most cheering to me, amid the opposition and slander I was then enduring, to read what he wrote :—

" I purchased one of the pamphlets entitled, 'Who is this Spurgeon?' and also your portrait (or a portrait sold as yours) for 3d. I brought these home, and exhibited them in my shop-window. I was induced to do so from a feeling of derisive pleasure. The title of the pamphlet is, naturally, suggestive of caricature, and it was especially to convey that impression that I attached it to your portrait, and placed it in my window. But I also had another object in view, I thought by its attraction to improve my trade. I am not at all in the book or paper business, which rendered its exposure and my motive the more conspicuous. I have taken it down now : *I am taken down, too.* . . . . I had bought one of your sermons of an infidel a day or two previously. In that sermon I read these words, 'They go on ;

that step is safe,—they take it ; the next is apparently safe,—they take that ; their foot hangs over a gulf of darkness.' I read on, but the word darkness staggered me ; it was all dark with me. I said to myself, 'True, the way has been safe so far, but I am lost in bewilderment ; I cannot go on as I have been going. No, no, no ; I will not risk it.' I left the apartment in which I had been musing, and as I did so, the three words, 'Who can tell?' seemed to be whispered to my heart. I determined not to let another Sunday pass without visiting a place of worship. How soon my soul might be required of me, I knew not ; but I felt that it would be mean, base, cowardly, not to give it a chance of salvation. 'Ay!' I thought, 'my associates may laugh, scoff, deride, and call me coward and turncoat, I will do an act of justice to my soul.' I went to chapel ; I was just stupefied with awe. What could I want there? The doorkeeper opened his eyes wide, and involuntarily asked, 'It's Mr. ——, isn't it?' 'Yes,' I said, 'it is.' He conducted me to a seat, and afterwards brought me a hymn-book. I was fit to burst with anguish. 'Now,' I thought, 'I am here, if it be the house of God, Heaven grant me an audience, and I will make a full surrender. O God, show me some token by which I may know that Thou art, and that Thou wilt in no wise cast out the vile deserter who has ventured to seek Thy face and Thy pardoning mercy !' I opened the hymn-book to divert my mind from the feelings that were rending me, and the first words that caught my eyes were—

"' Dark, dark indeed the grave would be
Had we no light, O God, from Thee !'"

After mentioning some things which he looked upon as evidences that he was a true convert, the man closed up by saying, " O sir, tell this to the poor wretch whose pride, like mine, has made him league himself with hell ; tell it to the hesitating and the timid ; tell it to the desponding Christian, that God is a very present help to all that are in need ! . . . Think of the poor sinner who may never look upon you in this world, but who will live to bless and pray for you here, and long to meet you in the world exempt from sinful doubts, from human pride, and backsliding hearts."

After that letter, I heard again and again from the good brother ; and I rejoiced to learn that, the following Christmas-day, he went into the market-place at Norwich, and there made a public recantation of his errors, and a profession of his faith in Christ. Then, taking up all the infidel books he had written, or that he had in his possession, he burned them in the sight of all the people. I blessed God with my whole heart for such a wonder of grace as that man was, and I afterwards had the joy of learning from his own lips what the Lord had done for his soul, and together we praised and magnified Him for His marvellous mercy.

Many singular things have happened in connection with the publication of the sermons. One brother, whose name I must not mention, purchased and gave away no less than 250,000 copies. He had volumes bound in the best style, and presented to every crowned head in Europe. He gave copies, each containing twelve or more sermons, to all the students of the Universities,* and to all the members of the two Houses of Parliament, and he even commenced the work of distributing volumes to the principal householders in the towns of Ireland. May the good results of his laborious seed-sowing be seen many days hence! The self-denial with which this brother saved the expense from a very limited income, and worked personally in the distribution, was beyond all commendation ; but praise was evaded and observation dreaded by him ; the work was done without his left hand knowing what his right hand did.

In the first days of our publishing, a city merchant advertised the sermons in all sorts of papers, offering to supply them from his own office. He thus sold large quantities to persons who might otherwise never have heard of them. He was not a Baptist, but held the views of the Society of Friends. It was very long before I knew who he was, and I trust he will pardon me for thus calling attention to a deed for which I shall ever feel grateful to him. By my permission, the sermons were printed *as advertisements* in several of the Australian papers, one gentleman spending week by week a sum which I scarcely dare to mention, lest it should not be believed. By this means, they were read far away in the Bush, and never were results more manifest, for numbers of letters were received—in answer to the enquiry as to whether the advertisements should be continued,—all bearing testimony to the good accomplished by their being inserted in the newspapers. A selection of these letters was sent to me, and made my heart leap for joy, for they detailed conversions marvellous indeed. Beside these, many epistles of like character came direct to me, showing that the rough dwellers in the wilds were glad to find in their secular paper the best of all news, the story of pardon bought with blood.

(Some particulars of these conversions will be given in a later volume, together with information concerning the numerous translations into foreign languages.)

In America, the sale of the first volume reached 20,000 in a very short time ; and, many years ago, it was calculated that half a million volumes had been sold

---

* Mr. Spurgeon's copy contains forty-two sermons; it is lettered on the back,—" A CURIOSITY IN RELIGIOUS LITERATURE." On the fly-leaf, in his handwriting, is the following inscription :—" Specimen of a collection of sermons given to all the crowned heads of Europe, and the students of Oxford; Cambridge ; Trinity College, Dublin; &c., &c."

During the compilation of this volume of the *Autobiography*, Mrs. Spurgeon received from a Church of England clergyman a letter containing the following reference to this distribution of sermons to the students in the Universities :—

"Over thirty years ago, when an undergraduate at Oxford, one of our men came into College with a volume of your husband's sermons, saying that someone was distributing them to the ' men ' who would accept them. I was one of those who had the privileged gift, and have since read it through and through with advantage. I have never preached knowingly other than the doctrines of grace ; and though the clergy round about are mostly Ritualists and Sacerdotalists, thank God the error taught by them has never tempted me ! "

there. Beside this, dozens of religious papers in the United States, and Canada, and elsewhere, appropriate the sermons bodily, and therefore it is quite impossible to tell where they go, or rather, where they do not go. For all these opportunities of speaking to so large a portion of the human race, I cannot but be thankful to God, neither can I refrain from asking the prayers of God's people that the gospel thus widely scattered may not be in vain

Brethren in the ministry will be best able to judge the mental wear and tear involved in printing one sermon a week, and they will most sympathize in the over-flowing gratitude which reviews between thirty and forty years of sermons, and magnifies the God of grace for help so long continued. The quarry of Holy Scripture is inexhaustible, I seem hardly to have begun to labour in it; but the selection of the next block, and the consideration as to how to work it into form, are matters not so easy as some think. Those who count preaching and its needful preparations to be slight matters, have never occupied a pulpit continuously month after month, or they would know better. Chief of all is the responsibility which the preaching of the Word involves : I do not wish to feel this less heavily, rather would I feel it more ; but it enters largely into the account of a minister's life-work, and tells upon him more than any other part of his mission. Let those preach lightly who dare do so ; to me, it is " the burden of the Lord,"—joyfully carried as grace is given ; but, still, a burden which at times crushes my whole manhood into the dust of humiliation, and occasionally, when ill-health unites with the mental strain, into depression and anguish of heart.

However, let no man mistake me. I would sooner have my work to do than any other under the sun. Preaching Jesus Christ is sweet work, joyful work, Heavenly work. Whitefield used to call his pulpit his throne, and those who know the bliss of forgetting everything beside the glorious, all-absorbing topic of Christ crucified, will bear witness that the term was aptly used. It is a bath in the waters of Paradise to preach with the Holy Ghost sent down from Heaven. Scarcely is it possible for a man, this side the grave, to be nearer Heaven than is a preacher when his Master's presence bears him right away from every care and thought, save the one business in hand, and that the greatest that ever occupied a creature's mind and heart. No tongue can tell the amount of happiness which I have enjoyed in delivering these sermons, and so, gentle reader, forgive me if I have wearied you with this grateful record, for I could not refrain from inviting others to aid me in praising my gracious Master. " Bless the Lord, O my soul, and all that is within me, bless His holy Name."

In my early experience as an author, I made one mistake which I have never repeated. For my volume, *The Saint and his Saviour*, which contained 480 small octavo pages, I accepted from Mr. James S. Virtue the sum of £50. At the time I entered into the agreement,—within about a year of my coming to London,—the amount seemed to me large ; but in comparison with what the book must have brought to the publisher, it was ridiculously small ; and as he never deemed it wise to add anything to it, I took good care not to put any other of my works into his hands, but entrusted them to publishers who knew how to treat me more generously. After the volume had been on sale for more than thirty years, the copyright was offered to me for considerably more than I had originally received for it ! Neither my publishers nor I myself thought it was worth while to buy it back under the circumstances, so it passed into the possession of my good friends, Messrs. Hodder and Stoughton.

(The book was issued in the United States soon after it was published in England, and it had a large sale there. In a letter to Mr. Spurgeon, dated " New York, Sept. 17, 1857," Messrs. Sheldon, Blakeman, & Co., who for many years republished his works on mutually advantageous terms, wrote :—" Messrs. Virtue and Son sold to D. Appleton & Co. the advance sheets of *The Saint and his Saviour*, and they have sold them to us. We have the book stereotyped as far as we have received the sheets ; we expect the rest from London by next steamer; and shall then immediately issue the book. We are delighted with it, and think it will take well with our people.")

My own experiences in the production of the work are faithfully described in the Preface :—

" Never was a book written amid more incessant toil. Only the fragments of time could be allotted to it, and intense mental and bodily exertions have often rendered me incapable of turning even those fragments to advantage. Writing is, to me, the work of a slave. It is a delight, a joy, a rapture, to talk out my thoughts in words that flash upon the mind at the instant when they are required ; but it is poor drudgery to sit still, and groan for thoughts and words without succeeding in obtaining them. Well may a man's books be called his ' works ', for, if every mind were constituted as mine is, it would be work indeed to produce a quarto volume. Nothing but a sense of duty has impelled me to finish this little book, which has been more than two years on hand. Yet have I, at times, so enjoyed the meditation which my writing has induced, that I would not discontinue the labour were it ten times more irksome ; and, moreover, I have some hopes that it may yet be a pleasure to me to serve God with the pen as well as the lip."

Those who are familiar with my literary career know how abundantly those "hopes" have been realized ; yet, at the time, my faithful friend, Dr. John Campbell, doubtless expressed what many beside himself felt when he wrote :—" Such hopes are innocent, and, should they never be realized, the disappointment will not be viewed as a calamity. We think it will be wise in Mr. Spurgeon, however, to moderate his expectations in this quarter. The number of those who, either in past or present times, have attained to eminence both with tongue and pen, is small. The Greeks produced none, and the Romans only one ; and Great Britain has hardly been more successful. Charles Fox, not satisfied with peerless eminence in the House of Commons, aspired to honour in the field of history. Thomas Erskine, without an equal at the Bar, also thirsted for literary renown. Each made the attempt, and gave to the world a fragment, presenting not the slightest impress of their towering genius as orators, and otherwise adding nothing to their fame. These illustrious men, however, were perfectly capable, had they foresworn eloquence, and given themselves to letters, in early life, to have taken a foremost place in the ranks of literature ; and so is Mr. Spurgeon ; but they were early ensnared by their rhetorical successes ; and so is he. By incessant speaking, they developed to the full, and cultivated to the highest extent, oral eloquence ; and so has he. After this, they could not endure the drudgery necessary to cultivate the habit of composition till it became a pleasure and a luxury ; and neither can he. Their indisposition to use the pen increased with time, and so will his ; and to such a length did their self-created incapacity grow on them, that they became almost incapable of correspondence ; and so will he. We believe he is well-nigh so now !

"If we might use the liberty, we would say, it is Mr. Spurgeon's wisdom to know his place, and be satisfied to occupy it. Let him rejoice in his glorious mission, and continue to fulfil, as he now does, its exalted obligations. It is surely enough to satisfy all the ambition for which there is room in the bosom of a Christian man, to remain supreme in the realm of sacred eloquence,—an instrument, beyond all others, intended to promote the salvation of sinners. . . . The volume throughout bears the stamp of a rhetorical genius, and indicates a practised speaker rather than writer, and breathes a most intense concern for the souls of men. This is everywhere the prominent idea, to the utter exclusion of everything that savours of display. We dismiss the work with the most cordial wish for its success in furtherance of the great object with which it was prepared, and doubt not that, however tame and gentle as compared with the powerful stream of life and fire which pervades the sermons, it will, in its own way, amply contribute to the same grand result,—the turning of men from darkness to light, and from the power of Satan unto God."

In the long interval which necessarily elapsed between my undertaking to write *The Saint and his Saviour* and the date of the publication of the volume, I had become so attached to my friends, Mr. Joseph Passmore and Mr. James Alabaster, that I had no wish to have any other publishers as long as I lived. Our relationship has been one of the closest intimacy, and I think they would join with me in saying that

it has been of mutual benefit; and our business arrangements have been such as Christian men would desire to make so that in all things God might be glorified. The young partners began in a very humble fashion in Wilson Street, Finsbury, and they were afterwards able to tell a wonderful story of how the Lord prospered and blessed them there. The very speedy and unprecedented success of the publications made it difficult at times to cope with the extraordinary rush of orders; but, by

setting themselves manfully to the task, and using all the help available, they were able to lay a solid foundation for the future well-being of the firm, which afterwards migrated to Little Britain, and then to Fann Street, Aldersgate Street. (See illustration on page 174.) I have often asked Mr. Passmore the question whether I write for him, or he prints for me;—whether he is my employer, or I am his. He says that I am "the Governor," so perhaps that settles the point.

(The following selection from the hundreds of letters written by Mr. Spurgeon to Mr. or Mrs. Passmore, during their long and intimate association, will afford just a glimpse of the happy friendship which existed between them, and also of the business relationship which remained throughout one of unbroken harmony. This communication was so characteristic that it was deemed worthy of reproduction in *facsimile* :—

This letter was written by Mr. Spurgeon at the close of one of the many Continental tours on which Mr. Passmore had been his companion :—

" Boulogne,
" Dec. 23.

" My Dear Mrs. Passmore,

"Your noble husband is sitting before the fire on one chair, with his legs up on another, and as it seemed to be a pity to disturb His Royal Highness, I offered to write to you for him, and he accepted the offer.   I am happy to say that our mutually respected and beloved Joseph is much better, and will, I hope, arrive at Park Lodge in first-rate condition about 7 or 8 o'clock on Friday.   The sea is in an excited condition, and I fear none of us will need an emetic when crossing to-morrow · but it will be better arranged than if we had the management of it, no doubt.

" I am very much obliged to you for lending me your worser half so kindly. He is a dear, kind, generous soul, and worth his weight in angels any day.   I hope all the young folk are quite well.   My dear wife says you are bonnie, which is vastly better than being bony.

" My kindest regards are always with you and yours.   Pray accept my love, and I daresay His Royal Highness, the King of Little Britain,* would send his also ; but he is so much engrossed in reading *The Standard*, that I have not asked about it.

"Yours ever truly,
" C. H. SPURGEON."

The two next letters need scarcely any explanation ; yet it would be interesting to know whether *all* authors write in as genial a spirit when promised " proofs " do not arrive at the appointed time, and whether *all* publishers possess such grateful acknowledgments of amounts paid to them by the writers whose works they have printed :—

" Dear Mr. Passmore,

"Have you retired from business ?   For, if not, I should be glad of proofs for the month of November of a book entitled *Morning by Morning* which, unless my memory fails me, you began to print.   I was to have had some matter on Monday ; and it is now Wednesday.   Please jog the friend who has taken your business, and tell him that you always were the very soul of punctuality, and that he must imitate you.

---

* Where the printing-offices were situated at that time.

"I send a piece for October 31, for I can't find any proof for that date.   Please let the gentleman who has taken your business have it soon.

"Yours ever truly,
"C. H. SPURGEON."

"P.S.—Has Mr. Alabaster retired, too?   I congratulate you both, and hope the new firm will do as well.   What is the name?   I'll make a guess,—MESSRS. QUICK AND SPEEDY."

"My Dear Mr. Passmore,

"As you have to-day paid to me the largest amount I have ever received from your firm at one time, I seize the opportunity of saying, what I am sure you know already, that I am most sincerely thankful to God for putting me into your hands in my publishing matters.   My connection with you has been one of unmingled satisfaction and pleasure.   Your liberality has been as great as it has been spontaneous.   Had I derived no personal benefit, it would have delighted me to see *you* prosper, for my interest in you is as deep as if you were my own brother, as indeed in the best sense you are.   From you and your partner, I have received nothing but kindness, courtesy, and generosity.   My share of profits has always exceeded my expectations, and the way it has been given has been even more valuable than the money itself.   God bless you both in your business and your families !   May your health be recruited, and as long as we live, may we be on as near and dear terms as we ever have been !   I am afraid I sometimes tease you when I grumble in my peculiar way; but I never intend anything but to let you know where a screw may be loose with your workmen, and not because I really have anything to complain of.   Your growing welfare lies very near my heart, and nothing gives me more pleasure than to see you advance in prosperity.

"I need not add my Christian love to you as my friend and deacon.

"Yours ever truly,
"C. H. SPURGEON."

Although the following letter is of much later date than the preceding ones, it is inserted here to show that Mr. Spurgeon had as much consideration for the welfare of a little messenger-boy as he had for the principals of the firm :—

"Westwood,
"Beulah Hill,
"Upper Norwood,
"March 11th, 1891.

"Dear Mr. Passmore,

"When that good little lad came here on Monday with the sermon, late at night, it was needful. But please blow somebody up for sending the poor little creature here, late to-night, in all this snow, with a parcel much heavier than he ought to carry. He could not get home till eleven, I fear; and I feel like a cruel brute in being the innocent cause of having a poor lad out at such an hour on such a night. There was no need at all for it. Do kick somebody for me, so that it may not happen again.

"Yours ever heartily,

"C. H. SPURGEON."

During his later years, Mr. Spurgeon inserted in *The Sword and the Trowel* portraits and sketches of his deacons and friends whom he afterwards intended to include in his *Autobiography.* This chapter may, therefore, be appropriately closed with the paragraph relating to Mr. Passmore which was published in the Magazine for April, 1891,—almost the last number that Mr. Spurgeon personally edited :—

" Fifty-eight years ago, Joseph Passmore was the first boy to be enrolled in the Sunday-school of the new chapel in New Park Street. He was a nephew of Dr. Rippon, who was then the venerable Pastor. March 1st, 1840, he joined the church by baptism, and in the January of 1862 he was elected deacon. He and his esteemed wife have been among the most faithful members of the church all these long years, and their children have followed in their footsteps. Mr. Joseph Passmore, Junr., of 'The Row,' has long been a valued member of the church, and Mr. James Passmore is a deacon. On the first Sunday evening of our visiting London, Mr. Passmore walked home with us to our lodgings in Queen's Square, and from that day to this our friendship has been of the most intimate character. With some trembling, the weekly publication of the sermons was commenced, but it has not been intermitted these six-and-thirty years ; neither has there been a jarring note in all our fellowship through the printing-press. Mr. Passmore has usually shared our journeys and our holidays, and we trust he will yet do so for many years. His partner, Mr. Alabaster, though a member of another denomination, is a brother in the Lord, whom we highly esteem , but it is a great comfort to find in Mr. Passmore at once a deacon, publisher, and friend. Mr. Passmore has thus seen, in the pastorate of our church, Dr. Rippon, Dr. Angus, James Smith, Mr. Walters, and ourselves. He has taken his share in the building and conduct of the Tabernacle, College, Almshouses, and Orphanage ; and all in so quiet and unobtrusive a manner that he has been always more useful than prominent, more felt than heard. God grant that such helpers may long be spared to us ! "

Mr. Passmore was spared to his beloved Pastor, and was one of the sincerest and deepest mourners when Mr. Spurgeon was " called home " on January 31, 1892.

In the following November, his partner and close personal friend for forty years, Mr. Alabaster, also received the summons, "Come up higher;" on August 1, 1895, the message came for Mr. Passmore; and on January 31, 1896, Mrs. Passmore rejoined the loved ones in the presence of the King.

It was Mr. Spurgeon's intention to include in his *Autobiography* illustrations of the buildings in which his works were printed and published. Accordingly, the accompanying view has been prepared.

For several years, the printing was done in the premises represented on the right-hand side of the picture; but this year—1898—the firm has erected new buildings in Whitecross Street. The publishing and sale of the works were for many years carried on at 23, and 18, Paternoster Row, and now that portion of the business has its headquarters at 4, Paternoster Buildings, which is represented on the left-hand side of the illustration.)

CHAPTER XLVIII.

Early Wedded Life.

By Mrs. C. H. Spurgeon.

Matrimony came from Paradise, and leads to it. I never was half so happy, before I was a married man, as I am now. When you are married, your bliss begins. Let the husband love his wife as he loves himself, and a little better, for she is his better half. He should feel, "If there's only one good wife in the whole world, I've got her." John Ploughman has long thought just that of his own wife ; and after thirty-five years, he is more sure of it than ever. There is not a better woman on the surface of the globe than his own, very own beloved.—*John Ploughman.*

GAIN the responsible task lies before me of interweaving my own dearest personal memories with my beloved's *Autobiography*, that the picture of his life's history may glow with the fair colours and present some of the finishing touches which are needed to render it as complete as possible. Alas, that his dear hand is powerless to furnish them ! Every line I write fills me with regret that I cannot better set forth the remembrance of his worth and goodness.

Someone wrote to me, lately, saying that it was impossible for a man's nearest friends to give a true and impartial idea of him ; they lived in too close proximity to him, their vision was interrupted by their admiration, they could not see many things that others, looking on from a remoter and broader coign of vantage, could distinctly discern. This seems to me a great mistake, except indeed in cases where "distance lends enchantment to the view ; " for who could so reasonably be supposed to understand and recognize the inner qualities and disposition of an individual's character as the one who lived in constant and familiar intercourse with him, and to whom his heart was as a clear, calm lake, reflecting Heaven's own light and beauty ? Those who knew my husband best, can testify that intimate knowledge of his character, and close companionship with him, did but more clearly reveal how very near, by God's grace, he had "come in the unity of the faith, and of the knowledge of the Son of God, unto a perfect man, unto the measure of the stature of the fulness of Christ." *Not in his own estimation*, be it well understood ;—he never spoke of himself as " having apprehended ; "—he was always "a poor sinner, and nothing at all." So pre-eminently and gloriously was " Jesus Christ his All-in-all " that his gracious, gentle, lovely life testified daily to the indwelling of the Holy Spirit in his heart, and the exceeding power of God which kept him through faith, and enabled him to "walk worthy of the vocation wherewith he was called." Robert Murray M'Cheyne used to pray :—"O God, make me as holy as a pardoned sinner can be made!" and, to judge by my husband's *life*, a similar petition must have been constantly in his heart if not on his lips.

Our brief wedding trip was spent in Paris; and, as I had made many previous visits to the fair city, beside spending some months in the Christian household of Pastor Audebez, in order to acquire the language, I felt quite at home there, and had the intense gratification of introducing my husband to all the places and sights which were worthy of arousing his interest and admiration. We had a cosy suite of rooms (by special favour) in the *entresol* of the Hôtel Meurice, and every day we explored some fresh *musée*, or church, or picture-gallery, or drove to some place of historic fame, all the charms of Paris seeming ten times more charming in my eyes than they had ever been before, because of those other loving eyes which now looked upon them with me.

The city was then in the days of her luxury and prosperity; no Communistic fires had scorched and blackened her streets, no turbulent mobs had despoiled her temples and palaces, and laid her glories in the dust; she was triumphant and radiant, and in the pride of her heart was saying, "I sit a queen, . . . and shall see no sorrow." Alas! there were days of calamity and tribulation in store for her, when war, and bloodshed, and fire, and famine ravaged her beauty, and laid waste her choice habitations. But no forecast of such terrible visitations troubled our hearts; the halo of the present illumined all the future. We went to Versailles, to Sèvres, to the Louvre, the Madeleine, the Jardin des Plantes, the Luxembourg, the Hôtel de Cluny; in fact, to every place we could find time for, where Christian people might go, and yet bring away with them a clear conscience. A peep at the Bourse interested us very much. What a scene of strife it was! What a deafening noise the men made! My husband quaintly depicted the excitement in a few words :—"The pot boiled more and more furiously as the hour of three approached, and then the brokers, like the foam on the top, ran over, and all the black contents followed by degrees!" Anyone acquainted with the place and its customs will recognize the accuracy and humour of this graphic description.

Naturally, the interiors of the churches attracted much of our attention; we always found something to admire, though, alas! there was also much to deplore. When we visited the Cathedral of Notre Dame, I was able to interest my companion by telling him that I had seen it in full gala dress on the occasion of the marriage of the Emperor Napoleon III. to his charming Empress Eugenie, and how glittering and gorgeous it then looked, with its abundant draperies of imperial purple velvet,

embroidered all over with golden bees! All the wealth and riches of the great
sanctuary were then pressed into service, and the result was magnificent. Without
such adornments, the church has a simple and solemn grandeur of its own, very
soothing to the mind; and, at the time of which I am writing, its sanctity was
enhanced—in the opinion of its Roman Catholic worshippers,— by its possession of
such sacred relics as part of the true cross, and the crown of thorns! These were
shown to visitors on payment of an extra fee, as was also an amazing number of
splendid vestments encrusted with gold and jewels, and worth a prince's ransom. I
believe that, at the time of the Commune, much of this treasure was carried away, or
ruthlessly destroyed.

EXTERIOR OF LA SAINTE CHAPELLE, PARIS.

The beauty of the Sainte Chapelle specially delighted us, and we went there
more than once. "It is a little heaven of stained glass," was my beloved's verdict;

and, truly, its loveliness looked almost celestial, as we stood enwrapped in its radiance, the light of the sinking sun glorifying its matchless windows into a very dream of dazzling grace and harmony of colour.

INTERIOR OF LA SAINTE CHAPELLE, PARIS.

Then there were St. Roch, St. Sulpice, Ste. Clotilde, and hosts of other churches, not forgetting St. Etienne du Mont, a grand edifice, containing the sumptuous shrine of Ste. Geneviève,—in its way, a perfect gem ;—nor St. Germain l'Auxerrois, with its ancient rose windows, and its pathetic memories of the betrayed Huguenots.

The Panthéon, too, once a temple, now a church, received a share of our interested attention. So far as I can remember, the building itself was almost empty, except for some statues ranged around it ; but we descended to the crypt, which contains the tombs of Rousseau, Voltaire, and other notable or notorious men, and we listened, with something like fear, to the thunderous echo which lurks there, and attracts visitors to these subterranean vaults. It is very loud and terrible, like a cannon fired off, and it gives one quite an uncanny feeling to hear such a deafening roar down in the bowels of the earth. After this experience, we were very glad to get into the fresh air again.

Of course, we went to St. Cloud (now, alas! in ruins). There is—or was—a lonely, lovely walk through the Park to the summit of an eminence crowned by the lantern of Diogenes. From there, the view was glorious. The Seine flowed far

CHURCH OF ST. GERMAIN L'AUXERROIS, PARIS.

(Where the tocsin was rung for the massacre of the Huguenots.)

below, the suburbs of the city lay beyond; Mont Valérien on the right, Paris straight before one's eyes, with the gilded dome of the Invalides shining in the clear air; St. Sulpice, and the Panthéon, and countless spires and towers forming landmarks in the great sea of houses and streets, the twin heights of Montmartre and Père la Chaise in the background; all these grouped together, and viewed from the hill, formed an indescribably charming picture.

I tried to be a good cicerone, and I think I fairly succeeded, for my companion was greatly delighted, and, in after years, in his frequent visits to the French capital with friends and fellow-voyagers, he took upon himself the *rôle* of conductor, with the happiest and most satisfactory results. He was never at a loss where to go, or how to spend the time in the most pleasant and profitable manner. A little note, written from Paris, twenty years after our wedding trip, contains the following sentences :— " My heart flies to you, as I remember my first visit to this city under your dear guidance. I love you now as then, only multiplied many times."

Ah ! " tender grace of a day that is dead," thy joy is not lessened by distance, nor lost by separation ; rather is it stored both in Heaven and in my heart's deepest chambers, and some day, when that casket is broken, it will " come back to me," not here, but in that happy land where the days die not, where " the touch of a vanished hand " shall be felt again, and " the sound of a voice that is still " shall again make music in my ravished ears !

'Twas a brief, bright season, this wedding trip of ours, lasting about ten days, for my husband could not leave his sacred work for a longer time, and we were both eager to return that we might discover the delights of having a home of our own, and enjoy the new sensation of feeling ourselves master and mistress of all we surveyed ! What a pure unsullied joy was that home-coming ! How we thanked and praised the Lord for His exceeding goodness to us in bringing us there, and how earnestly and tenderly my husband prayed that God's blessing might rest upon us then and evermore ! How we admired everything in the house, and thought there never was quite such a delightful home before, will be best understood by those who have lived in Love-land, and are well acquainted with the felicity of setting up house-keeping there. On the table, in the little sitting-room, lay a small parcel, which, when opened, proved to be a dainty card-case as a wedding present from Mr. W. Poole Balfern, accompanied by the following lines, which I have transcribed and recorded here since they were truly our first " Welcome Home," and, in a sense, prophetic of our future lives :—

" A NUPTIAL WISH.

" Dear friends, I scarce know what to say
  On this important nuptial day.
  I wish you joy ; and while you live,
  Such gifts as only God can give.
  Whether life be short or long,
  Dark with grief, or bright with song,
  Whether sorrowful or glad,
  Whether prosperous or sad,
  Oh, that you, through Christ, may be
  Heirs of immortality ;—

> Heirs of righteousness and peace,
> Heirs of life that ne'er shall cease,
> Heirs of glories yet to come,
> Heirs of the Eternal Home !
> In the valley, on the height,
> In the darkness, in the light ;
> Still possessed of living grace,
> Pressing on with eager pace ;
> Ever keeping Christ in view,
> Meek and humble, just and true ;
> Helpers of each other's faith,
> One in Him, in life and death ;
> By His Spirit taught and led,
> By His grace and mercy fed,
> Blessed and guarded by His love,
> Till with Him you meet above."

I think the circumstances under which my beloved and Mr. Balfern met, are also worthy of a passing notice One Saturday, the time for sermon-preparation had arrived, and the dear preacher had shut himself up in his study, when a ministerial visitor was announced.   He would not give his name, but said, " Tell Mr. Spurgeon that a servant of the Lord wishes to see him." To this my husband replied, " Tell the gentleman that I am so busy with his Master, that I cannot attend to the servant." Then word was sent that W. Poole Balfern was the visitor, and no sooner did Mr. Spurgeon hear the name, than he ran out to him, clasped his hand in both his own, and exclaimed, " W. Poole Balfern ! The man who wrote *Glimpses of Jesus !* Come in, thou blessed of the Lord ! " Describing that interview, long afterwards, Mr. Balfern said, " I learned then that the secret of Mr. Spurgeon's success was, that he was *cradled in the Holy Ghost.*" It was a very remarkable expression, which I do not remember to have met with anywhere else ; but it was as true as it was striking.

So many memories cling about our first home, and so many notable events of early married life transpired within its walls, that I must ask my readers kindly to refer to the view given in Vol. I., page 5, that they may the more readily understand the description which follows. On the ground floor, the single window—now almost hidden by a tree, planted since the days of which I write,—marks the little front parlour or "living-room", in old-fashioned parlance, where the greater part of the home-life was spent; above this, and boasting two windows, was a very fair-sized room, the best in the house, and, therefore, devoted to the best of uses,—the master's study; and the two windows immediately over this belonged to a bed-chamber of the same size, where afterwards our twin-boys first saw the light of day. It may not be out of place to say here that, in all the houses we have lived in,- four

THE LIBRARY AT "WESTWOOD."

in all,—we never encumbered ourselves with what a modern writer calls, "the draw-back of a drawing-room;" perhaps for the good reason that we were such homely, busy people that we had no need of so useless a place;—but more especially, I think, because the "best room" was always felt to belong by right to the one who "laboured much in the Lord."

Never have I regretted this early decision; it is a wise arrangement for a minister's house, if not for any other. When we first came to "Westwood," where there is a fine room for society purposes, there was much merry discussion as to how it should be furnished. Already, the large billiard-room was converted into a study, and filled with books from the floor to the arch of the ceiling; but more space was needed for my husband's precious volumes, and his heart was set on seeing the grand room turned into an equally grand library. I proposed, with great glee, that we should go on the "Boffin's Bower" plan ;—" She keeps up her part of the room in her way ; I keeps up my part of the room in mine ;" and with shouts of laughter we would amuse ourselves by imagining the big room fitted up for half its length as "my lady's parlour," the other half being devoted to literary pursuits, and so arranged that "Silas Wegg" could come and "drop into poetry" whenever it so pleased him ! In time, the question settled itself. It was quite twelve months before the huge bookshelves, which were to line the room, were completed, and put in place, and then, it looked so fine a *library*, that none could doubt its right or claim to this honourable appellation. But this is a digression.

We began housekeeping on a very modest scale, and even then had to practise rigid economy in all things, for my dear husband earnestly longed to help young men to preach the gospel, and from our slender resources we had to contribute somewhat largely to the support and education of Mr. T. W. Medhurst, who was the first to receive training for the work. From so small a beginning sprang the present Pastors' College, with its splendid record of service both done and doing, of which fuller account will be given in future chapters. I rejoice to remember how I shared my beloved's joy when he founded the Institution, and that, together, we planned and pinched in order to carry out the purpose of his loving heart ; it gave me quite a motherly interest in the College, and "our own men." The chief difficulty, with regard to money matters in those days, was to "make both ends meet ;" we never had enough left over to "tie a bow and ends ;" but I can see now that this was God's way of preparing us to sympathize with and help poor pastors in the years which were to come.

One of these good men, when recounting to me the griefs of his poverty, once said, " You can scarcely understand, for you have never been in the same position ;" but my thoughts flew back to this early time, and I could truly say, " I may not have been in such depths of need as seem now likely to swallow you up ; but I well remember when we lived on the 'do without' system, and only 'God's providence was our inheritance,' and when He often stretched forth His hand, and wrought signal deliverances for us, when our means were sorely straitened, and the coffers of both College and household were well-nigh empty." I recall a special time of need, supplied by great and unexpected mercy. Some demand came in for payment,—I think it must have been a tax or rate, for I never had bills owing to tradesmen,—and we had nothing wherewith to meet it. What a distressing condition of excitement seized us! " Wifey," said my beloved, " what can we do? I must give up hiring the horse, and walk to New Park Street every time I preach!" " Impossible," I replied, " with so many services, you simply could not do it." Long and anxiously we pondered over ways and means, and laid our burden before the Lord, entreating Him to come to our aid. And, of course, He heard and answered, for He is a faithful God. That night, or the next day, I am not sure which, a letter was received, containing £20 for our own use, and we never knew who sent it, save that it came in answer to prayer! This was our first united and personal home experience of special necessity provided for by our Heavenly Father, and our hearts felt a very solemn awe and gladness as we realized that He knew what things we had need of before we asked Him. As the years rolled by, such eventful passages in our history were graciously multiplied, and even excelled ; but perhaps this first blessed deliverance was the foundation stone of my husband's strong and mighty faith, for I do not remember ever afterwards seeing him painfully anxious concerning supplies for any of his great works ; he depended wholly on the Lord, his trust was perfect, and he lacked nothing.

CHAPTER XLIX.

Early Wedded Life *(Continued).*

Sometimes we have seen a model marriage, founded on pure love, and cemented in mutual esteem. Therein, the husband acts as a tender head; and the wife, as a true spouse, realizes the model marriage-relation, and sets forth what our oneness with the Lord ought to be. She delights in her husband, in his person, his character, his affection; to her, he is not only the chief and foremost of mankind, but in her eyes he is all-in-all; her heart's love belongs to him, and to him only. She finds sweetest content and solace in his company, his fellowship, his fondness; he is her little world, her Paradise, her choice treasure. At any time, she would gladly lay aside her own pleasure to find it doubled in gratifying him. She is glad to sink her individuality in his. She seeks no renown for herself; his honour is reflected upon her, and she rejoices in it. She would defend his name with her dying breath; safe enough is he where she can speak for him. The domestic circle is her kingdom; that she may there create happiness and comfort, is her life-work; and his smiling gratitude is all the reward she seeks. Even in her dress, she thinks of him; without constraint she consults his taste, and considers nothing beautiful which is distasteful to him. A tear from his eye, because of any unkindness on her part, would grievously torment her. She asks not how her behaviour may please a stranger, or how another's judgment may approve her conduct; let her beloved be content, and she is glad. He has many objects in life, some of which she does not quite understand; but she believes in them all, and anything that she can do to promote them, she delights to perform. He lavishes love on her, and, in return, she lavishes love on him. Their object in life is common. There are points where their affections so intimately unite that none could tell which is first and which is second. To watch their children growing up in health and strength, to see them holding posts of usefulness and honour, is their mutual concern; in this and other matters, they are fully one. Their wishes blend, their hearts are indivisible. By degrees, they come to think very much the same thoughts. Intimate association creates conformity; I have known this to become so complete that, at the same moment, the same utterance has leaped to both their lips.

Happy woman and happy man! If Heaven be found on earth, they have it! At last, the two are so blended, so engrafted on one stem, that their old age presents a lovely attachment, a common sympathy, by which its infirmities are greatly alleviated, and its burdens are transformed into fresh bonds of love. So happy a union of will, sentiment, thought, and heart exists between them, that the two streams of their life have washed away the dividing bank, and run on as one broad current of united existence till their common joy falls into the ocean of eternal felicity.—C. H. S.

HERE are one or two little pictures which memory has retained of events in that little front parlour whose window looks into the road. I will try to reproduce them, though the colours are somewhat faded, and the backgrounds blurred with age.

It is the Sabbath, and the day's work is done. The dear preacher has had a light repast, and now rests in his easy chair by a bright fire, while, on a low cushion at his feet, sits his wife, eager to minister in some way to her beloved's comfort. "Shall I read to you to-night, dear?" she says; for the excitement and labour of the Sabbath services sorely try him, and his mind needs some calm and soothing influence to set it at rest. "Will you have a page or two of good George Herbert?" "Yes, that will be very refreshing, wifey; I shall like that." So the book is procured, and he chooses a portion which I read slowly and with many pauses, that he may interpret to me the sweet mysteries hidden within the gracious words. Perhaps his enjoyment of the book is all the greater that he has thus to explain and open out to me the precious truths enwrapped in Herbert's quaint verse;—anyhow, the time is delightfully spent. I read on and on for an hour or more, till the peace of Heaven flows into our souls, and the tired servant of the King of kings loses his sense of fatigue, and rejoices after his toil.

Another Sabbath night, and the scene is somewhat changed in character. The dear Pastor is not only weary, but sorely depressed in spirit. "Oh, darling!" he says, "I fear I have not been as faithful in my preaching to-day as I should have been; I have not been as much in earnest after poor souls as God would have me be. O Lord, pardon Thy servant!" "Go, dear," he continues, "to the study, and fetch down Baxter's *Reformed Pastor*, and read some of it to me; perhaps that will quicken my sluggish heart." So I bring the book, and with deep sighs he turns the pages till he finds some such passage as the following:—"Oh, what a charge have we undertaken! And shall we be unfaithful? Have we the stewardship of God's own family, and shall we neglect it? Have we the conduct of those saints who must live for ever with God in glory, and shall we be unconcerned for them? God forbid! I beseech you, brethren, let this thought awaken the negligent! You that draw back from painful, displeasing, suffering duties, and will put off men's souls with ineffectual formalities; do you think this is an honourable usage of Christ's Spouse? Are the souls of men thought meet by God to see His face, and live for ever in His glory, and are they not worthy of your utmost cost and labour? Do you think so basely of the Church of God, as if it deserved not the best of your care and help? Were you the keepers of sheep or swine, you might better let them go, and say, 'They be not worth the looking after;' and yet you would scarcely do so, if they were your own. But dare you say so by the souls of men?"

I read page after page of such solemn pleadings, interrupted now and again by his stifled heart-sobs, till my voice fails from emotion and sympathy, my eyes grow dim, and my tears mingle with his as we weep together,—he, from the smitings of a very tender conscience towards God, and I, simply and only because I love him, and want to share his grief. Not for a moment do I believe there is any real cause for his self-upbraidings; but as that is a matter between himself and his God, I can only comfort him by my quiet sympathy. "The burden of the Lord" is upon his heart, and He lets him feel the awful weight of it for a time, that "the excellency of the power may be of God," and not of man. "Who teacheth like Him?"

In the same small room occurred also a touching little scene which I have described in *Ten Years After!* but which cannot be left out of this history, for it has a right to a place here, revealing, as it does, the tenderness of my beloved's heart, while he still consistently put "first things first." He was constantly away from home fulfilling preaching engagements of long or short duration, and these frequent absences were a trial to me, though I kept faithfully to my purpose of never hindering him in his work. But I remember how, while waiting for his return, late at night, from some distant place, I would tire of the cramped space of the tiny parlour, and pace up and down the narrow passage,—dignified by the name of a "hall,"—watching and listening for the dear footstep I knew so well, and praying,— oh, how fervently!—that the Lord would care for his precious life, and avert all danger from him as he travelled back by road or rail. I can even now recall the thrill of joy and thankfulness with which I opened the door, and welcomed him home.

One morning, after breakfast, when he was preparing to go out on one of his long journeys, the room looked so bright and cosy that a sudden depression seized me at the thought of its emptiness when he was gone, and the many anxious hours that must pass before I should see him again. Some tears would trickle down my cheeks, in spite of my efforts to restrain them. Seeing me look so sad, he said, very gently, "Wifey, do you think that, when any of the children of Israel brought a lamb to the Lord's altar as an offering to Him, they stood and wept over it when they had seen it laid there?" "Why, no!" I replied, startled by his strange question, "certainly not ; the Lord would not have been pleased with an offering reluctantly given." "Well," said he, tenderly, "don't you see, you are giving me to God, in letting me go to preach the gospel to poor sinners, and do you think He likes to see you cry over your sacrifice?" Could ever a rebuke have been more sweetly and graciously given? It sank deep into my heart, carrying comfort with it ; and, thenceforward, when I parted with him, the tears were scarcely ever allowed to show themselves, or if a stray one or two dared to run over the boundaries, he would say, "What! crying over your lamb, wifey!" and this reminder would quickly dry them up, and bring a smile in their place.

Ah, sweetheart ! was there ever one like thee ? These were the days of early married life, it is true, when love was young, and temper tranquil, and forbearance an easy task ; but "the wife of thy youth" can testify that, with thee, these lovely things of good report strengthened rather than diminished as time went on, and that, during all the forty years she knew and loved thee, thou wert the most tender, gracious, and indulgent of husbands, ruling with perfect love and gentleness, maintaining the Divinely-ordained position of "the head of the wife, even as Christ is the Head of the Church," yet permitting her heart and hand to influence and share in every good word and work.

And now that I am parted from thee, not for a few days only, as in that long-ago time, but "until the day break, and the shadows flee away," I think I hear again thy loving voice saying, "Don't cry over your lamb, wifey," as I try to give thee up ungrudgingly to God,—not without tears,—ah, no! that is not possible, but with that full surrender of the heart which makes the sacrifice acceptable in His sight.

An extraordinary incident occurred in this early period of our history. One Saturday evening, my dear husband was deeply perplexed by the difficulties presented by a text on which he desired to preach the next morning. It was in Psalm cx. 3: "Thy people shall be willing in the day of Thy power, in the beauties of holiness from the womb of the morning: Thou hast the dew of Thy youth;" and, with his usual painstaking preparation, he consulted all the Commentaries he then possessed, seeking light from the Holy Spirit upon their words and his own thoughts; but, as it seemed, in vain. I was as much distressed as he was, but I could not help him in such an emergency. At least, I thought I could not; but the Lord had a great favour in store for me, and used me to deliver His servant out of his serious embarrassment. He sat up very late, and was utterly worn out and dispirited, for all his efforts to get at the heart of the text were unavailing. I advised him to retire to rest, and soothed him by suggesting that, if he would try to sleep then, he would probably in the morning feel quite refreshed, and able to study to better purpose. "If I go to sleep now, wifey, will you wake me very early, so that I may have plenty of time to prepare?" With my loving assurance that I would watch the time for him, and call him soon enough, he was satisfied; and, like a trusting, tired child, he laid his head upon the pillow, and slept soundly and sweetly at once.

By-and-by, a wonderful thing happened. During the first dawning hours of the Sabbath, I heard him talking in his sleep, and roused myself to listen attentively. Soon, I realized that he was going over the subject of the verse which had been so obscure to him, and was giving a clear and distinct exposition of its meaning, with much force and freshness. I set myself, with almost trembling joy, to understand and follow all that he was saying, for I knew that, if I could but seize and remember the salient points of the discourse, he would have no difficulty in developing and enlarging upon them. Never preacher had a more eager and anxious hearer! What if I should let the precious words slip? I had no means at hand of "taking notes," so, like Nehemiah, "I prayed to the God of Heaven," and asked that I might receive and retain the thoughts which He had given to His servant in his sleep, and which were so singularly entrusted to my keeping. As I lay, repeating over and over again the chief points I wished to remember, my happiness was very great in anticipation of his surprise and delight on awaking; but I had kept vigil so long, cherishing my joy, that I must have been overcome with slumber just when the usual time for rising came, for he awoke with a frightened start, and seeing the tell-tale clock, said, " Oh, wifey, you said you would wake me very early, and now see the time! Oh, why did you let me sleep? What shall I do? What shall I do?" " Listen, beloved," I answered; and I told him all I had heard. "Why! that's just what I wanted," he exclaimed; "that is the true explanation of the whole verse! And you say I preached it in my sleep?" " It is wonderful," he repeated again and again, and we both praised the Lord for so remarkable a manifestation of His power and love. Joyfully my dear one went down to his study, and prepared this God-given sermon, and it was delivered that same morning, April 13, 1856, at New Park Street Chapel. It can be found and read in Vol. II. of the sermons (No. 74), and its opening paragraph gives the dear preacher's own account of the difficulty he experienced in dealing with the text. Naturally, he refrained from telling the congregation the special details which I have here recorded; but, many years after, he told the tale to his students at one of their ever-to-be-remembered Friday afternoon gatherings, and some of them still keep it fresh in their memories.

About this time, I recall a visit to Stambourne which I paid with my dear husband. I saw, and loved at first sight, the dear old grandfather, so proud of "the child" who had grown into a great and gracious preacher. How kindly he received his grandson's wife! With what tender, old-fashioned courtesy he cared for her! Everything about the place was then exactly as my beloved has described it in the first volume of this work; nothing had been altered. The old Manse was still standing, though not as upright as in its youth; the ivy grew inside the parlour, the old flowered chintz curtains still hung in their places, and the floor of the best bed-chamber where we slept was as "anxious to go out of the window" as ever; indeed, a watchful balancing of one's self was required to avoid a stumble or a fall. It was all very quaint, but very delightful, because of so many precious memories to him who had lived there. The occasion of our visit was the anniversary, either of the meeting-house, or the revered Pastor's ministry, and the house was crowded with visitors, and unremitting hospitality seemed the order of the day. How delighted and interested the home folks and neighbours all were, and how much loving fuss was made over the young Pastor and his wife! It was charming to see him in the midst of his own people. He was just " the child" again, the joy of the old man's heart; but when he preached, and the power of God's Spirit burned in his words, and he fed the people to the full, the grandfather's bliss must have been a foretaste of the joys of Heaven.

For my part, I had a considerable share of petting and kind attention, and but one black drop in my cup of pleasure. This I mean literally; I was enjoying a large cup of tea, and thinking how good and refreshing it was on a hot day, when, as the bottom of the cup was becoming visible, I saw, to my horror, a great spider,—my special detestation,—dead, of course, his black body swollen to a huge size, and his long legs describing a wheel-like circle in the remaining fluid. And I had been drinking the boiled juice of this monster! Oh, the disgust of it! Alas! that we can remember the evil, and let go the good! My beloved's *sermon* is forgotten; but the spider has the power to make me feel "creepy" even at this moment!

I make a passing reference to the birth of our twin-boys, in order to contradict emphatically a story, supposed to be very witty, which was circulated extensively, and believed in universally, not only at the time it was told, but through all the following years. It was said that my dear husband received the news of the addition to his household while he was preaching, and that he immediately communicated the fact to his congregation, adding in a serio-comic way,—

"Not more than others I deserve,
But God has given me more."

I am sorry to say there are persons, still living, who declare that they were present at the service, and heard him say it!

Now the truth is, that the boys were born on *Saturday* morning, September 20, 1856, and my dear husband never left the house that day; nor, so far as I know, did he ever preach on the seventh day at any time, so the statement at once falls to the ground disproved. But I think I have discovered how the legend was manufactured. Looking through the sermons preached near to this date, I find that, on Thursday evening, September 25,—five days after the event referred to,—Mr. Spurgeon delivered a discourse on behalf of the Aged Pilgrims' Friend Society, and in the course of it made the following remarks :—"When we take our walks abroad, and see the poor, he must be a very thankless Christian who does not lift up his eyes to Heaven, and praise his God thus,—

"'Not more than others I deserve,
But God has given me more.

'If we were all made rich alike, if God had given us all abundance, we should never know the value of His mercies; but He puts the poor side by side with us, to make their trials, like a dark shadow, set forth the brightness which He is pleased to give to others in temporal matters."

I have no doubt that some facetious individual, present at this Thursday evening service, and being aware of the babies' advent, on hearing these lines repeated, pounced upon them as the nucleus of an attractive story, linked the two facts in his own mind, and then proclaimed them to the world as an undivided verity! Most of the stories told of my dear husband's jocoseness *in the pulpit* were "stories" in the severe sense of the word; or possessed just so small a modicum of truth internally that the narrators were able, by weaving a network of exaggeration and romance around them, to make a very presentable and alluring fiction. It was one of the penalties of his unique position and gifts that, all through his life, he had to bear the cross of cruel misrepresentation and injustice. Thank God, that is all left behind for ever!

Though I am quite certain that the lines in question were not quoted by my beloved in public in reference to the double blessing God gave to us, I should scarcely be surprised if he made use of them when speaking to friends in private. If his heart were full of joy and gratitude, it would be sure to bubble over in some child-like and natural fashion. I have quite recently received a letter from a lady in the country, telling me of her visit to an old man,—an ex-policeman, named Coleman,—who, though bedridden, never tires of relating his memories of Mr. Spurgeon in those early days. He was stationed at New Park Street Chapel, on special duty, when the crowds came to hear "the boy-preacher," and he delights to tell how, after a short while, the street became so blocked that the chapel-gates had to be closed, and the people admitted a hundred at a time. "Ah!" said he, "he was a dear, good young man, he did not make *himself* anything; he would shake hands with anyone, he would give me such a grip, and leave half-a-crown in my hand; he knew that we policemen had a rub to get along on our pay. I know there were many he helped with their rent. *He did look pleased, that Sunday morning, when he said, ' Coleman, what do you think? God has blessed me with two sons!'* I used to go in and sit just inside the door, and get a feast for my soul from his discourses. I shall see him again soon, I hope."

Of course, this little story lacks the piquancy and sparkle of the former one; but it has the advantage of being *true.*

There was one other notable time in the front parlour. It recurs to me, at this moment, as the first falling of that black shadow of sorrow which the Lord saw fit to cast over our young and happy lives. It was again a Sabbath evening. I lay on a couch under the window, thinking of my dear one who had gone to preach his first sermon at the Surrey Music Hall, and praying that the Lord would bless his message to the assembled thousands. It was just a month since our children were born, and I was dreaming of all sorts of lovely possibilities and pleasures, when I heard a carriage stop at the gate. It was far too early for my husband to come home, and I wondered who my unexpected visitor could be. Presently, one of the deacons was ushered into the room, and I saw at once, from his manner, that something unusual had happened. I besought him to tell me all quickly, and he did so, kindly, and with much sympathy ; and he kneeled by the couch, and prayed that we might have grace and strength to bear the terrible trial which had so suddenly come upon us. But how thankful I was when he went away ! I wanted to be alone, that I might cry to God in this hour of darkness and death ! When my beloved was brought home, he looked a wreck of his former self,—an hour's agony of mind had changed his whole appearance and bearing. The night that ensued was one of weeping, and wailing, and indescribable sorrow. He refused to be comforted. I thought the morning would never break ; and when it did come, it brought no relief.

The Lord has mercifully blotted out from my mind most of the details of the time of grief which followed, when my beloved's anguish was so deep and violent that reason seemed to totter on her throne, and we sometimes feared he would never preach again. It was truly " the valley of the shadow of death " through which we then walked ; and, like poor Christian, we here " sighed bitterly," for the pathway was so dark " that, ofttimes, when we lifted up our foot to set forward, we knew not where or upon what we should set it next ! "

It was in the garden of a house belonging to one of the deacons, in the suburbs of Croydon, whither my beloved had been taken in hope that the change and quiet would be beneficial, that the Lord was pleased to restore his mental equilibrium, and unloose the bars which had kept his spirit in darkness. We had been walking together, as usual ;—he, restless and anguished ; I, sorrowful and amazed, wondering what the end of these things would be ;—when, at the foot of the steps which gave access to the house, he stopped suddenly, and turned to me, and with the old sweet light in his eyes, (ah ! how grievous had been its absence !) he said, " Dearest, how foolish I have been ! Why ! what does it matter what becomes of me, if the Lord shall but be glorified ?"—and he repeated, with eagerness and intense emphasis, Philippians ii. 9—11 : " Wherefore God also hath highly exalted Him, and given Him a Name which is above every name ; that at the Name of Jesus every knee should bow, of things in Heaven, and things in earth, and things under the earth ; and that every tongue should confess that Jesus Christ is Lord, to the glory of God the Father." " If Christ be exalted," he said,—and his face glowed with holy fervour,—" let Him do as He pleases with me ; my one prayer shall be, that I may die to self, and live wholly for Him and for His honour. Oh, wifey, I see it all now ! Praise the Lord with me ! "

In that moment, his fetters were broken, the captive came forth from his dungeon, and rejoiced in the light of the Lord. The Sun of righteousness arose once more upon him, with healing in His wings. But he carried the scars of that conflict to his dying day, and never afterwards had he the physical vigour and strength which he possessed before passing through that fierce trial. Verily, it was a thorny path by which the Lord led him. Human love would have protected him at any cost from an ordeal so terrible, and suffering so acute ; but God's love saw the end from the beginning, and "He never makes a mistake." Though we may not, at the time, see His purpose in the afflictions which He sends us, it will be plainly revealed when the light of eternity falls upon the road along which we have journeyed.

While staying at Mr. Winsor's hospitable home, where he so kindly received and sheltered us in the time of our trouble, it was decided that the babies should be there dedicated to the Lord, and His service. So, when our dear patient seemed sufficiently recovered to take part in the observance, a goodly number of friends gathered together, and we had a happy meeting for prayer and praise. Full details I am unable to give ; the only photograph which my memory retains is that of the two little creatures being carried round the large room,—after the dedicatory prayers were offered,—to be admired, and kissed, and blessed. What choice mercies, what special favours, their dear father asked for them then, I do not remember ; but the Lord has never forgotten that prayer, and the many petitions which followed it. He not only heard, but has been answering all through the years of their lives, and with the most abounding blessing since He saw fit to make them fatherless! No ceremonial was observed, no drops of "holy water" fell on the children's brows ; but in that room, that evening, as truly as in the house, "by the farther side of Jordan," in the days gone by, our infants were brought to Christ the Lord "that He would touch them ;" and it is not now a matter of faith, so much as of sight, that "He took them up in His arms, put His hands upon them, and blessed them."

Ah, me! it is not so many years ago, since the elder of those twin-boys brought his firstborn son to "Westwood," and my beloved, in one of those tender out-pourings of the heart which were so natural to him, gave the child to God :——and, not many months afterwards,—*God answered the prayer, and took him to Himself!* One of the brightest, bonniest babies ever seen, he was the delight and expectation of our hearts ; but the gift was claimed suddenly, and the child, who was to have done, according to our ideas, so much service on earth, went to sing God's praises with the angels! I wonder, sometimes, whether the little ransomed spirit met and welcomed his warrior grandfather on the shores of the Glory-land!

CHAPTER L.

The Great Catastrophe at the Surrey Gardens Music Hall.

SURREY GARDENS MUSIC HALL,—EXTERIOR.

Here the reader must pardon the writer if he introduces a personal narrative, which is to him a most memorable proof of the lovingkindness of the Lord. Such an opportunity of recording my Lord's goodness may never again occur to me; and therefore now, while my soul is warm with gratitude for so recent a deliverance, let me lay aside the language of an author, and speak for myself, as I should tell the story to my friends in conversation. It may be egotism to weave one's own sorrows into the warp and woof of this meditation; but if the heart prompts the act, and the motions of the Holy Spirit are not contrary thereto, I think I may venture for this once to raise an Ebenezer in public, and rehearse the praise of Jesus at the setting up thereof. Egotism is not such an evil thing as ungrateful silence; certainly, it is not more contemptible than mock humility. Right or wrong, here followeth my story.

On a night which time will never erase from my memory, large numbers of my congregation were scattered, many of them wounded and some killed, by the malicious act of wicked men. Strong amid danger, I battled against the storm; nor did my spirit yield to the overwhelming pressure while my courage could reassure the wavering, or confirm the bold; but when, like a whirlwind, the destruction was overpast, when the whole of its devastation was visible to my eye, who can conceive the anguish of my sad spirit? I refused to be comforted; tears were my meat by day, and dreams my terror by night.

I felt as I had never felt before. "My thoughts were all a case of knives," cutting my heart in pieces, until a kind of stupor of grief ministered a mournful medicine to me. I could have truly said, "I am not mad, but surely I have had enough to madden me, if I should indulge in meditation on it." I sought and found a solitude which seemed congenial to me. I could tell my griefs to the flowers, and the dews could weep with me. Here my mind lay, like a wreck upon the sand, incapable of its usual motion. I was in a strange land, and a stranger in it. My Bible, once my daily food, was but a hand to lift the sluices of my woe. Prayer yielded no balm to me; in fact, my soul was like an infant's soul, and I could not rise to the dignity of supplication. "Broken in pieces all asunder," my thoughts, which had been to me a cup of delights, were like pieces of broken glass, the piercing and cutting miseries of my pilgrimage. I could adopt the words of Dr. Watts, and say,—

> "The tumult of my thoughts
> Doth but enlarge my woe;
> My spirit languishes, my heart
> Is desolate and low.
>
> "With every morning-light
> My sorrow new begins.
> Look on my anguish and my pain,
> And pardon all my sins."

Then came "the slander of many,"—barefaced fabrications, libellous insinuations, and barbarous accusations. These alone might have scooped out the last drop of consolation from my cup of happiness; but the worst had come to the worst, and the utmost malice of the enemy could do no more. Lower they cannot sink who are already in the nethermost depths. Misery itself is the guardian of the miserable. All things combined to keep me, for a season, in the darkness where neither sun nor moon appeared. I had hoped for a gradual return to peaceful consciousness, and patiently did I wait for the dawning light. But it came not as I had desired; for He who doeth for us exceeding abundantly above all that we ask or think, sent me a happier answer to my requests. I had striven to think of the unmeasurable love of Jehovah, as displayed in the sacrifice of Calvary; I had endeavoured to muse upon the glorious character of the exalted Jesus; but I found it impossible to collect my thoughts in the quiver of meditation, or, indeed, to place them anywhere but with their points in my wounded spirit, or else at my feet, trodden down in an almost childish thoughtlessness.

On a sudden, like a flash of lightning from the sky, my soul returned unto me. The burning lava of my brain cooled in an instant. The throbbings of my brow were still; the cool wind of comfort fanned my cheek, which had been scorched in the furnace. I was free, the iron fetter was broken in pieces, my prison door was open, and I leaped for joy of heart. On wings of a dove, my spirit mounted to the stars,—yea, beyond them. Whither did it wing its flight, and where did it sing its song of gratitude? It was at the feet of Jesus, whose Name had charmed its fears, and placed an end to its mourning. The Name – the precious Name of Jesus, was like Ithuriel's spear, bringing back my soul to its own right and happy state. I was a man again, and what is more, a believer. The garden in which I stood became an Eden to me, and the spot was then most solemnly consecrated in my restored consciousness. Happy hour! Thrice-blessed Lord, who thus in an instant delivered me from the rock of my despair, and slew the vulture of my grief! Before I told to others the glad news of my recovery, my heart was melodious with song, and my tongue endeavoured tardily to express the music. Then did I give to my Well-beloved a song touching my Well-beloved; and, oh! with what rapture did my soul flash forth its praises! But all – all were to the honour of Him, the First and the Last, the Brother born for adversity, the Deliverer of the captive, the Breaker of my fetters, the Restorer of my soul. Then did I cast my burden upon the Lord; I left my ashes, and arrayed myself in the garments of praise, while He anointed me with fresh oil. I could have riven the very firmament to get at Him, to cast myself at His feet, and lie there bathed in the tears of joy and love. Never since the day of my conversion had I known so much of His infinite excellence, never had my spirit leaped with such unutterable delight. Scorn, tumult, and woe seemed less than nothing for His sake. I girded up my loins to run before His chariot, I began to shout forth His glory, for my soul was absorbed in the one idea of His glorious exaltation and Divine compassion.

After a declaration of the exceeding grace of God towards me, made to my dearest kindred and friends, I essayed again to preach. The task which I had dreaded to perform was another means of comfort, and I can truly declare that the words of that morning were as much the utterance of my inner man as if I had been standing before the bar of God. The text selected was in Philippians ii. 9—11. (See *The New Park Street Pulpit*, No 101, "The Exaltation of Christ") May I trouble the reader with some of the utterances of the morning, for they were the unveilings of my own experience?

"When the mind is intensely set upon one object, however much it may, by divers calamities, be tossed to and fro, it invariably returns to the place which it had chosen to be its dwellingplace. You have noticed this in the case of David. When the battle had been won by his warriors, they returned flushed with victory. David's mind had doubtless suffered much perturbation in the meantime ; he had dreaded alike the effects of victory and of defeat ; but have you not noticed how his thoughts, in one moment, returned to the darling object of his affections? 'Is the young man Absalom safe?' said he, as if it mattered not what else had occurred if his favourite son were but secure. So, beloved, is it with the Christian. In the midst of calamities, whether they be the wreck of nations, the crash of empires, the heaving of revolutions, or the scourge of war, the great question which he asks himself, and asks of others, too, is this,—'Is Christ's Kingdom safe?' In his own personal afflictions, his chief anxiety is,— Will God be glorified, and will His honour be increased by them? 'If it be so,' says he, 'although I be but as smoking flax, yet if the sun is not dimmed, I will rejoice ; and though I be a bruised reed, if the pillars of the temple are unbroken, what matters it if I am bruised?' He finds it to be sufficient consolation, in the midst of all the breaking in pieces which he endures, to think that Christ's throne stands fast and firm, and that, though the earth hath reeled beneath *his* feet, yet Christ standeth on a rock which never can be moved. Some of these feelings, I think, have crossed our minds. Amidst much tumult, and divers rushings to and fro of troublous thoughts, our souls have returned to the dearest object of our desires, and we have found it no small consolation, after all, to say, 'It matters not what shall become of us ; God hath highly exalted *Him*, and given *Him* a Name which is above every name ; that at the Name of *Jesus* every knee should bow.'"

Thus is the thought of the love of Jesus, in His delivering grace, most indelibly impressed upon my memory ; and the fact that this experience is to me the most memorable crisis of my life, must be my apology for narrating it.—C. H. S., in "*The Saint and his Saviour*," *published in* 1857

MANY of my friends are unacquainted with the transactions of the early years of my ministry in London, for a whole generation has passed away since then, and the mass of those who are with me now know little of "the brave days of old." Hence the necessity of telling the story, that later sympathizers and fellow-labourers may learn by what a wonderful way the Lord has led us. To return to New Park Street Chapel, greatly enlarged as it was during the time of our first sojourn at Exeter Hall, resembled the attempt to put the sea into a tea-pot. We were more inconvenienced than ever. To turn many hundreds away from the doors, was the general if not the universal necessity ; and those who gained admission were but little better off, for the packing was dense in the extreme, and the heat something terrible even to remember. My enemies continued to make my name more and more widely known, by means of pamphlets, caricatures,* and letters in the papers, which all tended to swell the crowd. Matters reached a crisis in the Spring of 1856, and at a church-meeting, held on May 26 in that year, two resolutions were passed, the first intended to meet the immediately pressing need of a larger meeting-place for our great congregation, and the second looking further ahead, and providing for the requirements of the future. The official record is as follows :—

" Resolved,—That arrangements be made, as early as possible, for this church to worship at Exeter Hall on the Sabbath evenings during the Summer months.

---

* The two caricatures—" Brimstone and Treacle " and " Catch-'em-alive-O !"—have been so often reproduced that they are not included in this volume ; but others that are less known are given,—"The Slow Coach and the Fast Train " (pages 48 and 49), "The Old Conductor and the New Conductor" (pages 208 and 209), and "The Young Lion of the Day and the Funny Old Woman of the Day " (Chapter LII).

" Resolved,—That the male members of this church be called together, as speedily as possible, to consult as to the best means of providing better accommodation for the vast crowds who are anxious to hear the gospel in connection with the ministry of our Pastor."

Accordingly, services were held at New Park Street Chapel on the Sabbath mornings from June 8 to August 24, and in the evenings at Exeter Hall, but this plan was very inconvenient ; and, therefore, in August, a fund was commenced to provide for the erection of a larger house of prayer, the first meeting in aid of that object being held at the house of " Father Olney." Meanwhile, the proprietors of Exeter Hall intimated that they were unable to let that building continuously to one congregation. Although we paid for the use of it, it was but natural that others should think that the Baptists were monopolizing a hall which pertained to all denominations. I felt this to be just, and began to look about for another shelter. It was an anxious time, for friends feared that it would be long before we could build a house of our own ; but the Lord had prepared for us a place where we sojourned for three years,—the Music Hall of the Royal Surrey Gardens.

Very curious is the story of the Surrey Gardens. Everybody has heard of the elephant and other animals which were to be seen at Exeter Change, near Waterloo Bridge. Mr. Cross, the proprietor of that exhibition, removed his menagerie, in 1831, to the Surrey Gardens. There were fountains, and caves, and summer-houses, a lake of three and a half acres, pleasant walks and lawns, and all the usual paraphernalia of public gardens. In Dr. Montgomery's *History of Ken-nington*, we read :—" Perhaps the most remarkable fact, for temperance folk, is that the proprietors of the Gardens never made application for a license to sell drink. It was started and made a success without the sale of intoxicants. This is a note-worthy fact. I do not know what happened in later years ; but during the time of Mr. Cross, up to 1844, no license was ever applied for. The hours kept were early. At the latest, in the middle of Summer, the Gardens closed at 10 p.m., and in the Autumn at 7 p.m. Our Queen, when she was quite a little girl, came here with the Duchess of Kent, and was shown over the Gardens by Mr. Warwick."

When I first came to London, the Zoological Gardens were a very respectable and quiet resort ; but few persons availed themselves of them. The age which could be content with quiet amusements, free from loose associations, was passing away, and giving place to a generation which looked for more flavour in its recreation. The Gardens were kept up in part by subscription from families in the neighbourhood, and partly by displays of fireworks. The affair did not pay in that form, so a company was formed to continue the zoological collection, and add thereto the far greater attraction of the popular concerts of M. Jullien. A very fine hall was erected, which had three galleries, and would accommodate from six to ten thousand people. I cannot speak exactly as to numbers, nor correct my estimate by personal inspection, for no vestige of the hall is now remaining. I recollect going with Mr. William Olney to see the place ; and though we felt it to be a venturesome experiment to attempt to preach in so large a building, we had faith in God, and dared to hope that He would bless an earnest attempt to proclaim the gospel to the multitude. One or two of our good members thought it wrong to go to what they persisted in calling " the devil's house." I did not agree with their hard names, but encouraged them to stop away, and not to violate their consciences. At the same time, I bade them not to discourage either their brethren or me, for we were willing to go even into " the devil's house " to win souls for Christ. We did not go to the Music Hall because we thought that it was a good thing to worship in a building usually devoted to amusement, but because we had no other place to go to.

On October 6, a special church-meeting was held, for the purpose which is thus recorded in our Minutes :—" This meeting was convened to consider the propriety of engaging the use of the large hall in the Royal Surrey Gardens for our Sabbath evening worship, the directors of Exeter Hall having refused the church the further use of that place. After several of the brethren had expressed their concurrence, it was resolved that the Music Hall of the Royal Surrey Gardens be engaged for one month, commencing the third Sabbath in October."

When the appointed day arrived, our anticipations ran high, but none of us dreamed of that which lay before us. Much prayer was offered, and I looked forward hopefully, but yet felt overweighted with a sense of responsibility, and filled with a mysterious premonition of some great trial shortly to befall me. In the Preface to Vol. II. of *The Pulpit Library*, I wrote :—" The first sermon in this volume—' Prove Me now,' Malachi iii. 10,—was preached at New Park Street Chapel in the morning of that Lord's-day on which the fatal accident occurred at the Surrey Gardens Music Hall By many readers it will now be perused with curiosity, but the preacher himself reviews each sentence with thrilling emotion. Its subject was entirely suggested by the enlarged sphere of labour he was about to occupy, and the *then* unprecedented number of souls he was expecting ere nightfall to address. If any passage seems to forestall the calamity, he can only say it is genuine,—a transcript from the reporter's notes. The Christian reader can understand many sore conflicts between the heart's feelings and its faith ; yet no one *can* know, as the author's own soul, how, amidst fightings without and fears within, he was enabled to proclaim the strongest confidence in God. He has made that proof, which he counselled others to make, of the Divine faithfulness ; and as to the result (notwithstanding a parenthesis of grievous tribulation), he dares to speak with abundant gratitude."

The sermon itself contained the following almost prophetic passage :—" Perhaps I may be called to stand where the thunder-clouds brew, where the lightnings play, and tempestuous winds are howling on the mountain-top. Well, then, I am born to prove the power and majesty of our God ; amidst dangers, He will inspire me with courage ; amidst toils, He will make me strong. . . . This old Bible speaks to me to-day. This sword of the Spirit hath been thrust into many of your hearts ; and though they were hard as adamant, it has split them in sunder. I have wielded it in your midst as God's soldier ; and some of you have had sturdy spirits broken in pieces by this good old Jerusalem blade. But we shall be gathered together, to-night, where an unprecedented mass of people will assemble, perhaps from idle curiosity, to hear the Word of God ; and His voice cries in my ears, ' Prove Me now.' Many a man has come, during my ministrations, armed to his very teeth, and having on a coat of mail, yet hath this tried weapon cleft him in twain, and pierced to the dividing asunder of the joints and marrow. ' Prove Me now,' says God, ' go and prove Me before blasphemers ; go and prove Me before reprobates, before the vilest of the vile, and the filthiest of the filthy ; go and "prove Me now." Lift up that life-giving cross, and let it again be exhibited ; into the regions of *death*, go and proclaim the Word of *life ;* into the most plague-smitten parts of the city, go and carry the waving censer of the incense of a Saviour's merits, and prove now whether He is not able to stay the plague, and remove the disease.'

"But what does God say to the church? ' You have proved Me aforetime, you have attempted great things ; though some of you were faint-hearted, and said, "We should not have ventured," others of you had faith, and proved Me. I say again, " Prove Me now." ' See what God can do, *just when a cloud is falling on the head of him whom God has raised up to preach to you*, go and prove Him now ; and see if He will not pour you out such a blessing as ye had not even dreamed of, see if He will not give you a Pentecostal blessing. ' Prove Me now.' Why should we be unbelieving? Have we one thing to make us so? We are weak ; what of that? Are we not strongest in our God when we are weakest in ourselves ? We are fools, it is said, and so we are, we know it ; but He maketh fools to confound the wise. We are base, but God hath chosen the base things of the world. We are unlearned,—

" ' We know no schoolman's subtle arts,'

yet we glory in infirmity when Christ's power doth rest upon us. *Let them represent us as worse than we are ;* let them give us the most odious character that hath ever been given to man, we will bless them, and wish them well. What though the weapon be a stone, or even the jawbone of an ass, if the Lord direct it ? ' Do you not know,' say some, ' what wise men say ?' Yes, we do ; but we can read their oracles backwards. Their words are the offspring of their wishes. We know *who* has instructed them, and we know he was a liar from the beginning. O fools, and slow of heart! do ye shrink from the truth, or do ye shrink from obloquy and disgrace? In either case, ye have not the love to your Master that ye should have. If ye be brave men and true, go on and conquer. *Fear not, ye shall yet win the day;* God's holy gospel shall yet shake the earth once more. The banner is lifted up, and multitudes are flocking to it; the Pharisees have taken counsel together,—the learned stand confounded,—the sages are baffled, they know not what to do. The little one, God has made great; and He that was despised, is exalted. Let us trust Him, then. He will be with us even to the end, for He has said, 'Lo, I am with you alway, even unto the end of the world.'"

I can never forget that terrible night. Having preserved all the pamphlets and papers connected with "the great catastrophe," I have just now perused them in order to write this memorial. I have thereby revived within myself much that is painful; but much more that causes me to praise the name of the Lord. When I was nearing the house in Manor Street, which was the office of the company, and was to serve me as a private entrance, I was exceedingly surprised to find the streets thronged for a long distance. With difficulty I reached the door. There was a long private road from the entrance of the Gardens to the Music Hall itself, and this appeared to be filled up with a solid block of people, who were unable to get into the building. I felt overawed, and was taken with that faintness which was, in my youth, the usual forerunner of every sermon. Still, I rallied, and was duly escorted to my pulpit in the midst of a dense throng. Here I was to pass through the greatest ordeal of my life.

But I will now give way to Dr. Campbell, then the Editor of *The British Banner;* for his is the description of an eye-witness, and of an impartial, self-possessed critic. He wrote:—" Ecclesiastically viewed, Sunday last (October 19th) was one of the most eventful nights that have descended upon our metropolis for generations. On that occasion, the largest, most commodious, and most beautiful building erected for public amusement in this mighty city was taken possession of for the purpose of proclaiming the gospel of salvation. There, where, for a long period, wild beasts had been exhibited, and wilder men had been accustomed to congregate, in countless multitudes, for idle pastime, was gathered together the largest audience that ever met in any edifice in these isles, to listen to the voice of a Nonconformist minister. The spectacle, of its kind, was one of the most imposing, magnificent, and awful ever presented to the human eye. No adequate idea of it can be conveyed by description; to be understood, it must have been seen; and they who beheld it received an impression which no time will ever obliterate. The sight of 10,000 or 12,000 people, more or fewer, assembled to listen to the Word of the living God, in such a place, at such a time, and addressed by a man with a voice of such power and compass that the remotest might hear with ease and pleasure, was sufficient to excite intense joy in the hearts of all good men who witnessed it ; nor is it extravagant to say, that it was enough to wake the attention of the angelic world !

"But, in proportion to the joy and the hope thus inspired, were the sorrow and disappointment arising from the terrible catastrophe by which the very first service was attended and cut short! At the most solemn moment of the occasion, the wicked rose in their strength, like a whirlwind, sin entered, followed by terror, flight, disorder, and death! The entire city has been filled with astonishment! From the cellar to the palace, the events of that dreadful night have been the theme of eager discourse. In the squares, the streets, the lanes, and alleys, as well as in the workshops and counting-houses, and all the chief places of concourse, it has been, through each successive day, the one great object of thought and converse.

"Imagination, as usual, has been active in the work of exaggeration, and malice in that of mendacity. At one time, the beautiful building has been wrapped in flames, and reduced to ashes! At another, the roof has fallen in, and entombed 10,000 people! The human mind, voracious of the tragical and the marvellous, has greedily devoured even the most preposterous accounts. The more horrible, the more credible and the more welcome; and the public press, as is its wont, has not been backward to pander to the morbid appetite of the excited millions. It has lied as well as exaggerated, most fearfully! Fancy pictures have been drawn, suited to 'the chamber of horrors.' Having ourselves not only witnessed the spectacle, but been in the very vortex, we are able to speak from observation touching the various points which the public are mainly concerned to know, and every way able to distinguish between truth and error. We, therefore, feel in duty bound to clear away the bewildering mist and darkness which have gathered around the character and conduct of honourable men. We were among the very first to enter the building, where we took up a position before the pulpit, which had been erected in front of the orchestra, so that we had a perfect command of the entire house, hearing and seeing everything of importance to be either heard or seen. The simple statement of facts as they occurred will form the best antidote to the flood of misrepresentation and falsehood which has welled forth from a portion of the metropolitan press.

"The house, considering its magnitude, might be said to be very speedily filled, leaving, it is supposed, an equal number outside unable to gain admission. The process of packing the hall, as may be presumed, was gone about in a somewhat tumultuous manner. The people were deeply excited by the violent struggle which had to be encountered and overcome at the doors to obtain an entrance, which naturally led, after admission, to rapid movements in every direction where there seemed a probability of gaining a seat, or, at least, standing-room. The aspect of the hall during this period was, of course, anything but like that which obtains in places of regular worship, and somewhat fitted to do violence to the sober spirit of orderly people ; but, certainly, it would have borne a very favourable comparison with the gatherings of the huge religious anniversary meetings at Exeter Hall, or any other vast place of general concourse. It was, ' Every man for himself ; ' and, as compared with the monster meetings of Whitefield on Kennington Common or Moorfields, in the High Churchyard, Glasgow, and the Orphan House Park, Edinburgh, so far as history has testified, there was nothing to complain of on the score of tumultuous levity.

"The hall having been filled in every part, things began to assume a perfectly settled aspect. The commotion ceased, and the air of the assembly was every whit as tranquil as that of our great philanthropic or even worshipping assemblies. The hall being thus gorged, Mr. Spurgeon considerately and wisely commenced the service about ten minutes before the appointed time, surrounded by a large number of most respectable people, composed of his officers and flock, who led the psalmody. After a few words of a highly pertinent character, he briefly offered prayer, and then gave out a thoroughly Evangelical hymn, with a force, a feeling, and an unction seldom witnessed in a worshipping assembly, and which threw an air of deep solemnity over the immense multitude by whom it was sung as with the voice of many waters. That hymn itself was an important proclamation of the gospel. The reading of the Sacred Scriptures immediately followed, with a running comment, as is the preacher's custom. The Scripture was well chosen, and the exposition admirably appropriate, and such as was well fitted to impress even the most frivolous. There was no dry disquisition, no curious criticism ; but an address directed to the hearts of the hearers, showing, from the first, that the speaker came strongly intent upon most important business, and that nothing was to be regarded short of its accomplishment.

"The general prayer next followed ; and here, too, the same pertinent and peculiar air was manifested. The one great motive which animated the preacher was, most obviously, the salvation of men. . . . This was the moment chosen by the emissaries of darkness to spring the mine of mischief, which, in effect, resulted in manifold murder ! To have made the attempt while the high praises of God were being sung, would have been certain failure. To have done so while a stream of eloquence was rolling on in the sermon, and all eyes open, would have been attended with no better success. Yes ; and the inhuman miscreants—cunning as they were impious and cruel,—knew it. They were obviously adepts in iniquity. They understood their business thoroughly. Their plans were skilfully formed, and executed with the precision of military science opening a masked battery. Just as the minds of the devout portion of the assembly were collected around the throne of the Great

Eternal, far away from earth and its grovellings, abstracted, absorbed, prostrate, suppliant, and adoring, the fiendish conspiracy broke forth with the rapidity of lightning and the fury of a tempest! The effect was such as was anticipated and desired. To say it began with one or two cries of 'Fire!' as we view the matter, is wholly to misrepresent it. For our own part, we heard no such cries. Such, however, there doubtless were; but they were only signals. The thing bore the impress of a plan to which some hundreds of persons at least appeared to be parties. The mere cry of 'Fire!' would have produced more or less of a general commotion extending to all parts of the house, which was but slightly moved; whereas, the indescribable and terrible outbreak was limited to a large portion of people in a given locality surrounding the great entrance. The outbreak could be likened to nothing but the sudden bursting forth of an immense body of trained singers, or a vast reservoir of water, whose sluices were opened, or whose banks had given way. It is impossible that any cries of two or three individuals could ever have produced so sudden, so simultaneous, and so sustained a display of fear, horror, and consterna- tion. We are strongly impressed with the conviction that the thing, from the adroitness of the performance, must have been well practised beforehand. So far as we could judge from appearances, the parties, or a portion of them, who led in the terrific uproar, also led in the rush, which appeared as an especial part of their infernal arrangement. Mr. Spurgeon, who instantly recovered from the horrible surprise with which he was overwhelmed, in the very act of prayer, of course saw in a moment that the alarm was false. There was no appearance whatever of fire; and the noble structure in no place gave any symptoms of fracture or rupture. His quick eye perceived in an instant the true origin of the movement, and he acted accordingly, adopting every method that seemed calculated to calm the tumult, and to reassure the assembly."

It may put the matter still more vividly before the reader, if I quote from a statement appended to a sermon, preached soon after the catastrophe, by the venerable Dr. Alexander Fletcher:—"As early as five o'clock, thousands of persons were filling up the approaches to the Surrey Gardens. By five minutes after six, the hall was filled to overflow; it is supposed that not fewer than 12,000 persons were present, and many thousands were on the outside, and still as many more were unable to gain admittance even to the Gardens. While the service was being con- ducted in Mr. Spurgeon's usual way, during the second prayer, all of a sudden there were cries simultaneously, doubtless preconcerted, from all parts of the building, of 'Fire!' 'The galleries are giving way!' 'The place is falling!' the effect of which on the audience it is impossible to describe. Many hundreds of persons rushed towards the place of exit, at the risk of their own lives, and sacrificing those of their fellow-creatures. In vain did Mr. Spurgeon, with his stentorian voice and self-possession, assure the alarmed multitude that it was a *ruse* on the part of thieves and pickpockets; the people in the galleries rushed down, precipitating themselves almost headlong over, or breaking down the balustrade of the stairs, killing some and fearfully wounding others. Those who fell through force, or fainting, were trampled under foot, and several lives were lost in the *mêlée*. To make 'confusion worse confounded,' it is also said that, as fast as one portion of the multitude made their exit, others from without entered. Mr. Spurgeon, who was ignorant of any of these fatal consequences, after a temporary lull, was persuaded to make an effort to preach ; but, after one or two attempts, he found it impossible to proceed, owing to the noises which the swell-mobsmen continued to make. Wishing to get the people gradually out of the hall, he gave out a hymn, requesting the congregation to withdraw while it was being sung. He then pronounced the Benediction, and, at length, overcome by emotion, which he had long striven to repress, he was led from the platform in a state of apparent insensibility. The results of this dreadful panic are most calamitous and distressing. Seven lives have been sacrificed, and serious bodily injury inflicted upon a great number of persons."

(Mr. Spurgeon felt that it was impossible, under the circumstances, to say what he had prepared, but, notwithstanding the tumult, the people clamoured for him to go on preaching, so he spoke as follows :—

" My friends, you bid me preach, but what shall I preach about? I am ready to do all I can ; but, in the midst of all this confusion, what shall be my subject? May God's Holy Spirit give me a theme suited to this solemn occasion! My friends, there is a terrible day coming, when the terror and alarm of this evening shall be as nothing. That will be a time when the thunder and lightning and blackest darkness shall have their fullest power, when the earth shall reel to and fro beneath us, and when the arches of the solid heavens shall totter to their centre. The day is coming when the clouds shall reveal their wonders and portents, and Christ shall sit upon those clouds in glory, and shall call you to judgment. Many have gone away to-night, in the midst of this terrible confusion, and so shall it be on that great day. I can, however, believe that the results of that time of testing will show that there will be many—not a less proportion than those who now remain to those who have left—who will stand the ordeal even of that day. The alarm which has just arisen has been produced, in some measure, by that instinct which teaches us to seek self-preservation ; but in the more numerous of the cases, it is not so much the dread of death which has influenced them, as 'the dread of something after death,—the undiscovered country, from whose bourn no traveller returns.' 'Tis conscience that has made cowards of them. Many were afraid to stop here, because they thought, if they stayed, they might die, and then they would be damned. They were aware—and many of you are aware—that, if you were hurried before your Maker to-night, you would be brought there unshriven, unpardoned, and condemned. But what are your fears now to what they will be on that terrible day of reckoning of the Almighty, when the heavens shall shrink above you, and hell shall open her mouth beneath you? But know you not, my friends, that grace, sovereign grace, can yet save you? Have you never heard the welcome news that Jesus came into the world to save sinners? Even if you are the chief of sinners, believe that Christ died for you, and you shall be saved. Do you not know that you are lost and ruined, and that none but Jesus can do helpless sinners good? You are sick and diseased, but Jesus can heal you; and He will if you only trust Him. I thought of preaching to-night from the third chapter of Proverbs, at the 33rd verse: 'The curse of the Lord is in the house of the wicked: but He blesseth the habitation of the just.' I feel that, after what has happened, I cannot preach as I could have wished to do; I fear that you will have another alarm, and I would rather that some of you would seek to retire gradually, in order that no harm may be done to anyone.'

Here there was a fresh disturbance; but after singing part of a hymn, comparative silence was obtained, and the preacher again attempted to begin his discourse :—" Although, my hearers, you may suppose that there are fifty different classes of persons in the world, there are, in the eyes of God, but two. God knows nothing of any save the righteous and the unrighteous, the wicked and the just."

In the confusion that again ensued it was useless to try to preach, so Mr. Spurgeon said :—" My brain is in a whirl, and I scarcely know where I am, so great are my apprehensions that many persons must have been injured by rushing out. I would rather that you retired gradually, and may God Almighty dismiss you with His blessing, and carry you in safety to your homes! If our friends will go out by the central doors, we will sing while they go, and pray that some good may, after all, come out of this great evil. Do not, however, be in a hurry. Let those nearest the door go first.")

All that I can remember of that awful night is the sight of a tumult, which I was then quite unable to understand. Even now it remains a mystery to me. I hope there was no concerted wickedness at the bottom of the sad event; though there may have been a love of mischief aiding at the first. We were all fresh to the place, and all more or less excited. I did my utmost to be calm, and to quiet the people, and I succeeded with the great mass of them; but away at the end of the building there was a something going on which I did not understand, while around the seated part of the hall there were rushes made by excited people again and again, for reasons quite incomprehensible to me. One can understand, now, that those who had seen the accident on the staircase may have been trying to call attention to it, thinking it a strange thing that the service should have been continued after persons had been killed. Of this dread calamity I was unaware till, as I was led down faint from the pulpit, I heard a whisper of it. I know no more, for I lost almost all consciousness, and, amid the weeping and cries of many, I was carried by a private garden into the street, and taken home more dead than alive. There were seven corpses lying on the grass, and many have since told me how grievous was the sight. This I never saw; but what I had seen might have been sufficient to shatter my reason. It might well seem that the ministry which promised to be so largely influential was silenced for ever. There were persons who said so exultingly; but they knew not what they said. I was taken away to the house of a friend, early the following morning, and as I was assisted out of the carriage at Croydon, a working-man caught sight of me, and, in a frightened fashion, stammered out, "Why, sir!—it's Mr. Spurgeon, isn't it?" I answered, "Yes." "Then," he rejoined, "it must be his ghost; for, last night, I saw him carried out dead from the Surrey Gardens Music Hall!" I was not dead, thank God; but the bystanders might well have imagined that the terrible shock had killed me.

Of course there was an inquest;—verdict, accidental death;—on the whole, the only safe conclusion to arrive at. A fund was raised for the sufferers, and all was done that lay in the power of our people to help the injured. Our friends were crushed in spirit, but not driven from their faith or love, nor divided from their youthful minister. I was, for a short time, incapable of any mental effort. Who would not be? How great a trial to have a number of one's hearers killed or maimed! A word about the calamity, and even the sight of the Bible, brought from me a flood of tears, and utter distraction of mind.

During that time, I was not aware of the ferocious assaults which were made upon me by the public press, indeed, I heard no word of them until I was sufficiently recovered to bear them without injury. As we read of David, that they spake of stoning him, so was it with me. Here is a specimen of what was said by a popular daily paper, which I will not name, for it has long been of quite another mind, and most friendly to me :—

"Mr. Spurgeon is a preacher who hurls damnation at the heads of his sinful hearers. Some men there are who, taking their precepts from Holy Writ, would beckon erring souls to a rightful path with fair words and gentle admonition; Mr. Spurgeon would take them by the nose, and bully them into religion. Let us set up a barrier to the encroachments and blasphemies of men like Spurgeon, saying to them, ' Thus far shalt thou come, but no further ;' let us devise some powerful means which shall tell to the thousands who now stand in need of enlightenment,—This man, in his own opinion, is a righteous Christian ; but in ours, nothing more than a ranting charlatan. We are neither strait-laced nor Sabbatarian in our sentiments ; but we would keep apart, widely apart, the theatre and the church ;—above all, would we place in the hand of every right-thinking man, a whip to scourge from society the authors of such vile blasphemies as, on Sunday night, above the cries of

THE OLD CONDUCTOR.

the dead and the dying, and louder than the wails of misery from the maimed and suffering, resounded from the mouth of Spurgeon in the Music Hall of the Surrey Gardens."

Many other utterances were equally cruel and libellous. A gentleman applied to the magistrate at Lambeth, seeking an investigation by his worship into the circumstances connected with the catastrophe, and into the necessity for a license to use the Music Hall as a place of worship. He was not aware that, on the previous Saturday, the building had been licensed as a place for Dissenting worship. He stated that persons collecting money in an unlicensed place were liable to be treated as rogues and vagabonds ; and went on to add that a further question might arise, as to whether the parties causing large congregations to assemble were not liable to a still graver charge. This liberal-minded person represented the mind of a considerable section whose thoughts of the preacher were bitterness itself. The

THE NEW CONDUCTOR.

magistrate, however, assured the applicant that the law permitted public buildings to be used as places of worship for temporary purposes.

The following article appeared in *The Saturday Review*, October 25, 1856 :—

"MR. SPURGEON AT THE SURREY GARDENS.

"If it be true, as has been said, that notables represent, rather than create, public opinion, Mr. Spurgeon and his doings are worth a more serious consideration than their intrinsic value would justify. The manners of an age or people do not follow its literature,—they produce it. Crebillon or Shaftesbury did not form the taste or principles of their contemporaries ;—Voltaire did not so much educate as embody his times ;—and, in like manner, Mr. Spurgeon does not create the state of feeling to which he owes his popularity. It is a melancholy reflection that such a personage is a notable at all. It is no new thing that there should be popular delusions ; but we had flattered ourselves that we had outlived the days of religious, or so-called religious, epidemics. Yet the age of spirit-rapping and of Mr. Spurgeon,—the times in which Dr. Cumming is an authority, and Joe Smith and Mr. Prince are prophets, —cannot cast stones at any 'dark ages.' Whatever legitimate weapons, be they of argument or ridicule, can be employed to arrest the progress of mere imposture, we hold to be justifiable. We should not deem Mr. Spurgeon entitled to the place which he at this moment occupies in public attention,—and certainly we should not trouble ourselves with any reference to his proceedings,—did we not consider him rather as a sign and a result than an original. His success is simply of the vulgarest and most commonplace type. Given a person of some natural talents, with matchless powers of acquired impudence, and a daring defiance of good taste, and often of common decency,—and he will always produce an effect. Anybody who will give himself out as some great one, will find followers enough to accept his leadership. A charlatan will never be without dupes. The crowds who flock to the various Spurgeon conventicles are only of the class who would follow the bottle conjuror, or anyone who chose to advertise that he would fly from the Monument to the dome of St. Paul's. Mr. Spurgeon is perfectly aware that human nature is much the same now as it was five hundred years ago, and it is with humiliation that we concur in his estimate. His crowded congregations are part of his stock-in-trade. He hires Exeter Hall or the Surrey Gardens merely in the way of an advertisement. If he could have the Coliseum at Rome, it would be a safe investment. His scheme for building a conventicle to hold fifteen thousand persons is all in the way of business, just like the big shop, *toute la Rue du Coq*, in Paris.

"All we can do is to warn the public ; but we are afraid it will be to little purpose. *Populus vult decipi.* It is, we fear, scarcely more useless to caution people against joint-stock banks and public companies when there is a plethora of money, than seriously to hold up Mr. Spurgeon to the world as a very ordinary impostor. The only effectual remedy is, in the one case, to provide safe and honest investments for capital ;—in the other, to offer more healthful and rational counter-attractions. We have been accused, in some quarters, of recommending Sunday amusements in the place of religion. As a fact, we have done no such thing, for our arguments were all based on the compatibility of religious exercises with healthful and innocent recreation, and the policy of combining them. But if the question is between Sunday bands and Sunday doings of the Spurgeon character at the Surrey

Gardens, by all means, we say, let the bands at least be admitted to unrestricted competition. We do not wish to silence Mr. Spurgeon; but, for the sake of the public safety, let there be a chance of thinning the crowds. Very judiciously, on a late occasion, we had fireworks simultaneously in the West End Parks, on Primrose Hill, and in the East of London; and we do not see why Mr. Spurgeon should have a monopoly of brazen instruments South of the Thames. Whitefield used to preach at fairs. In these days of open competition, we perceive no reason why this practice should not be inverted. The innovation would only be the substitution of one set of amusements for another;—or, rather, an addition to our list of Sunday sports. Let religious people ask themselves whether this is not in fact the true way of putting the case. It is a profanation to religion to imagine that, as regards the crowds who flock to the Spurgeon show, there is any higher influence at work than the common love of excitement. Mr. Spurgeon's doings are, we believe, entirely discountenanced by his co-religionists. There is scarcely a Dissenting minister of any note who associates with him. We do not observe, in any of his schemes or building operations, the names, as trustees or the like, of any leaders in what is called the religious world. Nor can we attribute to mere envy the feelings with which Mr. Spurgeon is apparently regarded by those respectable persons who are his brethren in the Dissenting ministry. Somehow, it is generally felt that religion is not benefited by his abnormal proceedings. There is, at any rate, this most remarkable *differentia* between him and other revivalists,—that he stands alone, or nearly so. The fact is an antecedent ground for grave suspicion and natural distrust.

" This hiring of places of public amusement for Sunday preaching is a novelty, and a painful one. It looks as if religion were at its last shift. It is a confession of weakness rather than a sign of strength. It is not wrestling with Satan in his strongholds,—to use the old earnest Puritan language;—but entering into a very cowardly truce and alliance with the world. After all, Mr. Spurgeon only affects to be the Sunday Jullion. We are told of the profanity which must have been at the bottom of the clerical mind when the Church acted miracle-plays, and tolerated the Feast of the Ass; but the old thing reappears when popular preachers hire concert-rooms, and preach Particular Redemption in saloons reeking with the perfume of tobacco, and yet echoing with the chaste melodies of *Bobbing Around* and the valse from the *Traviata*. And where is this to end? If, as Mr. Spurgeon doubtless argued, Exeter Hall can be hired by a clergyman of the Establishment to read Mr. Caird's sermon, and if the enterprising divine who performed this notable feat was rewarded for it by the judicious Archbishop of Canterbury with a living of £500 per annum, why should not he hire the Surrey Gardens? Mr. Spurgeon has outbid Mr. Mansfield; but why should not somebody outbid Mr. Spurgeon? Or why should he be content with his present achievements? The Surrey Gardens affair was a great *coup*. The deplorable accident, in which seven people lost their lives, and scores were maimed, mutilated, or otherwise cruelly injured, Mr. Spurgeon only considers as an additional intervention of Providence in his favour. 'This event will, I trust, teach us the necessity of'—being sober, rational, and decent?—No ;—'having a building of our own.' Preach another crowd into a frenzy of terror,—kill and smash a dozen or two more,—and then the speculation will have succeeded.

"Mr. Spurgeon, improving the occasion, is said to have remarked that 'this gathering had aroused Satan, and he would not allow the service to go on without endeavouring to interrupt it.' We do not profess that familiarity with Satan and his doings which is enjoyed by Mr. Spurgeon. Doubtless, he possesses more of Satan's confidence, and more knowledge of his character, than ordinary men ; at least, with our estimate of the power of evil, we should judge so from this mode of dealing with the deplorable result of his vanity and cupidity. We certainly believe that Satan was busy enough on Sunday evening last. The reporters tell us that the publicans and pickpockets 'reaped a rich harvest' from the occasion. These are, at any rate, new fruits of a gospel ministry, and strange triumphs of the cross. Expostulation and advice are thrown away upon one who can act as Mr. Spurgeon is reported to have acted in the very presence of these unusual seals to his ministry. Yet it is always a public duty to show up selfishness and vanity ; and we can only hope that it will prove in this instance to be a public benefit also."

Our church-book contains the following entry concerning the catastrophe ; it shows the way in which this great affliction was viewed by our own friends :— " Lord's-day, October 19, 1856. On the evening of this day, in accordance with the resolution passed at the church-meeting, October 6, the church and congregation assembled to hear our Pastor in the Music Hall of the Royal Surrey Gardens. A very large number of persons (about 7,000) were assembled on that occasion, and the service was commenced in the usual way, by singing, reading the Scriptures, and prayer. Just, however, after our Pastor had commenced his prayer, a disturbance was caused (as it is supposed, by some evil-disposed persons acting in concert), and the whole congregation was seized with a sudden panic. This caused a fearful rush to the doors, particularly from the galleries. Several persons, either in consequence of their heedless haste, or from the extreme pressure of the crowd behind, were thrown down on the stone steps of the north-west staircase, and were trampled on by the crowd pressing upon them. The lamentable result was that seven persons lost their lives, and twenty-eight were removed to the hospitals seriously bruised and injured. Our Pastor, not being aware that any loss of life had occurred, continued in the pulpit, endeavouring by every means in his power to alleviate the fear of the people, and was successful to a very considerable extent. In attempting to renew the service, it was found that the people were too excited to listen to him, so the service was closed, and those who had remained dispersed quietly. This lamentable circumstance produced very serious effects on the nervous system of our Pastor. He was entirely prostrated for some days, and compelled to relinquish his preaching engagements. Through the great mercy of our Heavenly Father, he was, however, restored so as to be able to occupy the pulpit in our own chapel on Sunday, November 2nd, and gradually recovered his wonted health and vigour. 'The Lord's name be praised!'

"The church desires to note this event in their Minutes, and to record their devout thankfulness to God that, in this sad calamity, the lives of their beloved Pastor, and deacons, and members were all preserved; and also with the hope that our Heavenly Father may, from this seeming evil, produce the greatest amount of real lasting good."

(Mr. Spurgeon did not approve of the printing of his prayers, as a rule; but the circumstances under which the church and congregation met on that Lord's-day morning,—November 2, 1856,—were so unusual, that an exception may be made in order to insert the record of the Pastor's first public utterance after the accident :—

"We are assembled here, O Lord, this day, with mingled feelings of joy and sorrow,—joy that we meet each other again, and sorrow for those who have suffered bereavements. Thanks to Thy Name! Thanks to Thy Name! Thy servant feared that he should never be able to meet this congregation again; but Thou hast brought him up out of the burning fiery furnace, and not even the smell of fire has passed upon him. Thou hast, moreover, given Thy servant special renewal of strength, and he desires now to confirm those great promises of free grace which the gospel affords. Thou knowest, O Lord, our feelings of sorrow! We must not open the sluices of our woe; but, O God, comfort those who are lingering in pain and suffering, and cheer those who have been bereaved! Let great blessings rest upon them,—the blessings of the covenant of grace, and of this world, too. And now, O Lord, bless Thy people! We have loved one another with a pure heart fervently;—we have rejoiced in each other's joy,—we have wept together in our sorrow. Thou hast welded us together, and made us one in doctrine, one in practice, and one in holy love. Oh, that it may be said of each individual now present with us that he is bound up in the bundle of life! O Lord, we thank Thee even for all the slander, and calumny, and malice, with which Thou hast allowed the enemy to honour us; and we pray Thee to grant that we may never give them any real cause to blaspheme Thy holy Name! We ask this for our Lord Jesus Christ's sake. Amen."

The opening sentences of the discourse delivered on that occasion have a special and permanent interest from the fact that the Lord so abundantly fulfilled Mr. Spurgeon's prophecy concerning future services and blessing in the Music Hall :—

"I almost regret, this morning, that I have ventured to occupy this pulpit, because I feel utterly unable to preach to you for your profit. I had thought that the quiet and repose of the last fortnight had removed the effects of that terrible catastrophe ; but on coming back to this chapel again, and more especially, standing here to address you, I feel somewhat of those same painful emotions which well-nigh prostrated me before. You will therefore excuse me, this morning, if I make no allusion to that solemn event, or scarcely any. I could not preach to you upon a subject that should be in the least allied to it ; I should be obliged to be silent if I should bring to my remembrance that terrific scene in the midst of which it was my solemn lot to stand. God will overrule it, doubtless. It may not have been so much by *the malice* of men, as some have asserted ; it was perhaps simple wickedness,—an intention to disturb a congregation ; but certainly with no thought of committing so terrible a crime as that of the murder of those unhappy creatures. God forgive those who were the instigators of that horrid act! They have my forgiveness from the depths of my soul. *It shall not stop us, however ;* we are not in the least degree daunted by it. I shall preach there again yet ; aye, and God will give us souls there, and Satan's empire shall tremble more than ever. God is with us ; who is he that shall be against us? The text I have selected is one that has comforted me, and, in a great measure, enabled me to come here to-day,—the reflection upon it had such a power of comfort on my depressed spirit. It is this :—'Wherefore God also hath highly exalted Him, and given Him a Name which is above every name : that at the name of Jesus every knee should bow, of things in Heaven, and things in earth, and things under the earth ; and that every tongue should confess that Jesus Christ is Lord, to the glory of God the Father.' I shall not attempt to preach upon this text ; I shall only make a few remarks that have occurred to my own mind ; for I could not preach to-day. I have been utterly unable to study, but I thought that even a few words might be acceptable to you this morning, and I trust to your loving hearts to excuse them. O Spirit of God, magnify Thy strength in Thy servant's weakness, and enable him to honour his Lord, even when his soul is cast down within him !")

I have many times used the great calamity as an illustration of the truth that accidents are not to be regarded as Divine judgments ; perhaps the most notable instance is the sermon I preached soon after the collision in the Clayton tunnel on the Brighton railway (See *Metropolitan Tabernacle Pulpit*, No. 408, "Accidents, not Punishments.") That discourse is to me the more memorable as I possess a copy of it which Dr. Livingstone had carried with him in his African journeys, and on the top of which he had written, "*Very good.*—D. L." It was found, after his death, in the volume of his Diary from November, 1861, to July, 1863, and was sent to me by his daughter, Mrs. Livingstone-Bruce. In the course of the sermon I said:—"It has been most absurdly stated that those who travel on the first day of the week, and meet with an accident, ought to regard that accident as being a judgment from God upon them on account of their violating the Christian's day of worship. It has been stated, even by godly ministers, that the late deplorable collision should be looked upon as an exceedingly wonderful and remarkable visitation of the wrath of God against those unhappy persons who happened to be in the Clayton tunnel. Now I enter my solemn protest against such an inference as that, not in my own name, but in the Name of Him who is the Christian's Master and the Christian's Teacher. I say of those who were crushed in that tunnel, Suppose ye that they were sinners above all the other sinners? 'I tell you, Nay: but, except ye repent, ye shall all likewise perish.' Or those who were killed last Monday, think ye that they were sinners above all the sinners that were in London? 'I tell you, Nay: but, except ye repent, ye shall all likewise perish.' Now, mark, I would not deny that there have been judgments of God upon particular persons for sin; sometimes, and I think but exceedingly rarely, such things have occurred. Some of us have heard, in our experience, instances of men who have b'asphemed God, and defied Him to destroy them, who have suddenly fallen dead; and in such cases, the punishment has so quickly followed the blasphemy that one could not help perceiving the hand of God in it. The man had wantonly asked for the judgment of God, his prayer was heard, and the judgment came. . . . But in cases of accident, such as that to which I refer, and in cases of sudden and instant death, again I say, I enter my earnest protest against the foolish and ridiculous idea that those who thus perish are sinners above all the sinners who survive unharmed. Let me just try to reason this matter out with Christian people; for there are some unenlightened Christians who will feel horrified by what I have said. Those who are ready at perversions may even dream that I would apologize for the desecration of the day of worship. Now, I do no such thing. I do not extenuate the sin, I only testify and declare that accidents are not to be viewed as punishments for sin, for punishment belongs not to this world, but the world to come. To all those who hastily look on every calamity as a judgment, I would speak in the earnest hope of setting them right.

"Let me begin, then, by saying, my dear brethren, do you not see that *what you say is not true*, and that is the best of reasons why you should not say it? Do not your own experience and observation teach you that one event happeneth both to the righteous and to the wicked? It is true, the wicked man sometimes falls dead in the street; but has not the minister fallen dead in the pulpit? It is true that a boat, in which men were seeking their own pleasure on the Sunday, has suddenly gone down; but is it not equally true that a ship, which contained none but godly men, who were bound upon an excursion to preach the gospel, has gone down, too? The visible providence of God has no respect of persons; and a storm may gather around the *John Williams* missionary ship, quite as well as around a vessel filled with riotous sinners. Why, do you not perceive that the providence of God has been, in fact, in its outward dealings, rather harder upon the good than upon the bad? For, did not Paul say, as he looked upon the miseries of the righteous in his day, 'If in this life only we have hope in Christ, we are of all men most miserable'? The path of righteousness has often conducted men to the rack, to the prison, to the gibbet, to the stake; while the road of sin has often led a man to empire, to dominion, and to high esteem among his fellows. It is not true that, in this world, God does, as a rule, and of necessity, punish men for sin, and reward them for their good deeds; for, did not David say, 'I have seen the wicked in great power, and spreading himself like a green bay tree;' and did not this perplex the psalmist for a little season, until he went into the sanctuary of God, and then he understood their end?

"Will you allow me also to remark that the supposition, against which I am earnestly contending, is *a very cruel and unkind one?* For, if it were the case, that all persons who thus meet with their death in an extraordinary and terrible manner were greater sinners than the rest, would it not be a crushing blow to bereaved survivors, and is it not ungenerous on our part to indulge the idea unless we are compelled by unanswerable reasons to accept it as an awful truth? Now, I defy you to whisper it in the widow's ear. Go home to her, and say, 'Your husband was a worse sinner than the rest of men, therefore he died.' You have not brutality enough for that. A little unconscious infant, which had never sinned, though, doubtless, an inheritor of Adam's fall, is found crushed amidst the *débris* of the accident. Now, think for a moment, what would be the infamous consequence of the supposition that those who perished were worse than others; you would have to make it out that this unconscious infant was a worse sinner than many in the dens of infamy whose lives are yet spared. Do you not perceive that the thing is radically false? And I might perhaps show you the injustice of it best by reminding you that it may, one day, turn upon your own head. Let it be your own case that you should meet with sudden death in such a way, are you willing to be adjudged to damnation on that account? Such an event may happen in the house of God. Let me recall to my own, and to your sorrowful recollection, what occurred when once we met together. I can say, with a pure heart, we met for no object but to serve our God, and the minister had no aim in going to that place but that of gathering many to hear who otherwise would not have listened to his voice; and yet there were funerals as a result of that holy effort (for holy effort still we avow it to have been, and the aftersmile of God hath proved it so). There were deaths, and deaths among God's people ;—I was about to say, I am glad it was with God's people rather than with others. A fearful fright took hold upon the congregation, and they fled ; and do you not see that, if accidents are to be viewed as judgments, then it is a fair inference that we were sinning in being there,—an insinuation which our consciences repudiate with scorn ? However, if that logic were true, it is as true against us as it is against others ; and inasmuch as you would repel with indignation the accusation that any were wounded or hurt on account of sin in being there to worship God, what you repel for yourself repel for others, and be no party to the accusation which is brought against those who have been destroyed, during the last fortnight, that they perished on account of any great sin.

"Here I anticipate the outcries of prudent and zealous persons who tremble for the ark of God, and would touch it with Uzzah's hand. 'Well,' says one, 'but we ought not to talk like this, for it is a very serviceable superstition, because there are many people who will be kept from travelling on the Sunday by the accident, and we ought to tell them, therefore, that those who perished, perished because they travelled on Sunday.' Brethren, I would not tell a lie to save a soul ; and this would be telling lies, for it is not the fact. I would do anything that is right to stop Sunday labour and sin, but I would not forge a falsehood even to do that. They might have perished on a Monday as well as on a Sunday. God gives no special immunity any day of the week, and accidents may occur as well at one time as at another; and it is only a pious fraud when we seek thus to play upon the superstition of men to make capital for Christ. The Roman Catholic priest might consistently use such an argument ; but an honest Christian man, who believes that the religion of Christ can take care of itself without his telling falsehoods, scorns to do it. These men did not perish because they travelled on a Sunday. Witness the fact that others perished on the Monday when they were on an errand of mercy. I know not why or wherefore God sent the accident. God forbid that we should offer our own reason when God has not given us His reason ; but we are not allowed to make the superstition of men an instrument for advancing the glory of God. You know, among Protestants, there is a great deal of Popery. I meet with people who uphold infant baptism on the plea, 'Well, it is not doing any hurt, and there is a great deal of good meaning in it, and it may do good ; and even confirmation may be blessed to some people, therefore do not let us speak against it.' I have nothing to do with whether the thing does hurt or not ; all I have to do with is whether it is right, whether it is Scriptural, whether it is true ; and if the truth does mischief,—which is a supposition we can by no means allow,—that mischief will not lie at our door. We have nothing to do but to speak the truth, even though the heavens should fall."

I thank God that, terrible as the great catastrophe was, there was never in my experience another like it, for I do not think I could have survived a second one. I have, on several occasions, seen some cause for alarm when I have been conducting services in places that have not seemed to me to be able to stand the strain of the multitudes gathered to hear the Word; and the sensation I felt at the Surrey Gardens has, in a moment, come over me again. Many years ago, I was preaching in a building which was exceedingly crowded; and, to my apprehension, there was a continuous tremor. I grew so anxious that I said to a friend, who understood such matters, "Go downstairs, and see whether this structure is really safe; for it seems hardly able to bear the weight of this crowd." When he returned, he looked anxious, but gave me no answer. The service ended quietly, and then he said, " I am so glad that everything has gone off safely. I do not think you should ever preach here again, for it is a very frail affair; but I thought that, if I frightened you, there would be more risk of a panic than there was in letting the service go on." The narrowest escape I ever had of a repetition of the Music Hall fatality was about eighteen months after the accident there; on the following Lord's-day morning,—April 11, 1858,—I thus described to my congregation the Lord's merciful interposition :—

" During this week, my mind has been much directed to the subject of providence, and you will not wonder when I relate a portion of one day's story. I was engaged to preach, last Wednesday, at Halifax, where there was a heavy snow-storm. Preparations had been made for a congregation of 8,000 persons, and a huge wooden structure had been erected. I considered that, owing to the severe weather, few persons could possibly assemble, and I looked forward to the dreary task of addressing an insignificant handful of people in a vast place. However, when I arrived, I found from 5,000 to 6,000 people gathered together to hear the Word; and a more substantial-looking place it has not been my lot to see. It certainly was a great uncomely building; but, nevertheless, it seemed well adapted to answer the purpose. We met together in the afternoon, and again in the evening, and worshipped God; and we separated to our homes, or rather, we were about to separate, and all this while the kind providence of God was watching over us. Immediately in front of me there was a huge gallery, which looked an exceedingly massive structure, capable of holding 2,000 persons. This, in the afternoon, was crowded, and it seemed to stand as firm as a rock. Again, in the evening, there it stood, and neither moved nor shook. But mark the provident hand of God; in the evening, when the people were retiring, and when there were scarcely more than a hundred persons there, a great beam gave way, and down came a portion of the flooring of the gallery with a fearful crash. Several people were precipitated with the planks, but still the good hand of God watched over us, and only two persons were severely injured with broken legs, which it is trusted will be set so as to avoid the necessity of amputation. Now, had this happened any earlier, not only must many more have been injured, but there are a thousand chances to one, as we say, that a panic must necessarily have ensued similar to that which we still remember, and deplore as having occurred in this place. Had such a thing happened, and had I been the unhappy preacher on the occasion, I feel certain that I should never have been able to occupy the pulpit again. Such was the effect of the first calamity, that I marvel that I ever survived. No human tongue can possibly tell what I experienced. The Lord, however, graciously preserved us ; the fewness of the people in the gallery prevented any such catastrophe, and thus a most fearful accident was averted. But there is a more marvellous providence still to record. Overloaded by the immense weight of snow which fell upon it, and beaten by a heavy wind, the entire structure fell with an enormous crash three hours after we had left it, splitting the huge timbers into shivers, and rendering very much of the material utterly useless for any future building. Now mark this,—had the snow begun three hours earlier, the hall must have fallen upon us, and how few of us would have escaped, we cannot guess. But mark another thing. All day long it thawed so fast, that the snow as it fell seemed to leave a mass, not of white snow, but of snow and water together. This ran through the roof upon us, to our considerable annoyance, and I was almost ready to complain that we had hard dealings from God's providence. But if it had been a frost, instead of a thaw, you can easily perceive that the place must have fallen several hours before it did ; and then your minister, and the greater part of his congregation, would probably have been in the other world. Some there may be who deny providence altogether. I cannot conceive that there were any witnesses of that scene who could have done so. This I know, if I had been an unbeliever to this day in the doctrine of the supervision and wise care of God, I must have been a believer in it at this hour. Oh, magnify the Lord with me, and let us exalt His Name together ! He hath been very gracious unto us, and remembered us for good."

(In his record of " The Life and Labours of Pastor C. H. Spurgeon," published by Messrs. Passmore & Alabaster under the title, *From the Usher's Desk to the Tabernacle Pulpit*, Mr. Shindler says, concerning the catastrophe at the Surrey Gardens :—" Twenty-five years afterwards, the writer witnessed the terribly depressing effect the memory of this sad event had on Mr. Spurgeon. During the session of the Baptist Union at Portsmouth and Southampton, in 1881, Mr. Spurgeon was announced to preach in the largest available room in the former town. Long before the service began, every available seat and all standing-room were occupied, and still there were hundreds pressing forward, and endeavouring to crowd in. There was some confusion just as the preacher was passing on to the platform to take his seat. He seemed entirely unmanned, and stood in the passage leaning his head on his hand. He told the writer that the circumstance so vividly recalled the terrible scene at the Surrey Music Hall, that he felt quite unable to preach. But he did preach, and preach well, though he could not entirely recover from the agitation of his nervous system. Prince Edward of Saxe-Weimar, a cousin of Queen Victoria, who was then the military commander of the district, was present with his suite, and cordially greeted ' the prince of preachers ' after his sermon."

Pastor W. Williams, in his *Personal Reminiscences of Charles Haddon Spurgeon*, writes :—"' What are you going to preach from to-morrow ?' he once asked me. ' " The curse of the Lord is in the house of the wicked : but He blesseth the habitation of the just ; " ' I answered. He gave a deep sigh ; his countenance changed even before I had finished the verse, brief as it was ; and he said, in tones of deep solemnity, ' Ah, me !' ' What is the matter, sir ?' I asked. ' Don't you know,' he replied, ' that is the text I had on that terrible night of the accident at the Surrey Music Hall ?' I did not know it, but I learned, from the mere mention of it, how permanent was the effect upon his mind of that awful night's disaster. I never alluded either to this text or to the Surrey Gardens calamity after that. I cannot but think, from what I then saw, that his comparatively early death might be in some measure due to the furnace of mental suffering he endured on and after that fearful night.")

CHAPTER LI.

Later Services at the Music Hall.

C. H. SPURGEON PREACHING IN THE SURREY GARDENS MUSIC HALL.

Standing in this pulpit, this morning, I recall to myself that evening of sorrow when I saw my people scattered, like sheep without a shepherd, trodden upon, injured, and many of them killed. Do you recollect how you cried for your minister, that he might be restored to a reason that was then tottering? Can you recollect how you prayed that, out of evil, God would bring forth good, that all the curses of the wicked might be rolled back upon themselves, and that God would yet fill this place with His glory? And do you remember how long ago that is, and how God has been with us ever since, and how many of those, who were injured that night, are now members of our church, and are praising God that they ever entered this hall? Oh! shall we not love the Lord? There is not a church in London that has had such answers to prayer as we have had; there has not been a church that has had such cause to pray. We have had special work, special trial, special deliverance, and we ought pre-eminently to be a church, loving God, and spending and being spent in His service.—C. H. S., *in sermon preached at the Surrey Gardens Music Hall, February* 27, 1859.

I cannot speak, as a grey-headed man, of the storms and troubles which many of you have endured; but I have had more joys and more sorrows, in the last few years, than any man in this place, for my life has been compressed as with a Bramah press,—a vast mass of emotion into one year. I have gone to the very bottoms of the mountains, as some of you know, in a night that never can be erased from my memory,—a night connected with this place. I have had also to pass through severe suffering and trial from the calumny and scorn of man, while abuse hailed pitilessly on my head. And I have had to endure acute bodily pain ; but, as far as my witness goes, I can say that the Lord is able to save unto the uttermost, and in the last extremity, and He has been a good God to me.—C. H. S., *in sermon at the Music Hall, May 22, 1859.*

In the best work for the Lord, we have no guarantee against accidents, and the losses which they occasion. The young prophet, in the days of Elisha, was most laudably engaged, yet the head of his axe flew off, and fell into the water. Those who conclude that every successful work has the smile of God upon it, should remember that Babylon was mistress among the nations, and none could stand against her, yet was she abhorred of the Lord. Those, on the other hand, who see, in every temporary calamity, a proof that an enterprise is not according to the Lord's mind, might condemn the preaching of the gospel itself, since in its very infancy it subjected so many to persecution and to cruel death. "Whom the Lord loveth, He chasteneth ;" and the works which He approves, He often renders difficult. When the preacher at the Surrey Music Hall saw his congregation scattered by the uproar of wicked men, and mourned over precious life which was so suddenly sacrificed, there were friends who read in that shocking disaster an omen that the work was not of God, and that the preacher must desist ; but the young man did not believe in omens, but in duty ; and, therefore, as soon as he could, he reappeared in his pulpit, and as the result of his after-ministry in that place, it is not too much to say that thousands found Christ by his direct teaching, while the preaching of the Word in cathedrals, abbeys, music-halls, and theatres, became a tolerated agency, and even a popular method of evangelization.—C. H. S., in *" The Sword and the Trowel," 1868.*

HE preaching in the Music Hall was resumed in the morning only, so that daylight prevented any further deed of darkness, although the evening would have been a time more favourable for the gathering of large congregations. Our first morning service there was held on November 23, 1856, and our last on December 11, 1859 In the providence of God, the great hall was ready exactly when it was needed, and it was available for use almost as long as it was required. The rent paid for its occupation, during the mornings only, was a respectable item in its accounts ; but Sunday takings were preferred to this sure income. The Sabbath before the gardens were opened to the public on the Lord's-day, we cleared out of the place, and with our occupancy, there departed from the company its chief source of revenue Its downward way to ruin was rapid enough from that hour ; both morally and financially it sank hopelessly. We, that is, preacher and people, are bound to commemorate the kind providence which found us such a shelter at a time when we could not otherwise have obtained one for ourselves. All classes —from the Prime Minister downwards—heard the Word there ; at no time have so many of the aristocracy made acquaintance with Nonconformist worship. The list of notable persons present on any one Sunday is a long one : statesmen, nobles, divines, great travellers, and all sorts of distinguished persons came to hear the preacher at the Surrey Gardens. Their presence and aid were hopeful signs that the building of our permanent house of prayer would be the provision of a necessity, and that we could accomplish the heavy task. As for the multitude, they were always there in force ; and these, not only from the religious section of society, but largely from those who never went to public worship. The reading of newspapers before the commencement of service, though in itself objectionable enough, was the proof that those were present for whom the effort was designed. The best of all is, that God was with us. Conversions were numerous, and some of them were of a very striking kind; they were mainly from that stratum of society which is not touched by ordinary religious services. Though the hall is completely swept away, it will never cease to hold a place in the memory of those to whom it was their spiritual birthplace. All along through the years in which we worshipped in it, there were continual additions to the church, perpetual discoveries of fresh workers, and constant initiations of new enterprises. The College, Orphanage, Colportage, Evangelists, College Missions, and our various branch mission-stations, have all benefited through the advance made by the church during those services. We have seen good brought out of evil; and in our case we have been made to say with the psalmist, "Thou hast caused men to ride over our heads : we went through fire and through water ; but Thou broughtest us out into a wealthy place."

When I began to preach at the Surrey Gardens, I had such a diversified congregation as few men have ever had to address from Sabbath to Sabbath. God alone knows what anxiety I experienced in selecting my subjects and arranging my appeals for such a vast fluctuating assembly. There was a time when my brain was all in a whirl at the very thought of ascending that pulpit, while for all the services among my own people I enjoyed the greatest liberty. With the confidence of one who felt his heart at ease amidst the home-circle of his own family, I spoke as if my perfect love to the brotherhood had cast out all fear of missing the mark, or failing in the true work of a Pastor. There was all the difference between preaching in the hall, and in the chapel, that might be expected from the contrast between the neutral ground occupied in the one case and the sacred prestige enjoyed in the other.

(After a time, in addition to the great numbers of strangers who always flocked to the Music Hall, so large a part of the assembly consisted of Mr. Spurgeon's regular hearers that he felt almost as much at home there as in New Park Street Chapel, and he adapted his preaching to the altered condition of affairs. In a discourse delivered on Lord's-day morning, February 28, 1858, he said:— "When first I preached in this hall, my congregation assumed the appearance of an irregular mass of persons collected from all parts of this city to listen to the Word. I was then simply an evangelist, preaching to many who had not heard the gospel before. By the grace of God, the most blessed change has taken place ; and now, instead of having an irregular multitude gathered together, my congregation is as fixed as that of any minister in the whole of London. I can, from this pulpit, observe the countenances of my friends, who have occupied the same places, as nearly as possible, for these many months ; and I have the privilege and the pleasure of knowing that a very large proportion, certainly three-fourths of the people who meet together here, are not persons who stray hither from curiosity, but are my regular and constant hearers. And, observe, that my character also has been changed. From being an evangelist, it is now my business to become your Pastor in this place, as well as in the chapel where I labour in the evening. I think, then, it will strike the judgment of every person that, as both the congregation and myself have now changed, the teaching itself should in some measure show a difference. It has been my wont to address you from the simple truths of the gospel; I have very seldom, in this place, attempted to dive into the deep things of God. A text, which I have thought suitable for my congregation in the evening, I should not have made the subject of discussion in this hall in the morning. There are many high and mysterious doctrines which I have often taken the opportunity of handling in my own place, but which I have not felt at liberty to introduce here, regarding you as a company of people casually gathered together to hear the Word. But now, since the circumstances are changed, the teaching will be changed also. I shall not now simply confine myself to the doctrine of faith, or the teaching of believers' baptism; I shall not stay upon the surface of truth, but shall venture, as God shall guide me, to enter into those things that lie at the basis of the religion that we hold so dear. I shall not blush to preach before you the doctrine of God's Divine Sovereignty; I shall not hesitate to proclaim, in the most unreserved and unguarded manner, the doctrine of election. I shall not be afraid to propound the great truth of the final perseverance of the saints; I shall not withhold that undoubted teaching of Scripture, the effectual calling of God's elect; I shall endeavour, as God shall help me, to keep back nothing from you who have become my flock. Seeing that many of you have now 'tasted that the Lord is gracious,' we will endeavour to go through the whole system of the doctrines of grace, that saints may be edified and built up in their most holy faith."

The following Sabbath, the Pastor preached on "Human Inability," from our Lord's words, "No man can come to Me, except the Father which hath sent Me draw him." A little later, he discoursed upon "Human Responsibility," taking for his text another of Christ's most weighty sayings: "If I had not come and spoken unto them, they had not had sin: but now they have no cloke for their sin." Not long afterwards, he sought to set forth both sides of Divine truth in a sermon entitled, "Sovereign Grace and Man's Responsibility," in which he avoided the errors of Arminianism on the one hand, and those of Hyper-Calvinism on the other. In course of time, either at the Surrey Gardens or at New Park Street Chapel, Mr. Spurgeon had expounded all the doctrines of grace; and one result of that method of teaching the truth was thus described by him:—

"Among the many candidates for baptism and church-membership, who came forward every month, there were great numbers of young people, and others of riper years who had but recently found the Saviour; and I was delighted to hear them, one after another, not only express themselves clearly upon the great fundamental truth of justification by faith, but also give clear evidence that they were well instructed in the doctrines that cluster around the covenant of grace. I believe that one reason why our church has been, for these many years, so signally blessed of God, is that the great majority of those who have been added to our ranks have been well established in the old-fashioned faith of the Puritans and the Covenanters, and therefore have not been turned aside or drawn away from us. It used to be said, in those early days, that we were taking into the church 'a parcel of girls and boys.' I remember, long afterwards, at one of our great gatherings in the Tabernacle, reminding our friends of this contemptuous remark, whereat they laughed, and then I added, 'I am happy to have around me, still, those very same girls and boys,—they are a good deal older now,—and many of *their* sons and daughters have followed their parents' example, while some even of the grandchildren of my early converts are already united with us.'")

So far as the general public was concerned, the Music Hall services were a great evangelistic campaign, in which "the slain of the Lord" were many. I determined that, whether my hearers would receive the gospel, or reject it, they should at least understand it; and therefore I preached it in plain, homely Saxon that a child could comprehend, and with all the earnestness of which I was capable. I recollect a friend saying to me, one Sabbath, as we went down the stairs from the hall, "There are eight thousand people, this morning, who will be without excuse at the day of judgment;" and I hope that was the case many another time as the vast multitude dispersed from the Surrey Gardens. I did not please everybody even then; and some found fault who ought to have been my best friends. I recollect great complaint being made against my sermon on the words, "Compel them to come in," in which I was enabled to speak with much tenderness and compassion for souls. The violent, rigid school of Hyper-Calvinists said that the discourse was Arminian and unsound; but it was a small matter to me to be condemned by the judgment of men, for my Master set His seal very clearly upon that message. I think I never preached another sermon by which so many souls were won to God, as our church-meetings long continued to testify; and all over the world, wherever the printed discourse has been scattered, sinners have been saved through its instrumentality; and, therefore, if it be vile to exhort sinners to come to Christ, I purpose to be viler still. I am as firm a believer in the doctrines of grace as any man living, and a true Calvinist after the order of John Calvin himself; and probably I have read more of his works than any one of my accusers ever did; but if it be thought an evil thing to bid sinners "lay hold on eternal life," I will be yet more evil in this respect, and herein imitate not only Calvin, but also my Lord and His apostles, who, though they taught that salvation is of grace, and grace alone, feared not to speak to men as rational beings and responsible agents, and to bid them "strive to enter in at the strait gate," and "labour not for the meat which perisheth, but for that meat which endureth unto everlasting life."

Among the sermons preached in the Music Hall, another which was very greatly blessed was the one entitled, "Looking unto Jesus." It was often mentioned by converts who were brought to the Lord through hearing it delivered; and when it was published, and scattered abroad, I received many testimonies that the reading of it had been attended with a like unction from on high. This fact I do not wonder at, for it is but another proof of the Sovereignty of God, since the discourse is one of the most simple of the series, and would probably be overlooked by those who were seeking for anything original and striking. The Master is in the sermon; and, therefore, it has rejoiced the hearts of His people, when applied by the Holy Spirit. I value a discourse, not by the approbation of men, nor by the ability manifest in it; but by the effect produced in comforting the saint, and awakening the sinner. The sermon on "The Shameful Sufferer" was the means of a great blessing to very many. Christ bleeding always makes the heart bleed, and His shame makes men ashamed of sin. Let but the Holy Spirit open the eyes of men to behold a sorrowing Saviour, and they will at once sorrow for sin.

There were many instances of remarkable conversions at the Music Hall; one especially was so singular that I have often related it as a proof that God sometimes guides His servants to say what they would themselves never have thought of uttering, in order that He may bless the hearer for whom the message is personally intended. While preaching in the hall, on one occasion, I deliberately pointed to a man in the midst of the crowd, and said, "There is a man sitting there, who is a shoemaker; he keeps his shop open on Sundays, it was open last Sabbath morning, he took ninepence, and there was fourpence profit out of it; his soul is sold to Satan for fourpence!" A city missionary, when going his rounds, met with this man, and seeing that he was reading one of my sermons, he asked the question, "Do you know Mr. Spurgeon?" "Yes," replied the man, "I have every reason to know him, I have been to hear him; and, under his preaching, by God's grace I have become a new creature in Christ Jesus. Shall I tell you how it happened? I went to the Music Hall, and took my seat in the middle of the place; Mr. Spurgeon looked at me as if he knew me, and in his sermon he pointed to me, and told the congregation that I was a shoemaker, and that I kept my shop open on Sundays; and I did, sir. I should not have minded that; but he also said that I took ninepence the Sunday before, and that there was fourpence profit out of it. I did take ninepence that day, and fourpence was just the profit; but how he should know that, I could not tell. Then it struck me that it was God who had spoken to my soul through him, so I shut up my shop the next Sunday. At first, I was afraid to go again to hear him, lest he should tell the people more about me; but afterwards I went, and the Lord met with me, and saved my soul."

I could tell as many as a dozen similar cases in which I pointed at somebody in the hall without having the slightest knowledge of the person, or any idea that what I said was right, except that I believed I was moved by the Spirit to say it; and so striking has been my description, that the persons have gone away, and said to their friends, " Come, see a man that told me all things that ever I did; beyond a doubt, he must have been sent of God to my soul, or else he could not have described me so exactly." And not only so, but I have known many instances in which the thoughts of men have been revealed from the pulpit. I have sometimes seen persons nudge their neighbours with their elbow, because they had got a smart hit, and they have been heard to say, when they were going out, " The preacher told us just what we said to one another when we went in at the door."

Several persons who joined the church at New Park Street, traced their conversion to the ministry in the Surrey Gardens Music Hall, but they said it was not the preaching alone, but another agency co-operating with it that was the means of bringing them to decision. They were fresh from the country, and one of our friends, who is in Heaven now, met them at the gate, spoke to them, said he hoped they had enjoyed what they had heard, asked them if they were coming to the chapel in the evening, and told them he would be glad if they would be at his house to tea; they went, he had a word with them about the Master, and then brought them again to our service. The next Sunday the same thing occurred; and at last, those whom the sermons had not much impressed, were brought to hear with other ears, till, through the good old man's persuasive words, and the good Lord's gracious work, they were converted to God.

While I was preaching at the Music Hall, an unknown censor, of great ability, used to send me a weekly list of my mispronunciations and other slips of speech. He never signed his name, and that was my only cause of complaint against him, for he left me with a debt which I could not discharge. With genial temper, and an evident desire to benefit me, he marked down most relentlessly everything which he supposed me to have said incorrectly. Concerning some of his criticisms, he was himself in error; but, for the most part, he was right, and his remarks enabled me to perceive many mistakes, and to avoid them in the future. I looked for his weekly memoranda with much interest, and I trust I am all the better for them. If I repeated a sentence which I had used two or three Sundays before, he would write,

"See the same expression in such-and-such a sermon," mentioning the number and page. He remarked, on one occasion, that I too often quoted the line,—

"Nothing in my hand I bring,"—

and he added, "we are sufficiently informed of the vacuity of your hand." He demanded my authority for calling a man *covcchus;* and so on. Possibly, some young men might have been discouraged, if not irritated, by such severe criticisms; but they would have been very foolish, for, in resenting such correction, they would have been throwing away a valuable aid to progress.

(The last service at the Surrey Gardens was held on Lord's-day morning, December 11, 1859. Mr. Spurgeon preached, on that occasion, from Paul's farewell to the Ephesian elders: "Wherefore I take you to record this day, that I am pure from the blood of all men. For I have not shunned to declare unto you all the counsel of God." That discourse so well summarizes his three years' ministry in the Music Hall that an extract from it may be appropriately inserted here :—

" If any of us would clear our conscience by delivering all the counsel of God, we must take care that we preach, in the first place, *the doctrines of the gospel.* We ought to declare that grand doctrine of the Father's love towards His people from before all worlds. His sovereign choice of them, His covenant purposes concerning them, and His immutable promises to them, must all be uttered with trumpet tongue. Coupled with this, the true evangelist must never fail to set forth the beauties of the person of Christ, the glory of His offices, the completeness of His work, and, above all, the efficacy of His blood. Whatever we omit, this must be in the most forcible manner proclaimed again and again. That is no gospel which has not Christ in it; and the modern idea of preaching THE TRUTH instead of Christ, is a wicked device of Satan. Nor is this all, for as there are three Persons in the Godhead, we must be careful that They all have due honour in our ministry. The Holy Spirit's work in regeneration, in sanctification, and in preservation, must be always magnified from our pulpit. Without His power, our ministry is a dead letter, and we cannot expect His arm to be made bare unless we honour Him day by day.

" Upon all these matters we are agreed, and I therefore turn to points upon which there is more dispute, and consequently more need of honest avowal, because more temptation to concealment. To proceed then :—I question whether we have preached all the counsel of God, unless predestination, with all its solemnity and sureness, be continually declared,—unless election be boldly and nakedly taught as being one of the truths revealed of God. It is the minister's duty, beginning from the fountain-head, to trace all the other streams ; dwelling on effectual calling, maintaining justification by faith, insisting upon the certain perseverance of the believer, and delighting to proclaim that gracious covenant in which all these things are contained, and which is sure to all the chosen, blood-bought seed. There is a tendency in this age to throw doctrinal truth into the shade. Too many preachers are offended with that stern truth which the Covenanters held, and to which the Puritans testified in the midst of a licentious age. We are told that the times have changed, that we are to modify these old (so-called) Calvinistic doctrines, and bring them down to the tone of the times ; that, in fact, they need dilution, that men have become so intelligent that we must pare off the angles of our religion, and make the square into a circle by rounding off the most prominent edges. Any man who does this, so far as my judgment goes, does not declare all the counsel of God. The faithful minister must be plain, simple, pointed, with regard to these doctrines. There must be no dispute about whether he believes them or not. He must so preach them that his hearers will know whether he preaches a scheme of free-will, or a covenant of grace,—whether he teaches salvation by works, or salvation by the power and grace of God.

"But, beloved, a man might preach all these doctrines to the full, and yet not declare all the counsel of God. It is not enough to preach doctrine ; we must preach *duty*, we must faithfully and firmly insist upon *practice*. So long as you will preach nothing but bare doctrine, there is a certain class of men, of perverted intellect, who will admire you ; but once begin to preach responsibility,—say outright, once for all, that if the sinner perish, it is his own fault, that if any man sinks to hell, his damnation will lie at his own door, and at once there is a cry of 'Inconsistency ; how can these two things stand together?' Even good Christian men are found who cannot endure the whole truth, and who will oppose the servant of the Lord who will not be content with a fragment, but will honestly present the whole gospel of Christ. This is one of the troubles that the faithful minister has to endure ; but he is not faithful to God,—I say it solemnly, I do not believe that any man is even faithful to his own conscience, who can preach simply the doctrine of Sovereignty, and neglect to insist upon the doctrine of responsibility. I do assuredly believe that every man who sinks into hell shall have himself alone to curse for it. The apostle Paul knew how to dare public opinion, and on one hand to preach the duty of man, and on the other the Sovereignty of God. I would borrow the wings of an eagle, and fly to the utmost height of high doctrine when I am preaching Divine Sovereignty. God hath absolute and unlimited power over men to do with them as He pleases, even as the potter doeth with the clay. Let not the creature question the Creator, for He hath given no account of His matters. But when I preach concerning man, and look at the other aspect of truth, I dive to the utmost depth. I am, if you will so call me, a low doctrine man in that, for as an honest messenger of Christ I must use His own language, and cry, ' He that believeth not is condemned already, because he hath not believed in the Name of the only begotten Son of God.'

"Moreover, if a man would declare all the counsel of God, and not shun to do so, he must be very outspoken concerning the crying sins of the times. The honest minister does not merely condemn sin in the mass, he singles out separate sins in his hearers ; and without drawing the bow at a venture, he puts an arrow on the string, and the Holy Spirit sends it right home to the individual conscience. He who is true to his God looks to his congregation as separate individuals ; and he endeavours to adapt his discourse to men's consciences, so that they will perceive he speaks of them. If there be a vice that you should shun, if there be an error that you should avoid, if there be a duty that you ought to fulfil, if all these things be not mentioned in the discourses from the pulpit, the minister has shunned to declare all the counsel of God. If there be one sin that is rife in the neighbourhood, and especially in the congregation, should the minister avoid that particular vice in order to avoid offending you, he has been untrue to his calling, dishonest to his God.

" But, then, let me remark further, the true minister of Christ feels impelled to preach the whole truth, because it and it alone can meet the wants of man. The believer in Christ, if he is to be kept pure, simple, holy, charitable, Christ-like, is only to be kept so by the preaching of the whole truth as it is in Jesus. And as for the salvation of sinners, ah ! my hearers, we can never expect God to bless our ministry to the conversion of sinners, unless we preach the gospel as a whole. Let me get but one part of the truth, and always dwell upon it, to the exclusion of every other, and I cannot expect my Master's blessing ; but if I preach as He would have me preach, He will certainly own the Word ; He will never leave it without His own living witness. But let me imagine that I can improve the gospel, that I can make it consistent, that I can dress it up and make it look finer, I shall find that my Master has departed, and that ' Ichabod ' is written on the walls of the sanctuary. How many there are kept in bondage through neglect of gospel invitations ! They go up to the house of God, longing to be saved, and there is nothing but predestination for them. On the other hand, what multitudes are kept in darkness through practical preaching ! It is, ' Do ! Do ! Do ! ' and nothing but ' Do ! ' and the poor soul comes away, and says, ' Of what use is that command to me ? I can do nothing. Oh, that I had the way of salvation pointed out as available for me ! '

" I must now address to you A VERY FEW EARNEST, SINCERE, AND AFFECTIONATE WORDS BY WAY OF FAREWELL. I wish not to say anything in self-commendation ; I will not be my own witness as to my faithfulness ; but I appeal to you, I take you to witness this day, that ' I have not shunned to declare unto you all the counsel of God.' Often have I come into this pulpit in great weakness, and I have far more often gone away in great sorrow, because I have not preached to you as earnestly as I desired. I confess to many errors and failings, and more especially to a want of earnestness when engaged in prayer for your souls; but there is one charge of which my conscience acquits me, this morning, and I think you will acquit me, too, 'for I have not shunned to declare unto you all the counsel of God.' If in anything I have erred, it has been an error of judgment. I may have been mistaken; but, so far as I have learned the truth, I can say that no fear of public opinion, nor of private opinion, has ever turned me aside from that which I hold to be the truth of my Lord and Master. I have preached to you the precious things of the gospel. I have endeavoured, to the utmost of my ability, to preach grace in all its fulness, I know the preciousness of that doctrine in my own experience; God forbid that I should preach any other! If we are not saved by grace, we can never be saved at all. If, from first to last, the work of salvation be not in God's hands, none of us can ever see His face with acceptance. I preach this doctrine, not from choice, but from absolute necessity; for if this doctrine be not true, then are we lost souls; your faith is vain, our preaching is vain, and we are still in our sins, and there we must continue to the end. But, on the other hand, I can also say, I have not shunned to exhort, to invite, to entreat; I have bidden the sinner come to Christ. I have been urged not to do so, but I could not resist it. With bowels yearning over perishing souls, I could not conclude without crying, 'Come to Jesus, sinner, come.' With eyes weeping for sinners, I am compelled to bid them come to Jesus. It is not possible for me to dwell upon doctrine without invitation. If you come not to Christ, it is not for want of calling, or because I have not wept over your sins, and travailed in birth for the souls of men. The one thing I have to ask of you is this,—Bear me witness, my hearers, bear me witness that, in this respect, I am pure from the blood of all men, for I have preached all that I know of the whole counsel of God. Have I known a single sin which I have not rebuked? Has there been a doctrine that I have believed which I have kept back? Has there been a part of the Word, doctrinal or experimental, which I have wilfully concealed? I am very far from perfect, again with weeping I confess my unworthiness, I have not served God as I ought to have done, I have not been so earnest with you as I could have desired to be. Now that my three years' ministry here is over, I could wish that I might begin again, that I might fall on my knees before you, and beseech you to regard the things that make for your peace; but here, again, I do repeat it that, while as to earnestness I plead guilty, yet as to truth and honesty I can challenge the bar of God, I can challenge the elect angels, I can call you all to witness, that I have not shunned to declare unto you all the counsel of God.

" In a little time, some of you may be frequenting places where the gospel is not preached, you may embrace another and a false gospel; I only ask this thing of you,

—Bear me witness that it was not my fault, that I have been faithful, and have not shunned to declare unto you all the counsel of God.   Possibly, some here, who have been restrained from evil by the fact of having attended a place of worship, seeing the chosen minister has gone, may not go anywhere else afterwards.   You may become careless.   Perhaps, next Sabbath-day you may be at home, lolling about, and wasting the day; but there is one thing I should like to say before you make up your mind not to attend the house of God again,—Bear me witness that I have been faithful with you.   It may be that some here, who have professedly run well for a time while they have been hearing the Word, may go back; some of you may go right into the world again, you may become drunkards, swearers, and the like.   God forbid that it should be so !   But I charge you, if you plunge into sin, do at least say this one thing for him who desired nothing so much as to see you saved, say I have been honest to you ; that I have not shunned to declare unto you all the counsel of God.   O my hearers, some of you in a little time will be on your dying beds ! When your pulse is feeble, when the terrors of grim death are round about you, if you are still unconverted to Christ, there is one thing I shall want you to add to your last will and testament, it is this,—the exclusion of the poor minister, who stands before you this day, from any share in that desperate folly of yours which has led you to neglect your own soul.   Have I not implored you to repent?   Have I not bidden you look to Christ ere death surprises you ?   Have I not exhorted you, my hearers, to lay hold upon the hope set before you in the gospel?   O sinner, when thou art wading through the black river, cast back no taunt on me as though I was thy murderer, for in this thing I can say, ' I wash my hands in innocency ; I am clear of thy blood.'   But the day is coming when we shall all meet again ; this great assembly shall be merged into a greater one, as the drop loses itself in the ocean ; and, in that day, if I have not warned you, if I have been an unfaithful watchman, your blood will be required at my hands ; if I have not preached Christ to you, and bidden you flee to Him for refuge, then, though you perish, your soul shall be required of me.   I beseech you, if you laugh at me, if you reject my message, if you despise Christ, if you hate His gospel, if you will be damned, yet at least give me an acquittal of your blood.   I see some before me who do not often hear me ; and yet I can say concerning them that they have been the subject of my private prayers ; and often, too, of my tears, when I have seen them going on in their iniquities.   Well, I do ask this one thing, and as honest men you cannot deny it me ; if you will have your sins, if you will be lost, if you will not come to Christ, at least, amid the thunders of the last great day, acquit me of having helped to destroy your souls.

"What can I say more?   How shall I plead with you?   Had I an angel's tongue, and the heart of the Saviour, then would I plead ; but I cannot say more than I have often done. In God's name, I beseech you, flee to Christ for refuge. If all hath not sufficed before, let this suffice thee now. Come, guilty soul, and flee away to Him whose wide-open arms are willing to receive every soul that fleeth to Him in penitence and faith. In a little time, the preacher himself will lie stretched upon his bed. A few more days of solemn meeting, a few more sermons, a few more prayers, and I think I see myself in yon upper chamber, with friends watching around me. He who has preached to thousands now needs consolation for himself; he who has cheered many in the article of death is now passing through the river himself. My hearers, shall there be any of you, whom I shall see upon my death-bed, who shall charge me with being unfaithful? Shall these eyes be haunted with the visions of men whom I have amused, and interested, but into whose hearts I have never sought to convey the truth? Shall I lie there, and shall these mighty congregations pass in dreary panorama before me; and as they subside before my eyes, one after the other, shall each one curse me as being unfaithful? God forbid! I trust you will do me this favour that, when I lie a-dying, you will allow that I am clear of the blood of all men, and have not shunned to declare unto you all the counsel of God. Thunders such as have never been heard before must roll over this poor head, and lightnings more terrific than have ever scathed the fiend shall blast this heart, if I have been unfaithful to you. My position—if I had but once preached the Word to these crowds, not to speak of many hundreds of times, —my position were the most awful in the whole universe if I were unfaithful. Oh, may God avert that worst of ills—unfaithfulness—from my head! Now, as here I stand, I make this my last appeal: 'I pray you, in Christ's stead, be ye reconciled to God.' But if ye will not be, I ask you this single favour,—and I think you will not deny it me,—take the blame of your own ruin, for I am pure from the blood of all men, since I have not shunned to declare unto you all the counsel of God."

On page 222, Mr. Spurgeon states that, after the preaching at the Surrey Music Hall was discontinued, "both morally and financially it sank hopelessly." A remarkable confirmation of this assertion came to hand while this volume was in course of preparation. It was contained in a letter written by a Christian man who was baptized in the Metropolitan Tabernacle, in November, 1897, but who had long before been employed at the hall under the circumstances which he describes. In his communication, the names of all the persons mentioned are given in full; he writes:—

"Having spent my last sovereign of compensation for the loss of the sight of my right eye while in the 'nigger' business, I was given to understand that Mr. ———, the manager of the Alhambra, Leicester Square, was going to re-open the Music Hall as a theatre with a capital of £63,000; no expense was to be spared to make the venture a brilliant financial speculation. The opera (a burlesque) was entitled *Eurydice,* and was a shameful travesty on Holy Writ; some of the characters portrayed lost souls in hell. Knowing the principal manager, Mr. ———, at Norwood, I applied to him for something to do; he engaged me, and suggested that I should go, under ———, the decorator and property-master, at sixpence an hour, and two shillings for the evening, attending to the female Blondin. When the rehearsals were on, the performers were constantly enquiring, 'What will Spurgeon think about it? What will Spurgeon say about it? What will Spurgeon do about it?' We had not long to wait before we heard what Mr. Spurgeon was doing; it came in this wise. On learning that the tenants of the houses overlooking the Gardens were nearly all members of Mr. Spurgeon's flock, and that they were going to petition against what they considered an intolerable nuisance, Mr. ——— tried to mollify them by sending free passes of admission for themselves and their lodgers. He received the passes back by post, with tracts and letters urging him not to attempt to wage war against Christ; the writers, in many instances, adding these significant words, ' *We are praying for you.*' This all leaked out through the manager's confidants when drinking at the theatre bars.

"Well, from the opening, everything connected with the venture of converting that place from a temporary hospital to a theatre and pleasure gardens, went wrong. The performers played to paper (admission free by ticket); the money lavished on the speculation to reproduce the gods and goddesses of heathen mythology went out of Mr. ———'s pocket, never to be returned, and failure upon failure came thick and fast. The very elements assisted in keeping the people away, the violent thunderstorms (almost phenomenal while they lasted) caused the visitors to exclaim, 'There is a judgment on this place; it will never pay,' while every fresh financial disaster was met by the usual cynical phrase, ' *They're praying again,*'—meaning Mr. Spurgeon and his congregation. As I write this true account, it seems but last week that it all happened. Poor ———, who died of a broken heart, always put his failure down to the prayers of C. H. Spurgeon and his flock. We rallied round him, and got what scenery, etc., we could away from the Surrey Gardens, and tried the Satanic venture again at the Royal Amphitheatre, Holborn, but with the same result, nothing but disaster.

"Perhaps you wonder why I never mentioned all this to you before; it was because I had gone back to the 'nigger' business, and being a servant of the devil, I did not wish to furnish you with anything in the shape of testimony which would only make you more importunate in urging me to come to the Saviour. But now, being a child of God, through the blood of Jesus, I do what I can to show forth His power over sin and Satan."

After this chapter was in the hands of the printer, the following interesting letter was received. The writer of it was evidently a most appreciative member of the great congregations that assembled at the Music Hall, and it contains such a graphic description of the Surrey Gardens services, that a place is gladly found for it here, with heartiest thanks to the unknown correspondent :—

" Dear Mrs. Spurgeon,

"As I believe there will shortly be issued a second volume of Mr. Spurgeon's *Autobiography*, I thought I would venture to send you some of the impressions I had concerning him at the Music Hall, Royal Surrey Gardens. I have always been of opinion that his ministry there was the most wonderful and the most romantic that ever fell to the lot of any Christian minister. The vast concourse of people, the almost-dramatic excitement experienced by them when expecting to see the youthful preacher appear, the sudden hush and impressive silence of the great throng (composed of all classes, from the aristocracy to the very humblest,) as he was seen to approach the pulpit stairs, the solemn and pale face contrasting with the black hair, and the beautiful voice that charmed every ear as he said, ' Let us commence the worship of God by prayer,'—all this, though it occurred forty years ago, is as vivid in my recollection as if it had only happened recently.

" I am sorry that I cannot recall *the first time* I heard Mr. Spurgeon. I know I had done so before a certain Sunday, in April, 1857, when my father came home full of admiration for the sermon entitled, ' David's Dying Prayer,' which, for its matchless preface, and the stirring character of the whole discourse, must have been one of the most notable ever delivered. But the first sermon of which I have a distinct recollection is No. 133, ' Heavenly Rest,' preached in the following month. How well I remember enjoying that sermon, and his reference to the ' Stitch, stitch,' of the poor needlewoman! I believe Mr. John Ruskin was present on that occasion.

" I attended a Sunday-school in Camberwell, but I had such a passionate enthusiasm for C. H. Spurgeon that I obtained permission to leave a few minutes after ten, which enabled me to reach the Gardens in time for service. I only missed one Sunday morning, and that was through ill-health. I remember how solemn was the sermon entitled, ' The Warning Neglected,' preached November 29 ; and how happy he was on December 20, when he preached on ' The First Christmas Carol,' and wound up his sermon by wishing all his hearers the happiest Christmas they had ever had in their lives. It made me wonder whether the assembled thousands would not verbally reciprocate the kind wish. Nor can I ever forget the discourse, ' What have I done ? ' delivered on the last Sabbath of the year 1857. With what burning eloquence he condemned the sin of men who were leading others astray, and warned them that they would have a double hell unless they repented. He seemed to speak like one of the old prophets or apostles, and several persons in the galleries, and other parts of the building where they were not able to see him when seated, rose to look at the preacher who was uttering such wondrous words. In the sermon about Felix trembling, Mr. Spurgeon made some remarks about the workings of the Holy Spirit which received strong censure from a preacher at Kennington. He said that, if the Holy Spirit acted in the way Mr. S. said He did, he would shut up his Bible, and never read it again. I know, however, that, in after years, the same minister had the highest opinion of C. H. S., just as a good many others subsequently gravitated towards him whom they had originally opposed.

"During the months of February and March, 1858, I thought he seemed sad. It was about this time that he told his audience that he looked upon them as a fixed congregation, and that he would shape his discourses accordingly. Still, he seemed troubled; and, one Sunday morning, he commenced his sermon by saying that the prophets in the olden times spoke of the message they had to deliver as 'the burden of the Lord;' and I thought to myself, 'You seem to have the burden of the Lord resting upon you also.' I shall never forget the way in which, about this period, he quoted those words of our Lord, 'My God, My God, why hast Thou forsaken Me?' The piercing, wailing, almost shrieking cry, and the sorrowful tones of his voice, must have gone to many another heart as they did to mine. Very enjoyable was it to notice how grateful Mr. Spurgeon was for having escaped a serious accident, mentioned in the discourse entitled, 'Providence.' It was in April, 1858, that he preached from John xvii. 24; and, coming from the hall, I told a friend my opinion of the sermon; and an old man, a stranger to me, hearing what I said, remarked, 'Ah, my lad! does it not make one wish to go to Heaven?' I was very much impressed by the discourse on 'The Wicked Man's Life, Funeral, and Epitaph;' there was something specially solemn about it. In the introduction, the preacher spoke of children playing among the graves in a churchyard, and recalled some of his early memories of Stambourne. But how happy he was when he preached, in the month of August, from that text, 'As thy days, so shall thy strength be.' He had been unwell a few days previously, and I well remember two lines of a hymn we sang then,—

" 'Tis He that heals thy sicknesses,
And makes thee young again.'

"In September, the sermon entitled, 'His Name—Wonderful!' was listened to by a lady-relative of mine who, for years after, whenever I saw her, always referred to it in terms of admiration; and the following month, as you are aware, Mr. Spurgeon was laid aside by severe suffering, which necessitated his being absent from the Music Hall for three Sundays. I recollect his coming back, the first Sabbath after his illness, and being almost carried up the pulpit stairs; the preliminary part of the service was conducted very efficiently by Mr. Probert, of Bristol. The sermon about Samson, delivered in November, I did not hear, as I was unwell; and you may smile when I tell you how I endeavoured to sing to myself, during the Sunday morning, such hymns as 'Grace, 'tis a charming sound,' and 'Blow ye the trumpet, blow,'—both being great favourites with C. H. S.

"On December 19, 1858, the congregation at the Surrey Gardens suddenly dwindled down to very small dimensions; the weather was not bad, but the platform was only half-full, there was scarcely anyone in the third gallery, and the area was only three-parts filled. Mr. Spurgeon preached a delightful discourse on God's love, and I so wondered what effect the reduced audience would have on his mind that I went to New Park Street in the evening. He certainly appeared sad, but his spirits rose as he went on with his sermon. I was rather anxious, during the week, as to how the Music Hall would look on the following Sabbath; and when that day came, and with it rain, I was still more concerned. However, my sister and I walked to the service all in the wet, and I remember that she said, 'Well, there will be two of us present, at any rate.' But I had been only meeting trouble half-way, for, on arriving, I found that the congregation was much larger than on the previous Sunday, and, in a short time, it reverted to its original dimensions. Early in the New Year (1859), it was rumoured that Mr. Spurgeon was going to America, and he confirmed the truth of the report by telling his hearers that he might be away for some time. However, we know he never went there. About this time, he preached a very able sermon, which was entitled, 'Reform,' parts of which were aimed at some of the amusements of the people, such as dancing and the theatre. Were any in his audience offended, I wonder?

"A month or two later, during the singing of a hymn, he suddenly stopped, and said, 'A little while ago, when I was worshipping in a Jewish synagogue, I kept on my hat in accordance with the custom of the friends meeting there; I notice two gentlemen, probably of the Jewish persuasion, who have their hats on; will they kindly take them off as we do when we meet for worship?' I could not see the parties referred to; but, doubtless, they did as the preacher requested, for, after a moment's pause, the service was resumed. Not many could have conveyed a reproof in such a kind manner to the irreverent individuals who, possibly out of bravado, had kept on their hats after the service had commenced.

"On the first Sabbath in July, Mr. Spurgeon delivered a very pathetic sermon from the text, 'Kiss the Son, lest He be angry,' &c. On the following Sunday afternoon, he preached on Clapham Common, under a tree where a man had been killed by lightning a fortnight previously. I shall never forget the sermon on July 17, 1859, 'The Story of God's Mighty Acts.' I believe the Music Hall authorities had proposed to open the place for concerts on Sunday evening; but Mr. S.'s threat to leave prevented them doing so. How he revelled in preaching that morning! It was very hot, and he kept on wiping the perspiration from his forehead; but his discomfort did not affect his discourse, his words flowed on like a torrent of sacred eloquence.

" As you are aware, in August was laid the foundation stone of the Tabernacle, the ruins of which can now be regarded with feelings similar to those experienced by the old Jew when he thought of the destruction of the first Temple, for the new Tabernacle can never be quite the same as the old one. I was present at the last service held in the Music Hall, on December 11, 1859. It was very foggy, but the place was crowded, as much indeed as it could be. I had a front seat in the second gallery, and therefore enjoyed a splendid view of the people. Mr. S. preached an earnest sermon on declaring the whole counsel of God. There is always something sad about last things; and, as I came away, I felt that one of the happiest experiences of my youth belonged to the past. So also—in my opinion—passed away the most romantic stage even in Mr. Spurgeon's wonderful life.

" I have thus finished conveying to you some of my impressions of your dear husband's ministry at the Royal Surrey Gardens. You may ask what useful purpose has been served by my writing about those facts with which you, of course, were well acquainted; but when I read that the second volume of *C. H. Spurgeon's Autobiography* would cover his experience at the Music Hall, I felt an irresistible desire to send you these recollections. The other day, I stood opposite what used to be the entrance to the old Gardens. I could not help thinking of more than forty years since, when the carriages, like a stream, used to roll up and down the neighbourhood with their fashionable occupants, and the thousands of people coming away from the hall when the service was over; also of the number who used to wait to see the young minister take his departure; and when he was seen to approach, with head uncovered, a section of the crowd, kindly and respectfully, would call out, ' Put on your hat, sir; put on your hat, sir.' All is now changed; and where there was once life, excitement, and curiosity, nothing but dulness, and apathy, and lifelessness reign.

" Were not C. H. Spurgeon in his *youth*, and W. E. Gladstone in his *old age*, the two most wonderful phenomena of the nineteenth century? Both are gone; but I shall always count it a great privilege, as well as a high honour, to have lived under the influence of those good and noble men. I am aware of the general objection there is to anonymous communications; but, for several reasons, I prefer to abstain from giving my name and address, which I trust you will excuse. I may mention that I am a perfect stranger to you, although, on one occasion, shortly after the Tabernacle was opened, I had the pleasure of conversing with you.

"With every expression of respect,

"Believe me,

"Yours very faithfully,

"S. J. C.")

THE FAST-DAY SERVICE AT THE CRYSTAL PALACE.

During the time of our sojourn at the Surrey Gardens, it was my privilege to conduct one service which deserves special mention, for it was the occasion on which I addressed the largest congregation to which I ever preached in any building. This was on Wednesday, October 7, 1857, when 23,654 persons assembled in the Crystal Palace to join in the observance of the day appointed by proclamation, "for a solemn fast, humiliation, and prayer before Almighty God : in order to obtain pardon of our sins, and for imploring His blessing and assistance on our arms for the restoration of tranquillity in India." About a month previously, in my sermon at the Music Hall on "India's Ills and England's Sorrows," I had referred at length to the Mutiny, and its terrible consequences to our fellow-countrymen and women in the East. The Fast-day had not then been proclaimed ; but when it was announced, I was glad to accept the offer of the Crystal Palace directors to hold a service in the centre transept of the building, and to make a collection on behalf of the national fund for the sufferers through the Mutiny.

The Lord set His seal upon the effort even before the great crowd gathered, though I did not know of that instance of blessing until long afterwards. It was arranged that I should use the Surrey Gardens pulpit, so, a day or two before preaching at the Palace, I went to decide where it should be fixed ; and, in order to test the acoustic properties of the building, cried in a loud voice, "Behold the Lamb of God, which taketh away the sin of the world." In one of the galleries, a workman, who knew nothing of what was being done, heard the words, and they came like a message from Heaven to his soul. He was smitten with conviction on account of sin, put down his tools, went home, and there, after a season of spiritual struggling, found peace and life by beholding the Lamb of God. Years after, he told this story to one who visited him on his death-bed.

A complete record of the service is preserved in Nos. 154-5 of *The New Park Street Pulpit,* so I need not give details here, but simply mention that the text was, "Hear ye the rod, and who hath appointed it." The collection amounted to nearly £500, to which the Crystal Palace Company added £200, beside contributing £50 to the Tabernacle Building Fund, as I declined to accept any fee for preaching. It was a service that I was not likely ever to forget, and one result upon my physical frame was certainly very remarkable. I was not conscious, at the close of the service, of any extraordinary exhaustion, yet I must have been very weary, for after I went to sleep that Wednesday night, I did not wake again until the Friday morning. All through the Thursday, my dear wife came at intervals to look at me, and every time she found me sleeping peacefully, so she just let me slumber on until—

"Tired nature's sweet restorer, balmy sleep,"

had done its work. I was greatly surprised, on waking, to find that it was Friday morning; but it was the only time in my life that I had such an experience. Eternity alone will reveal the full results of the Fast-day service at the Crystal Palace.

C. H. SPURGEON PREACHING AT THE CRYSTAL PALACE.

CHAPTER LII.

Varying Voices—Pro and Con.

It is not by the power of *eloquence* that souls are saved. I believe every man who preaches the gospel from his heart is eloquent, so I have used a wrong word; I mean, however, that great oratorical powers are seldom made use of by God to produce great spiritual results. You have heard of the preaching of Whitefield; but did you ever read his sermons? If you did, you will say they were by no means remarkable productions; there is nothing in them that I should think could have approached to oratory, it was only the man's earnestness that made him eloquent. Have you heard any preacher who has been blessed by God to move the multitude? He has been eloquent, for he has spoken earnestly; but as to oratory, there has been none of it. I, for my own part, must eschew every pretension thereunto. I am certain I never think, when I come into this pulpit, "How shall I talk to these people in a grand fashion?" I think, when I come up here, "I have something to say which these people ought to hear;" but how I will tell it to them, does not signify much to me; I find the words, somehow or other, God helping me; but about any of the *graces* of eloquence, or the tricks of oratory, I am utterly and quite in the dark; nor do I wish to imitate any who have been masters in that art. I believe that the men, whom we call eloquent now they are dead, were laughed at in their day as poor bungling speakers; now they are buried, they are canonized, but in their lives they were probably abused.

Now, my brethren, God, I do think, will generally cast a slur upon fine speaking, and grand compositions, and so on, in order that He may show that the blessing comes not by any human power, but by His Spirit. I could stand here, and point my finger in a certain direction, and I could pause at such-and-such a chapel, and say, "There is a man preaching there whose compositions are worthy to be read by the most intellectual persons, but whose chapel contains, this morning, perhaps a hundred people." I could point you to another, of whose preaching I could say that it was the most faultless oratory to which I ever listened, but his congregation were nearly all of them asleep. I might point you to another, of whom I could say that there was the most chaste simplicity, the most extraordinary beauty in the compositions he delivered, but there has not been a soul known to be saved in the chapel for years. Now, why is that? I think it is because God says, it shall not be by any earthly power. And I will also say that, whenever God is pleased to raise up a man by individual power to move the world, or to work any reform, He invariably selects one whose faults and whose errors are so glaring and apparent to everyone, that we are obliged to say, "I wonder that man should do it; surely it must be of God, it could not be of the man himself." No, there are some men who are too great for God's designs, their style is too excellent. If God blessed them, the world would cry,—especially the literary world,—it is their talent that God blesses; but God, on the other hand, takes up some rough fellow, and just shakes the whole world by him. People say, "We do not see how it is, it is certainly not in the man." The critic takes up his pen, dips it in gall, writes a most fearful character about the preacher; he reads it, and says, "It is quite true, and I am glad of it, for if it had not been true, God would not have used me. I glory in my infirmities, because Christ's own power rests on me. If I had not those weaknesses, so much could not have been done; but the very infirmities have insured me against men's saying, 'It was the man.'" I have often been delighted at some of my opponents; they have sneered at everything in me,—from the crown of my head to the sole of my foot, I have been all over bruises and putrefying sores;—every word has been vulgarity, every action has been grotesque, the whole of it has been abominable and blasphemous; and I have said, "Well, that is delightful;" and while some persons have said, "Now we must defend our minister," I have thought, "You had better let it alone; for suppose it is true,—and it is, the most of it,—there is all the more glory to God; for who can deny that the work is done?" And he is a great workman that can use bad tools, and yet produce a fine piece of workmanship; and if the conversion of hundreds of souls now present, if the sobriety of drunkards, if the chastity of harlots, if the salvation of men who have been swearers, blasphemers, thieves, and vagabonds from their youth up, is not a grand result, I do not know what is. And if I have been the unwieldy, uncouth, unworthy tool employed in doing it, I bless God, for then you cannot honour me, but must give all the glory to Him, and to Him all the glory belongs. He will have it proved that it is "not by might, nor by power, but by My Spirit, saith the Lord of Hosts."—C. H. S., *in sermon preached at the Surrey Gardens Music Hall, August 31, 1857.*

IN Chapter L., mention was made of the cruel and libellous articles which appeared in various newspapers after the great catastrophe at the Music Hall, and extracts from two of them were given as specimens of the rest. There were other secular papers which published more favourable comments, one of the first being *The Evening Star*, November 5, 1856, which said:—

"Other questions than that of the structure of the building, or the self-protection of the startled assemblage, are raised by the Surrey Gardens calamity. The vocation of the preacher, and the secret of his power, are brought by it within the range of every man's thoughts, and, therefore, of newspaper discussion. The worldly-minded are forced to reflect on the nature of an institution which survives the most sweeping changes, defies alike persecution and rivalry, and is no less conspicuous in this nineteenth century, to which the press and platform are almost peculiar, than in the twelfth or sixteenth, when the altar and the pulpit had no competitors but in the throne. The devout, moreover, who prefer to think of all religious exercises as more or less supernatural, and the result of direct or indirect inspiration from on high, are compelled to observe the very different operations of the same Divine Spirit working through different human instrumentalities; so that, while a host of good, and perhaps able men, are discoursing from Scripture texts to their few hundreds of hearers each, one—and he a comparatively untrained youth—draws the multitude by ten and fifteen thousand at a time, and is even besought to continue his preaching while the dead and wounded are being carried from the doors of the meeting-house.

"No one can go into a well-filled church, or into the majority of chapels, without being tempted to ask,—'Where are the poor?' Preacher and hearers are alike emphatically of the middle class. The grey-headed, white-neckclothed, and otherwise respectable-looking men, in conspicuous seats, are prosperous traders, lawyers, or doctors. The younger fathers of families are clerks or shopkeepers. A few Sunday-school teachers, unmarried shopmen and clerks, make up the males of the congregation. The female portion greatly preponderate in number, are almost exclusively connections of the before-mentioned; though, here and there, is some solitary wife or widowed mother, who has slipped away from a penurious home to snatch consolation from the lips that speak of Heaven. But where are the artizan classes,—that keen-eyed, strong-minded race, who crowd the floor at political meetings or cheap concerts, fill the minor theatres, and struggle into the shilling gallery of the Lyceum or Princess's? So very scanty is their attendance upon the most noted preachers, that it is their adhesion to Mr. Spurgeon which has made that gentleman a prodigy and a phenomenon. The first that we heard of him, two or three years since, was that the Bankside labourers went to hear him on Sundays and week-nights. The summer before last, we found the artizans of Bethnal Green—a much more fastidious race—flocking round him in a field at Hackney. And in the list of the killed and wounded at the Music Hall, are journeymen painters, tanners, and milliners' girls. It is worth while to ask the reason why.

"A single hearing is sufficient to answer the question,—supposing the hearer can also see. There never yet was a popular orator who did not talk more and better with his arms than with his tongue. Mr. Spurgeon knows this instinctively. When he has read his text, he does not fasten his eyes on a manuscript, and his hands to a cushion. As soon as he begins to speak, he begins to act,—and that not as if declaiming on the stage, but as if conversing with you in the street. He seems to shake hands with all around, and put everyone at his ease. There is no laboured exordium, making you wonder by what ingenious winding he will get back to his subject ; but a trite saying, an apt quotation, a simple allegory, one or two familiar sentences, making all who hear feel interested and at home. Then there is no philosophical pomp of exposition,—but just two or three catch-words, rather to guide than to confine attention. Presently comes, by way of illustration, a gleam of humour,—perhaps a stroke of downright vulgarity,—it may be, a wretched pun. The people are amused, but they are not left at liberty to laugh. The preacher's comedy does but light up his solemn earnestness. He is painting some scene of death-bed remorse, or of timely repentance ; some Magdalene's forgiveness, or some prodigal's return. His colours are taken from the earth and sky of common human experience and aspiration. He dips his pencil, so to speak, in the veins of the nearest spectator, and makes his work a part of every man's nature. His images are drawn from the homes of the common people, the daily toil for daily bread, the nightly rest of tired labour, the mother's love for a wayward boy, the father's tenderness to a sick daughter. His anecdotes are not far-fetched, they have a natural pathos. He tells how some despairing unfortunate, hastening with her last penny to the suicide's bridge, was stopped by the sound of psalmody, and turned into his chapel ; or how some widow's son, running away from his mother's home, was brought back by the recollection of a prayer, and sits now in that pew. He does not narrate occurrences, but describes them, with a rough, graphic force and faithfulness. He does not reason out his doctrines, but announces, explains, and applies them. He ventures a political allusion, and it goes right to the democratic heart. In the open air, someone may interrupt or interrogate, and the response is a new effect. In short, this man preaches Christianity—his Christianity, at any rate,—as Ernest Jones preaches Chartism, and as Gough preaches temperance. Is it any wonder that he meets with like success ? Or is he either to be blamed or scorned ? Let it first be remembered that Latimer was not less homely when he preached before the king,—nor South less humorous when he cowed Rochester,—nor Whitefield less declamatory when he moved Hume and Franklin,—nor Rowland Hill less vulgar, though brother to a baronet. To us, it appears that dulness is the worst fault possible to a man whose first business it is to interest,—that the dignity of the pulpit is best consulted by making it attractive,—and that the clergy of all denominations might get some frequent hints for the composition of their sermons from the young Baptist preacher who never went to College."

Soon after the services were resumed at the Music Hall, a correspondent of *The Sun* newspaper wrote:—"If what we heard, last Sunday, be a specimen of Mr. Spurgeon's usual preaching, there was certainly nothing at all more extravagant than would be heard from most of the Evangelical clergymen and Dissenting preachers in the country. There were no outrageous descriptions of Divine anger and future punishment, nor any wiredrawn refinements on the theology of repentance. His statements on the latter point were characterized by remarkable common sense; they were forcibly expressed and illustrated, as were his arguments for the necessity of repentance. Indeed, there was little in which preachers of all creeds would not have concurred. His voice is a noble one, filling the whole place with the greatest ease; at the further end of the building, we did not miss a syllable. His manner was perfectly unrestrained, but not irreverent. His command of language is very considerable, but does not lead him, for an extempore speaker, into verbosity. His style is unfettered, homely, forcible, and abounds in pointed remarks. There was a total absence of anything humorous or ludicrous. The secret of his popularity, taking last Sunday as a specimen, appeared to us to be something very different.

"It was impossible not to feel that the preacher was absorbed, not in himself, but in his audience. The formal separation of the pulpit did not separate him from his hearers. He conversed with them, he was one of them. He did not lecture them *ex cathedrâ*, or indulge in disquisitions or topics out of their line of thought; but spoke with them as he would have done on a solemn subject in their own houses. Most of our pulpits 'die of dignity;' but, while there was nothing unbecoming on Sunday, the preacher placed himself on a level with all. Of course, a vivid fancy, and considerable powers of expression, aided by a first-rate voice, will account for much; but we think what we have pointed out was the chief reason why, among so many thousands of hearers, we could not —and we looked carefully—detect a single sleeper.

"Our more dignified preachers might study with advantage the phenomenon of this youth's popularity. We can only say that, for our part, his manner disarmed criticism, and we could think only of his probable usefulness to the thousands present who, we are confident, by their appearance, are not listeners to our customary pulpit prosaics.   Lord Chief Justice Campbell, with his son, was present on the platform, and seemed to take the same view with ourselves ; he remarked several times to one of the managers, after the service, in our hearing, and also to Sir Richard Mayne (Commissioner of Police), who was likewise present, ' He is doing great good, sir,—great good.'   London could find room for twenty such preachers ; they are just what the populace needs."

Dr. John Campbell reprinted the foregoing letter in *The British Banner*, and added the following remarks :—

"Such a testimony, from such a quarter, possesses a special value, and the deliberate language of the Lord Chief Justice of England will be duly estimated wherever it shall be read.   There is no living man from whom a ranting, raving enthusiast would have so much to fear.   A better judge of teaching, or preaching, or eloquence, than Lord Campbell, is nowhere to be found.   The friends of Mr. Spurgeon, therefore, may congratulate themselves on having anticipated the decision of this great legal luminary."

The famous *Greville Memoirs* contain the following record relating to the period now under consideration :—" 8th February, 1857.—I have just come from hearing the celebrated Mr. Spurgeon preach in the Music Hall of the Surrey Gardens. It was quite full.   He told us from the pulpit that there were 9,000 persons present. The service was like the Presbyterian,—psalms, prayer, expounding a Psalm, and a sermon.   He is certainly very remarkable ; and, undeniably, a fine character ;—not remarkable in person ; in face, rather resembling a smaller Macaulay ;—a very clear and powerful voice, which was heard through the hall ; a manner natural, impassioned, and without affectation or extravagance ; wonderful fluency and command of language, abounding in illustration, and very often of a very familiar kind, but without anything either ridiculous or irreverent.   He gave me an impression of his earnestness and sincerity ; speaking without book or notes, yet his discourse was evidently very carefully prepared.   The text was, ' Cleanse Thou me from secret faults,' and he divided it into heads,—the misery, the folly, the danger (and a fourth, which I have forgotten,) of secret sins, in all of which he was very eloquent and impressive.   He preached for about three-quarters of an hour ; and, to judge by the use of the handkerchiefs and the audible sobs, with great effect."

The letter on pages 247 and 248 was published in *The Times*, April 13, 1857. Mr. Spurgeon thought it was worthy of preservation, for it came from the pen of a learned professor, and did much to turn the tide of public opinion in his favour.

THE YOUNG LION OF THE DAY   AND   THE FUNNY OLD WOMAN OF THE DAY.

" PREACHING *and* PREACHING.

"To the Editor of *The Times,*

"Sir,—One Sunday morning, about a month ago, my wife said, 'Let us send the children to St. Margaret's, to hear the Archbishop of —— preach on behalf of the Society of Aged Ecclesiastical Cripples, which is to celebrate to-day its three hundredth anniversary.' So the children went, though the parents, for reasons immaterial to mention, could not go with them. 'Well, children, how did you like the Archbishop of ——, and what did he say about "the Aged Ecclesiastical Cripples"?' Here the children—for it was during their dinner,—attacked their food with great voracity; but never a word could we get out of their mouths about the spiritual feast of which they had just partaken. No! not even the text could they bring out. The more they were pressed, the more they blushed, and hung their heads over their plates, until, at last, in a rage, I accused them of having fallen asleep during the service. This charge threw my first-born on his defence, and he sobbed out the truth, for, by this time, their eyes were full of tears. 'Why, papa! we can't say what the Archbishop of —— said, because we could not hear a word. He is very old, and has got no teeth; and, do you know, I don't think he has got any tongue either, for, though we saw his lips moving, we could not hear a single word.' On this I said no more, but I thought a good deal of ' the Aged Ecclesiastical Cripples,' and their venerable advocate, and, being something of a philologist, I indulged in dreamy speculations on the possibility of an alphabet composed entirely of labials; and if my wife had not roused me from my dream by some mere matter-of-fact question, I almost think I should have given my reflections to the world in the shape of a small pamphlet entitled, 'The Language of Labials; or, how to preach sermons without the aid of either tongue or teeth; published for the benefit of the Society of Aged Ecclesiastical Cripples, and dedicated, of course by permission, to the Archbishop of ——.'

" Now listen to another story. A friend of mine, a Scotch Presbyterian, comes up to town, and says, ' I want to hear Spurgeon; let us go.' Now, I am supposed to be a High Churchman, so I answered, 'What! go and hear a Calvinist,—a Baptist,—a man who ought to be ashamed of himself for being so near the Church, and yet not within its pale?' 'Never mind, come and hear him.' Well, we went yesterday morning to the Music Hall in the Surrey Gardens. At first, I felt a strange sensation of wrong-doing. It was something like going to a morning theatrical performance on Sunday; nor did a terrific gust of wind (which sent the Arctic Regions, erected out of laths and pasteboard in a style regardless of expense, flying across the water of the lake,) tend to cheer a mind depressed by the novelty of the scene. Fancy a congregation, consisting of ten thousand souls, streaming into the hall, mounting the galleries, humming, buzzing, and swarming,—a mighty hive of bees,—eager to secure at first the best places, and at last, any place at all. After waiting more than half-an-hour,—for if you wish to have a seat, you must be there at least that space of time in advance,—Mr. Spurgeon ascended the tribune. To the hum, and rush, and trampling of men, succeeded a low, concentrated thrill and murmur of devotion, which seemed to run at once, like an electric current, through the breast of everyone present; and by this magnetic chain, the preacher held us fast bound for about two hours. It is not my purpose to give a summary of his discourse. It is enough to say of his voice, that its power and volume are sufficient to reach everyone in that vast assembly; of his language, that it is neither high-flown nor homely; of his style, that it is at times familiar, at times declamatory, but always happy, and often eloquent; of his doctrine, that neither the Calvinist nor the Baptist appears in the forefront of the battle which is waged by Mr. Spurgeon with relentless animosity, and with gospel weapons, against irreligion, cant, hypocrisy, pride, and those secret bosom sins which so easily beset a man in daily life; and to sum up all in a word, it is enough to say of the man himself that he impresses you with a perfect conviction of his sincerity.

"But I have not written so much about my children's want of spiritual food when they listened to the mumbling of the Archbishop of ——, and my own banquet at the Surrey Gardens, without a desire to draw a practical conclusion from these two stories, and to point them by a moral. Here is a man not more Calvinistic than many an incumbent of the Established Church, who 'humbles and mumbles,' as old Latimer says, over his liturgy and text. Here is a man who says the complete immersion, or something of the kind, of adults is necessary to baptism. These are his faults of doctrine; but, if I were the examining chaplain of the Archbishop of ——, I would say, 'May it please your Grace, here is a man able to preach eloquently, able to fill the largest church in England with his voice, and, what is more to the purpose, with people. And may it please your Grace, here are two churches in the metropolis, St. Paul's and Westminster Abbey. What does your Grace think of inviting Mr. Spurgeon, this heretical Calvinist and Baptist, who is able to draw ten thousand souls after him, just to try his voice, some Sunday morning, in the nave of either of those churches? At any rate, I will answer for one thing that, if he preaches in Westminster Abbey, we shall not have a repetition of the disgraceful practice, now common in that church, of having the sermon *before* the anthem, in order that those who would quit the church when the arid sermon begins, may be forced to stay it out for the sake of the music which follows it.' But I am not, I am sorry to say, examining chaplain to the Archbishop of ——, so I can only send you this letter from the devotional desert in which I reside, and sign myself,—

" HABITANS IN SICCO."

" Broad Phylactery, Westminster."

The Times, of the same date, had the following leading article upon the letter :—
"Society, like the private individual, has its grievances,—certain old-established
sores, any allusion to which is sure to excite general sympathy in all companies. The
extortions of cabmen, inn charges, rates and taxes,—any reference to these veteran
impositions kindles a spark of genial hostility in every circle. Everyone has had his
particular collision with these offensive claims, and has his story to tell. Those
compositions called sermons belong to this class of veteran grievances. An allusion
to them will revive a drooping conversation, and awaken a spirit of rebellion in every
breast. Everybody has suffered from this quarter, and a long vista of recollection
opens out before every eye the retrospect of a yoke long borne,—the image of yourself
sitting in a pew or stall after or before an anthem, with a look of calm resignation,
which vaguely betrays, however, the general impression that something or other—
we do not say what,—will be over in half-an-hour, or three-quarters of an hour, or
even an hour from the present moment. A series of tableaux, representing yourself
in formal relations with a sounding-board, is produced by the machinery of the brain.
The relation is one of temporary subjugation. There are one or two others near
you with the same mixed expression that you have yourself, indicative of transient
and bearable adversity. The sky is lowering overhead, but the horizon is clear. We
will not call this ' smiling at grief,' because, to say the truth, the attitude of the figures
is rather too comfortable to be sentimental. It is unnecessary to say what sympathy
the same pictorial representation pervading the whole company creates. 'A fellow-
feeling makes us wondrous kind.' It is, indeed, curious to observe the extraordinary
difficulty which some of our most respectable writers—nay, our ablest moralists,—
seem to have had in encountering this particular ordeal. Dr. Johnson repented,
most sincerely and devoutly, but still annually, over his very rare use of this great
opportunity and privilege. We hardly know whether it is fair to notice the same
delinquency in the valetudinarian Coleridge. Certainly, to hear the remarks that are
generally made, a good preacher does seem to be a very rare production, and to
require the lantern of Diogenes to discover him. The fact of the excessive dulness
of sermons being indeed taken for granted, people are lost in perplexity how to
account for it. Do the Canons require it? Do the Bishops enjoin it? The evil is
altogether mysterious, and broods over the public like a nightmare. Its origin, like
that of the source of the Nile, is unknown. Is it the result of volcanic influences?
Will the same discovery explain it that will, some day, explain the phenomenon of
the tides? Or does the enigma await a meteorological solution? There appears
also to be something mysterious in the sensations of the sufferers. Language can
give the superficial characteristics of what is experienced, but there seems to be
something at the bottom which is indescribable. In fact, the whole thing is very
mysterious, and we feel out of our depth when we attempt to penetrate it analytically.

But, as metaphysicians say, the facts of consciousness in this department are plain ; and, so long as we keep quite close to them, we feel ourselves tolerably safe.

" Now, undoubtedly, preachers have something to say on their side of the question. As a class of public exhibitors, they labour under peculiar difficulties. For example, a good lecture and a good theatrical piece can be repeated, and we have Mr Albert Smith and *The Corsican Brothers* night after night. But a good sermon has only one existence. It goes off like a rocket, and disappears for ever. The preacher cannot advertise a second delivery. If it takes place, it is by stealth. But success is not so frequent that it can afford this waste and extravagance without serious results. In other departments, the failures escape notice, because they are merely tentative, and are withdrawn as soon as they are discovered not to take, while one good hit is hammered for months running into the public mind. In the case of sermons, good and bad are on the same exhibitory level, and human nature is pinned forcibly to its average mark.

" The reputation, however, of this class of compositions being thus low, it is not surprising if the sudden phenomenon of a monster preacher excites some astonishment ; and if our correspondent, 'HABITANS IN SICCO,' regrets that the Church has not the benefit of similar services, it is quite natural to ask why should such demonstrations be confined to Dissent? Why cannot the Church have a monster preacher drawing his crowds ?

" Physically speaking, there can be no reason why the Church should not have, at any rate once or twice in a generation, a natural orator in its clerical ranks endowed with a voice as loud as Mr. Spurgeon's ; and, if she has, there can be no cogent reason why she should not use him. A loud voice is a decided gift, an endowment ; it may be thrown away in the prodigality of nature upon a man who has no purpose to turn it to, no thought to utter from that splendid organ ; upon a man, in fact, who is a mere pompous Stentor in a pulpit ; but give it to one who has thought and a purpose, and see the effect. It collects a crowd to listen, but that is only the first step. Another crowd comes because there is a crowd to begin with, and a third follows the second. But this is not all. A multitude listens with a different feeling to a speaker from that with which a roomful of people or a churchful of people listen, for the multitude *feels* itself a multitude ; it is conscious of its numbers, and every individual partakes in some degree the gigantic vibrations of the mass. The addition of power which is thus gained is immense ; and, therefore, how is it that the Church never has a monster preacher?

" The reason is, that a loud voice requires its proper material to exert itself upon. The voice is notoriously the most sympathetic thing in nature. It cannot be loud and soft indiscriminately. Some things are made to be shouted, and others to be whispered. Nobody shouts out an axiom in mathematics ; nobody balances probabilities in thunder,—*Nemo consilium cum clamore dat.* There must be a strong sentiment, some bold truth, to make a man shout. In religion, there must be something rather extravagant in the shape of doctrine. The doctrine of sudden conversion or of irresistible grace can be shouted ; but if a man tried ever so hard to shout in delivering a moderate and sensible discourse on free-will, he would find himself talking quietly in spite of himself. A loud voice, then, must have ' loud ' doctrine to develop it. But the Church of England has rather a distaste for 'loud' doctrine ; her general standard is opposed to it, her basis is a balanced one, mixing opposite truths, and qualifying what she teaches with judicious protests and disclaimers. She preaches Catholicity with a protest against Rome, and Protestantism with a protest against Geneva. This is very sensible, and very true ; but it is not favourable to popular preaching. Of the two parties into which she is divided, one thinks it wrong to shout, as being against the principle of reverence. This school specially contrasts itself in this respect with ' the rude world,' which is supposed to be always shouting, and doing everything that is noisy and vulgar, and with heretics who are audacious and immodest ; and it plumes itself on its refinement and good taste in the delivery of religious truth, which it thinks ought to be done in a sort of veiled and fragmentary way, so as to reach the sensitive ears of the good, and pass over those of the profane. All this is very excellent and refined, but it is against popular preaching. So much for one party. The other party might speak loud if it liked ; it has no theory against it, and its doctrines admit of it, but it does not like the trouble. And, besides, this party, though it professedly holds strong doctrine, practically tempers it considerably, and bends to the moderate standard of the Church. Thus, what with the fear of criticism, the deference to a recognized standard, idleness, reverence, and a great many other things,—what with some thinking it heretical to shout, and others thinking it unpolite to be popular,—there is no monster preaching in the English Church. It does certainly admit of a question whether, in our general policy, we are not over-cautious, and gain greater theoretical correctness at the cost of much practical efficiency. It admits of a question whether a little extravagance and a little onesidedness might not be tolerated for the sake of a good, substantial, natural, telling appeal to the human heart. We should have no objection, for our part, to an Evangelical clergyman, with a strong voice, doing what Mr. Spurgeon does. The doctrines of the two are in reality much the same ; and, that being the case, why should fear of criticism prevent the Evangelical school. from making themselves as effective as they can ? But such is the influence of a conventional standard, which, like conscience, ' makes cowards of us all.' "

The British Quarterly Review, June, 1857, contained a long article, of which the following were the opening and closing paragraphs :—

"CHARLES SPURGEON AND THE PULPIT.

" Mr. Spurgeon is a notability. He filled Exeter Hall with eager listeners for months together. He has since done the same in the great Music Hall of the Surrey Gardens, though spacious enough to receive 9,000 persons. Hitherto, the prophets have been in the wrong. The feeling does not subside. The crowds gather even more than before. The 'common people' are there, as at the first; but with them there are now many who are of a much higher grade. Professional men, senatorial men, ministers of state, and peers of the realm, are among Mr. Spurgeon's auditory. These are facts that cannot be questioned. That there is something very extraordinary in them, everyone must feel. How is the matter to be explained? . . .

"We believe that, to explain the fact presented in the Sunday meetings at the Surrey Gardens, we must go beyond the personal as found in the preacher, beyond the scheme of truth which he propounds,—and we must rest in nothing short of the Divine hand itself. The All-wise has often worked by instruments, and in ways which would seem to have been chosen for the purpose of making a mock of the world's wisdom. He did so when he founded Christianity,—He may do much like it again.

" Certainly, a choice rebuke has been administered to a course of speculation which has become somewhat rife among us of late, especially among parties who account themselves as belonging to the far-seeing of their generation. It has come to be very much in fashion, with some persons, to speak of all things connected with religion as beset with great difficulty and mystery. On all such questions, we are told, there must be two sides ; and the negative side, it is said, is generally much more formidable than is commonly imagined. It is assumed, accordingly, that, to be in a state of some hesitancy and doubt, is the sign of intelligence, while to be positive, very sure about anything, is the sign of a vulgar and shallow mind. Our people are said to be familiar with phrases about the doctrines of the gospel, but with little more. They may become bigots in their conceit on such subjects, and know nothing. Educated men now must not be expected to be content with phrases, or with assertions. The preacher, in consequence, owes it to himself to deal with matters much otherwise than formerly. To insist on the authority of Scripture now, as in past times, it is said, would be in vain. To set forth the doctrines of the gospel now as formerly, would be wasted labour. The preacher must be more considerate, more candid, more forbearing. He must acquit himself with more intelligence, more independence, and in a more philosophical spirit, presenting his topics on broader and more general grounds. In other words, the old mode of presenting what is called 'the old truth' has had its day. Whitefield himself, were he to come back, would produce little impression on our generation.

" But here comes a man—no Whitefield in voice, in presence, in dignity, or genius, who, nevertheless, as with one stroke of his hand, sweeps away all this sickly sentimentalism, this craven misbelief. It is all to him as so much of the merest gossamer web that might have crossed his path. He not only gives forth the old doctrine of Paul in all the strength of Paul's language, but with exaggerations of his own, such as Paul would have been forward to disavow. This man knows nothing of doubt as to whence the gospel is, what it is, or wherefore it has its place amongst us. On all such subjects his mind is that of a made-up man. In place of suspecting that the old accredited doctrines of the gospel have pretty well done their work, he expects good from nothing else, and all that he clusters about them is for the sake of them.

" The philosophical precision, the literary refinements, the nice discriminations between what we may know of a doctrine and what we may not, leaving us in the end, perhaps, scarcely anything to know about it,—all this which, according to some, is so much needed by the age, is Mr. Spurgeon's utter scorn. He is the direct, dogmatic enunciator of the old Pauline truth, without the slightest attempt to soften its outline, its substance, or its results ; and what has followed? Truly, Providence would seem once more to have made foolish the wisdom of this world. While the gentlemen, who know so well how people ought to preach, are left to exemplify their profound lessons before empty benches and in obscure corners, the young man at the Surrey Gardens can point to his 9 000 auditors, and ask, 'Who, with such a sight before him, dares despair of making the gospel, the good old gospel, a power in the great heart of humanity ? ''

The following extracts from an article written by Mr. J. Ewing Ritchie ("Christopher Crayon"), and published in his volume entitled, *The London Pulpit*, will show that, even in 1857, "all men" did not "speak well" of the young preacher :—

"THE REV. C. H. SPURGEON.

" I fear there is very little difference between the Church and the world. In both, the tide seems strongly set in favour of ignorance, presumption, and charlatanism. In the case of Mr. Spurgeon, they have both agreed to worship the same idol. Nowhere more abound the vulgar, be they great or little, than at the Surrey Music Hall on a Sunday morning. Mr. Spurgeon's service commences at a quarter to eleven, but the doors are opened an hour and a half previously, and all the while there will be a continuous stream of men and women,—some on foot, some in cabs, many in carriages,—all drawn together by this world's wonder. The motley crowd is worth a study. . . A very mixed congregation is this one at the Surrey Gardens. The real flock—the aborigines from Park Street Chapel—are a peculiar people,—very plain, much given to the wearing of clothes of an ancient cut,—and easy of recognition. The men are narrow, hard, griping, to look at ;—the women stern and unlovely ;—yet they, and such as they alone, if we are to believe them, are to walk the pearly streets of the New Jerusalem, and to sit down with martyrs and prophets and saints,—with Abraham, and Isaac, and Jacob,—at the marriage supper of the Lamb. . . .

"Here is a peer, and there his tailor. Here Lady Clara Vere de Vere kills a weary hour, and there is the poor girl who sat up all night to stitch her ladyship's costly robe. Here is a blasphemer come to laugh ; there, a saint to pray. Can these dry bones live ? Can the preacher touch the heart of this listening mass? Breathed on by a spell more potent than his own, will it in its anguish and agony exclaim, 'What must we do to be saved?' You think how this multitude would have melted beneath the consecrated genius of a Chalmers, or a Parsons, or a Melville, or an Irving,—and look to see the same torrent of human emotions here. Ah, you are mistaken !—Mr. Spurgeon has not the power to wield 'all thoughts, all passions, all delights.' It is not in him to 'shake the arsenal, and fulmine over Greece.' In the very midst of his fiercest declamation, you will find his audience untouched ; so coarse is the colouring, and clumsy the description, you can sit calm and unmoved through it all ;—and all the while the haughty beauty by your side will fan herself with a languor Charles Matthews in 'Used Up' might envy. Look at the preacher ;—the riddle is solved. You see at once that he is not the man to soar ; and, soaring, bear his audience, trembling and enraptured, with him in his Heavenward flight. . . .

"Of course, at times, there is a rude eloquence on his lips, or, rather, a fluent declamation, which the mob around takes for such. The orator always soars with his audience. With excited thousands waiting his lightest word, he cannot remain passionless and unmoved. Words and thoughts are borne to him from them. There is excitement in the hour ; there is excitement in the theme ; there is excitement in the living mass ; and, it may be, as the preacher speaks of a physical hell and displays a physical heaven, some sensual nature is aroused, and a change may be effected in a man's career.

"Little causes may produce great events ; one chance word may be the beginning of a new and a better life ; but the thoughtful hearer will learn nothing, will be induced to feel nothing, will find that, as regards Christian edification, he had much better have stayed at home. At the best, Mr. Spurgeon will seem to him a preacher of extraordinary volubility. Most probably he will return from one of Mr. Spurgeon's services disgusted with the noisy crowding, reminding him of the Adelphi rather than the house of God ; disgusted with the commonplace prayer ; disgusted with the questionable style of oratory ; disgusted with the narrowness of the preacher's creed, and its pitiful misrepresentations of ' the glorious gospel of the blessed God ;' disgusted with the stupidity that can take, for a Divine afflatus, brazen impudence and leathern lungs. Most probably, he will come back confessing that Mr. Spurgeon is the youngest, and the loudest, and the most notorious preacher in London,—little more ; the idol of people who dare not go to theatres, and yet pant for theatrical excitement. . . .

"Will not Mr. Spurgeon's very converts, as they become older,—as they understand Christianity better,—as the excitement produced by dramatic dialogues in the midst of feverish audiences dies away,—feel this themselves? And yet this man actually got nearly 24,000 to hear him on the Day of Humiliation. Such a thing seems marvellous. If popularity means anything, which, however, it does not, Mr. Spurgeon is one of our greatest orators. It is true, it is not difficult to collect a crowd in London. If I simply stand stock still in Cheapside, in the middle of the day, a crowd is immediately collected. The upper class of society requires finer weapons than any Mr. Spurgeon wields ; but he preaches to the people in a homely style, and they like it, for he is always plain, and never dull. Then, his voice is wonderful ; of itself, a thing worth going to hear ; and he has a readiness rare in the pulpit, and which is invaluable to an orator. Then, again, the matter of his discourses commends itself to uneducated hearers. We have done with the old miracle-plays, wherein God the Father appeared upon the stage in a blue coat, and wherein the devil had very visible hoofs and tail ; but the principle to which they appealed— the love of man for dramatic representations rather than abstract truths—remains, and Mr. Spurgeon avails himself of it successfully. Another singular fact—Mr. Spurgeon would quote it as a proof of its truth,—is that what is called high doctrine, —the doctrine Mr. Spurgeon preaches,—the doctrine which lays down all human pride,—which teaches us we are villains by necessity, and fools by a Divine thrusting on,—is always popular, and, singular as it may seem, especially on the Surrey side of the water.

"In conclusion, let me not be understood as blaming Mr. Spurgeon. We do not blame Stephani when Caliban falls at his feet, and swears that ' he's a brave god, and bears celestial liquor.' Few ministers get people to hear them. Mr. Spurgeon has succeeded in doing so. It may be a pity that the people will not go and hear better preachers ; but, in the meanwhile, no one can blame Mr. Spurgeon that he fearlessly and honestly preaches what he deems the truth."

In the Preface to the volume, *From the Usher's Desk to the Tabernacle Pulpit,* Mr. Shindler thus writes concerning the group represented on page 256 :—" In the hall at ' Westwood ' there hangs a picture, of considerable size,—containing the portraits of one hundred and ninety-three men and women of mark, almost

(For key to above illustration, see page 257; for description, see pages 255 and 256.)

1 Edward Ashburner, M.A.
2 Dr. Andrews.
3 George Burder, D.D.
4 Sir Edward Buxton.
5 John Butterworth.
6 William Bull.
7 William Bates, D.D.
8 William Burkitt.
9 John Brown.
10 J. Brown (Commentator).
11 T. Brown.   (Son of J. B.)
12 Isaiah Birt.
13 John Bunyan
14 Samuel Brewer.
15 H. Blair, D.D.
16 George Betts.
17 Benjamin Brook.
18 J. Bradford (Martyr, 1555).
19 Abraham Booth.
20 Theodore Beza.
21 John Berridge, M.A.
22 T. Cranmer (Martyr, 1556).
23 Cornelius Cayley.
24 Thomas Craig.
25 John Carter.
26 William Carey, D.D.
27 Richard Cecil.
28 Thomas Charles.
29 Dr. Chalmers.
30 Tobias Crisp, D.D.
31 William Cowper.
32 George Campbell.
33 Ingram Cobbin.
34 Miles Coverdale, D.D.
35 John Clayton, Sen.
36 "Cupido."
37 Doctor Collyer.
38 John Cooke.
39 William Cooper.

40 Edmund Calamy, B.D.
41 James Hoby, D.D.
42 Stephen Charnock.
43 William Burrows.
44 John Calvin.
45 Charles Drelincourt.
46 R. M. M'Cheyne.
47 R. De Courcy, M.A.
48 Dr. Dick.
49 Dr Dillon.
50 Dr. Dodlridge.
51 Timothy Dwight.
52 Edward VI.
53 John Evans, D.D.
54 Andrew Fuller.
55 Dr. Fletcher.
56 Professor Francke.
57 Dr. Fawcett.
58 William Fox.
59 John Gill, D.D.
60 S. Greathead.
61 Colonel Gardener
62 W. A. Gunn.
63 Thomas Goodwin, D.D.
64 G. H. Geddin.
65 W. M. Goode, M.A.
66 J. Hooper, D D. (Mtr. 1555.)
67 Elizabeth Rowe.
68 George Herbert, B.A.
69 John Howe.
70 Joseph Fussey.
71 John Hyatt.
72 William Huntington.
73 J. Huss D.D. (Mtr. 1415.)
74 Charles Hyatt.
75 Rowland Hill, M.A.
76 R. Hawker, D.D.
77 Thomas Hawies, D.D.
78 Richard Hurd, D.D.

79 Dr. Horneck.
80 Matthew Henry.
81 James Hamilton, D.D.
82 Joseph Irons.
83 Jerome (Martyr, 1416).
84 James Janeway.
85 John Chin.
86 Benjamin Keach.
87 William Kiffin.
88 Dr. Latimer (Martyr, 1555)
89 Robert Lowth. D D.
90 Martin Luther.
91 Philip Melancthon.
92 John Macgowan.
93 Samuel Medley.
94 William Mason.
95 Erasmus Middleton.
96 James Montgomery.
97 John Newton.
98 Felix Neff.
99 John Milton.
100 John Owen, D.D.
101 William Paley, D.D.
102 Jonathan Edwards
103 Robert Pearsall.
104 Dr. Ridley (Martyr, 1555).
105 William Roby.
106 John Ryland, Sen.
107 John Ryland, Jun, D.D
108 John Rippon, D.D.
109 John Rees.
110 Edward Reynolds, D.D.
111 William Romaine.
112 Robert Raikes, Esq
113 Samuel Stennett, D.D
114 C. C. Sturm.
115 Dr. Sibbes.
116 William Newman, D.D.
117 Walter Shirley.

118 Augustus Toplady, B.A.
119 Lord Teignmouth.
120 H. Tanner.
121 Henry Thornton, M.P.
122 James Upton.
123 William Wilberforce.
124 John Williams.
125 John Witherspoon.
126 Matthew Wilks.
127 Mark Wilks.
128 George Whitefield.
129 Isaac Watts, D.D.
130 Griffith Williams.
131 Dr Young.
132 John Wycliffe.
133 W. Wilkinson, M.A.
134 John Howard.
135 David Denham.
136 T. T. West.
137 John Knox, M A.
138 Richard Hale, M.A.
139 Lady S. Huntingdon.
140 Henry Fowler.
141 James Hervey, M A.
142 John Warburton.
143 Joseph Kinghorn.
144 T. Sharp.
145 John Wesley.
146 William Groser.
147 Thomas Scott.
148 Dr Yates
149 William Lepard.
150 W. Tyndal (Martyr, 1536).
151 Joseph Hughes, M.A.
152 Joseph Hall, D.D.
153 Walter Row.
154 Duchess of Ferrara.
155 J. H. Hinton, M.A.

156 John Flavel.
157 Reginald Heber, D.D.
158 General Sir H Havelock.
159 Frederick Trestrail, D.D.
160 B. W. Noel, M.A.
161 Edward Steane, D D.
162 Robert Hale, M.A.
163 W. B. Gurney.
164 S. Pearce.
165 Dr. Kitto.
166 J. Thomas.
167 Archbishop Usher.
168 John Angell James.
169 Dr. Cumming.
170 Robert Maguire, M.A.
171 Dr. Livingstone.
172 J. H. Evans, M A.
173 Dr. Cox.
174 Joseph Ivimey.
175 Sir S. M. Peto, M.P.
176 William Brock D.D.
177 George Murrell.
178 Charles Stovel.
179 C. Elven.
180 H. J. Betts.
181 H. S. Brown.
182 J. P. Chown.
183 Richard Baxter.
184 W. Poole Balfern.
185 Joseph Mountford.
186 T. Winter.
187 Christmas Evans.
188 William Knibb.
189 Thomas Burchell.
190 Eustace Carey.
191 C. H. Spurgeon.
192 W. Barker.
193 James Smith.

exclusively divines of the Protestant Church,—in the centre of which is a large likeness of Mr. Spurgeon, when about twenty-three years of age, and when hardly the promise of a beard adorned his face. The portraits were pieced together, in a very neat and ingenious manner, by the Rev. Joseph Mountford, then of Sevenoaks, and afterwards of Leighton Buzzard, where he died in 1867. Mr. Mountford presented the picture to Mr. Spurgeon, and it was photographed and sold for the benefit of the Metropolitan Tabernacle Fund, when the building was in course of erection. In the picture, Mr. Spurgeon stands in the attitude in which he was commonly represented at that time,—the right arm raised, and the forefinger of the right hand pointing upwards. It might have seemed to some too great an honour conferred on the young Pastor to place him so conspicuously among the learned doctors and great divines of the Puritan and later times; but his subsequent career has fully justified the position then assigned to him. He has eclipsed in popularity and usefulness the greatest of them all, though no one could have dreamed, at that time, to what vast dimensions his influence, his fame, and his varied and marvellous usefulness would extend."

Beside the historic interest attaching to the group of portraits, readers of the *Autobiography* will be able to pick out the likenesses of many ministers and prominent laymen who were more or less closely associated with Mr Spurgeon, and whose names are mentioned in this or the preceding volume.

CHAPTER LIII.

The "Down-grade" Controversy Foreshadowed.

It is frequently objected that the preacher is censorious : he is not desirous of defending himself from the charge He is confident that many are conscious that his charges are *true*, and if true, Christian love requires us to warn those who err ; nor will candid men condemn the minister who is bold enough to point out the faults of the Church and the age, even when all classes are moved to anger by his faithful rebukes, and pour on his head the full vials of their wrath. IF THIS BE VILE, WE PURPOSE TO BE VILER STILL.—C. H. S., 1856.

I have often thought, the best answer to the new theology is, that the true gospel was always preached to the poor : "The poor have the gospel preached to them." I am sure that the poor will never learn *the gospel* of these new divines, for they cannot make head or tail of it ; nor will the rich either.   After you have read one of their volumes, you have not the least idea what the book is about until you have gone through it eight or nine times, and then you begin to think you are very stupid for having ever read such inflated heresy, for it sours your temper, and makes you feel angry, to see the precious things of God trodden under foot. Some of us must stand out against these attacks on truth, although we love not controversy. We rejoice in the liberty of our fellow-men, and would have them proclaim their convic ions ; but if they touch these precious things, they touch the apple of our eye. We can allow a thousand opinions in the world, but that which infringes upon the doctrine of a covenant salvation, through the imputed righteousness of our Lord Jesus Christ,—against that we must, and will, enter our hearty and solemn protest, as long as God spares us.—C. H. S., *in sermon preached at New Park Street Chapel, April* 15, 1860. (*See quotation on page* 273.)

As good stewards, we must maintain the cause of truth against all comers. "Never get into religious controversies," says one ; that is to say, being interpreted, "Be a Christian soldier, but let your sword rust in its scabbard, and sneak into Heaven like a coward." Such advice I cannot endorse If God has called you by the truth, maintain the truth which has been the means of your salvation We are not to be pugnacious, always contending for every crotchet of our own ; but wherein we have learned the truth of the Holy Spirit, we are not tamely to see that standard torn down which our fathers upheld at the peril of their lives. This is an age in which truth must be maintained zealously, vehemently, continually. Playing fast and loose, as many do, believing this to-day and that to-morrow, is the sure mark of children of wrath ; but having received the truth, to hold fast the very form of it, as Paul bids Timothy to do, is one of the duties of heirs of Heaven. Stand fast for truth, and may God give the victory to the faithful !—C. H. S., 1867

WHEN, in 1887, there arose the great "Down-grade" controversy, in which Mr. Spurgeon was to prove himself Christ's faithful witness and *martyr*, many people were foolish enough to suppose that he had adopted a new *rôle*, and some said that he would have done more good by simply preaching the gospel, and leaving the so-called "heretics" to go their own way ! Such critics must have been strangely unfamiliar with his whole history, for, from the very beginning of his ministry, he had earnestly contended for the faith once for all delivered to the saints.   Long before *The Sword and the Trowel* appeared, with its monthly " record of combat with sin and of labour for the Lord," its Editor had been busily occupied both in battling and building,—vigorously combating error in all its forms, and, at the same time, edifying and establishing in the faith those who had been brought to a knowledge of the truth as it is in Jesus.

While the church under Mr. Spurgeon's pastoral charge was worshipping in New Park Street Chapel, there were two notable controversies,—the first was caused by the issue of a book of hymns, written by the Rev. Thomas Toke Lynch, and entitled, *The Rivulet; or, Hymns for the Heart and Voice.* The other arose from the publication of a volume of sermons by Rev. James Baldwin Brown, B.A., entitled, *The Divine Life in Man.* Mr. J. Ewing Ritchie, whose adverse opinion concerning Mr. Spurgeon, at that period, is given on page 253, wrote at about the same time in this friendly fashion with regard to Mr. Lynch :—

"Some few years back, when Professor Scott, then of University College, London, now of Owen's College, Manchester, was in town, it seemed as if an honest attempt was made to meet and win to Christianity the philosophy that was genuine and earnest and religious, though it squared with the creed of no church, and took for its text-book the living heart of man rather than the written Word. In our time, the same thing is attempted. The man who has had the courage to make the attempt,—and to whom honour should be given for it,—is the Rev. Thomas Lynch."

The Baptist Messenger, May, 1856, in reviewing Mr. James Grant's pamphlet upon "The Rivulet Controversy," gave the following *résumé* of the dispute, which will enable present-day readers to understand the merits of the subject then under discussion :—

"A volume of poetry by Rev. T. T. Lynch, has lately been published. These 'hymns' were very highly commended in *The Eclectic Review*, and subsequently in *The Patriot*, and *The Nonconformist*. The Editor of *The Morning Advertiser* (Mr. James Grant), who has in his day done much service to the cause of Evangelical truth, also reviewed the volume ; and while referring most respectfully to Mr. Lynch and his poetry, pronounced these 'hymns' to be seriously defective with regard to the essentials of vital Christianity ; that, while in them there was no distinct recognition of the Divinity of Christ, or of the mediatorial work and vicarious sacrifice of the Saviour, or of the personality, office, and work of the Holy Ghost ; at the same time there was an implied denial of the doctrine of innate and total depravity. In proof of this latter charge, the following stanzas, from one of the hymns in question, were quoted by Mr. Grant :—

> " 'Our heart is like a little pool,
> Left by the ebbing sea;
> Of crystal waters still and cool,
> When we rest musingly.

<blockquote>
" ' And see what verdure exquisite,
Within it hidden grows;
We never should have had the sight,
But for this brief repose.'
</blockquote>

" 'Only imagine,' says the Editor of *The Morning Advertiser*, 'this and other such kind of hymns being sung in a place of public worship, or being quoted to or by a person in the near prospect of the world to come. There is poetry,' says Mr. Grant, 'in the 63rd hymn, but we look in vain for the least atom of practical religion in it ;' and he adds, ' if the materials of the reverend gentleman's sermons be substantially similar to those of his hymns, we should be much surprised were not the instances very rare indeed of persons crying out in intense agony of soul, under his ministrations, "What must we do to be saved ?" '

" In a subsequent notice of the work, the same writer expressed his regret that *The Eclectic Review* should have endorsed this 'modified Deism' of Mr. Lynch, hoping that the objectionable article had crept into the pages of that Magazine unawares. To these animadversions, the Editor of *The Eclectic* replied, not ingenuously enough to escape further remonstrances from his sturdy opponent, at which *The Eclectic* took great umbrage, and accused Mr. Grant of being guilty of 'sordidness and calumny,' and of being influenced by 'extreme personal prejudice.' For ourselves, we have no hesitation in saying that, from all we know of the Editor of *The Morning Advertiser*, we can testify that he is too much of a Christian and a gentleman to be influenced by mean and unworthy motives. So far from this, Mr. Grant has not been in the least degree backward to acknowledge the literary taste which the volume displayed, and spoke of Mr. Lynch as being both amiable and highly intellectual. It was his *theology* only that was condemned.

" In the March number of *The Eclectic*, the strife was renewed with more than tenfold vigour. On this occasion, some fifteen of the leading metropolitan ministers, headed by the Revs. Allon, Binney, and Newman Hall, came to the help of the Editor of *The Eclectic*, and their *protégé*, the Rev. T. T. Lynch. The literary and devotional merits of these hymns, as well as the orthodoxy of their author, they endorsed and commended in the form of a protest signed by all the fifteen.

" The Editor of *The Morning Advertiser*, nothing daunted by the *status* or talents of his reverend assailants, met the combined forces—an imposing phalanx,—with a simple interrogatory :—' Can Mr. Newman Hall, Mr. Binney, Mr. Martin, or either of the remainder of the fifteen reverend protesters reconcile it with his views of right, to give out the " hymn " we have just quoted in his chapel? No one of the number will venture to return an affirmative answer to the question.' If this be so, then we ask, wherefore do these reverend gentlemen appear in the field at all ? It had been far better for themselves, and for *The Eclectic Review*, had they heeded the counsel of the wise man, 'Leave off contention, before it be meddled with,' and had left the criticism and remonstrances of Mr. Grant to their own merits, than for them to have interfered at all in the affair. We do most deeply deplore the position these fifteen reverend gentlemen have voluntarily and needlessly taken in this business, inasmuch as we greatly fear it betokens, on their part, an evident leaning towards a transcendental theology, the blighting influences of which have proved most fatal to many once-flourishing churches.

"In a series of powerfully-written articles, which have appeared in *The Banner*, headed 'The Theology of Nonconformity,' Dr. Campbell has given the results of his searching analysis of Mr. Lynch's volume, which he pronounces to be as destitute of poetic excellence as it is of the elementary principles of Christian doctrine, containing hymns which any infidel might compose or use. We thank Mr. Grant for the outspoken truths contained in his pamphlet. Although but a layman, he has, in its pages, contended nobly and earnestly for the faith once delivered to the saints,—'an effort,' to adopt his own words, 'which may the Almighty be pleased to crown with eminent success!'"

In *The Christian Cabinet*, May 23, Mr. Banks published the following article written by Mr. Spurgeon :—

"MINE OPINION.

"The appearance of a volume entitled *The Rivulet* has excited a controversy of the most memorable character. I shall not enter into the details of that fierce affray ; the champions on either side have been of noble rank, have done their best, and must await the verdict of the Master for whom they profess to strive. Some of the fighting has not appeared quite in keeping with fairness, and there are a few persons who have gained little but disgrace in the battle, while there are others who deserve the eternal thanks of the faithful for their valiant defence of the truth. It is my business, not to review the controversy, but the book of poems. Another time I may possibly give 'mine opinion' upon that subject. Suffice it here to say that my mind on doctrinal points is wholly with the men who have censured the theology of the writer of the hymns.

"With the leave of Mr. Editor, I will forget the past for a moment, and give 'mine opinion.' It may be of little worth, but there are not a few who will give it a patient hearing. Concerning this book,—*The Rivulet*,—let me say, in the first place, I believe that, except in Kentish Town (Mr. Lynch's residence), there is scarcely to be found an individual who would ever think of using these *Hymns for the Heart and Voice* in the public assembly. A book may be very excellent, and yet unfit for certain purposes. Who would dream of giving out a verse from quaint old Quarles ?

Imagine tne precentor saying, ' Let us sing to the praise and glory of God the ode on the 150th page of Quarles' *School of the Heart.*—

"'What!
Shall I
Always lie
Grov'ling on earth,
Where there is no mirth?
Why should I not ascend,
And climb up where I may mend
My mean estate of misery?
Happiness, I know, is exceeding high ;
Yet sure there is some remedy for that.'

"We should not find fault with Milton's *Paradise Lost,* Herbert's *Temple,* or Young's *Night Thoughts,* because we cannot sing them in our houses of prayer, for such was not their design. But *The Rivulet* professes to be a book of hymns 'suitable for the chamber or the church ;' they may be 'said or sung ;' and to facilitate their use in song, the author has appended tunes from *The Psalmist.* We are, therefore, called upon to judge it as a hymn-book ; and it is our firm opinion that, until Butler's *Hudibras* is sung in Heaven, Mr. Lynch's *Rivulet* will not be adopted in the assemblies of the saints below.

" There is scarcely an old woman in our churches who would not imitate that ancient dame in Scotland who hurled her stool at the minister's head, should any of us venture to mount our pulpits, and exclaim, ' Let us commence the present service by singing the 34th hymn in *The Rivulet,*—

"'When the wind is blowing
Do not shrink and cower ;
Firmly onward going,
Feel the joy of power :
Heaviest the heart is
In a heavy air,
Every wind that rises,
Blows away despair.'

" I ask, without fear of any but a negative reply,—Could any man in Christendom sing the concluding 'l'Envoi'? I believe I shall never find an advocate for the singing of these hymns in churches, and will therefore have done with that point, only remarking that, if a book be not what it professes to be, it is a failure, however excellent it may be in other respects. One would fain hope that the intelligent author, should another edition be demanded, will preface it with other words, purporting another object for his book, and then one great objection would be quietly removed, while he could still use his work himself as a hymn-book, if any could be found to sing with him.

" It is said that the new hymn-book matter omens badly ; well, it is very likely, but that is not my business just now.

"In the second place, when reading these hymns, simply as literary compositions, I found them far from despicable. There is true poetry in some of them, of a very delicate and refined order. Every now and then, the voices of the flowers or of the rain-drops are clear and soft, and perpetually the thinkings of the poet wake an echo in the soul. There is much mist, and a large proportion of fog; but, nevertheless, there is enough of poetic light to cheer the darkness. I believe there is a moderate quantity of unintelligible writing in the book. At any rate, there are many sentences of which I cannot see the connection; but, no doubt, these are grand thoughts which broke the backs of the words, or frightened them out of their propriety. There is nothing very wonderful in the book. We hope to see many productions far superior to it before we are very much older, and we hope at least to see many volumes which can endure the criticism of a daily journal, and yet keep up their spirits without the potent cordial of fifteen ministerial recommendations.

"I should set this *Rivulet* on my shelf somewhere near Tennyson for its song, and sundry nondescript labyrinthine divines for its doctrine; but should I place it in the same bookcase with Watts, Cowper, Hart, and Toplady, I should be on the look-out for a tremendous hubbub if the worthy authors should arouse themselves from the covers of their volumes; and should it show itself in the region sacred to Owen, Baxter, Howe, Charnock, Bunyan, Crisp, Gill, &c., I am sure their ancient effigies would scarcely be able to display their indignation in the absence of those lists whereof the antique oval frame has bereaved them. Apart from all theological consideration, a man of reading would not regret the purchase of this volume; but the mass of book-skimmers would, with some qualification, apply to the present book the words of the wit concerning Tennyson's Maud,—

"'Dreadfully dry and dreadfully dawdling,
Tennyson's Maud should be Tennyson's maudlin.'

"This, I am aware, is no argument against the book; in fact, many writers think themselves complimented when they are told that only the few can appreciate them. I am midway between the many and the few; I shall not exclaim against a man's poem because I have not culture of mind enough to sympathize with his mode of expression, nor can I hope to claim the privilege which allows to the discerning few the right of decisive criticism. I can only say, I had rather have written *Divine and Moral Songs for Children* than these fine but comparatively useless verses. No man of even moderate education can despise the talent, the mind, and the research, which have together produced this 'rivulet singing as it flows along;' but he who desires to see talent well applied, and mind put out to the largest interest, will never consider the writing of these verses a profitable employment. A minister of Christ's holy gospel should ever be seeking after the conversion of his fellow-men; and I would be sorry to write so much, and expend so much labour, on a work so little calculated to arouse the careless, guide the wanderer, comfort the desponding, or edify the believer.

" In the next place, what have I to say of the hymns theologically? I answer, there is so little of the doctrinal element in them that I am at a loss to judge ; and that little is so indefinite that, apart from the author's antecedents, one could scarcely guess his doctrinal views at all. Certainly, some verses are bad,—bad in the most unmitigated sense of that word ; but others of them, like noses of wax, will fit more than one face.

" There are sweet sentences which would become the lips of those rich poets of early times in whom quaintness of style and weight of matter were united, but an unkind observer will notice that even these are not angular enough to provoke the hostility of the Unitarian, and might be uttered alike by the lover and the hater of what we are well known to regard as the gospel.

" Frequently, an honest tongue must pronounce unhesitating condemnation ; but in many other places, one must pause lest, while cutting up the tares, we destroy the wheat also. The scale one moment descends with good truth, and for many a long hour it hangs aloft with emptiness for its only glory. There is nothing distinct in the book but its indistinctness ; and one becomes painfully nervous while wandering through this pretty valley, lest it should turn out to be what some of its waymarks betoken,—an enchanted ground full of ' deceivableness of unrighteousness.' There are in it doctrines which no man who knows the plague of his own heart can tolerate for a moment, and which the believer in free-grace will put aside as being nothing but husks, upon which he cannot feed. ' It is not my book,' the convinced sinner will exclaim ; and the matured believer will say, ' Nor is it mine,' and yet it is more covertly unsound than openly so.

" These hymns rise up in the *Rivulet* like mermaids,—there is much form and comeliness upon the surface, but their nether parts, I ween, it were hard to describe. Perhaps they are not the fair things they seem : when I look below their glistening eyes and flowing hair, I think I discern some meaner nature joined with the form divine, but the surface of this *Rivulet* is green with beautifully-flowering weeds, and I can scarcely see into the depths where lurks the essence of the matter.

" This much I think I can discover in this volume,—viz., that it is not the song of an Isaiah speaking more of Jesus than all the rest, nor a canticle of Solomon concerning ' my Well-beloved.' It is doubtful who is the mother of this babe ; and so little claim will orthodoxy ever lay to it, that its true parent may receive it into her loving arms, and there will be no demand for the half thereof. But, then, the writer never asked us to grant him the reputation of our orthodoxy ; we need not, therefore, dispute with him concerning that to which he makes no claim.

" If I should ever be on amicable terms with the chief of the Ojibewas, I might suggest several verses from Mr. Lynch as a portion of a liturgy to be used on the next occasion when he bows before the Great Spirit of the West wind, for there are some most appropriate sonnets for the worship of the God of nature which the unenlightened savage would understand quite as well as the believer in Revelation, and might perhaps receive rather more readily.   Hark! O ye Delawares, Mohawks, Choctaws, Chickasaws, Blackfeet, Pawnees, Shawnees, and Cherokees, here is your primitive faith most sweetly rehearsed,—not in your own wild notes, but in the white man's language :—

> "'My God, in nature I confess
> A beauty fraught with holiness;
> Love written plainly I descry
> My life's commandment in the sky;
> Oh, still to me the days endear,
> When lengthening light leads on the year!

"It is, I conceive, but a fair judgment to which even the writer would give his assent that these are more the hymns of nature than the songs of Zion, though I am far from believing that even the voice of nature is here at all times faithfully interpreted.   This rivulet runs through fair meadows, and between glorious hills, but it flows rather too far away from 'the oracle of God' to please me.   It has some pure drops of God's own rain within its bosom, but its flood is not drawn from the river, 'the streams whereof shall make glad the city of God.'   It has good thoughts, holy thoughts, from God's glorious temple of nature, commingled with a few of the words of the inspired prophets of the Lord ; but, in the main, its characteristic is not Revelation, but nature.   As such, it can never suit the taste of the spiritually-minded who delight in fellowship with the Divine Jesus.   Those who would crown the Head of their Maker with wreaths of thought, may here find some little assistance ; but she who would wash the feet of the God-man, Christ Jesus, with her tears, will never find a companion in this book.   I can talk with it for an hour, and learn much from it ; but I cannot love it as I do my favourite Herbert, and it does not open the door of Heaven to me as does the music of Zion which it is my wont to hear.   But why am I to condemn a book because it does not touch a chord in my own soul?   Why should I blame a man because he has not written for the old-fashioned piety which some of us inherit from our fathers?   Why murmur if he speaks his own much-puzzled mind in language which the repose of an anchored faith cannot interpret?   It were unfair to burn this book because it came forth, like some other queer things, on the fifth of November; and it is not very brave to be so desperately afraid of a plot because, on that day, a man was discovered, with a dark lantern, singing in the vaults beneath the house which ancient people call *the truth, against which the gates of hell shall not prevail.*

" Liberty of conscience is every man's right; our writer has spoken his mind, why should he alone provoke attack when many others, who agree quite as little with our views, are allowed to escape? The battle is either a tribute to superior ability, or else a sign of the times; I believe it to be both. The work has its errors, in the estimation of one who does not fear to subscribe himself a Calvinistic Christian, but it has no more evil leaven than other books of far less merit. No one would have read it with a jealous eye unless it had been made the centre of a controversy, for we should either have let it quietly alone, or should have forgotten the deleterious mixture, and retained the little good which it certainly contains. The author did not write for us; he wrote for men of his own faith, he tells his little book,—

" ' Thy haven shall the approval be
Of hearts with faith like thine.'

" The only wonder is, that men, whom we thought to be of other mind, should endorse all therein ; but private friendship operates largely, and perhaps some of them may have sympathized more with the *man censured* than with the *man singing*. This deed of men, who in standing are eminent, is not a theme for our present discussion. We must, however, observe that we cannot wonder that they themselves are attacked, and we cannot think that any other course was open to the original censor than to reply *with spirit*.

" We are sure this book could not cheer us on a dying bed, or even nerve us with faith for a living conflict. Its sentiments are not ours ; its aims, its teachings, are not enough akin to any which we hold dear to give us any aid in our labours ; but if there be any goodness, doth not the bee suck honey from the nettle? We would do the same, believing it to be a nettle still ; but one which does not grow in our garden, and is not of very gigantic stature, and therefore no great object of abhorrence. Had the author claimed to be one of the old school, we might be up in arms ; but we know the men and their communications, therefore we need not read what we do not approve.

" The book is out of our line as a theological work, it does not advocate what *we* believe ; having said that, we have been but honest ; and those who think with us need not malign the author ; but, seeing that the fight is now in another quarter, let them respect the man, however much they may oppose the sentiments which have been for a while brought into fellowship with his volume. This controversy is but one volcano indicative of seas of latent fire in the bosom of our churches. It will, in a few more years, be hard to prove the orthodoxy of our churches if matters be not changed. It has manifested what existed already ; it has dragged to light evils which were before unseen.

" Would to God that the day were over when our churches tamely endure false doctrine ; and would, moreover, that all champions of truth would keep the one point in view, and cease from all personalities !   May God, of His infinite mercy, preserve the right ; and may those who err from the faith be brought to the fold of Jesus, and be saved !   The old doctrines of free-grace are gracious doctrines still ; there are none of these in this book, what then ?   They are in our hearts, I trust ; and the outspoken enunciation of them will do ten times more for these truths than the high-flying language of the pseudo-intellectual few can ever do against them.   This book is important only as the hinge of a controversy, as such alone ought it to excite our minds ; but the less we observe the hinge, and the more we look to the matter itself, the more easy will be our victory.

"As long as the fight is thought to be concerning a man, or a book, the issue is doubtful, but let it be for God and for His truth, and the battle is the Lord's.   The time is come for sterner men than the willows of the stream can afford ; we shall soon have to handle truth, not with kid gloves, but with gauntlets,—the gauntlets of holy courage and integrity.   Go on, ye warriors of the cross, for the King is at the head of you.   *The Evening Star* exhorts the ministers to stand fast in the liberty wherewith Cromwell and Milton have made them free ; but the apostle of the Son of God bids you stand fast in the liberty wherewith *Christ* has made you free.   THE OLD FAITH MUST BE TRIUMPHANT.

"C. H. SPURGEON."

Mr. Lynch thus commented on this article :—"This review of Mr. Spurgeon's enjoys the credit with me of being the only thing on his side—that is, *against* me,—that was impertinent, without being malevolent.   It evinced far more ability and appreciation than Grant or Campbell had done, and indicated a man whose eyes, if they do not get blinded with the fumes of that strong, but unwholesome, incense, popularity, may glow with a heavenlier brightness than it seems to me they have yet done.   Mr. Spurgeon concluded by remarking that 'the old faith must be triumphant,' in which I entirely agree with him, doubting only whether he is yet old enough in experience of the world's sorrows and strifes to know what the old faith really is.   He says, 'We shall soon have to handle truth, not with kid gloves, but with gauntlets,—the gauntlets of holy courage and integrity.'   Aye, that we shall, and some of us now do !   And, perhaps, the man who has a soul that 'lights to music,'—

"'Calm 'mid the bewildering cry,
Confident of victory,'—

is the likeliest to have a hand with a grip for battle, and a grasp for friendship alike strong and warm."

The controversy continued for a long time ; *The Freeman* and *The Wesleyan*

Times joined the other papers that had supported Mr. Lynch; but so powerful was the protest of Mr. Grant and Dr. Campbell, that the Congregational Union actually had to postpone its autumnal session. The ultimate result of this long-past "fight for the faith" appears to have been very much the same as followed the "Down-grade" controversy more than thirty years later: many ministers, and their people, too, were led back to the fundamental doctrines from which they had begun to wander; Evangelical truth was, at least for a time, more widely proclaimed; and, although some strayed yet further away from the great central verities of the inspired Word, yet, on the whole, the discussion was declared by contemporary and reliable witnesses to have been productive of "an untold amount of good to the Church of God."

Nearly four years elapsed before the next historic controversy, which was produced by Mr. Baldwin Brown's volume of sermons. The veteran Baptist minister, Rev. J. Howard Hinton, M.A., wrote two articles, which were published in *The Baptist Magazine*, March and April, 1860, under the title, "Strictures on some passages in the Rev. J. B. Brown's *Divine Life in Man*." The conclusion of his protest is such a pattern and justification of Mr. Spurgeon's similar action, twenty-seven years afterwards, that it must be inserted here. Mr. Hinton wrote :—

"I offer no apology for these 'Strictures', since the matter on which they are made is before the public. I have written them with a feeling of perfect respect towards Mr. Brown; and I trust nothing inconsistent with that feeling has escaped from me. I submit them respectfully to my brethren in the ministry, and in 'the kingdom and patience of Jesus Christ,' deeply feeling the importance of the subjects to which they relate, and not without hope that they may be deemed worthy of serious consideration.

"To my own conviction, I am pleading for vital Evangelical truth, — for the truth of God, and for the souls of men. I speak because I would fain contribute somewhat, however little, to withstand what I take to be the first open inroad, into English Evangelical Nonconformist churches, of a theology fatally deficient in the truth and power of the gospel. Whether this, or any similar system may have privately diffused itself to any considerable extent, I neither know, insinuate, nor conjecture; but, assuredly, I should regard the prevalence of it as a mischief of the gravest character; and whether I am heard or not, I cannot but lift up my voice against it.

"It is true, I am now an old minister, and perhaps I ought, as is said to have been pleasantly suggested by some fast spirit of the rising generation of divines concerning old ministers in general, to be 'hung up in God's armoury,' as the armour

of ancient heroes is in the Tower; but words of truth and soberness may find a
response, if breathed low from the verge of the grave. The aspect of the times
emboldens me. It is not now, dear brethren,—above all times, it is not now, when
'the end' must be so near, and when so many cheering tokens of revival enkindle
our hopes, that a perversion, or even a dilution, of the truth as it is in Jesus should
find welcome or entrance among us; and I trust in God it will be given to us to
'contend earnestly for the faith which was once delivered unto the saints.'"

The articles were afterwards reprinted, and issued as a pamphlet. The review
of the "Strictures", published in *The Freeman*, was considered by several prominent
Baptist ministers to be of so unsatisfactory a character that seven of them signed the
following joint-protest, which duly appeared in the denominational paper on
April 11:—

"THE REV. J. B. BROWN, AND THE REV. J. H. HINTON.

"To the Editors of *The Freeman*,

"Dear Sirs,

"We are constrained to address you by considerations which, if we
may not say they are imperative, appear to us too urgent and weighty to be
resisted. We entertain, however, so high a sense of the value of free and
unbiassed criticism, and are so jealous of infringing on the proper liberty of a
public journal, that we address you with great reluctance, and only under the
influence of what we deem our duty, at once to ourselves and to what we regard
as important theological truth.

"Our duty to ourselves seems to us to require that we should, with your
permission, explicitly state in your columns that the review, in your last number, of
Mr. Hinton's 'Strictures' on the recent work of the Rev. J. B. Brown, is so far from
expressing *our* sentiments that we altogether disagree with the writer's estimate,
both of the theological principles Mr. Brown avows, and of the services which Mr.
Hinton has rendered to Evangelical truth by his strictures upon them. *The Freeman*
is so generally assumed to be connected with the Baptist denomination that, but for
such a disclaimer as we now send you, that review might be supposed to speak the
sense of the body. A more erroneous opinion could not, so far as we know, be
entertained. At all events, *our* position as Baptist ministers is well known, and we
speak for ourselves.

"We shall not indulge in any indefinite censures on the character and tendency
of Mr. Brown's volume; but we feel constrained to say that the passages on which
Mr. Hinton founds his 'Strictures' contain, in our judgment, pernicious error. We
would not hold an author responsible for the inferences which may seem to another

fairly deducible from his statements, and we entertain the hope that Mr. Brown does not see the consequences which we think inevitably follow from some of his principles. But we do not hesitate to avow our conviction, that both the principles and their consequences, whether categorically stated, or involved in a metaphor, go to subvert the whole scheme of God's moral government as revealed in the sacred Scriptures, and with it those precious truths which cluster round the cross and centre in it, and which, for that reason, are most distinctive of the gospel, and most fundamental to it.

" In our judgment, therefore, Mr. Hinton has rendered a timely and valuable service to Evangelical Christianity by his animadversions on those portions of Mr. Brown's book ; and, for our part, we thank God that our brother's pen has been so well and so ably employed. We are no more lovers of controversy in the Church than is your reviewer ; but if errors subversive of the gospel are advocated by some of her ministers, it is the duty of others to withstand them ; and we honour Mr. Hinton that, at a period of life when he might be naturally desirous of repose, he has stepped forward in the vindication and defence of some of the vital doctrines of the faith.

" Nor, in conclusion, can we refrain from expressing our earnest hope that our pulpits may be preserved from the sentiments which Mr. Brown has published, and which *we cannot but fear your reviewer approves.* Without conjuring up any 'phantasmal hydra' of heterodoxy, as your reviewer speaks, and imagining that it is beginning to be rampant in our churches, which we do not for a moment suppose or believe, we take the liberty of saying that we trust our ministers will continue to be students of Howe, and Charnock, and Hall, and Fuller, rather than draw their theology from Maurice, Professor Scott, and others of the same school, whom Mr. Brown so strongly recommends.

"Above all, we desire affectionately to caution those in the ministry, who are younger than ourselves, against that style of preaching which, under the pretentious affectation of being intellectual, grows ashamed of the old and vulgar doctrines of man's guilt, as well as of his total depravity, of Christ's atonement and satisfaction for sin, of justification by the imputation of His righteousness through faith, of the new birth by the agency of the Holy Spirit, and, in a word, of that scheme of dogmatic Christian truth which is popularly known under the designation of ' the doctrines of grace.' Those doctrines are dear to us as epitomising and concentrating the theology of the Bible, and as constituting, through the presence and power of the Christian Comforter, the spiritual life of our churches.

" Pardon us in one final word to yourselves. By whomsoever the evil work of lowering the estimate entertained of the value of these doctrines, and so diminishing their influence, may be perpetrated, let it be far from you as the conductors of one of our public denominational journals, to further it with your countenance, or to lend even the semblance of your aid.

"We are,

"Dear Sirs,

"Yours very faithfully,

"EDWARD STEANE.
"DANIEL KATTERNS.
"C. H. SPURGEON.
"CHARLES STANFORD.
"W. G. LEWIS, JUNR.
"WILLIAM BROCK.
"JOSEPH ANGUS."

"London,

"April 9, 1860."

To this communication the Editors of *The Freeman* added the following note:—

"We have no hesitation in giving insertion to the above letter. Notwithstanding that it is somewhat unusual, and generally inconvenient, to admit of discussion respecting reviews, the spirit of our brethren who have favoured us with the above letter is at the same time so excellent, and so kindly respectful to ourselves, that we should be doing both ourselves and them an injustice if we hesitated about admitting this expression of their views. At the same time, we cannot but be somewhat surprised that they should have considered such an expression necessary. In whatever sense *The Freeman* may be regarded as 'the organ of the Baptist denomination, *we* had never been so vain as to suppose that the editoral 'we' in our columns meant Messrs. Steane, Katterns, Spurgeon, Stanford, Lewis, Junr., Brock, and Angus; still less had we imagined that any judgment respecting a work, which was formed and expressed by our reviewer, would be regarded by anybody as the judgment of the Baptist denomination. The modesty of our reviewer, at least, is so shocked at the very idea of being supposed to review in this representative character, that he begs us to state, once for all, that his judgment of the works which come before him is simply *his own*, and that, neither the brethren who have favoured us with the above letter, nor any other brethren, are at all responsible for opinions of books which probably they have not seen, and about which, assuredly, he has not consulted them.

"As to our friend's review of Mr. Brown's book, we do not think it is needful to say anything. Our reviewer has already given *his* opinion of that work at considerable length, and his objections to the volume were by no means 'indefinite.' Indeed, he pointed out its deficiencies, in relation to the person and work of the Redeemer, with a precision that ought, we venture to say, to have secured him from the censures of our brethren. If he felt it his duty, as an impartial critic, to object to some things, also, in Mr. Hinton's 'Strictures', everyone who read the review would see at once that it was not the *doctrine* of the 'Strictures' that he had any doubt about,—for the 'doctrine' he declared emphatically to be 'important to be upheld,'—but the *style and character* of the 'Strictures', upon which he still retains his own opinion.

"We hope it is not necessary for *us* to say that we also 'trust'—without thinking we are 'taking a liberty' in saying so,—that 'our ministers will continue to be students of Howe, and Charnock, and Hall, and Fuller? We trust—and, what is more, *we thoroughly believe*—that our ministers will not grow ashamed of 'the old' (*we* will not venture to say, 'vulgar') doctrine of man's guilt as well as of his total depravity, of Christ's atonement and satisfaction for sin, of justification by the imputation of His righteousness through faith, of the new birth by the agency of the Holy Spirit, and, in a word, of that scheme of dogmatic Christian truth which is popularly known under the designation of 'the doctrines of grace.' At the same time, we must be permitted still to doubt whether 'our younger ministers' have given any cause to their 'elder' brethren,—amongst whom, it seems, are Mr. Spurgeon, Mr. Stanford, and Mr. Lewis, Junr.,—to 'caution' them publicly against becoming 'ashamed' of these doctrines. To our 'younger' ministers as well as to their 'elders', these doctrines are 'dear.' In the pulpits of our 'younger' ministers, as much, if not as ably as in those of their elders, these doctrines are preached. We so far sympathize with our reviewer as to hope that 'the last days of our elder brethren may not be embittered by suspicions of their younger brethren's orthodoxy, from which souls such as theirs must naturally recoil.'—*Eds.*"

Preaching at New Park Street Chapel, on Lord's-day evening, April 15, from the text, "For He hath made Him to be sin for us, who knew no sin; that we might be made the righteousness of God in Him," the Pastor, in commencing his discourse, thus referred to the burning question of the hour :—

"Some time ago, an excellent lady sought an interview with me, with the object, as she said, of enlisting my sympathy upon the question of 'Anti-Capital Punishment.' I heard the reasons she urged against hanging men who had committed murder; and, though they did not convince me, I did not seek to answer them. She proposed that, when a man committed murder, he should be confined for life. My remark was, that a great many men, who had been confined half their lives, were not a bit the better for it, and as for her belief that they would necessarily be brought to repentance, I was afraid it was but a dream. 'Ah!' she said, good soul as she was, 'that is because we have been all wrong about punishments. We punish people because we think they deserve to be punished. Now, we ought to show them that we love them; that we only punish them to make them better.' 'Indeed, madam,' I replied, 'I have heard that theory a great many times, and I have seen much fine writing upon the matter, but I am no believer in it. The design of punishment should be amendment, but the ground of punishment lies in the positive guilt of the offender. I believe that, when a man does wrong, he ought to be punished for it, and that there is a guilt in sin which justly merits punishment.' She could not see that. Sin was a very wrong thing, but punishment was not a proper idea. She thought that people were treated too cruelly in prison, and that they ought to be taught that we love them. If they were treated kindly in prison, and tenderly dealt with, they would grow so much better, she was sure. With a view of interpreting her own theory, I said, 'I suppose, then, you would give criminals all sorts of indulgences in prison. Some great vagabond, who has committed burglary dozens of times,—I suppose you would let him sit in an easy chair in the evening, before a nice fire, and mix him a glass of spirits and water, and give him his pipe, and make him happy, to show how much we love him.' Well, no, she would not give him the spirits; but, still, all the rest would do him good. I thought that was a delightful picture, certainly. It seemed to me to be the most prolific method of cultivating rogues which ingenuity could invent. I imagine that you could grow any number of thieves in that way; for it would be a special means of propagating all manner of wickedness. These very beautiful theories, to such a simple mind as mine, were the source of much amusement; the idea of fondling villains, and treating their crimes as if they were the tumbles and falls of children, made me laugh heartily. I fancied I saw the Government resigning its functions to these excellent persons, and the grand results of their marvellously kind experiments,—the sword of the magistrate being transformed into a gruel-spoon, and the jail becoming a sweet retreat for people with bad reputations.

" Little, however, did I think I should live to see this kind of stuff taught in the pulpit; I had no idea that there would arise teaching which would bring down God's moral government from the solemn aspect in which Scripture reveals it, to a namby-pamby sentimentalism, which adores a deity destitute of every masculine virtue. But we never know to-day what may occur to-morrow. We have lived to see a certain sort of men,—thank God, they are not Baptists!—though I am sorry to say there are a great many Baptists who are beginning to follow in their trail,— who seek to teach, nowadays, that God is a universal Father, and that our ideas of His dealing with the impenitent as a Judge, and not as a Father, are remnants of antiquated error. Sin, according to these men, is a disorder rather than an offence, an error rather than a crime. Love is the only attribute they can discern, and the full-orbed Deity they have not known. Some of these men push their way very far into the bogs and mire of falsehood, until they inform us that eternal punishment is ridiculed as a dream. In fact, books now appear which teach us that there is no such thing as the vicarious sacrifice of our Lord Jesus Christ. They use the word atonement, it is true; but, in regard to its meaning, they have removed the ancient landmark. They acknowledge that the Father has shown His great love to poor sinful man by sending His Son; but not that God was inflexibly just in the exhibition of His mercy, nor that He punished Christ on the behalf of His people, nor that, indeed, God ever will punish anybody in His wrath, or that there is such a thing as justice apart from discipline. Even *sin* and *hell* are but old words employed henceforth in a new and altered sense. Those are old-fashioned notions, and we poor souls, who go on talking about election and imputed righteousness, are behind our time. Aye, and the gentlemen who bring out books on this subject applaud Mr. Maurice, and Professor Scott, and the like, but are too cowardly to follow them, and boldly propound these sentiments. These are the new men whom God has sent down from Heaven, to tell us that the apostle Paul was all wrong, that our faith is vain, that we have been quite mistaken, that there was no need for propitiating blood to wash away our sins; that the fact was, our sins needed discipline, but penal vengeance and righteous wrath are quite out of the question! When I thus speak, I am free to confess that such ideas are not boldly taught by a certain individual whose volume excites these remarks, but as he puffs the books of gross perverters of the truth, I am compelled to believe that he endorses such theology.

"Well, brethren, I am happy to say that sort of stuff has not gained entrance into this pulpit. I dare say the worms will eat the wood before there will be anything of that sort sounded in this place; and may these bones be picked by vultures, and this flesh be rent in sunder by lions, and may every nerve in this body suffer pangs and tortures, ere these lips shall give utterance to any such doctrines or sentiments ! We are content to remain among the vulgar souls who believe the old doctrines of grace. We are willing still to be behind in the great march of intellect, and stand by that unmoving cross, which, like the pole star, never advances, because it never stirs, but always abides in its place, the guide of the soul to Heaven, the one foundation other than which no man can lay, and without building upon which no man shall ever see the face of God and live.

"Thus much have I said upon a matter which just now is exciting controversy. It has been my high privilege to be associated with six of our ablest brethren in the ministry, in a letter of protest against the countenance which a certain newspaper seemed willing to lend to this modern heresy. We trust it may be the means, in the hands of God, of helping to check that downward march,—that wandering from truth which seems, by a singular infatuation, to have unsettled the minds of some brethren in our denomination."

So far as that particular publication *(The Freeman)* was concerned, the protest was unavailing; and a few weeks later, Mr. Spurgeon forwarded to at least two other papers the following letter, which appears to have been his final contribution to the controversy :—

"Clapham,

" May 21, 1860.

" Sir,

" The fulfilment of irksome duties is the test of sincere obedience. When pleasure and service are identical, it is easy to be diligent in Heavenly business ; but when flesh and blood rebel against a known duty, it is time to invoke the aid of Divine grace. Every personal feeling and private affection must give way before the imperative demands of our Lord and Master. Contention for the faith is far less pleasant than communion with Christ ; but the neglect of the precept may involve the withdrawal of the privilege.

" In the matter of *The Freeman* newspaper, I most sorrowfully enter upon a work as distasteful to my feelings as it is inconvenient to my circumstances. Excuses for silence have utterly failed me. Although my respect for the gentlemen who conduct that journal has given me great readiness in suggesting arguments for peace, my conscience permits me no longer to purchase peace at the expense of the truths in which my soul finds its solace and delight. Private resentment I have none ; but, on the contrary, I cherish feelings of personal regard, which restrain me in this controversy from the use of a more vigorous style, and seriously encumber me in the conflict which lies before us. Can we not honour the gentlemen in their private capacity, and yet regret the fact that they have officially occupied a position which exposes them to severe criticism ? I can honestly say that I can meet, with cordial charity, many men from whom I differ widely ; and I never consider a blow dealt against my opinions in the light of a personal attack ;—nay, I respect an honest antagonist, and only despise the man who mingles resentment with public debate. We have solemn matters to discuss,—in some degree, connected with one of the most serious heresies which ever afflicted the Christian Church ;—and it behoves us to use language which shall become the lips of men who know the value of the doctrines upon which they debate ; and it will be our wisdom to cherish the spirit which shall be in consonance with the sentiments which we maintain. Solemnly, as in the sight of God, I believe *The Freeman* to have been very guilty ; but to our own Master we must stand or fall. It is ours to reprove, but not to condemn ; it will be the duty of the offender to defend, and not to recriminate.

"The fact that seven brethren among the London Baptist ministers, led by one of the most venerable fathers of the denomination, had unitedly dissented from their opinion upon an important question, should have had some weight with the Editors. They are not so conspicuous for learning, ability, or success, as to be beyond the reach of friendly admonition ; and surely they are not so immodest as to hold in contempt a solemn protest signed by brethren whom they are compelled to regard as honoured servants of Christ. Was the document in which that protest was contained insulting, contemptuous, or unfriendly ? Far from it. Was it not written by one whose amiable spirit might rather tempt him to laxity than lead him to severity ? What but the most weighty reasons and powerful motives could compel the most loving spirit in the universe, at a time of life when age and painful infirmity have brought him very low, to spend a great part of a weary night in penning a deliberate protest against a dangerous evil ? This may be a joke to some men ; to us, it was as devout an act as our baptism into the name of our Lord Jesus. Freely would I have signed that letter with my blood had it been needed ; and I think I speak the sentiments of all. We saw in the matter before us one of the ramifications of a deadly evil, which has commenced by polluting our literature, and may conclude by debauching our pulpits. We wrote under a strong sense of duty as in the sight of God, and there has not been a moment since in which I would not have signed it again with all my heart. We did not attack *The Freeman;* we only deprecated its patronizing the new school of theology. It is true, we expressed our fear that the reviewer was a personal believer in the sentiments we denounced ; that fear has since ripened into conviction ; but it did not involve a suspicion of the Editors, as we had reason to believe the reviewer to be a person totally distinct from the managers of the journal. At the risk of being considered egotistical, I do not hesitate to say that a more judicious, generous, gentlemanly, and Christian letter was never written. It was worthy of its author, and honourable to the cause it vindicated.

"But now the evil begins. How, think you, was the admirable document received ? Why, Sir, it was supplemented by an editorial postscript, the marrow of which consisted in a joke upon the juvenility of three of the brethren, who are yet old enough to know some who are their juniors in years, and a few who are far more their juniors in decency. A ghastly smile, like that which flickers upon the face of a man who is confused and confounded, but who longs to conceal his fears with the mask of levity, was the only answer we received. We were dealing with Divine realities, and with verities which concern the very basis of our holy religion ; the reply was a play upon a harmless sentence, highly appropriate in the mouth of most of the seven, and not indecorous upon the lip of any one of them.   This absurd trifling was esteemed to be so terrible a piece of artillery that it must needs be fired off again at Exeter Hall on the missionary occasion, to the disgust of many of the audience, by a gentleman who was so alarmed at the stupendous engine with which he was entrusted, that the echo of his own voice seemed to startle him, and one word from an indignant hearer extorted a trembling apology.

"A silence ensued.   Discretion mounted guard, and hushed alike review and article, save one faint growl, which showed the animus within more surely than the most laboured writing.   We will not hint that conscience was at work ; and yet this is a better supposition than some have hinted at.   However, the quietude was at last broken, and *The Freeman* came forth in a new and unexpected character.   It refused to be styled an organ, or even to be suspected of such a relation to the body.   Who in his senses could have thought it possible that a paper could represent even seven men, much less a denomination ?   The question was a singularly refreshing one.   We had certainly been unreasonable enough to assist in the first circulation of the paper, and some of us in its continued maintenance, under the hallucination that it was, in some sense, the representative of the denomination.

" In this belief, we wrote our letter.   We now find that we were all the victims of a mistaken, if not ridiculous, idea.   It is true that the irrational conception of a representative newspaper is embodied in scores of journals which are the advocates and organs of bodies political and religious ; but facts, however stubborn, must give way before the powerful satire of *The Freeman.*   It is equally true that the circulation of that paper is mainly owing to the absurd notion which our Editors so merrily repudiate ; but, when a protest presents no other assailable point, common sense and interest are alike invaluable, and must be slaughtered if they stand in the way of revenge.   Oh, sad result of this most rebellious protest ! It has achieved its purpose in a manner the most unexpected.   We thought to screen ourselves from complicity with error, and it is done more effectually than we could desire when *The Freeman* rejects the representative standing which was its greatest honour and the very breath of its nostrils.   This is committing suicide in order to be avenged.   The worst enemies of the paper could not have uttered a sentiment more damaging to it than that which it reiterates *ad nauseam.*   The Member has taken his seat in the Parliament of the Press, but he is not now the representative of the men whose suffrages he sought.   He laughs in your face if you have the impertinence to show him kindness in that capacity.   Be it so, Mr. *Freeman :* follow your own sweet will, and utter your own opinions without restraint.   From this day forth, we will never slander you by the supposition that there is any connection between you and our churches ; you are your own spokesman, and not ours. We would not have touched the subject if we had not believed ourselves compromised ; and, as we find we were labouring under a delusion, now happily dispelled, there is no need for protesting in a friendly manner. The field of battle now divides us ; and, if the old Lutheran spirit be not buried for ever, we will be clear of the blood of all men by clearing ourselves each day from the errors of the times.

"But, Sir, it seems that, in the performance of *The Freeman*, tragedy must always be followed by a farce. This marvellously-free actor has mounted the judgment-seat, put on the wig and gown, and tried the brethren who gently rebuked him, as if they had been guilty of misdemeanour. In mimic justice, he condemns ; but, in comic mercy, he offers pardon. Forgive me, Sir, if I leave my place as a minister for a moment, and answer these brethren according to their folly. What brilliant wits these men are ! They seem to expect the whole seven of us to perform a penitential pilgrimage to *The Freeman* office, and, with ropes about our necks. plead for pardon at the hands of the offended Editors. In truth, the offence is very grievous, and demands punishment the most exemplary. It is all in vain to plead that witnessing was of old an honoured service, and that protesting is sanctioned by the very name of our Protestant theology. It is equally in vain to hint that the opinions of seven ministers may be, in some cases, equal in value to the *dicta* of two or even three Editors. This is not to the point ; the criminals are guilty, and let them plead so, that mercy may step in. It is a memorable proof of the longsuffering of a paper which, not long ago, pretended to exercise a sort of archiepiscopal over-sight and authority, that the seven culprits were not executed upon the spot, and that space for repentance is still allowed. We are assured (and I do not doubt it) that our retractation, when tendered, will be received with all the lovingkindness with which the yearning bowels of our tender parent are so abundantly surcharged. Oh, hasten to be wise, my erring brethren, sorrowful comrades in crime ! We have but to confess our great iniquity, and the forgiveness, which we so ill deserve, shall be poured in unctuous abundance upon our heads, low as they must be in the very dust. *The Freeman*, glorious in magnanimity, stretches out to you the hand of mercy ; run into its gracious arms, and be smothered by its suffocating compliments. By dint of steady obedience, you may recover your lost position, and once more receive the paternal approbation. Yes, gentle *Freeman ;* when we retract, when we ask your pardon, when we confess that our protest was anything but a needed tribute to the soundness of the Baptist denomination, and a most proper warning to yourself, then, and not till then, put us all in your portrait gallery, from which some of our ablest ministers have prayed to be excluded, and dandle us upon your knee in blissful companionship with Kingsley and J. B. Brown.

"However agreeable this comedy may be to *The Freeman*, I am completely weary with it, and once more return to the sobriety which our subject demands. I must now refer to the injurious insinuations with which we have been personally assailed. *The Freeman* affirms that some of us had never read the book to which we referred. I am sure I had both read and marked it ; but, as to inwardly digesting it, I am not nearly enough allied to an ostrich to be able to accomplish that feat. Next, it unfairly takes it for granted that the letter of Dr. Angus was a joint affair, although it is his writing, and his alone. Admirable as it is, that letter is no more the composition of the whole seven than is this epistle, which the Editor will take care to observe is mine, and mine alone.

"A worse act than this imperiously demands enquiry. *The Freeman* must make good a statement to which I am now about to refer, or tacitly admit that its courage and truthfulness have vanished. *It dares to say that one of us had previously approved of Mr. Brown's book.* Name the man. Why stab the whole seven in the dark? In the name of common honesty, not to say religion, point out the individual. None of us would take the pains to deny an accusation so indefinitely worded. The charge is so serious that, to whomsoever it may be falsely applied, it will be his duty, for the protection of society, to visit the author of the libel with the fullest punishment the laws of his country can enforce, unless an ample apology be forthcoming. The imputation is tantamount to calling a man dishonest, if not a liar, and what remains to any of us when such charges are allowed to pass unchallenged?

"This last item is weighty enough to allow me to pause for a reply. I have written to you rather than to *The Freeman*, because this last matter is a barrier to communication too serious to be overleaped.

"I am, Sir,

"Yours very truly,

"C. H. SPURGEON."

Mr. Brown wrote the following letter to the Editors of *The Freeman :*—

"Sirs,

"I hold no controversy with the six Baptist ministers who have joined Mr. Spurgeon in a deliberate effort to prejudice my ministry, and the book which I have recently published on *The Divine Life in Man.*

"So many Christian brethren have testified to me that they find the book full of the light of those truths which I am said to weaken or deny, that I am able to bear with great composure the judgment of my critics.

"I content myself with declaring, in the belief that there are men in the Baptist ministry candid enough to find my words credible, that the doctrines of grace, in the broad, full, Evangelic sense of the term, have for nearly twenty years been the great theme of my ministry, and, if I know my own heart, will be till I die.

" I pray these seven to bear more faithful witness to their Master's words in their ministry, than they have borne to mine, and am,

" Yours faithfully,

" J. BALDWIN BROWN."

" P.S.—Is it too much to expect that those papers which have copied the protest, will do me the justice to insert this brief reply ? "

One of the papers which published Mr. Brown's letter added this significant comment :—

"While we feel it to be a matter of simple justice to give insertion to Mr. Baldwin Brown's letter, it is, to say the least of the matter, not a little remarkable that Mr. Brown should hold to ' the doctrines of grace, in the broad, full, Evangelic sense of the term,' as he here professes to do ; and that he should, at the same time, declare his full appreciation of Professors Maurice and Scott, as model teachers of truth, whose published works are most decidedly antagonistic to, and subversive of, the fundamental truths of the gospel."

" *The Inquirer*, a Unitarian paper, in an article on the controversy, fully justified the protests of Mr. Hinton, and his seven brother-ministers, when it said :—" It is not a little encouraging to us, who have maintained a faithful confession through long years of ill-report, to find the most thoughtful and earnest of the younger school of orthodox ministers gradually and painfully struggling, amid much opposition, towards the recognition of the same conclusions which we have long advocated as the highest truth of the Scriptures. With deep sympathy do we watch their struggles, praying that they may have strength from above to quit themselves like true men in the contest, and to follow *the whole truth* faithfully wheresoever it may lead them."

The Dial, in quoting this extract, very pertinently adds :—" Mr. Brown will probably say, ' Save me from my friends ! '" The writers in the Unitarian paper could see clearly enough whither his teaching was tending, just as, a whole generation afterwards, their successors plainly perceived the drift of the " Down-gradeism " which broke the heart of the brave champion of the faith,—C. H. Spurgeon,—who counted not even his life dear unto him if he might, in any degree, stem the torrent that was bearing away so much that he regarded as the priceless truth of the living God.

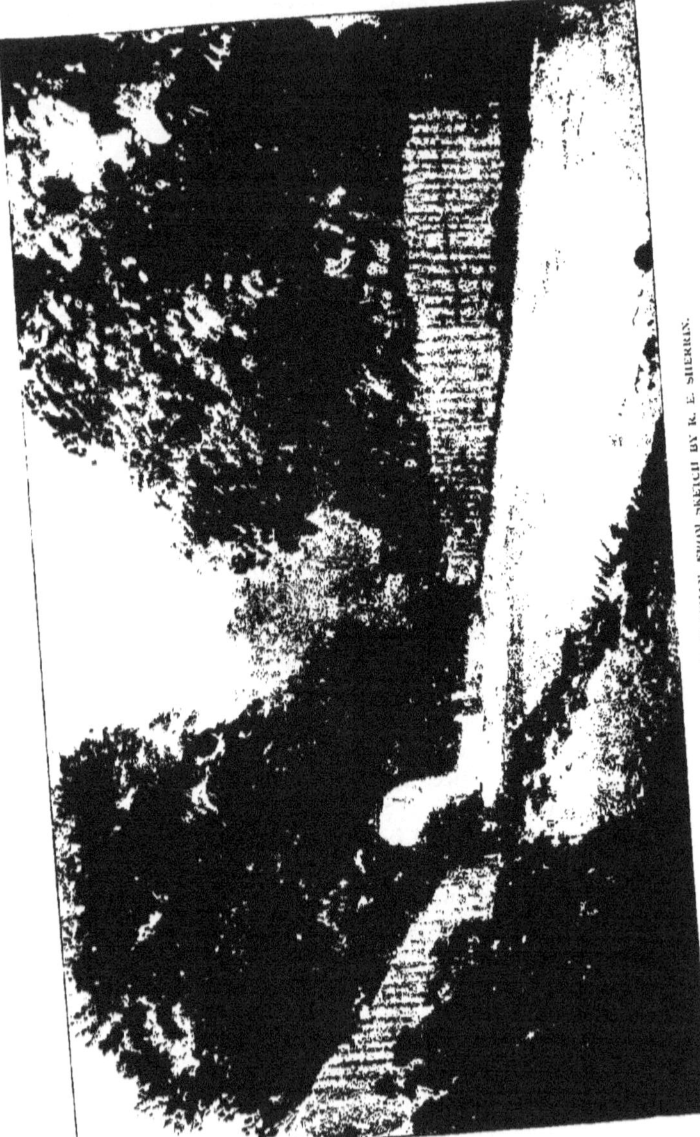

NIGHTINGALE LANE, CLAPHAM, FROM SKETCH BY K. E. SHERRIN.

CHAPTER LIV.

" Helensburgh House" and Garden.

By Mrs. C. H. Spurgeon.

HUSBAND AND WIFE IN THE GARDEN.

 WELL-KNOWN writer of to-day, in one of his pleasant little sketches, says:—" There are certain scenes in one's early life which come before us in a somewhat confused fashion. One is quite sure of the facts; but where to place them as to time, and how to connect them with relation to other facts, is not easy. It is a curious medley that memory gives back to one, passing quickly ' from grave to gay, from lively to severe.' "

This exactly describes my experience while trying to chronicle the further events of our early married life. I am embarrassed with the multitude and variety of the recollections which crowd upon me; but many of them are not important enough to be written down, and some are so disjointed that I fail to reproduce them connectedly. I seem to have before me a mass of bright, shining webs of precious memories, hopelessly disarranged and entwisted ; and the question is,—How can I bring these rebellious threads into something like order and beauty ?   I remember a story of my childhood's days, in which a little maiden— for a punishment of untidy habits, I think,—was given a basket full of tangled skeins of silk, and told that she must, by a certain time, have them all sorted out, and laid in regular rows.   The fairy "Order", pitying her distress, came to her relief ; and, with a touch of her wand, did the work deftly, and thus disposed of all her difficulties.   I want better help than a fairy could give.   "Order" and dates are some little aid to me ; but, beside this, I have earnestly asked to have brought to my full remembrance only those incidents, the relation of which shall not tend so much to gratify natural curiosity, as to render some immediate and lasting benefit to those who read them.   My husband's whole life was "an example of the believers, in word, in conversation, in charity, in spirit, in faith, in purity ;" and if, in any of the pages I have written, I have failed to set this bright example forth with due prominence, the fault is mine, and will be deeply grieved over ;—but if I have at all succeeded in magnifying the grace of God in him, it is simply because the Lord, for His own glory, has given skill for the service. I can say with Ezra, "I was strengthened as the hand of the Lord my God was upon me."

We left the New Kent Road, in 1857, to reside in Nightingale Lane, Clapham. This was then a pretty and rural, but comparatively unknown, region ; and our delight in the change and interest it afforded, was unbounded.   The sketch on page 282 (the original being a water-colour by our late friend, Mr. Sherrin,) gives a good idea of the umbrageous beauty of the locality.   On the right hand of the road, if the visitor came from Clapham, stretched a glorious park, which, with its residential mansion, was then the property of J. Dent, Esq.   Our house stood on the left side, facing the park and its palings ; it was just below and behind the spot where the angle of a cottage wall is shown in the picture.   I do not think there were more than five or six houses, beside our own, the whole length of the "Lane" from one end to the other !   This secludedness was a great attraction to my beloved, for he felt the need of absolute quiet and rest after the labours and toils of the day ; and he found them here.   We could walk abroad, too, in those days, in the leafy lanes, without fear of being accosted by too many people, and this privilege brought us very great pleasure.   In one of these wanderings, an incident occurred which my dear husband has so tenderly described, and so aptly turned into an encouragement for a seeking sinner, that I introduce it here, as a diamond among my rock-crystals, praying that some longing soul may find it, appropriate it, and be rich for ever :—

"We were walking up the lane near where I live, and there was a poor woman, who stopped us. She spoke in French. This poor soul had some children at Guildford, and she was wanting to find her way to them, but did not know a single sentence of English. She had knocked at the doors of all the gentlemen's houses down the lane, and of course the servants could do nothing for her, for they did not understand a word she said. So she went from one place to another, and at last she

"HELENSBURGH HOUSE," NIGHTINGALE LANE (FRONT VIEW).

did not know what would become of her. She had some thirty miles to walk; she did not mind that, but then, she could not tell which way to go; so I suppose she had made up her mind she would ask everybody. All she knew was, she had written on a piece of paper the word 'Guildford,' and she held it up, and began to ask in French which was the right road.

"When, at last, she had met with someone who could tell her the path she must take, beautifully did she express both her distress and her gratitude; she said she felt like a poor little bird who was hunted about, and did not know how to find her way to the nest. She poured a thousand blessings on us when we told her the way; and, I thought,—how much this is like the sinner when he wants to find the way to Heaven! All he knows is, he wants Christ; but where to find Him, and how to get to Him, he cannot tell; and he knocks, first at one door, and then at another; and perhaps the minister at the place of worship does not know the language of human sympathy. He cannot comprehend the sinner's need, for there are many servants in my Master's house, I am sorry to say, who do not understand the language of a sinner's cry. O sinner, thou shalt surely find Christ though thou knowest not how to find Him! He will ask thee, 'Whom seekest thou?' and thou wilt answer, 'I seek Jesus,' and He will say, 'I that speak unto thee am He.' I am much mistaken if He who speaks in thy heart is not the very Jesus whom thou art seeking. His speaking in thy heart is a token of His love. Trust Him, believe in Him, and Thou shalt be saved."

The house was a very old one; and, in its first estate, I should judge it had been an eight-roomed cottage, with underground cellars afterwards turned into kitchens. Some bygone owner had built another story, and thrown the eight small rooms into four better-sized ones; but, even with this improvement, they were narrow and incommodious. To us, however, they were then all that we could desire, and the large garden made up for all the inconveniences indoors. Oh, what a delightsome place we thought it, though it was a very wilderness through long neglect,—the blackberry bushes impertinently asserting themselves to be trees, and the fruit trees running wild for want of the pruning-knife! It was all the more interesting to us in this sweet confusion and artlessness because we had the happy task of bringing it gradually into accord with our ideas of what a garden should be. I must admit that we made many absurd mistakes both in house and garden management, in those young days of ours; but what did that matter? No two birds ever felt more exquisite joy in building their nest in the fork of a tree-branch, than did we in planning and placing, altering and rearranging our pretty country home.

What a boon such a retreat was to my beloved, can be well understood by all zealous workers who know the penalties exacted by weary brains and jaded powers. At this time, Mr. Spurgeon's sermons were having a phenomenal sale both at home and abroad, and the generous arrangements of the publishers, together with the increased income from the church, made possible the purchase of the freehold of this house and grounds; and the fact of the place being old and long untenanted, enabled him to obtain it on very easy terms. It had some queer corners in it, which we peopled with mysterious shadows for the mere gratification of afterwards dispersing them. A large brewhouse sort of erection at the side was a great puzzle to us, with its flagged floor, its great boiler in one corner, and its curious little rooms, like cells, which we converted into apple-chambers.

But *the* sensation of the place was *the well*, which altogether fascinated us, and did not withdraw its spell till the demolition of the old house broke the charm by covering it up entirely, and leaving only a common pump-handle "en évidence." It was a wonderful well ; the water came up pure, sparkling, and cold as ice. The story of it was, as far as I can recollect, as follows :—A former occupant of the house had resolved, at any cost, to have water at that particular spot. So he hired well-diggers, and they began to dig. At one hundred feet depth, they stopped. There was no sign of water. "Go on," said the master; "you must go deeper." They dug another two hundred feet, and came to the solid rock ! " Now," said he, "you must *bore*, for I am going to have water here if I bore to the centre of the earth for it." So they bored, and bored, and got quite disheartened, for they had now gone 460 feet into the bowels of the earth ! But the master insisted that they should continue their efforts ; and, one day, they came up as usual to have their dinner, but they never went down to the rock again, for the water had burst through, and covered up their tools, and risen high in the well ! Was not the man right glad that he had not relinquished his object, and was he not well rewarded for his perseverance ? He was a benefactor to succeeding generations, too, for the delicious water had quite a fame round about the place, and residents in our time used to send and beg the favour of a large jugful of "water from the well."

Many years afterwards, when the main drainage works were in progress, its generous abundance diminished ; and when the new house was built, though its services were still secured, it lost, as I have said, all its ancient attractiveness,—*and danger*. Yes, there was danger in the old well, as we painfully realized, one day, when a man, while making some repairs, a short way down, lost his footing, and fell through many of the wooden stages (erected inside the well, and reached by ladders), and would have been precipitated into the deep water, with a very faint chance of life, but that, by God's great mercy, he was caught by the arms on one of the stagings, and there hung suspended, in horror and darkness, till his mates could reach and rescue him ! I can never forget my dear husband's anguish of mind on that occasion. He paced to and fro, before the well-house door, in an agony of suspense. We were all white and trembling, and sick with frightful fears. But it pleased the Lord to avert the threatened tragedy ; and, after a time, the man was brought up from the depths, to see again the blessed light of the sun. He looked more like a dead than a living creature when he was safely on *terra firma ;* but, beyond being much bruised, he was uninjured. After that, my dear husband allowed no one to go down the well without having a stout rope round his body, securely fastened, or held by other men. We never again had an accident there.

In the little parlour of this old house,—see the window of the room to the left of the porch in the picture,—there occurred, one day, an incident of much interest, which, though it concerns a notable and still living author (Mr. John Ruskin), I think I may be permitted to reveal. It will but disclose the existence, at that time, in a very noble and gifted heart, of a sweet spring of brotherly love, which has long remained sealed-up and hidden. Towards the end of the year 1858, my beloved had a serious illness, which kept him out of his pulpit for three Sabbaths. In those early days, Mr. Ruskin was not only a frequent attendant at the Surrey Music Hall services, and a loving friend to my dear husband, but I believe he was also an ardent admirer of him as a preacher of the gospel. When Mr. Spurgeon was partly convalescent, but still painfully weak, Mr. Ruskin, knowing of his condition, called to see him. My beloved was downstairs for the first time that day, and was lying on the couch in the room I have indicated. How well I remember the intense love and devotion displayed by Mr. Ruskin, as he threw himself on his knees by the dear patient's side, and embraced him with tender affection and tears. "My brother, my dear brother," he said, "how grieved I am to see you thus!" His sorrow and sympathy were most touching and comforting. He had brought with him two charming engravings,—gems of artistic taste, which still adorn the walls of one of the rooms at "Westwood,"—and some bottles of wine of a rare vintage, which he hoped would prove a cordial to the sufferer's much-weakened frame. My husband was greatly moved by the love and consideration so graciously expressed, and he very often referred to it afterwards in grateful appreciation ; especially when, in later years, there came a change of feeling on Mr. Ruskin's part, and he strongly repudiated some of the theological opinions to which Mr. Spurgeon closely clung to the end of his life.

I am not sure that it was on the occasion of the visit I have now described, or at some other time, that Mr. Ruskin told my husband a very remarkable story, for the truth of which he himself could answer. I think they had been talking together of the interpositions of God's providence, of His care over His people, and of the singular deliverances which He had vouchsafed to them when in danger or distress ; and Mr. Ruskin then related, with an impassioned tenderness and power which my pen cannot possibly imitate, the following instance of direct and Divine preservation from a dreadful death.

A Christian gentleman, a widower, with several little ones, was in treaty for the occupancy of an old farm-house in the country, for the sake of his children's health. One day, he took them to see their new residence, before finally removing into it. While he talked with the landlord or agent, the young people set off on a tour of inspection, and scampered here, there, and everywhere over the garden and grounds. Then they proceeded to examine the house, and rushed up and down stairs, looking into every room, dancing with delight, full of fun and frolic, and shouting out their joy over every new discovery. Presently, when they seemed to have exhausted the wonders of the old house, one of them suggested that the underground premises had not yet been explored, and must therefore be visited at once. So the merry band went helter-skelter in search of a way below, found a door at the head of some dark stairs, and were rushing down them at great speed, when, midway, they suddenly stopped in startled amazement, for, standing at the bottom of the steps, they saw *their mother*, with outstretched arms and loving gesture, waving them back, and silently forbidding their further passage. With a cry of mingled fear and joy, they turned, and fled in haste to their father, telling him that they had seen " Mother," that she had smiled lovingly at them, but had eagerly motioned them to go back. In utter astonishment, the father listened to the children's tale, and at once perceived that something unusual had happened. Search was made, and close at the foot of those narrow, gloomy stairs, they found a deep and open well, entirely unguarded, into which, in their mad rush, every child must inevitably have fallen and perished, had not the Lord in His mercy interposed.

Stories of the supernatural are seldom worthy of credence ; but, in this case, both my dear husband and Mr. Ruskin were convinced that God permitted the appearance of their mother to those dear children, in order to save them from a terrible death ; and that nothing else, and nothing less than such a vision could have attained this object, and prevented the calamity.

I find, from data kindly supplied to me by Pastor J. W. Davies, of Lee, that on one occasion, " under the Oak " at " Westwood," the question was asked of Mr. Spurgeon, " Do you believe in supernatural visitations ?" and for answer he repeated this story ot Mr. Ruskin's. The students listened with eager interest, and then promptly requested their President to give his theory of the nature of the appearance. He replied that he could not explain it, but he thought that God had impressed on the retina of the children's eyes an object which would naturally cause them to return at once to their father, thus ensuring their safety.

There have been many other well-authenticated instances of similar appearances permitted by the Lord in seasons of special danger to His children ; and the calm and reverent consideration of such a subject, by devout minds, might have the happy effect of bringing the soul very close to the veil which separates the things that are seen, and are temporal, from the things that are not seen, and are eternal.

CHAPTER LV.

"Helensburgh House" and Garden (*Continued*).

FATHER AND SONS IN THE GARDEN.

I took my little boys, a few years ago, to a churchyard, and we carried with us a piece of tape. I told them to measure some of the little graves, for I wanted them to learn practically how soon they might die. They found there were several which were shorter than they themselves were. Ah! there are many who are taken away before they are your age, my young friends, and why may not you be so taken? It is early with you, but it is not too early for Death to be even now pointing his darts at you.—C. H. S., *in sermon to senior scholars, at John Street Chapel, Bedford Row, May 1, 1867.*

E lived in the dear old house in Nightingale Lane for many happy years; and, looking back upon them from this distance of time, I think they must have been the least shadowed by care and sorrow of all the years of our married life. We were both young, and full of high spirits. We had fairly good health, and devoutly loved each other. Our children grew apace in the sweet country air, and my whole time and strength were given to advance my dear husband's welfare and happiness. I deemed it my joy and privilege to be ever at his side, accompanying him on many of his preaching journeys, nursing him in his occasional illnesses,—his delighted companion during his holiday trips, always watching over and tending him with the enthusiasm and sympathy which my great love for him inspired. I mention this, not to suggest any sort of merit on my part, but simply that I may here record my heartfelt gratitude to God that, for a period of ten blessed years, I was permitted to encircle him with all the comforting care and tender affection which it was in a wife's power to bestow. Afterwards, God ordered it otherwise. He saw fit to reverse our position to each other; and for a long, long season, suffering instead of service became my daily portion, and the care of comforting a sick wife fell upon my beloved. How lovingly he fulfilled so sorrowful a duty, will be fully seen in future pages.

HUSBAND AND WIFE AT HOME.

I have already said what a great joy the garden was to us. At first, there was always something fresh and new to interest us; and when, by degrees, the novelty of its possession wore off, then we loved it all the better, because we knew more about it. Here my dear husband enjoyed, not only rest and recreation for the body, but stimulus and quickening for the mind. Original illustrations for sermons,—side-lights on texts,—metaphors and parables, whereby the hearts of hearers might be moved or impressed,—all these Mr. Spurgeon found ready to his hand in this old pleasaunce, which ungrudgingly laid its stores at his feet. It mattered not to him how commonplace was the figure which could supply a barb or a feather to the arrow which he designed to send straight home to the heart of a saint or a sinner.

He did not disdain to employ the simplest incidents or similes to further the important purposes of illustration and instruction.

He himself gives a notable instance of the working of this life-long habit, in one of the lectures to his students, where he says :—" If you keep your eyes open, you will not see even a dog following his master, nor a mouse peeping up from his hole, nor will you hear even a gentle scratching behind the wainscot, without getting something to weave into your sermons if your faculties are all on the alert. When you go home to-night, and sit by your fireside, you ought not to be able to take up your domestic cat without finding that which will furnish you with an illustration. How soft are pussy's pads, and yet, in a moment, if she is angered, how sharp will be her claws ! How like to temptation, soft and gentle when it first cometh to us, but how deadly, how damnable the wounds it causeth ere long !

" I recollect using, with very considerable effect in a sermon in the Tabernacle, an incident that occurred in my own garden. There was a dog which was in the habit of coming through the fence, and scratching in my flower-beds, to the manifest spoiling of the gardener's toil and temper. Walking in the garden, one Saturday afternoon, and preparing my sermon for the following day, I saw the four-footed creature,—rather a scurvy specimen, by-the-by,—and having a walking-stick in my hand, I threw it at him with all my might, at the same time giving him some good advice about going home. Now, what should my canine friend do but turn round, pick up the stick in his mouth, bring it, and lay it down at my feet, wagging his tail all the while in expectation of my thanks and kind words ! Of course, you do not suppose that I kicked him, or threw the stick at him any more. I felt quite ashamed of myself, and told him that he was welcome to stay as long as he liked, and to come as often as he pleased. There was an instance of the power of non-resistance, submission, patience, and trust, in overcoming even righteous anger. I used that illustration in preaching the next day, and I did not feel that I had at all degraded myself by telling the story."

If my memory does not play me false, there used to be sundry crusts, or even bones, secretly conveyed to that mongrel cur after this memorable encounter.

Here, too, the young Pastor could peacefully enjoy all the ordinary sights and sounds of an open space in the country. The song of birds was sweetest music to him, and the commonest flowers gave him joy, because they both revealed to him the love of his Father's heart. "When I go into my garden," he once said, referring to this same old place of which I am writing, "I have a choir around me in the trees. They do not wear surplices, for their song is not artificial and official. Some of them are clothed in glossy black, but they carol like little angels ; they sing the sun up, and wake me at break of day ; and they warble on till the last red ray of the sun has departed, still singing out from bush and tree the praises of their God. And all the flowers,—the primroses that are almost gone,—convey to my heart deep meanings concerning God till the last one shuts his eye. And now the mignonette, and the wallflowers, and the lilac, and the guelder-roses, and a host of sweet beauties are pouring out their incense of perfume, as if they said, 'Thank the God that made us! Blessed be His Name! The earth is full of His goodness.'"

On another occasion he wrote :—"On summer evenings, the queen of our little kingdom spreads a banquet in our great green saloon which the vulgar call a lawn ; it is opposite the parlour window, and her guests punctually arrive, and cheerfully partake, while their hostess rejoices to gaze upon them. Some of them are now so tame that, when fresh provision is brought out to them, they take no more notice of the lady-servitor than a child at table does of a servant who brings in a fresh joint. We do not allow a gun in our garden, feeling that we can afford to pay a few cherries for a great deal of music ; and we have now quite a lordly party of thrushes, blackbirds, and starlings upon the lawn, with a parliament of sparrows, chaffinches, robins, and other minor prophets. Our summer-house is occupied by a pair of blue martins, which chase our big cat out of the garden by dashing swiftly across his head one after the other, till he is utterly bewildered, and makes a bolt of it."

'DICK.'

He was no insignificant enemy, as the accompanying faithful likeness of him will prove ; yet again and again have I, too, seen him reduced to abject fear by the little creatures who were bravely defending their home. He was a splendid specimen of *Felis domestica*, and a great favourite with his master. He weighed nearly eighteen pounds, and was singularly intelligent and affectionate. He had a trick of helping himself to milk, which highly diverted Mr. Spurgeon. His depredations were carried on for some time before the culprit was discovered ; but there was so serious a loss of milk in the usual morning supply, that a watch was set to see what became of it, since a thief of some sort was an uncomfortable certainty. Judge of the spy's surprise, when he saw this great creature march slowly across the yard, push open the lid of the can, insert his huge paw into it, and deliberately lick the creamy member till it needed recoating by another dip ! This process was repeated till puss was satisfied, and all the while he showed no fear of punishment, or sense of wrong-doing.

When Mr. Spurgeon heard of this escapade, he was much amused, and had the cat and a can of milk brought to him that he might see "how it was done." Dick was nothing loth to show him, and thereafter became quite a hero in his master's eyes ! He would try to induce him to show off this trick at the tea-table, when guests were present ; and if Dick indulged him by a repetition of the performance, he would greatly applaud and pet him.

There were some curiosities of ornamentation in this old garden of ours. The pulpit stairs, pictured in Vol. I., page 367, led up to a breezy and delightful seat in the heart of the willow tree ; and there, in summer-time, we could always be sure of a shadow from the heat. However sultry the weather might be, there were cool and gentle zephyrs frolicking amid the branches, and waiting to fan the hot cheeks of those who cared to climb to their playground. We never knew the cause of this singular movement of the air in that particular spot, but it was a very pleasant fact, and "the sound of a going" in the big tree was one of our most delightful mysteries.

We had also what I should imagine must be a very unusual addition to the charms of a Baptist minister's garden,—the font out of a High Church building, which one of the early students secured for Dissenting worship when it was vacated by its Ritualistic congregation for a more imposing structure. My dear husband used to point it out to visitors, calling it "one of the spoils of the Holy War," and I am sure he heartily rejoiced that, in its changed position, it was at least unable ever again to assist in deluding people into the errors of baptismal regeneration.

As I am writing, there flashes across my mind the remembrance of a great surprise in the adornment (!) of our garden which once awaited us on our return from a Continental trip. After the bustle and joy of the home-coming, of asking and answering innumerable questions, of kissing and petting the boys, and generally making ourselves amiable, we strolled into the garden, to renew our acquaintance with its old-fashioned enticements and delights. We thought it looked very quiet, peaceful, and lovely ; and we felt the sweetness of God's mercy to us, in bringing us back in safety to such a fair and comely home.   But our serenity was to be quickly disturbed   Close by the spot where Mr. Spurgeon interviewed the little dog, there were some steps leading under an archway to slightly lower ground, and two large vases were placed, one on each side of the descent.   When we came near to this turn in the path, we saw before us a sight which nearly took our breath away; our amazement was so great that we stood for a minute or two without speaking, looking from one to the other, and then at the innocent vases which caused us such consternation.   Someone *had painted them a bright blue, relieved here and there with yellow !*

"Who could have been guilty of such Vandalism?" we wondered.   Fresh from the land of art and artists, and from beholding all that skill and good taste combined could provide of beauty of design and charm of colouring in every small detail of decoration and embellishment, our recoil from our disfigured belongings can be easily imagined.   Passing round the garden, we found more stone

THE GARDEN WHERE THE FONT STOOD.

or stucco work treated in the same way,—*the font included !*   We made enquiries within the house, and learned that these brilliant tints were intended to be a special "Welcome Home" to the travellers from the hands of our gardener, who thought to give us immense pleasure by the contemplation of his artistic skill! Unfortunate man! Still more unfortunate possessors of the too-gaily-bedecked garden! I cannot remember when the gardener was shown his error, nor how soon the unsightly ornaments were restored to their original purity; but I know that only dear Mr. Spurgeon could have successfully negotiated such a delicate piece of business as to secure for them a return to their former whiteness without, by a single word, hurting the feelings of the man who had unwittingly wrought the mischief.

Every Saturday morning, for a good many years, the quiet seclusion of our happy home was changed into a scene of rather noisy activity in consequence of the visits of the early students of the Pastors' College, who came to spend an hour or two with their President. First, one young brother; then, two; a little later, three; and, by-and-by, quite a company of these good soldiers of Jesus Christ marched down to Nightingale Lane for a season of special drill under the direction of their loved and loving leader. They were the forerunners of successive generations of "our own men" who were to be influenced throughout their whole lives by being brought into close personal contact with him who was neither the last nor the least of the Puritans. The earliest " Record of the Lord's Work in connection with the Pastors' College," written in 1863 by Professor Fergusson, contained the following reference to these visits :—

"Whilst resident at Mr. Rogers' house, once every week the students assembled at that of the Pastor, and were there instructed in theology, pastoral duty, preaching, and other practical subjects. Here was the nucleus of the present Monday and Friday classes, conducted by Mr. Spurgeon himself, in which his wide experience in church matters is presented to the young men, and furnishes them with the most essential preparation for their future work." I may add, that here was also the nucleus of those never-to-be-forgotten *Lectures to my Students*, which still continue to be of untold value in the equipment of Christian ministers of all denominations, and which are among the most precious monuments of the peerless President's consecrated genius, wit, and wisdom.

As an appropriate ending to this chapter, I have inserted, in *facsimile*, the beautiful love-song which my dear husband wrote at Hull, during one of his many evangelistic journeys, and which reached me at " Helensburgh House," one happy morning in September, 1865. None can be expected to feel the same rapturous delight in the sweet verses as I did when I first read them; I was far more proud of them than I should have been of chains of gold or strings of pearls; and they have still the power to move my soul to an overwhelming tenderness both of memory and anticipation;—but they may at least touch a chord of sympathy in some loving heart, and set it trembling with the tones of the long-forgotten music of bygone years.

Married Love — To my wife
by C.H. Spurgeon.

Over the space which parts us, my wife,
I'll cast me a bridge of song.
Our hearts shall meet, O joy of my life,
On its arch unseen but strong.

As the river never forgets the sea,
But hastes to the ocean's breast,
My constant soul flows onward to thee,
And finds in thy love its rest.

The swallows must plume their wings to greet
New summers in lands afar;
But dwelling at home with thee I meet
No winter my year to mar.

The wooer his new love's name may wear
Engraved on a precious stone;
But in my heart thine image I wear,
That heart has been long thine own.

The glowing colours on surface laid,
Wash'd out in a shower of rain,
Thou need'st not be of rivers afraid,
For my love is dyed ingrain.

And as every drop of Garda's lake
Is tinged with the sapphire's blue,
So all the powers of my mind partake
Of joy at the thought of you.

The glittering dewdrops of dawning love
Exhale as the day grows old,
And fondness, taking the wings of a dove,
Is gone like a tale of old;
But mine for thee, from the chambers of joy,
With strength came forth as the sun;
Nor life nor death shall its force destroy,
For ever its course shall run.

All earthborn love must sleep in the grave,
To its native dust return;
What God hath kindled shall death outbrave,
And in Heav'n itself shall burn.

Beyond & above the wedlock tie
Our union to Christ we feel,
Uniting bonds wh. were made on high
Shall hold us when earth shall reel.

Though He who chose us all worlds before,
Must reign in our hearts alone,
We fondly believe that we shall adore,
Together before His throne.

CHAPTER LVI.

Early Pastoral Epistles.

URING Mr. Spurgeon's illness, mentioned on page 288, he wrote the following letters, which are interesting, not only for their own sake, but because they are probably the first of that long series of epistles from the sick room, or from the sunny South, in which the beloved Pastor manifested his deep affection and tender care for the large flock committed to his charge :—

" Clapham,

" October 26th, 1858.

" Beloved Friends and Kindred in Christ,

"The days seem like weeks, and the weeks seem like months, since I went up to the house of the Lord. My heart and my flesh are crying out for the assembly of the saints. Oh, how I long to hear once more the solemn shout of the festal throng, who, with the voice of joy and praise, keep holy day! I am slowly rallying. My great struggle now is with weakness. I feel as if my frail bark had weathered a heavy storm which has made every timber creak. Do not attribute this illness to my having laboured too hard for my Master. For His dear sake, I would that I may yet be able to labour more. Such toils as might be hardly noticed in the camp, for the service of one's country, would excite astonishment in the Church, for the service of our God.

"And now, I entreat you, for love's sake, to continue in prayer for me. When ye find access to God, remember me. Mind, it is not by the words of your mouth, nor yet by the cravings of your heart, but it is by the precious blood of Christ you must draw nigh to God. And when you are in His sweet presence, and are bedewed with His holy anointing, then pour out your souls before Him, and make mention of me in your supplications.

" Yours, to love and serve in the gospel,

"C. H. SPURGEON."

"Clapham,

"November 2nd, 1858

"Dearly-beloved Friends,

"I am a prisoner still. Weakness has succeeded pain, and languor of mind is the distressing result of this prostration of my physical powers. It is the Lord's doing. In some sense, I might say with Paul, 'I am a prisoner of Jesus Christ.' But, ah! my bonds are more easy and less honourable to wear than his. Instead of a dungeon, my lot is cast in an abode of comfort. I am not restrained from my accustomed ministry by a chain forged by man, but by the silken cord of God's providence; no rough jailer, but loving relatives and friends attend upon me in these tedious hours of my bondage. I beseech you therefore, my beloved, let your many prayers to God on my behalf be each and all mingled with thanksgiving. Gratitude should ever be used in devotion, like salt of old was in sacrifice, 'without prescribing how much.'

"And now, though unable to stand in the pulpit, I will endeavour to give you a short address,—or rather, I will attempt to express the kindlings of my heart in a few broken sentences.

"And, first, to you my well-beloved and trusty brethren and sisters in Christ, and in the family tie of church-fellowship; to you I tender my fondest regards, my sincerest thanks, my sweetest love. I feel refreshed by your sympathy, and my heart is overwhelmed at the estimation in which you hold me. It brings the hot blush to my cheek, and well it may. Tenderly as a husband thinks of the doting affection of his wife, as the father receives the fond homage of his children, as a brother when he is held in honour by all the family circle,—so tenderly, and even more tenderly, I remember your care of me. The tone of your supplications during my affliction has made me beyond measure thankful. I rejoice that you have, with humble submission, kissed the rod, not impatiently asking for my recovery, but meekly acquiescing in the providence of our Heavenly Father, craving most of all that the Lord would sanctify the pains of your Pastor, and guard the flock with His own watchful eye. 'Grace and peace be multiplied unto you through the knowledge of God, and of Jesus our Lord.'

"Yet again, in the still chamber of retirement, I anxiously remember some who would have been, ere this, baptized on a profession of their faith, and received into membership with the church, had not my health been thus impaired. Be not fretful concerning this delay; accept it as an ordained trial of your patience. If a farmer has a field of corn severed by the sickle from its native earth, but not yet housed in the garner, is he not concerned lest he suffer loss? How much more, as a minister of Christ, am I concerned for you,—the converts God hath given me! O beloved, be steadfast! Commit not the great sin of apostasy. Beware lest Satan take advantage of you: 'for we are not ignorant of his devices.' Draw not back. It is written in the law, 'No devoted thing, that a man shall devote unto the Lord of all that he hath, shall be sold or redeemed : every devoted thing is most holy unto the Lord.' The Israelite might not take back for his own use the beast that he had dedicated from his flock or his herd for an offering unto the Lord ; far less may the Christian, when he hath resolved to yield up his heart, his life, his soul, to Jesus, withhold any part of the sacrifice. I write not thus to grieve you. Think not that my jealousy bodes a suspicion, but rather that it betokens my love. 'We are not of them who draw back unto perdition ; but of them that believe to the saving of the soul.' 'My little children, these things write I unto you, that ye sin not.'

"To those who have worshipped with us, during the past two years, in the Surrey Music Hall, the preacher sends his greetings and his love. Ye have heard how the prophet Samuel set up a stone, and called the name of it EBENEZER, saying, 'Hitherto hath the Lord helped us.' That stone marked the place where the Lord gave the children of Israel a great victory over the Philistines ; but it likewise marked the very place where, twenty years before, the Israelites were defeated, and the ark of God was taken. Let us rejoice, O my people, with trembling ! Two years ago, the Music Hall was the scene of such discomfiture, such dire calamity and death, as we hardly dare to think of. Surely that was the night of my heart's bitterest anguish. 'Howbeit our God turned the curse into a blessing.' For ninety-nine successive Lord's-days was I enabled to supply the pulpit ; no congregation could have been more evenly sustained ; never were sermons more widely echoed. God has owned these services to the quickening of many souls, to the establishing of many in our most holy faith, and by them, through His goodness, hath the blessed Spirit stirred up many of my brethren in the ministry to a righteous emulation. 'According to this time it shall be said, What hath God wrought !' Ah, sirs ! if ye knew in what fear we began, and with what anxiety we have continued,—if ye knew the unrequited exertions of those beloved brethren, whose names are unknown to fame, but whose good offices were essential to keep the place open,—if ye knew, once more, how many a time your minister has prostrated himself as a broken-hearted sinner before God to renew his first vows of unreserved self-dedication,—if ye knew these things, ye would not be backward in adopting the psalmist's ascription of praise, 'Not unto us, O Lord, not unto us, but unto Thy Name give glory.' 'Therefore, my beloved brethren, be ye steadfast, unmovable, always abounding in the work of the Lord, forasmuch as ye know that your labour is not in vain in the Lord.'

"Yet I have other friends. They are scattered far and wide throughout this country, and the sister isles. To you also let me write a word. Ye have received me most kindly ; faster friendships were surely never made in fewer hours than I have cemented with some of you. Ye are my spiritual kith and kin. I take you to record that my God hath graciously proportioned my strength to my days, while I have been among you 'in labours more abundant.' When I have laboured most for His glory, I have feasted most on the provisions of His grace. And, blessed be God, when ofttimes called to visit a people heretofore unknown to me, He hath given me the key of David, to unlock the secret springs of your heart; nay, rather, He holdeth the key in His own hand; He openeth, and no man can shut. Keep, beloved, the Word of His patience, and He will keep you 'from the hour of temptation, which shall come upon all the world, to try them that dwell upon the earth.'

" Finally, my brethren, I am cheered and comforted beyond measure by the joyous hope that, on the coming Sabbath, I shall again appear among you. This prospect is as oil to my bones ; and, although I cannot hope to fulfil my ministry with my wonted vigour, yet to attempt to address you will be to me as strengthening medicine, a tonic to my fluttering heart. ' Brethren, pray for us.'

"Yours in covenant,

"C. H. SPURGEON."

In the early years of his London ministry, it was Mr. Spurgeon's custom to write an annual letter to his people. This series of pastoral epistles, from 1857 to 1862, covers rather more than the period described in this volume, and gives a bird's-eye view of the progress of the work from the memorable night of the great catastrophe in the Music Hall to the happy settlement of the congregation in the Metropolitan Tabernacle. All of the letters show the Pastor's intense desire for the growth in grace of the brethren and sisters in fellowship with the church, and for the ingathering of those who were still " out of the way." With the exception of the last one, they were all addressed " To the Church in New Park Street," so it is only necessary to give the date of the year to which each one belongs.

1857.

" Dearly-beloved,

" We have hitherto been assisted by our Covenant Head ; let us pause and thank Him. Dark have been some of the dealings of providence towards us ; but however much we may lament, we cannot alter, let us therefore give our time to action rather than regret.

" Our numbers have been multiplied, and our zeal maintained ; for this let us be grateful. And now that we enter upon another period of time, what shall we do in it ? Let our answer be, that, through God's grace, we will be devoted to His cause, and seek out means of glorifying Him. Our hearts are set upon A LARGER

TABERNACLE. Will we not labour to immortalize this year by laying the foundation stone thereof? I am persuaded that God demands it; will we not delight to give Him all His cause requires?

"The Lord has been on our side, and through much opposition He has preserved us unscathed. Let us build Him a house to His honour, which will be the means of making known His glory, and discomfiting His enemies.

"The Church of Christ will help us; but, if all forsake us, by God's help let us do it alone. We have hitherto had the answer to that prayer of Moses, 'Let his hands be sufficient for him;' and it shall not fail us now. We will toil together with one warm heart until the topstone be laid, and then our prayer shall be, 'Lord, fill the house with Thy glory!'

"May every blessing attend you in your families, in your businesses, and especially in your souls; and may Pastor and people meet in glory!

"'*Trust in the Lord, and do good.*'"

1858.

"Dearly-beloved,

"We again acknowledge the goodness of our Covenant Lord. Last year, we wrote in faith. Surrounded by dark clouds, we believed that all things would work for our good; and now, rejoicing in hope, we record the fulfilment of the promise. The huge waves which Satan stirred against us have not caused us damage; but, by God's good grace, we have surmounted every billow, and are still sailing on to our desired haven. This has been the greatest year of all. Every Sabbath, crowds have filled the Music Hall; and every month the pool of baptism has witnessed that they have not heard in vain.

"Let us be grateful for past indulgence, and let us be on the look-out for trial. We must not expect to be let alone. Satan has many plots; and though signally foiled in one, another may be ready. Be prayerful, that trial come not upon us as a thief in the night; be watchful, lest we ourselves should, by our sloth, become the instruments of our own ruin.

"The Tabernacle Fund progresses beyond our hopes. It is most probable that, before the end of the year, we shall have far exceeded £5,000, which is no small sum. Another year of earnest effort, and the work will be nearing a conclusion. 'Bless the Lord, O my soul: and all that is within me, bless His holy Name.' The Lord will prosper that which concerneth us; we shall continue in loving labour, knit together as the heart of one man; and, by-and-by, we shall raise the topstone to its place amidst the shouts of the people.

"I am anxious beyond measure for your purity and unity. I pray you, watch over one another in the Lord, and may the Master Himself keep us all by His grace! Accept your minister's most hearty love, with every good wish for yourselves and your families ; and be not unmindful to offer fervent prayer for our success and preservation. Your minister's motto is,—

"'ON! ON! ON!'"

" Let yours be,—

"'GO FORWARD.'"

1859.

" Dearly-beloved and longed-for, my joy and crown,

"May the blessing of the Most High God descend upon you in answer to my earnest prayers ! This has been a year of prayer. I thank God for the daily supplications which you have presented at the throne of grace. Rest assured that your Pastor appreciates your affectionate earnestness on his behalf, and is greatly strengthened and encouraged thereby. It often brings tears of joy to my eyes when, in the midst of weary labour and cruel abuse, I remember your united prayers. May God hear you, and make me a better preacher, causing my labours among you to be more successful, both in your edification and increase !

" Permit me to counsel you as to the training of your families. I would have all our children fully taught the Word of God. Let me strongly recommend to you the use of *The Assembly's Catechism.* Many a minister has derived his first doctrinal knowledge from that book ; and, indeed, it has in it the very life-blood of the gospel. Let our youths and maidens study the Scriptures daily, and let them use *The Baptist Confession of Faith,* which they will find to be a useful compendium of doctrinal knowledge. My desire is, that I may have around me a well-instructed people, who shall be able to give a reason for the hope which is in them.

" There are many among us who are, at present, cold or lukewarm ; may the Divine fire, which is in some of you, be kindled in their hearts also ! Cleave to the Lord with purpose of heart, and the fellowship of the Holy Ghost be with you !"

1860.

" My Very Dear Friends,

" I am glad of this opportunity to assure you of the continuance and increase of my hearty and undissembled love to you. Each year unites us more firmly. We have suffered together, and we have also rejoiced together. In the cause of our common Master, we have alike endured the reproach of men, and the reviling of the people ; and in the success which has attended us, we have had to rejoice in the smile of a Covenant God, and in the energy of His Spirit. Comrades in battle, we are also co-heirs of victory. May the Lord, whom I serve in the gospel of His Son, abundantly bless you, and return into your bosoms a thousand-fold those acts of love, and those words of affection, by which you so perpetually prove your earnest attachment to me! Never had pastor a better flock; never did minister more sincerely long for the good of his people. And now, brethren, suffer the word of exhortation which I address to you :—

" 1. *In relation to myself.* I beseech you, cease not to plead with God on my behalf. I have always acknowledged and recognized the value of the supplications of my church, and I feel the necessity of your earnest prayers more than ever. I entreat you, as the spiritual father of very many of you, cease not to intercede with God on my behalf.

" 2. *In relation to the deacons ana elders.* Let me indulge the hope that our church shall become as Scriptural in its order as in its doctrines; and let me go further, let me hope that we may not only walk in Scriptural order, but in spiritual power. Seek unitedly the purity and increase of the whole body. Rally round the officers of our little army, and submit yourselves to their guidance and counsel. Let every member know the elder who presides over his district; and should that brother fail to visit him, let the member visit the elder, and remind him that he has overlooked one of the sheep of his flock. Endeavour to maintain meetings for prayer in each district of this great city; and if there be a door for other agencies, use them to the utmost of your ability. Each district, with its elder, should be a regiment with its officer; and then all the different bands, when called to united action, would be ready to achieve an easy victory. Honour the brethren who serve you in the gospel, and esteem them very highly in love, for the Lord's sake.

" 3. *In relation to one another.* I admire the liberality of our poor brethren to the cause, and the zeal of all for the spread of the truth, and the love which exists among you one toward another. ' Let brotherly love continue.' We are none of us perfect, and therefore need forbearance from others; our fellow-members are like ourselves, and therefore we must exercise the like charity towards them. We must mutually seek the comfort and sanctification of each other, ' endeavouring to keep the unity of the Spirit in the bond of peace.'

" A meek and quiet temper will always tend to sustain you under injuries from others, and will prevent your dealing harshly with brethren. The character of Archbishop Leighton is one which it would be a noble thing for us to imitate to the letter. Speaking of his humility, Burnet says 'that he seemed to have the lowest thoughts of himself possible, and to desire that all other persons should think as meanly of him as he did of himself; and he bore all sorts of ill-usage and reproach, like a man that took pleasure in it.' And again, of his temperament, ' he had so subdued the natural heat of his temper that, in a great variety of circumstances, and in the course of intimate conversation with him for twenty years, he never observed the least sign of passion in him, but upon one occasion. The accidents and behaviour which usually disturb the temper had no power to ruffle the equanimity of Leighton. Whilst living at Dunblane, his man-servant, being desirous of fishing, went off one morning very early, locking the door, and taking the key with him, thus making his master a prisoner; nor did he return until the evening, when the only rebuke which he received from the Bishop was, "John, when you next go a-fishing, remember to leave the key in the door."' Perhaps it is too much to expect so great a degree of gracious temper in all; but, nevertheless, let us strive after it. This will make it easy work to maintain cordial and joyous communion.

"4. *In relation to other churches.* Be careful to maintain your orthodoxy, and bear your witness against all error; but be even more mindful to secure the communion of saints, and avoid all bigotry and bitterness.

"5. *With regard to the world.* Let it not seduce you; come out from it daily, and be separate; but strive daily for the salvation of souls; and may the Lord make you, in His hands, the salt of the earth, and the instructors of the people! Huge is our city, and hideous its sin; labour for the good of men, and, finally, when the chief Shepherd shall appear, may we all appear with Him in glory!"

1861.

• "Brothers and Sisters,

"Bless God for the past, and trust Him for the future. It is far better to prepare for what lies before us than to congratulate ourselves upon that which is already accomplished. Great as have been the blessings with which Almighty God has favoured us, we are longing and looking for larger displays of His goodness. Permit me very lovingly to thank all of you for your hearty assistance in labours already performed, and allow me to entreat your continued aid in our new undertakings. Above all things, I most earnestly crave your prayers; and I am sure you will not deny them to me.

"*Pray for me in my ministry.* It is no narrow sphere to which my Lord has called me. Nothing but all-sufficient grace can enable me to discharge the labours which devolve upon me. Oh, I beseech you, as Aarons and Hurs, hold up my hands, that my pulpit power may not abate!

"*Pray for me as Pastor.* The church is of so great a magnitude, that no eye but that of Omniscience can oversee it all. As a company of fallible men, we have many infirmities; and it is a matchless favour to deal faithfully with all, and yet maintain perfect peace; to be ever active in stirring up the whole company, and yet very tender and pitiful to the lambs of the flock. Pray for me, my beloved, for I would rather renounce my office than lack your prayers.

"*Pray for me as an evangelist.* I am incessantly itinerating through the cities, towns, and villages of this land. There are few large towns in which I have not uplifted the cross of Christ. These frequent journeyings require much physical strength ; and constant preaching demands great mental power, and spiritual might. Ask of my Lord that, everywhere, His Word may have free course, run, and be glorified. There are lifeless churches to be aroused, and careless sinners to be called. Entreat our Heavenly Father that my preaching may have a share of success in promoting these most important objects.

"*Pray for me as a teacher of teachers.* The Lord put it into my heart to commence an Institution for the training of young ministers. With a very able coadjutor, I have constantly increased the number of young men. Prayer and faith have always supplied the means so far, although I have no society or regular funds to depend upon. I would rejoice greatly if my gracious Lord would send me pecuniary aid to enable me to increase the number at once to twenty. This I must leave with Him. Much wisdom is needed in training uncultivated but earnest minds, and in finding suitable spheres for the men when they are ready for the work. Let this matter, then, be remembered at the mercy-seat so often as it shall be well with you.

"*Pray for me as an intercessor for others.* Beg that the Lord may give *me* power in prayer. The most of a minister's work must be done upon his knees. Weak here, we are weak everywhere. I desire to bear you ever on my heart before the throne ; but how can I do this unless you shall pray the Lord to enable me ? For this, I appeal to you, and beg your perpetual remembrances.

"Finally, brethren, wait for the appearance of the Lord from Heaven, and be ye found with well-trimmed lamps and well-girt loins, that, when He cometh, you may rejoice before Him."

1862.

"To the Church in the Metropolitan Tabernacle, over which the Lord has made me overseer.

"Beloved Friends,

"Your faithfulness and affection are gratefully remembered in my daily thanksgivings, and in this public manner I tender you my warmest gratitude. Truly, I have no cause to complain of fickle or lukewarm friends in the church. No abuse, however venomous, has shaken your confidence ; no misrepresentations, however ingenious, have perverted your opinions ; and no slanders, however scurrilous, have loosened your attachment. We have borne equally and cheerfully the cross of Christ. You have not repudiated the burden, as though it belonged only to the Pastor ; but you have felt that an attack upon him was an assault upon yourselves, and any wounds which he might suffer have rankled in your spirit as well as in his own. Persecution has been greatly blessed to us, for it has made us a united people ; and we may add, a separated company, who are constantly constrained to contend for one another against the world, both religious and profane. A thousand times have the haters of our holy cause uttered the most villainous calumnies against your Pastor ; but, as one by one you have heard their report, they have no more alarmed you than the crackling of thorns in the fire, or the noise of summer insects among the trees. We can afford to endure this 'trial of cruel mockings,' for a clear conscience, prevalence in prayer, and abundant success, are an armour quite sufficient for the church in her worst condition.

"During the past year, we have entered upon our new Tabernacle, having no debt to encumber our future action. What a cause for gratitude to our all-gracious, prayer-hearing God! And what a claim upon us to exercise abundant faith and entire consecration to His cause! The Lord hath not dealt thus with every people ; let *us* be glad and rejoice in Him.

"Since the opening of the building, very many necessary works have been performed which have engrossed the larger part of the annual revenue ; and much remains still to be done before the Tabernacle can be called complete ; hence there will be little or nothing to spare for the College, and the Pastor must look to your thankofferings for the support of this great cause. You have not been backward aforetime, and will certainly be ready now.

"With regard to our spiritual interests, let us ask ourselves whether we have grown in grace this year, whether, like the living tree, we have put forth fresh branches and leaves, or whether we have stood like posts, on which the rain descends and the dew distils, but they remain as dead and unfruitful as before. Is our faith stronger? Is our love warmer? Is our hope brighter? Have we advanced in courage, patience, virtue, and true holiness? Has grace in the blade become grace in the ear? Have we a deeper sense of the depravity of our nature? Are we more habitually looking out of self into Christ, and do we walk in closer fellowship with Him? Let us answer these questions, and then remember the injunction of the apostle. 'See then that ye walk circumspectly, not as fools, but as wise, redeeming the time, because the days are evil.'

"And now that the lion-standard of the tribe of Judah is uplifted for another march, let us confidently and joyously follow it. Jehovah is with us, and the God of Jacob is our Refuge. Rise up, Lord, and let Thine enemies be scattered ; and let them that hate Thee flee before Thee ! We shall tread upon the lion and adder ; the young lion and the dragon shall we trample under our feet. 'They that wait upon the Lord shall renew their strength ; they shall mount up with wings as eagles ; they shall run, and not be weary ; and they shall walk, and not faint.'"

CHAPTER LVII.

Building "Our Holy and Beautiful House."

How can the poor have the gospel preached to them, if they cannot come and listen to it? And yet how many of our places of worship there are into which they cannot come, or into which, if they are admitted, they only come as inferior creatures! They may sit in the back seats, but they are not to be known and recognized as being like other people. Hence the absolute necessity of having places of worship large enough to accommodate the multitude; and hence, moreover, the obligation to go out into the highways and hedges. If the poor are to have the gospel preached to them, then we must take it where they can hear it. If I wanted to preach to English people, it would be of no use for me to go and stand on one of the peaks of the Himalayas, and begin preaching; they could not hear me there. And it is of little avail to build a gorgeous structure for a fashionable congregation, and then to think of preaching in it to the poor; they cannot come there any more than the Hottentots can make the journey from Africa, and listen to me here. I should not expect them to come to such a place, nor will they willingly enter it.

The gospel should be preached, then, where the poor will come. We should have houses of prayer where there is accommodation for them, and where they are regarded and respected as much as any other rank and condition of men. It is with this view alone that I have laboured earnestly to be the means of building a large place of worship, because I feel that, although the bulk of my congregation in New Park Street Chapel consists of poor people, yet there are many in the humbler ranks of society who can by no possibility enter the doors, because we cannot find room for the multitudes that desire to come.

You ask me, perhaps, why I do not preach in the street. I reply, I would do so, and am constantly doing so in every place except London; but here I cannot do it, since the enormous crowds that would probably assemble would be likely to cause a breach of the peace. I trembled when I saw twelve thousand persons on the last occasion when I preached in the open air; therefore I have thought it best, for the present at least, to desist, until haply there shall be fewer to follow me. – C. H. S., *in sermon preached at the Music Hall, Royal Surrey Gardens, January 25, 1857, from the text, "The poor have the gospel preached to them."*

IN June, 1856, the Building Committee for the proposed new Tabernacle was appointed. Their first meeting was held on June 16, and they were able so far to put their recommendations into practical form that it was possible to hold the first public meeting in aid of the project in New Park Street Chapel, on Monday evening, September 29. In view of the ultimate expenditure of over £31,000, it is interesting to read the official account of that early gathering, and the estimate then formed as to the probable financial responsibility the church and congregation thought of incurring :—" Resolutions were unanimously passed (1) that a Tabernacle, holding 5,000 sittings, should be erected, and (2) that subscription lists should be opened. Upwards of £3,000 was promised, and the Committee are very sanguine in their expectation that the sum of £12,000 (the amount required) will be speedily forthcoming. They earnestly solicit the hearty co-operation of the Christian public in this undertaking. Their chief object in this movement is the welfare of the masses, who hitherto have been neglectful of their souls Steady, earnest assistance is required, that the building may be erected. It would be gratifying to the Committee if every church in the kingdom had a brick or a beam in the new Tabernacle."

No one in the densely-crowded and enthusiastic audience, on that Monday evening, could have imagined that, just three weeks later, a sorrow-stricken assembly would be gathered in the same place, without the beloved Pastor, who had been utterly prostrated by " the great catastrophe" at the Surrey Gardens Music Hall. Among the many comments and criticisms of that trying period, several newspapers, including *The Times, The Daily News,* and *The Saturday Review,* stated that the contemplated new Tabernacle was to hold 15,000 people ; so, at the first service in the Music Hall, after the accident, Mr. Spurgeon corrected this exaggeration, and explained the need for a large permanent home for his church and congregation. He said :—

"There have been a great many rumours abroad respecting the new chapel, the building of which has been contemplated by a number of my friends. It has been asserted that we want to erect a Tabernacle capable of holding 15,000 people. With respect to that assertion, I will only say that some truthful ( ) person has thought fit to put a ' 1 ' before the ' 5,' for we have never entertained even a thought of building such a place. It has, however, been judged that a place of worship capable of accommodating about 5,000 persons is necessary. For my own part, I have no wish for such a large sanctuary ; only I cannot bear to see, Sabbath after Sabbath, as many people go away as are able to enter the chapel where we have been accustomed to assemble for worship. It is the will of people to come in great multitudes to listen to my proclamation of the truths of the gospel ; I have not asked them to come, it is of their own free will that they meet with us ; and if it is a sin for me to have so many hearers, it is at least an uncommon sin, which many others would like to commit if they could. It has been said, ' Let those who wish to hear Mr. Spurgeon pay for their seats ;' but that method would defeat the object I have in view. I want to preach to those who cannot afford to pay for seats in a chapel, and it is my wish to admit as many of the general public as possible. Many of my friends, I know, are most anxious on the subject of a larger place of worship than we have at present, and would give double what they have done if they could afford it. It is much to the inconvenience of my congregation to attend here. We have a comfortable place of worship at New Park Street. There we are very happy together, and I have as many hearers and church-members as any man need desire. It is only with a view of winning more souls to God that we have come to this larger building, and that we wish to erect our proposed Tabernacle. Should we be charged with seeking any other objects, the judgment-day will declare what our motives have truly been."

The next large meeting in aid of the Building Fund was held on Monday evening, March 23, 1857, at New Park Street Chapel, which was again quite crowded. The chairman was W. Joynson, Esq., of St. Mary Cray, whose donations, during the evening, reached altogether £200. The amount paid in or promised at the meeting was over £500, making the total to that date about £4,500. Mr. Spurgeon, in his address, recounted the history of the enlargement at New Park Street, and of the services at Exeter Hall and the Surrey Gardens Music Hall. Of the latter gatherings, and of the need of the new Tabernacle, he said :—

"In the Music Hall, we have reason to believe that the Lord has gathered great numbers to His Heavenly Shiloh. Few have witnessed the teeming multitudes who have assembled there to join in the praises of God, but have done so with tears ; and it has well-nigh overpowered me many a time. Truly, the Lord hath done wonderful things for us, whereby we are laid under solemn obligation to Him. The Lord having given me favour in the eyes of the people, and blessed me with not a little success, the number of members has so increased as well-nigh to fill this place ; indeed, we have 300 more friends, whose names are on the church-book, than are able to sit down in the area of the chapel to partake of the communion ; and if the Lord should continue to bless my labours in the years to come, as He has done in those that are past, very soon there will not be room for an unconverted sinner to get into the chapel. What should I do then ? 'Oh !' you say, 'there is the work of building up God's people.' I know there is, but I also know what it is to travail in soul for the unsaved, and I cannot bear the thought of not having sinners to speak to. Therefore it becomes me to look for a large place where they can be permanently gathered. The Music Hall has been made a trap for many a soul ; but, then, it would not do always to worship there. Many of the converts want to join the church, and to come regularly under my ministry ; but we have no room for them here ; our chapel is altogether out of proportion to the crowds that gather with us at the Surrey Gardens. Where do they spend their Sabbath evenings ? It is my duty to look after them. Long ago, I made up my mind that either a suitable place must be built, or I would resign my pastorate : you by no means consented to the latter alternative ; yet I sternly resolved that one or the other must be done,—either the Tabernacle must be erected, or I would become an evangelist, and turn rural dean of all the commons in England, and vicar of all the hedge-rows. Some nobleman, speaking or writing of this matter, said, 'Who knows whether the place will ever be built ?' I wrote to him, and said, 'You need not ask that question, my lord ; there's a man alive who will earn the money.' Yes, it shall be had. I have prayed to the Lord, and I shall keep on praying ; and I know He will not refuse my request.'

A newspaper *canard*, in *The Morning Star*, June 10, 1857, might have checked the flow of contributions for the Tabernacle ; but the Pastor promptly contradicted the story, and so neutralized its effects. A contemporary suggested that, instead of Mr. Spurgeon being " done " by the person referred to, it was the Editor of the *Star* who had himself been " done " by a penny-a-liner. The paragraph was as follows :—

" MR. SPURGEON DONE BY A PICKLE-SELLING TARTUFFE.—Most persons have observed in the newspapers, and on the walls of the metropolis, announcements of a reward for the apprehension of Mr. ———, an oil and pickle merchant in the Borough, who has not surrendered to his bankruptcy, but has left the country in company with, it is said, his governess. It may not be known that, in Mr. ———, we have to add another to the unhappily long list of persons who have traded on religion for the purpose of deluding the world in general. Mr. ———, who was accustomed to wear a white neckcloth among his other personal adornments, was Treasurer of the funds in process of collection for the new chapel about to be erected for Mr. Spurgeon,—by whose teaching, it would seem, he has profited but little ;—and has absconded, it is said, with over £2,000 of the popular young Baptist's money."

Mr. Spurgeon wrote the following letter, which the Editor at once published :—

" Nightingale Lane,
" Clapham,
June 10, 1857.

" Sir,

" I beg to call your immediate attention to several errors in an article in this morning's *Star*, headed ' Mr. Spurgeon done by a pickle-selling Tartuffe.' I cannot imagine the origin of so extraordinary a statement, for it might as well have been said that Adam robbed my orchard as that Mr. ——— had appropriated our funds. I am happy to say that the moneys for the new Tabernacle are ' preserved ' in the London and Westminster Bank, in two good names, and have never been placed in any jeopardy up to the present. It is very probable that Mr. ——— was a hearer of mine ; for, in a congregation of such magnitude, he may have been sometimes included ; but he was not a member of my church, he did not hold a seat, nor did he regularly attend. He may have worn a white neckcloth, but he did not purchase it out of our funds, for he was in no way whatever connected with us beyond being an occasional attendant. If ever your informant has been under the sound of my ministry, I can only regret that I must put him down, with ———, as one who did not hear to profit. Men should be cautious in their repetition of unfounded tales, and especially so in cases where the sacred name of religion is concerned.

> "I am,
>> "Yours faithfully,
>>> "C. H. SPURGEON."

On September 7, 1857, a meeting was held at New Park Street Chapel, for the double purpose of giving thanks to God for the success that had attended the Pastor's labours in gathering funds for the new Tabernacle, and of encouraging the people to do their utmost for the same object. On this occasion, Mr. Spurgeon said that the many thousands of hearers, who regularly worshipped at the Music Hall, proved that, as soon as a building could be erected to seat 5,000 persons, that number of friends might be safely calculated upon to fill it, and they would then have the best and strongest church in London. Sir Morton Peto had promised to get his agent to look out for a suitable site, and he had also guaranteed substantial help to the Building Fund, which continued to grow, though not as rapidly as the young Pastor desired.

The following resolution, preserved in the church-book, shows that, in July, 1858, the time appeared to have arrived for making a further advance in connection with the much-needed new Tabernacle :—

> "Meeting of the male members of the church,
>> "Monday, July 26th, 1858.

"Our Pastor convened this meeting in order to acquaint the church with the position of the great design for erecting a new Tabernacle, and also to obtain the opinion of the church as to immediate progress.

"The church unanimously resolved,—That the Committee be desired to proceed with all prudent speed, and agree that our Pastor should leave us alternate months, if he saw it necessary to do so, in order to collect the needful funds.

"The meeting afforded a most pleasing proof of the unity and zeal of the brethren."

This was the memorable gathering of "the men members of the church" (in accordance with the provisions of the Trust Deed), to which Mr. Spurgeon often referred when relating the history of the building of the Tabernacle. His account of it will be found, with other autobiographical paragraphs, at the close of the present chapter.

It was not long after this time that the public announcement was made concerning the purchase of the freehold site for the new sanctuary; and on December 13, 1858, New Park Street Chapel was once more crowded with an eager and expectant audience, which had assembled " to hear a statement of the progress made, and to devise steps for recruiting the funds necessary for building the proposed Tabernacle." The venerable Deacon James Low, presided; and Deacon Thomas Cook, the Honorary Secretary, presented a report which contained the following information with regard to the financial and other progress made by the Building Committee :—

"Their first efforts were directed to adopt measures for raising funds, and obtaining a site for the building, in both of which they have met with abundant success. Since the opening of the account, in September, 1856, to the present date, a period of 27 months, the sum of £9,418 19s. 7d. has been received, or an average of £348 17s. per month. The object, however, of paramount importance to the Committee was obtaining an eligible site for the building. This was, indeed, surrounded with innumerable difficulties; which seemed at times to be beyond the power of the Committee to overcome. At length, however, their labours were crowned with complete success, and they were rewarded for their long and tedious negotiation by obtaining the promise of the Fishmongers' Company to sell a portion of their land at Newington.* In announcing this, the Committee cannot refrain

THE FISHMONGERS' ALMSHOUSES, NEWINGTON BUTTS.

---

* The site was formerly occupied by the Fishmongers' Company's Almshouses. They bore the name of St. Peter's Hospital, and were built in 1618-36, out of the Kneseworth and other trusts; and consisted of three courts, a chapel, and a hall. They were rebuilt, in 1850-1, at East Hill, Wandsworth; and, after their removal, the land presented such a forlorn appearance that the building of the Tabernacle upon it was regarded as a great public improvement. It proved to be that in more senses than one. In the list of contributions for the Tabernacle Building Fund, is the name of the Worshipful Company of Fishmongers,—one hundred guineas.

from expressing their high appreciation of the service rendered by W. Joynson, Esq., of St. Mary Cray, who, when it was stated that an Act of Parliament would, in all probability, be required to legalize the sale of the land, in the most generous manner offered to meet the expense which might be incurred in so doing, to the extent of £400. The Committee feel that the completion of this great and important work, which is now brought to so satisfactory a state, must rest entirely with the Christian public; and it only remains for those who desire to see the Kingdom of Christ extended in this our world of sin and iniquity, to co-operate with them, and the house shall be built; and long may the sure and certain message of salvation echo within its walls!"

After several other ministers had addressed the meeting, Mr. Spurgeon said :—

"I do not feel in speaking order to-night, because I seem to have something in my heart so big that I am not able to get it out. I cannot, however, resist the temptation of saying a few words on a topic which you may think far remote from the object of the meeting. The times in which we live are most wonderful; and I wish that this church should be in the future what it has been in the past,—the advance-guard of the times. I cannot help observing that, during the last four or five years, a remarkable change has come over the Christian mind. The Church of England has been awakened. How has this been accomplished, and what means have been used? I cannot help remembering that God honoured us by letting us stand in the front of this great movement. From our example, the blessed fire has run along the ground, and kindled a blaze which shall not soon be extinguished. When I first heard that clergymen were to preach in Exeter Hall, my soul leaped within me, and I was ready to exclaim, 'Lord, now lettest Thou Thy servant depart in peace!' When I heard that Westminster Abbey was opened on Sunday evenings for the preaching of the gospel, and then St. Paul's Cathedral, I was overwhelmed with gratitude, and prayed that only the truth as it is in Jesus might be preached in those places; and that the ministers might travail in birth for souls, that Christ might be formed in them the hope of glory. I never felt such union to the Church of England as I now do. The fact is that, when a youth in the country, I was accustomed to associate with the name of clergyman, fox-hunting and such-like amusements; I abhorred them, for I thought they were all like that. Now I see them anxious to win souls to Christ, I cannot help loving them; and as long as they go on to feel the value of souls, I shall continue to pray for them. Now, seeing that the Lord has thus honoured us to be leaders of others, we must continue to lead; we must not take one step backwards, but must still be the very van of the army. What if God should spread the late revival, and let the New Park Street Church still go on as the advance-guard of the host?

" Now, as to the Tabernacle, I am quite certain that it will be built, and that I shall preach in it ; and I have no doubt that the money will be forthcoming,—that matter is no burden to me.   Some of you have done a great deal, but you ought to have done a great deal more.   There are others who, if measured by oughts, ought not to have done so much.   We have not done badly, after all ; for, after paying £5,000 for the site, we have a balance in hand of £3,600.   I hope that you will all agree that the spot is a most eligible one ; though some recommended Kensington, others Holloway, and others Clapham.   Having secured the ground, the next thing we did was to advertise for plans, and the following is the circular issued to architects :—

" ' The Committee for building the new Tabernacle for the congregation of the Rev. C. H. Spurgeon give notice that they are prepared to receive designs or models from architects or others, for the erection of a building on land situate near " The Elephant and Castle," Newington, for which they offer the following premiums :— £50 for the best design, £30 for the second, and £20 for the third.   The following are the conditions :—The building to contain on basement floor (which is to be five feet below the level of footway) school-rooms, twelve feet high, for boys and girls, and lecture-hall to seat 800 persons.   The chapel above to seat 3,000 persons, with standing-room for not less than 1,000, and with not more than two tiers of galleries. Each sitting to be not less than two feet six inches by one foot seven inches.   Gothic designs will not be accepted by the Committee.   The plan of the Surrey Music Hall has proved to be acoustically good, and will be decidedly preferred.   The total cost, including architect's commission, warming, ventilation, lighting, boundary walls, fences, paths, fittings, and every expense, to be about £16,000.   If the architect, to whom a premium may be awarded, shall be employed to superintend the execution of the work, he will not be entitled to receive such premium.   Each architect to state the commission he will require on outlay,—such commission to include all expenses for measuring, superintendence, etc.   The designs in respect of which premiums may be given are, thereupon, to become the property of the Committee.   The designs to be addressed to the Building Committee, New Park Street Chapel, Southwark, and delivered, carriage free, on or before the 31st day of January, 1859.   Each design to be inscribed with a motto, and an envelope,—with the same motto on the outside,— containing the name and address of the competitor, to be also sent to the Committee. The envelopes will not be opened until the premiums are awarded.   The architects competing will be requested to act as judges, and to award the first and third premiums.   The second premium to be awarded by the Committee.   No architect will be allowed to select his own design.'   More than 250 architects have applied for this circular, all of whom appear desirous to build the place ; so that I anticipate we shall have a very pretty Tabernacle picture-gallery by-and-by.   There are many friends with us to-night who attend the Music Hall ; they cannot get in here on a

Sabbath evening, so they are obliged to be content with half a loaf. For their sake, I want to see the new chapel built, for I cannot bear the thought that so many should come here Sabbath after Sabbath, unable to get inside the doors.

"Now, as to money; we say that the building is to cost about £16,000; but depend upon it, it will be £20,000. Someone asks, perhaps, 'How are we to get it?' Pray for it. When I thought of the large sum, I said to myself, 'It may as well be twenty thousand as ten; for we shall get one amount as readily as the other.' Brethren, we must pray that God will be pleased to give us the money, and we shall surely have it. If we had possessed more faith, we should have had it before now; and when this Tabernacle is built, we shall find money enough to build a dozen. Look at what Mr. Müller, of Bristol, has done by faith and prayer. When this land was threatened with famine, people said, 'What will you do now, Mr. Müller?' 'Pray to God,' was the good man's answer. He did pray, and the result was, that he had an overwhelming increase. Do you ask, 'What is required of me to-night?' Let me remind you that all you possess is not your own; it is your Master's; you are only stewards, and must hereafter give an account of your stewardship."

Evidently many who were present were touched by the Pastor's words, for the sums collected and promised during the evening amounted to nearly £1,000.

It will be noticed that the date for sending in plans, models, and estimates, was *January* 31,—a day which was afterwards to become sadly memorable in the history of the church at the Metropolitan Tabernacle, for on that day, in 1892, its beloved Pastor heard the call, "Come up higher," and went to join "the general assembly and church of the first-born, which are written in Heaven." Careful readers will also note that, although " about £16,000 " was the amount the architects were to allow for the total cost of the building and its fittings and surroundings, Mr. Spurgeon said, " Depend upon it, it will be £20,000 ;" and so it was, and more, too.

In February, 1859, the competing architects' drawings (sixty two sets and one model) were exhibited in the Newington Horse and Carriage Repository, and proved exceedingly attractive both to the New Park Street congregation and the general public. By a vote taken among themselves, about forty of the competitors assigned the first premium (£50) to the design submitted by Mr. E. Cookworthy Robins. The following letter from Mr. Spurgeon to Mr. Robins shows that the Pastor himself placed the prize design among the first three, but that the drawings submitted by Mr. W. W. Pocock had been selected by himself and the Committee :—

" Dear Sir,

"I am requested by the Committee to forward the enclosed cheque for £50 as the first premium. In so doing, allow me to congratulate you upon the

architectural taste which is so manifest in your drawings. In my own personal
selection, your design was one of three which I considered to be pre-eminent among
the many. We have inspected the designs with great care, and long deliberation ; and,
although we are compelled to prefer Mr. Pocock's design as the best basis for our
future building, we could not but regret that we were thus compelled to lose your
services in the erection. You may not be aware that we have received from private
friends of yours, and persons for whom you have erected buildings,' the most
flattering testimonials of your ability. Since these were unsolicited on your part,
and probably unknown to you, we thought them worthy of the highest consideration,
and should have felt great pleasure in entrusting our great undertaking to your
hands. Wishing you every prosperity,

"I am,

"Yours heartily,

"C. H. SPURGEON."

THE ACCEPTED DESIGN FOR THE METROPOLITAN TABERNACLE.

The Committee awarded the second premium (£30) to Mr. W. W. Pocock, and
the Tabernacle was erected after his design, though with considerable modifications,
including the abandonment of the towers at the four corners of the building. When

Mr. Spurgeon found that they would probably cost about £1,000 each, he thought that amount of money could be more profitably expended, and therefore had them omitted, and the style of the structure was altered to the form which has since become familiar to hundreds of thousands of earnest worshippers from all quarters of the globe. The motto on the envelope accompanying Mr. Pocock's drawings was the word " Metropolitan "—a singularly appropriate one, for the building erected under his superintendence was to contain that word in its official designation,—The Metropolitan Tabernacle.*

When the plans were finally settled, and the tenders were received and opened, it was found that the highest amounted to £26,370, and the lowest to £21,500, with a saving of £1,500 if Bath instead of Portland stone should be used. This was the tender of Mr. William Higgs ; and at the net estimate of £20,000, the very figures the Pastor had stated some months before, the contract was signed. Mr. Spurgeon often said that it was one of his chief mercies that Mr. Higgs was the builder of

THE METROPOLITAN TABERNACLE.

---

* After the disastrous fire, on April 20, 1898, which almost destroyed the beautiful building he designed forty years before, Mr. Pocock kindly offered to do anything in his power towards the rebuilding of the Tabernacle, and very generously lent to the Committee his original drawings free of charge.

the Tabernacle, and it was a special cause of joy to many that the contract was secured by one of the Pastor's own spiritual children, who afterwards became an honoured deacon of the church, and one of the dearest personal friends and most generous helpers his minister ever had.

All needful preparations for the great building having been made, the foundation stone was laid by Sir Samuel Morton Peto, Bart., M.P., on Tuesday afternoon, August 16, 1859. About 3,000 persons were present at the ceremony, which was commenced with the singing of the hundredth Psalm, and prayer by Mr. Spurgeon ; after which Mr. B. W. Carr read the statement, which he had drawn up on behalf of the deacons, rehearsing the history of the church, as summarized in Chapter XXVIII. of the *Autobiography.* The closing paragraph, narrating the unparalleled advance made during the five years from 1854 to 1859 at New Park Street, Exeter Hall, and the Surrey Gardens, has been anticipated in the former part of the present volume ; but a brief extract from it will show the tenor of the deacons' testimony to their Pastor's usefulness throughout the whole period of his ministry among them :—

"The antecedents of many generations, and the cherished reminiscences of the older members, prepared for the Rev. CHARLES HADDON SPURGEON that enthusiastic welcome with which he was spontaneously hailed by this church. From the day he commenced his labours in our midst, it pleased the Lord our God to grant us a revival which has steadily progressed ever since. Among the earliest additions to our number, there were not a few disciples of Christ, who, after making a profession under faithful ministers long ago departed to their rest, had wandered about, and found no settled home. Many such were gathered into the fold of our fellowship. Here their souls have been restored, while they have found the presence of the good Shepherd, who maketh us to lie down in green pastures, and leadeth us beside the still waters. But the greater work was that of conversion. So did the Holy Ghost accompany the preaching of the gospel with Divine power, that almost every sermon proved the means of awakening and regeneration to some who were hitherto ' dead in trespasses and sins.' Thus our church became an asylum for the aged, as well as a nursery for the babes of our Saviour's family. . . .

" The prejudice against entering a Nonconformist sanctuary has, in many instances, been laid aside by those who have worshipped within the walls of an edifice that is justly accounted neutral ground, it being sacred or profane according to the temporary use it is made to serve. Every week has borne testimony to the saving influence of the gospel, as it has been proclaimed in the Music Hall to an assembly of 5,000 persons. Still, with so large a congregation, and so small a chapel, the inconvenience of a temporary meeting-place becomes more and more grievously felt. There is, and has been for the past two years, as fair an average of that large congregation, who are devout persons, and regular attendants, as in any sanctuary in London. Yet not one-third of them can find a place under the same ministry for more than one service during the week. The church-members far exceed the extent of accommodation in our own chapel to provide all of them with sittings. It is only by having two distinct services that we can admit our communicants to the table of the Lord. The necessity therefore for the undertaking that we assemble to inaugurate, must be perceived by all. Every attempt to trace the popular demand for Evangelical teaching to spasmodic excitement, has failed. The Pastor of New Park Street Church has never consciously departed from the simple rule of faith recorded in the New Testament. The doctrines he has set forth are identical with those which have been received by godly men of every section of the Church since the days of the apostles. The services of religion have been conducted without any peculiarity or innovation. No musical or æsthetic accompaniments have ever been used. The weapons of our warfare are not carnal, but they are mighty. The history of our progress for five years is patent to the world. The example has been found capable of successfully stimulating other churches in their aggressive efforts to save perishing souls. With earnest individual and united prayer, each step has been taken ; and to the exclusive honour and praise of our God, our stone of Ebenezer is this day laid."

After the reading of the paper, Mr. Spurgeon said :—" In the bottle which is to be placed under the stone, we have put no money,—for one good reason, that we have none to spare. We have not put newspapers, because, albeit we admire and love the liberty of the press, yet that is not so immediately concerned in this edifice. The articles placed under the stone are simply these :—the Bible, the Word of God, we put that as the foundation of our church. Upon this rock doth Christ build the ministration of His truth. We know of nothing else as our standard. Together with this, we have put *The Baptist Confession of Faith*, which was signed in the olden times by Benjamin Keach, one of my eminent predecessors. We put also *the declaration of the deacons*, which you have just heard read, printed on parchment. There is also an edition of Dr. Rippon's Hymn Book, published just before he died ; and then, in the last place, there is a programme of this day's proceedings. I do not suppose that the New Zealander who, one day, is to sit on the broken arch of London Bridge, will make much out of it. If we had put gold and silver there, it is possible he might have taken it back to New Zealand with him ; but I should not wonder, if ever England is destroyed, these relics will find their way into some museum in Australia or America, where people will spell over some of our old-fashioned names, and wonder whoever those good men could be who are inscribed here, as Samuel Gale, James Low, Thomas Olney, Thomas Cook, George Winsor, William P. Olney,

George Moore, and C. H. Spurgeon.   And I think they will say, ' Oh ! depend upon it, they were some good men, so they put them in stone there.'   These deacons *are* living stones, indeed ; they have served this church well and long.   Honour to whom honour is due.   I am glad to put their names with mine here ; and I hope we shall live together for ever in eternity."

Sir Morton Peto,* having duly laid the stone, addressed the assembly as follows:— " My Christian friends, I congratulate my excellent friend, Mr. Spurgeon, the deacons, the church, and all assembled here, on this interesting event.   It is one to which you have looked forward for some time.   It is the commencement of an edifice in which we trust that the era of usefulness inaugurated by your Pastor's ministry will be continued, and largely increased.   That admirable paper, which was read before the stone was laid, gave you a succinct but interesting account of the church up to the present time ; we hope that those glories, which have been so remarkably shown in the earlier history of the church, may not only be continued in the salvation of a larger number than has ever yet been known, but that, in years to come, those glories may be even surpassed, and that all who live may have the happiness of feeling that the work, which has been begun to-day, was one which the Lord had eminently blessed.   I could not but feel, during the reading of that paper, that the fact there stated, that the church at New Park Street is larger, at the present time, than can be accommodated in the building, that there is practically no room in the chapel for the world, is one which, to every Christian heart, must show that there remained nothing but for the church to arise and build.   I know it may be said that the Music Hall, and other large places, might have given Mr. Spurgeon an opportunity of making known the unsearchable riches of Christ ; but then there are other institutions in connection with an edifice of this kind, which are of equal importance with that to which I have referred.   We have not only the assembly of the church within its walls, but we must have an opportunity of gathering the young for instruction ; and when we look to the fact that this new Tabernacle will accommodate about two thousand Sunday-school children, and also place nearly five thousand people in the position of hearing the gospel of Christ, we not only feel that the world will be accommodated to hear, and the church amply provided for, but the young will be trained up in the way in which they should go.   When my excellent friend, Mr. Spurgeon—as I have no doubt he will if spared (and I trust he will be spared),—opens this place, and

---

* Sir Morton Peto was a most generous supporter of religious and philanthropic movements of all kinds, and he was a special benefactor to the Baptists.   In later days, when reverses came upon him through no fault of his own, he was greatly cheered by the reception of the following letter from Mr. Spurgeon :—

"A little time ago, I thought of writing to condole with you in the late tempests; but I feel there is far more reason to congratulate you than to sympathize.   I have been all over England, in all sorts of society, and I have never heard a word spoken concerning you, in connection with late affairs, but such as showed profound esteem and unshaken confidence.   I do not believe that this ever could have been said of any other man placed in similar circumstances.   The respect and hearty sympathy which all sorts of persons bear towards you could never have been so well known to you as they now are by means of the past difficulties."

declares the full, free, and finished gospel of our Lord Jesus Christ as the basis of his ministry in years to come, as it has been the basis of his ministry in the past,—I hope that it will be in a chapel free from debt. I know there is no testimony which his loving heart would so freely acknowledge, as that testimony to himself, or rather to his Lord through him, which would enable him to feel, when he first ascends the pulpit of this new chapel, 'I am here preaching the gospel to a people who are assembled in an edifice which has no claim whatever to discharge.' Accept my sincere congratulations on this event, my hearty prayers that every wish of yours may be more than abundantly realized in all the future, that my dear friend, Mr. Spurgeon, and his deacons and friends, may not only live to see this house completed without accident, but that they and you, occupying it together, may have what, after all, is of the greatest importance, a rich baptism of the Holy Spirit, without whom all that we undertake is worthless."

Mr. Spurgeon then said :—" My dear friends, this is not the first time that I have borrowed light from Sir Morton Peto. I have often cheered the darkness of a long railway journey by a most excellent lamp of his own manufacture, which he kindly presented to me, that I might see to read by it as I was travelling. I am very glad to see him blazing forth again to-day; in the light of his countenance many of us have been made glad. It is my earnest prayer that, while God is pleased to bless him with wealth, and rank, and influence, he may find it quite as easy to serve his God in the future as he has done in the past. We owe him much, as Dissenters, for his great zeal and wisdom in having brought through the House of Commons an Act whereby our chapels are well secured to us. I pray that God may give him grace, every day, that he may know his own title to the Kingdom of Heaven to be clearer and clearer as years come upon him.

" Before I speak about the building we are going to erect here, I want just to mention that I had a sweet letter from that eminent servant of God, John Angell James, of Birmingham, in reply to one I had written asking him to come to this meeting. He said, ' I would have done so if I had been well enough, but I am unable to travel. My work is almost done, I cannot serve my Master much longer; but I can still do a little for Him. I preach perhaps once on the Sabbath, and I still continue to do what I can with my pen. What a mercy,' he adds, ' to have been permitted to serve my Master so long!' We frequently exchange notes, and in his last letter to me he said, ' My dear brother, be on your watch-tower, and gird your sword on your thigh. The devil hates you more than most men, for you have done so much damage to his kingdom; and, if he can, he will trip you up.' I am sure what good Mr. James says is true, but I know that he, and you, and many more of the Lord's people are praying that I may be upheld, and that we may successfully carry through this great undertaking. I never answer any slanders against myself, and very seldom answer any questions about what I mean to do. I am obliged to be a self-contained man, just going on my own way, and letting other people go in their own way. If I am wrong, I will be accountable to my own Master, but to no flesh living ; and if I am right, the day will declare it. God knows how sincere are my intentions even when I may have acted unwisely.

"I said, some time ago, when our brethren were half afraid, 'The Tabernacle is to be built, and it will be built, and God will fill it with His presence and glory.' There is no doubt whatever about the money being obtained. I scarcely know that I have asked an individual to give anything, because I have such a solid conviction that the money must come. I suppose that, out of all that is now in our hands, I have myself collected more than half through my preaching ; and I daresay that is how the larger part of the remainder will come, through the kindness of the provincial and metropolitan churches, who have almost all treated me with the noblest generosity. I give this day my hearty thanks to all who have helped me ; and I do not know but what I may as well add, to all who have not helped me. Many of them mean to do so, and therefore I will thank them beforehand. There is one gentleman here to-day who is to address you. I think (albeit that he can speak admirably,) the best part of his speech will be made with his hand, for he has three thousand pounds with him to give as a noble donation from an aged servant of Christ, long sick and confined to his house, but who loves Christ's ministers, and desires to help Christ's cause. He would not like me to mention his name, and therefore I shall not do it.

"And now, my dear friends, as to the place to be erected here. I have a word or two to say with regard to *its style*, with regard to *its purposes*, and with regard to *our faith and our prospects*.

"It is to me a matter of congratulation that we shall succeed in building in this city a Grecian place of worship. My notions of architecture are not worth much, because I look at a building from a theological point of view, not from an architectural one. It seems to me that there are two sacred languages in the world. There was the Hebrew of old, and I doubt not that Solomon adopted Jewish architecture for the Temple,—a Hebrew form and fashion of putting stones together in harmony with the Hebrew faith. There is but one other sacred language,—not Rome's mongrel tongue—the Latin ; glorious as that may be for a battle-cry, it is of no use for preaching the gospel. The other sacred language is the Greek, and that is dear to every Christian's heart. Our fullest revelation of God's will is in that tongue ; and so are our noblest names for Jesus. The standard of our faith is Greek ; and this place is to be Grecian. I care not that many an idol temple has been built after the same fashion. Greek is the sacred tongue, and Greek is the Baptist's tongue ; we may be beaten in our own version, sometimes ; but in the Greek, never. Every Baptist place should be Grecian,—never Gothic. We owe nothing to the Goths as religionists. We have a great part of our Scriptures in the Grecian language, and this shall be a Grecian place of worship ; and God give us the power and life of that master of the Grecian tongue, the apostle Paul, that here like wonders may be done by the preaching of the Word as were wrought by his ministry !

" As for our faith, as a church, you have heard about that already. We believe in the five great points commonly known as Calvinistic ; but we do not regard those five points as being barbed shafts which we are to thrust between the ribs of our fellow-Christians. We look upon them as being five great lamps which help to irradiate the cross ; or, rather, five bright emanations springing from the glorious covenant of our Triune God, and illustrating the great doctrine of Jesus crucified. Against all comers, especially against all lovers of Arminianism, we defend and maintain pure gospel truth. At the same time, I can make this public declaration, that I am no Antinomian. I belong not to the sect of those who are afraid to invite the sinner to Christ. I warn him, I invite him, I exhort him. Hence, then, I have contumely on either hand. Inconsistency is charged against me, by some people, as if anything that God commanded could be inconsistent ; I will glory in such inconsistency even to the end. I bind myself precisely to no form of doctrine. I love those five points as being the angles of the gospel, but then I love the centre between the angles better still. Moreover, we are Baptists, and we cannot swerve from this matter of discipline, nor can we make our church half-and-half in that matter. The witness of our church must be one and indivisible. We must have one Lord, one faith, and one baptism. And yet dear to our hearts is that great article of the Apostles' Creed, ' I believe in the communion of saints.' I believe not in the communion of Episcopalians alone ; I do not believe in the communion of Baptists only, I dare not sit with them exclusively. I think I should be almost strict-communionist enough not to sit with them at all, because I should say, ' This is not the communion of saints, it is the communion of Baptists.' Whosoever loves the Lord Jesus Christ in verity and truth hath a hearty welcome, and is not only permitted, but invited to communion with the Church of Christ. However, we can say, with all our hearts, that difference has never lost us one good friend yet. I see around me our Independent brethren ; they certainly have been to Ænon to-day, for there has been ' much water' here ; and I see round about me dear strict-communion brethren, and one of them is about to address you. He is not so strict a communionist but what he really in his own heart communes with all the people of God. I can number among my choicest friends many members of the Church of England, and some of every denomination ; I glory in that fact. However sternly a man may hold the right of private judgment, he yet can give his right hand with as tight a grip to everyone who loves the Lord Jesus Christ.

" Now with regard to *our prospects*. We are to build this place, and the prospect I anticipate is, that it will be paid for before it is opened. I think it is likely to be so; because, if we carry out our intention, as a Committee, we have a notion that, if our friends do not give us liberal contributions, we will put up the carcass and roof it in, and allow them to come in and stand. Those who want seats can buy them. I am sure my people would soon get me a pulpit, and such is the zeal of our brethren that they would soon build me a baptistery. I leave it open for any generous friend here, who pleases to do so, to engage to provide some part of the Tabernacle, and to say, ' I will give that.' Churchmen give painted windows for their places of worship ; and if some of you agree to give different parts of the chapel, it may be so erected. You must understand that our large expenditure is caused partly by the fact that we have immense school-rooms underground, and also a lecture-hall, holding between 800 and 900 persons, for church-meetings. This is necessary, because our church is of such an immense size, and our members come out to every service if possible ; there is no church-edifice in London so well used as ours is ; they hack it to pieces. We must build this Tabernacle strongly, I am sure, for our friends are always with us. They love to be at the prayer-meetings. There are no people who take out their quarter's seat-money so fully. They say, ' We will hear all that we can ;' and, depend upon it, they never give me a chance of seeing the seats empty. But our desire is, after we have fitted up our vestry, schools, and other rooms, that we shall be able to build other chapels. Sir Morton Peto is the man who builds one chapel with the hope that it will be the seedling for another ; and we will pretty soon try *our* hands at it. Our people have taken to chapel-building, and they will go on with it. They built a chapel, that held ' near a thousand hearers, in Horse-lie-down,' for Benjamin Keach ; then they built one in Carter Lane, for Dr. Gill ; then one in Park Street, for Dr. Rippon ; and now we have set about building one here. God sparing my life, if I have my people at my back, I will not rest until the dark county of Surrey is covered with places of worship. I look on this Tabernacle as only the beginning ; within the last six months, we have started two churches,—one in Wandsworth and the other in Greenwich, and the Lord has prospered them, the pool of baptism has often been stirred with converts. And what we have done in two places, I am about to do in a third, and we will do it, not for the third or the fourth, but for the hundredth time, God being our Helper. I am sure I may make my strongest appeal to my brethren, because we do not mean to build this Tabernacle as our nest, and then to be idle. We must go from strength to strength, and be a missionary church, and never rest until, not only this neighbourhood, but our country, of which it is said that some parts are as dark as India, shall have been enlightened with the gospel."

Mr. Inskip, of Bristol, said :—" I appear to-day as the representative of one, who is confined to a sick chamber, and has not seen the outside of the city for some years past; but that chamber is enlivened and enlightened by the bright illumination of the Eternal Spirit. That man's large fortune has been dedicated to his Lord. He is eighty-three years of age, and he has given away upwards of eighty thousand pounds. And he has sent me here to say that he will give you *three thousand pounds;* and, what is more, if twenty gentlemen will come forward with one hundred pounds each upon the opening of this chapel, I am prepared to put down twenty hundreds to meet theirs. It is not for me to laud the man, and therefore I leave him in his solitude, with an earnest prayer, in which no doubt many of you will unite, that the Lord will grant to him the bright shinings of His countenance in his last declining hours. As regards this building which is about to be erected, it is a matter of considerable delight to me to be able to forward in the least degree the views of my friend, Mr. Spurgeon. It has been my happiness to hear of many sinners, in the West of England, brought to a knowledge of Christ through his ministry. Let me now place on this stone, in accordance with the mission with which I am entrusted, not a painted window, but a printed piece of paper."

Many other donations were laid upon the stone, before the assembly dispersed. About two thousand persons sat down to tea in the Repository, and at half-past six the chair was taken by the Lord Mayor, Alderman Wire, when other addresses were delivered, and large additional contributions given, the total proceeds of the day amounting to between £4,000 and £5,000. In due time, the full amount required to claim the extra £2,000 from Bristol was forthcoming, and the generous friend there gave the amount he had authorized Mr. Inskip to promise on his behalf.

At the close of the entry in the church-book, from which the above account is condensed, there is, in Mr. Spurgeon's handwriting, under date September 5, 1859, the following paragraph :—

"As a record of the laying of the first stone, the accompanying report is inserted. We were highly favoured with the smile of our Heavenly Father, and desire to raise a joyful Ebenezer in remembrance of the happy event. May God speed the work, and permit us to meet for His service within the walls of the spacious edifice thus joyously commenced!"

In January, 1860, the total receipts had grown to £16,868 6s. 2d., and on Monday evening, April 2, one more crowded meeting was held at New Park Street Chapel, under the presidency of the Pastor, "to hear a statement as to the progress of the Building Fund, and to adopt measures for obtaining additional contributions."

Mr. Spurgeon mentioned that the number of members had nearly reached 1,500, and that there was a constant and regular stream of enquirers and candidates for church-fellowship; and he had no doubt that, soon after the new Tabernacle was opened, and all the organizations were in operation, they would have over 3,000 members in full communion with them. Mr. Cook reported that there had been received, up to that date, £18,904 15s. 2d., but it was estimated that a further sum of £12,000 would be required before the Tabernacle could be opened free of debt. Towards this amount, upwards of £500 was contributed that evening.

(The remainder of this chapter consists of autobiographical paragraphs which Mr. Spurgeon had intended to use in narrating this portion of his life-story.)

It has always been a subject of satisfaction to me that Newington Butts was the site selected for the erection of the Tabernacle. It appears that, in the old days of persecution, some Baptists were burnt "at the Butts at Newington,"—probably on or near the very spot where thousands have been brought to the Lord, and have confessed their faith in the identical way which cost their predecessors their lives. If this is not actually an instance in which " the blood of the martyrs " has proved to be " the seed of the Church," it is certainly a most interesting and pleasing coincidence. Our district seems to have furnished other martyrs, for in a record, dated 1546, we read :—" Three men were condemned as Anabaptists, and brente in the highway beyond Southwark towards Newington." Though that description is not very explicit, the region referred to could not have been very far from the place where, these many years, there has been gathered a great congregation of those believers whom some people still erroneously persist in calling " Anabaptists ', though we most strenuously hold to " one Lord, one faith, one baptism."

Our friends were at first not at all agreed as to the position which they thought would be most suitable for the new sanctuary. Some would have liked to go as far West as Kensington, others would have preferred the Northern district of Holloway, while some would have gone nearer to Clapham ; but, as soon as I found that it was possible for us to obtain the site formerly occupied by the Almshouses belonging to the Fishmongers' Company, I set my heart upon securing that position. I could see that it was a great advantage to be so near the spot where many great public roads converged, and in a region from which we might reasonably expect to draw a large part of our future congregation.

When the male members of the church were summoned to attend a special meeting for the transaction of important business in connection with the site for the new Tabernacle, the sisters, who were unable to be present on the occasion, were greatly concerned ; and when it, somehow, leaked out that the Pastor wished to buy the land in a certain position, and that some of the members of the Building Committee wanted to go elsewhere, every one of our brethren who had a wife, or daughter, or sister, or sweetheart, before he started for that memorable meeting received some such injunction as this :—" Never you mind what anybody else says, you vote for what the Pastor proposes." So it came to pass that, as soon as I described the advantages of the Newington Butts site, there was such an emphatic endorsement of my recommendation that it was quite useless for any other position to be mentioned, and the meeting decided accordingly.

I had said to the friends on the Committee who would have preferred some other site, " I have two plans for carrying out my proposal ; the first is, to call the male members together, and to consult them about the matter." When the special church-meeting had been held, and its verdict was so very decisive, one of the objectors said to me, " You told us that you had two plans for carrying out your proposal ; what was the second one?" "Oh!" I replied, "simply that I had made up my mind not to go elsewhere, as I felt sure that we had been Divinely guided to the right spot." The brother was rather amused at my answer to his question, but he and all the rest soon came round to my way of thinking, and we all rejoiced together that the Lord had so graciously prepared the place on which we were to erect "our holy and beautiful house" to His praise and glory. It was, certainly, by the special providence of God that Mr. James Spicer and other friends were placed upon the Court of the Fishmongers' Company just when their services were needed to enable us to secure the land ; and it was also a matter for sincere congratulation that the Company was able to sell the freehold, for I would never have built the Tabernacle on leasehold or copyhold ground, as so many other places of worship have been erected.

Soon after the building operations commenced, I went to the site with Mr. Cook, the Secretary of our Committee, and there, in the midst of the bricks, and mortar, and stone, and scaffold poles, and so on, we two knelt down, and prayed for the Lord's blessing on the whole enterprise, and also asked that no one of the many workmen employed might be killed or injured while they were helping to rear our new place of worship ; and I was afterwards able to testify that our prayer-hearing God had graciously granted both of our requests.

I have one, among many reasons, for speaking with 'bated breath as to anything which God has wrought by me, because, in my heart of hearts, I am made to feel that the true honour belongs to unknown helpers, who serve the Lord, and yet have none of the credit of having done so. I cannot help being pushed to the front ; but I envy those who have done good by stealth, and have refused to have their names so much as whispered. I do not think I ever told in public, until the night of my pastoral silver-wedding celebration (May 19, 1879), one fact which will ever live in my memory. The Tabernacle was to be built, and some £30,000 would be wanted. We did not know, when we started, that it would be so much; we thought about £12,000 or £15,000 would suffice, and we felt that we were rather bold to venture upon *that*. When we came to the undertaking of responsibilities, there was a natural shrinking on the part of the Committee with which we started. No one could be blamed; it was a great risk, and, personally, I did not wish anyone to undertake it. I was quite prepared for any risk; but then I had no money of my own, and so was a mere man of straw. There was, in some of our friends, a measure of fear and trembling, but I had none; I was as sure upon the matter as possible, and reckoned upon paying all the cost. This quiet assurance, however, had a foundation which reflects credit upon one who has for some years gone to his reward. When I was riding with a friend to preach in the country, a gentleman overtook us, and asked me if I would get out of the trap, and ride with him in his gig, as he wished to speak with me. I did so. He said, "You have got to build that big place." I said, "Yes." He said, "You will find that many friends will feel nervous over it. Now, as a business man, I am sure you will succeed; and, beside that, God is with the work, and it cannot fail. I want you never to feel anxious or downcast about it." I told him that it was a great work, and that I hoped the Lord would enable me to carry it through. "What do you think," he asked, "would be required, at the outside, to finish it off altogether?" I replied, "£20,000 must do it in addition to what we have." "Then," he said, "I will let you have the £20,000, on the condition that you shall only keep what you need of it to finish the building. Mark," he added, "I do not expect to give more than £50; but you shall have bonds and leases to the full value of £20,000 to fall back upon." This was truly royal. I told no one, but the ease of mind this act gave me was of the utmost value. I had quite as much need of faith, for I resolved that none of my friend's money should be touched: but I had no excuse for fear. God was very good to me; but, by this fact, I was disabled from all personal boasting. My friend gave his £50, and no more, and I felt deeply thankful to him for the help which he would have rendered had it been required. There were others who did like generous deeds anonymously, and among them was the giver of £5,000. If there be honours to be worn by anyone, let these dear brethren wear them.

CHAPTER LVIII.

Week-day Services, 1858—1860.

Preach, preach twice a day, I can and will do; but, still, there is a travailing in preparation for it, and even the utterance is not always accompanied with joy and gladness; and God knoweth that, if it were not for the good that we trust is to be accomplished by the preaching of the Word, it is no happiness to a man to be well known. It robs him of all comfort to be from morning to night hunted for labour, to have no rest for the sole of his foot or for his brain,—to have people asking, as they do in the country, when they want to get into a cart, " Will it hold us? " never thinking whether the horse can drag them;—so they ask, "Will you preach at such-and-such a place? You are preaching twice, couldn't you manage to go to the next town or village, and preach again?" Everyone else has a con-stitution, the minister is supposed not to have any; and if he kills himself by overwork, he is condemned as imprudent. I bless God that I have a valiant corps of friends who, day and night, besiege God's throne on my behalf. I would beseech you again, my brethren and sisters, by our loving days that are past, by all the hard fighting that we have had side by side with each other, not to cease to pray for me now. The time was when, in hours of trouble, you and I have bent our knees together in God's house, and we have prayed that He would give us a blessing. You remember what great and sore troubles rolled over our head; and now that God has brought us into a large place, and so greatly multiplied us, let us still cry unto the living God, asking Him to bless us. What shall I do if you cease to pray for me? Let me know the day when you give up praying for me, for then I must give up preaching, and I must cry, " O my God, take me home, for my work is done!"—C. H. S., *in sermon preached at the Music Hall, Royal Surrey Gardens, June 28, 1857.*

I can say, and God is my witness, that I never yet feared the face of man, be he who or what he may; but I often tremble—yea, I always do,—in ascending the pulpit, lest I should not faithfully proclaim the gospel to poor perishing sinners. The anxiety of rightly preparing and delivering a discourse, so that the preacher may fully preach Christ to his hearers, and pray them, in Christ's stead, to be reconciled to God, is such as only he knows who loves the souls of men. It is no child's play to be the occupant of a pulpit; he who finds it to be so may find it to be something more fearful than devil's play when the day of judgment shall come.—C. H. S., *in sermon preached at Belfast, August, 1858.*

HEN the project for the building of the Tabernacle was fairly launched, the Pastor set to work most energetically in gathering the funds needed for the great enterprise. By means of his preaching, speaking, and lecturing, a very large proportion of the required amount was collected. In many cases, half the proceeds were devoted to local objects, and the remainder given to Mr. Spurgeon for his new chapel; but, in other instances, the whole sum was added to the Building Fund. Scarcely a single monthly list of contributions was issued without the inclusion of several of these items. The congregation at the Surrey Gardens Music Hall was of such a special character that it was only on rare occasions that the young minister could be absent on the Lord's-day. Once, when he did spend a Sabbath, as well as some week-days in Scotland, he was able, on his return, to pay into the treasury the sum of £391 as the net result of his visit to Glasgow and Edinburgh. He also continued, as far as he was able, to preach on behalf of various provincial churches which sought his aid; and it sometimes happened that where the collections had been given one year towards the new Tabernacle, the next year Mr. Spurgeon would go again, and raise as large a sum as possible for the funds of those who had previously helped him.

A bare outline of these week-day services, even if it could be made, would occupy far more space than can be spared in this work. There is no need to attempt the task, for that campaign of love is recorded on high, and it is gladly and gratefully remembered in thousands of the cities, and towns, and villages of the United Kingdom; and the story of it has been told, again and again, from sire to son, in almost every part of the land. Eternity alone will reveal how great was the young evangelist's influence upon the religious life of that portion of the nineteenth century; and those who formed a part of his vast audiences may well treasure in their memories, and hand on to their descendants, reminiscences of the notable incidents of those long-past days. Just a few representative instances only can be given, from which may be gathered something of the character of the "labours more abundant" in which the New Park Street Pastor was engaged in addition to his arduous occupation in connection with his ever-growing church and work.

In London, Mr. Spurgeon's services were constantly in request every day or hour that was not required to meet the claims of his pastorate; and he was ever the ready and willing advocate of all who were downtrodden and oppressed. In a discourse upon Isaiah lxii. 10,—"Gather out the stones,"—delivered at the Scotch Church, Regent Square, on February 22, 1858, in aid of the Early Closing Association, he gave utterance to sentiments which are as appropriate to the present time as to the occasion when they were first spoken, although "early closing" has made great advances during the intervening period. After trying to remove, out of the way of those who desired to tread the Heavenly road, such "stones" as these,— (1) the supposed sacred character of the buildings in which the gospel was preached, (2) the obscure and learned language of many of the preachers, (3) the inconsistencies or gloominess of professors of religion,—Mr. Spurgeon thus referred to the object for which he had been asked to preach :—

"And now, what else have you to say? Perhaps you reply, 'What you say is well and good; no doubt religion is a holy and Heavenly thing; but, sir, there is one more stone in my path,—can you take that away? I am so engaged in business that it is utterly impossible for me to attend to the concerns of my soul. From Monday morning to Saturday night,—or, rather, till Sunday morning,—it is work,

work, work, and I scarcely seem to throw myself upon my bed before I have to rise in the morning, and resume my tasks. You invite me to come to your place of worship on the Sabbath morning; do you wish me to go there to sleep? You ask me to come and listen to the minister; if you fetched an angel from Heaven, and gave him Gabriel's trumpet, with which he could wake the dead, then I might listen; but I require something almost as powerful as that to keep my poor eyelids open. I should be snoring while the saints were singing; why should I come to mar your worship? What is the use of the minister telling me to take the yoke of Christ upon me, because His yoke is easy, and His burden is light? I know not whether Christ's yoke be easy, but I know that the yoke a so-called Christian population puts upon me is not easy. I have to toil as much as if I were a slave, and the Israelites in the brick-kilns of Egypt could hardly have sweated more fearfully under the taskmaster's lash than I do. Oh, sir, this is the great stone in the midst of my path; and it so impedes me, that it is all in vain for you to talk to me of Christianity while this obstacle is in my way!'

" I tell you all, that this barrier is like the great stone that was laid at the door of the sepulchre of the dead Christ. Unless you try to remove it, where is the hope of getting these people under the sound of the Word? It is for this reason that I came, this evening, to preach a sermon on behalf of the Early Closing Movement. I felt that I could not make that matter the staple of my discourse; but that I might bring it in as one of the points to which I would ask your very special attention, and I am endeavouring to do so. I do think, Christian people, that you ought to take this stone out of the path of those who are without; and to do so, you must put a stop to that evil but common custom of visiting shops and houses of business at a late hour. If you make a man work so many hours in the six days,—really, it is twelve days in six, for what is it better than that when he has two days' labour crowded into every one? —how can you expect the Sabbath to be kept sacred by him? And even if the man is willing so to keep it, how can you imagine that he can be in a proper frame of devotion when he comes into the house of God? Our Lord Jesus Christ is able to save to the uttermost; were He not, the salvation of poor dressmakers, and young men employed in drapers' and other shops, would be impossible; for it is saving to the uttermost when He saves them nothwithstanding their exhaustion, and gives them strength to feel and repent, when they have scarcely physical and mental power enough left for any effort at all. O brethren and sisters, gather out the stones! If you cannot take them all away, do not strew the road more thickly with them by unthinkingly keeping your fellow-creatures at work when they ought to be at rest.

" There are many young men and women, who are seeking something higher than the dust and ashes of this world, who might be converted to Christ, and who might be happy, but who are restrained because they have not the time which they

desire for seeking the Lord. I say not that it is a valid excuse for them to make,—
for very little time is needed for the exercise of repentance and faith ;—but I do say that
there are hundreds and thousands who are hindered from coming to Christ, and have
their early religious impressions checked and damped, and their convictions stifled,
and the first dawn of a better life quenched within them, because of the cruel system
of the present state of society. I remember seeing a good farmer stop his chaise,
and let his old grey pony stand still while he got down to pick off the road the
bottom of a glass bottle. and throw it over the hedge. ' Ah !' he said, ' I remember
how my pony cut his foot by stepping on a glass bottle, and I should not like anyone
to lame a valuable horse in the same way, so I thought I would get out, and remove
the cause of danger.' Let all of us act in the same fashion as that old farmer did,
and gather out all stones that may be an occasion of stumbling to any of our
brothers and sisters."

It must have been a memorable sight for those who saw the Surrey Gardens
Music Hall packed on a week-day morning,—April 28, 1858, when Mr. Spurgeon
preached the annual sermon of the Baptist Missionary Society from Psalm xlvi. 8, 9 :
"Come, behold the works of the Lord, what desolations He hath made in the earth.
He maketh wars to cease unto the end of the earth ; He breaketh the bow, and
cutteth the spear in sunder ; He burneth the chariot in the fire." The discourse is
published in *The New Park Street Pulpit*, under the title, " The Desolations of
the Lord, the Consolation of His Saints," so it need not be described at length ;
but it is interesting to note Dr. Campbell's comment on the new era which had
dawned in connection with the Society's anniversary :—

"The missionary sermon of Mr. Spurgeon, on Wednesday, at the Surrey
Music Hall, was a magnificent affair. The immense edifice was crowded to
overflowing at the early hour of 11 o'clock in the forenoon. The great preacher
was, as usual, completely at home, full of heart, vivacity, and business. Mr. Spurgeon
cannot devote weeks, if not months, to the preparation of such a sermon, and then
take a fortnight's rest to recruit his strength before the great day. All his days are
great, and they come in such rapid succession as to exclude the possibility of finish
and elaboration, even if he aspired to it. But, with him, there is no aiming at
greatness : exhibition has no place in his thoughts. He scorns it. What the
occasion supplies, amid ceaseless toils, past and coming, is all that he seeks, and all
that he gives. In the proper sense, he preaches ; and preaches, not to the ministers,
but to the people ; and he has his reward. He has no conception of reading a
treatise, by way of a May Meeting sermon, extending to two or three hours ! This
he would deem a perversion of his office, and an insult to his hearers. His discourse
on Wednesday was of the usual length, and of the usual character, only throughout

highly missionary.   Common sense in this, as in most of Mr. Spurgeon's doings, obtained for once a thorough triumph.   The collection amounted to nearly £150."

Two notable week-day sermons were preached by Mr. Spurgeon, on Friday, June 11, 1858, on the Grand Stand, Epsom race-course.   The text in the afternoon was singularly suitable to such a place : " So run, that ye may obtain ;" in the evening, the discourse was a powerful gospel invitation founded upon Isaiah lv. 1 : " Yea, come, buy wine and milk without money and without price."   There was a large congregation on each occasion, £60 was contributed towards the funds of a chapel in Epsom, and none who were present were likely to forget the unusual purpose to which " Satan's seat " was that day devoted.

In August, 1858, Mr. Spurgeon paid his first visit to IRELAND, and preached four sermons in Belfast.   He gave his services freely, in order that the whole of the proceeds might help the Young Men's Intellectual Improvement Association to build new school-rooms.   That he was in a very unfit state of health for making such an effort, is evident from his remarks at the Music Hall service on the Sabbath morning after his return.   Preaching on the words, " As thy days, so shall thy strength be," he said :—" Children of God, cannot you say that this has been true hitherto? *I* can.   It might seem egotistical if I were to talk of the evidence I have received of this during the past week ; but, nevertheless, I cannot help recording my praise to God.   I left this pulpit, last Sunday, as sick as any man ever left the pulpit ; and I left this country, too, as ill as I could be ; but no sooner had I set my foot upon the other shore, where I was to preach the gospel, than my wonted strength entirely returned to me.   I had no sooner buckled on the harness to go forth to fight my Master's battle, than every ache and pain was gone, and all my sickness fled ; and as my day was, so certainly was my strength."

The first sermon was an earnest appeal to the undecided, the text was Mark xii. 34 : " And when Jesus saw that he answered discreetly, He said unto him, Thou art not far from the Kingdom of God."   Twenty-three years afterwards, Mr. Spurgeon received, from a missionary, the following cheering note :—

" Your first sermon in Belfast caused me to decide finally to enter the ministry. Since then, I have given ten years to mission work in Damascus, where I built the first church ever erected for the spiritual worship of the true God in that city.   I built two churches on Mount Hermon, and again and again I have preached there your sermons in Arabic ; one of them was delivered on the top of Mount Hermon at a picnic given to our different villagers."

The second discourse was upon a subject of which Mr. Spurgeon was especially fond.   In those early days, if he was preaching several sermons at any place, one of them was almost certain to be founded upon Revelation xiv. 1—3 :—" And I looked, and, lo, a Lamb stood on the Mount Sion, and with Him an hundred forty and four thousand, having His Father's Name written in their foreheads. And I heard a voice from Heaven, as the voice of many waters, and as the voice of a great thunder : and I heard the voice of harpers harping with their harps : and they sung as it were a new song before the throne, and before the four beasts, and the elders : and no man could learn that song but the hundred and forty and four thousand, which were redeemed from the earth ;"—and in the course of the sermon, Mr. Spurgeon usually introduced a few sentences describing his love for the harp. It was so at Belfast, as the following extract shows :—

"John says, 'I heard the voice of harpers harping with their harps.' Surely, of all instruments, the harp is the sweetest. The organ has a swelling grandeur, but the harp has a softness and sweetness about it that might well make it a fit instrument for a royal musician like David. I must confess that a harp has so great a charm for me that I have sometimes found myself standing in the street, listening to some old harper making music on his harp. I have bidden him come into the house and play to me, that I might prepare a sermon while he played ; and I have found comfort, and my heart has been stirred within me, as I have listened to the thrilling strains. The singing in Heaven has all the tender melody of the harp, while it thunders like the rolling sea. Why is this? Because there are no hypocrites there, and no formalists there, to make a jarring noise, and spoil the harmony. There are—

> "' No groans to mingle with the songs
> Which warble from immortal tongues.'

No pain, nor distress, nor death, nor sin, can ever reach that blessed place ; there is no drawback to the happiness of the glorified spirits above. They all sing sweetly there, for they are all perfect ; and they sing all the more loudly, because they all owe that perfection to free and sovereign grace."

The text of the third sermon was Matthew xxviii. 5 :—" The angel answered and said unto the women, Fear not ye : for I know that ye seek Jesus, which was crucified,"—and was specially aimed at finding out and comforting true seekers.

The last of the four services was held in the Botanic Gardens, when it was estimated that 7,000 persons heard the discourse delivered from Matthew i. 21 : " Thou shalt call His Name JESUS : for He shall save His people from their sins." Towards the end of the sermon, Mr. Spurgeon told the story of Jack the Huckster, whose theology was comprised in the familiar lines,—

> "I'm a poor sinner, and nothing at all,
> But Jesus Christ is my All-in-all."

In closing the service, the preacher said .—" I have to thank you all for the kindness with which I have been received, and especially I have to thank the ministers of Belfast. I never was in a town in my life where I met with such a noble body of men who love the good old truth, and I can say that I love every one of them. I thank them for all the kind things they have said to me and concerning me, and I wish them and all my friends a hearty good-bye, and may the day come when we shall all meet in Heaven!"

Mr. Spurgeon went to Ireland many times after this, and Irish friends contributed very generously to the building of the Tabernacle. On one of his visits, after the great revival, when preaching in Exeter Hall, from Amos ix. 13,— " Behold, the days come, saith the Lord, that the plowman shall overtake the reaper, and the treader of grapes him that soweth seed ; and the mountains shall drop sweet wine, and all the hills shall melt,"—he said : —

" Here we are told that ' the mountains shall drop sweet wine ; ' by which we are to understand that conversions shall take place in unusual quarters. Brethren, this day is this promise literally fulfilled to us. I have this week seen what I never saw before. It has been my lot, these last six years, to preach to crowded congregations, and to have many, many souls brought to Christ ; it has been no unusual thing for us to see the greatest and noblest of the land listening to the Word of God ; but this week I have seen, I repeat, what mine eyes have never before beheld, used as I am to extraordinary sights. I have seen the people of Dublin, without exception, from the highest to the lowest, crowd in to hear the gospel ; and I have known that my congregation has been composed in a considerable measure of Roman Catholics, and I have beheld them listening to the Word with as much attention as though they had been Protestants. I have noticed military men, whose tastes and habits were not like those of the Puritanic minister, but who have nevertheless sat to listen ; nay, they have come again, and have made it a point to find the place where they could hear the best, and have submitted to be crowded if they might but hear the Word. I have heard, too, cheering news of men, who could not speak without larding their conversation with oaths, who have come to hear the Word ; they have been convinced of sin ; and I trust there has been a work done in them which will last throughout eternity.

" But the most pleasing thing I have seen is this, and I must tell it to you. Hervey once said, ' Each floating ship, a floating hell.' Of all classes of men, the sailor has been supposed to be the one least likely to be reached by the gospel. In crossing over from Holyhead to Dublin and back,—two excessively rough passages,—I spent the most pleasant hours that I ever remember. The first vessel that I entered, I found my hand very heartily shaken by the sailors. I thought, ' What can these men know of me ?' They began calling me ' *Brother.*' Of course, I felt that I was their brother ;

but I did not know how they came to talk to me in that way. It is not usual for sailors to call a minister 'Brother.' They paid me the utmost attention; and when I made the enquiry, 'What makes you so kind?' 'Why!' said one, 'because I love your Master, the Lord Jesus.' I enquired, and found that, out of the whole crew, there were but three unconverted men; and that, though the most of them had been before without God, and without Christ, yet, by a sudden visitation of the Spirit of God, they had nearly all been converted. I talked to many of these men; and more spiritually-minded men, I never saw. They have a prayer-meeting every morning before the boat starts, and another prayer-meeting after she comes into port; and on Sundays, when they lie-to off Kingstown or Holyhead, a minister comes on board, and preaches the gospel. Service is held on deck when it is possible; and an eye-witness said to me, 'The minister preaches very earnestly, but I should like you to hear the men pray; I never heard such pleading before, they pray as only sailors can pray.' My heart was lifted up with joy, to think of a ship being made a floating church,—a very Bethel.

"When I came back by another steamer, I did not expect to have my previous experience repeated; but it was. The same kind of work had been going on among these sailors; I walked among them, and talked to them. They all knew me. One man took out of his pocket an old leather-covered book in Welsh, and said to me, 'Do you know the likeness of that man in front?' 'Yes,' I replied, 'I think I do; do you read those sermons?' 'Yes, sir,' he answered, 'we have had your sermons on board ship, and I read them aloud as often as I can. If we have a fine passage coming over, I get a few around me, and read them a sermon.' Another man told me the story of a gentleman who stood laughing while a hymn was being sung; so one of the sailors proposed that they should pray for him. They did so, and the man was suddenly smitten down, and on the quay began to cry for mercy, and plead with God for pardon. 'Ah! sir,' said the sailors, 'we have the best proof that there is a God here, for we have seen this crew marvellously brought to a knowledge of the truth; and here we are, joyful and happy men, serving the Lord.'

"Now, what shall we say of this blessed work of grace, but that the mountains drop sweet wine? The men who were loudest with their oaths, are now loudest with their songs; those who were the most daring sons of Satan, have become the most earnest advocates of the truth; for, mark you, once get sailors converted, and there is no end to the good they can do. Of all men who can preach well, seamen are the best. The sailor has seen the wonders of God in the deep; the hardy British tar has got a heart that is not made of such cold stuff as many of the hearts of landsmen; and when that heart is once touched, it gives big beats, and sends great pulses of energy right through his whole frame; and with his zeal and energy, what may he not do, God helping him, and blessing him?"

So far as can be ascertained, Mr. Spurgeon's first sermons to a WELSH audience were delivered in the ancient village of Castleton, midway between Newport and Cardiff, on Wednesday, July 20, 1859. Pastor T. W. Medhurst, who kindly forwards this information, says :—

" This visit is still greatly talked about by the aged people in the district ; I have often been delighted to see their glistening eyes as they have related their recollections of this red-letter day in their past experience. Never in the annals of the village, either before or since, has there been anything at all approximating to the scene which was witnessed that day. For some time previously, it had been made known through Monmouthshire and Glamorganshire that the popular preacher, C. H. Spurgeon, would deliver two discourses in the open air at Castleton. The excitement among the people, and especially among the inhabitants of the hill-districts, in anticipation of the services, was immense. The question, 'Are you going to hear Spurgeon?' took the place of the usual remarks about the weather. The various railway companies ran excursion trains, and the result was an enormous gathering of people from all parts.

" The first service began at eleven o'clock in the morning, in a field which was admirably adapted for the occasion, as it gradually sloped to a level at the bottom. The seats were arranged in a semi-circular form. Everyone had a full view of the preacher, and his powerful voice was distinctly heard by the nine or ten thousand persons assembled. Before announcing his text Mr. Spurgeon said :—' My dear friends, I most earnestly and humbly entreat your prayers that I may be enabled to preach the gospel with power this day. I do not know that at any time I ever felt my own weakness more than I do now. I recollect to what mighty men of God some of you have sometimes listened, ministers whose names ought to be held in reverence as long as any man's name endures on the face of the earth. I can scarcely hope to tread in the footsteps of many of those preachers whom you have heard. This, however, I can say to you,   you may have men in Wales who can preach the gospel *in a better manner* than I can hope to do, but you have no one who can preach A BETTER GOSPEL. It is the same gospel from first to last, and tells of the same Saviour, who is ready to receive the meanest, the feeblest, the most guilty,. and the most vile, who come unto God by Him. May the Holy Spirit graciously rest upon us now! I will read my text to you from the Gospel according to Matthew, the twenty-eighth chapter, and the fifth verse, and then Mr. Davies, of Haverfordwest College, will read it to you in Welsh,—a feat which I cannot accomplish.'

" The sermon was a most powerful discourse, delivered with impassioned earnestness and fire, never surpassed by the most eloquent of the Welsh preachers. The text in the evening was Revelation xiv. 1—3. Every word of the preacher was plainly audible to the whole of the vast audiences at both the services ; and at the close of the day it was remarked that his voice was as clear and as vigorous as at the commencement."

Mr. Spurgeon preached in the Principality on several occasions afterwards ; the service to which he refers on page 93 was probably the one held at Abercarne on Wednesday, May 30, 1860, when it was estimated that 20,000 persons heard the discourse which he delivered in the open air.

Among all the notable week-day services in his earlier years, few were more memorable to both preacher and people than those held in PARIS, on Tuesday, Wednesday, and Thursday, February 7—9, 1860. The record of them is preserved in a pamphlet of thirty-two pages. On the title-page of Mr. Spurgeon's own copy is inscribed, in his handwriting :—" By Rev. Wm. Blood, who escaped at the burning of the *Amazon*." This gentleman was temporarily officiating as minister of the American Church in Paris, and he thus narrates the circumstances which resulted in Mr. Spurgeon's visit :—

" I had not been long in Paris, when it occurred to me that a good opportunity presented itself for inviting my friend, the Rev. C. H. Spurgeon, to preach in the French capital ; hoping that, thereby, with the blessing of God, a revival might commence in this land of superstition and error. And well knowing that France and the Continent offered a fine field for missionary enterprise, though awfully neglected since the days of the Reformation, I did not see why an attempt should not be made to enkindle the smoking embers of pure religion, which might eventually send forth a flame of light and heat which would spread over the entire country. It was a solitary monk, in his lonely cell, who, discovering the Word of God, read it, and, finding that it cheered his otherwise dismal hours, and gave light and warmth to his heart, determined that others should be made happy by the celestial fire. He snatched the torch of Divine truth, went forth from his darkness, and held it up, that all might see the living light ; other hearts were illumined by the same flame ; and, soon, a blaze of Heavenly truth spread all over Germany. Why should there not be another and even a better Luther raised up in beautiful France ? Why not many ? Why should not the ministry of the Lord's servant, which has been blessed to the conversion of so many souls in Great Britain, be also blessed in this great country ?

" Still, there were obstacles to encounter. Mr. Spurgeon had engagements made for almost every day for two years to come, and he had refused to go to America, even for a short time, although £20,000 had been offered to help build his chapel in London. I had, it is true, preached for him under peculiar circumstances when he had been seized with severe illness. But would it not be ' *uncanonical* ' for a clergyman to invite one to preach not 'in holy orders'? But is he not 'in holy orders,' God having evidently '*ordered*' him to preach the gospel of peace; for he can already point to thousands of sinners made '*holy*' by his preaching, and say, 'The seals of my ministry are ye, in the Lord.' The matter was then decided. I at once applied to my friend, Mr. Curtis,—a generous and noble-spirited American, who had originated the erection of the American Chapel,—for the use of that building, expressing the desire that, if any collection were made, it might be given to liquidate the debt on the chapel, or for the poor. The Committee met immediately, when the following resolution was agreed to :—

"'Paris, January 18, 1860.—The Committee have unanimously resolved to give up the American Chapel to the Rev. William Blood, to be disposed of as he thinks proper for the use of his friend, the Rev. C. H. Spurgeon; but they decline the collection for the American Chapel, preferring to give it towards the erection of the chapel for Mr. Spurgeon.'

"Application was next made to the *Consistoire* of the Reformed Church of France for the use of a much larger building,—the *Église de l'Oratoire*, nearer the centre of Paris. The application was at once responded to by the following resolution :—

"'The *Consistoire* held a council last night, and decided to lend the *Église de l'Oratoire* to the Rev. W. Blood, for the *prédications* of his friend, the Rev. C. H. Spurgeon.'

"This was accompanied by a few lines from one of the venerable Pastors, the Rev. Dr. Grandpierre, in which he said :—'I fervently pray that the Holy Spirit may bless the *prédications* of our brother, Mr. Spurgeon, to the conversion of many souls, and the strengthening of the regenerate in the faith.'"

Mr. Spurgeon was then asked if he would go to Paris, and he cheerfully consented to preach three sermons. To the further request that he would deliver two discourses on each of the three days of his visit, he replied :—

" My Dear Mr. Blood,

" I am willing to preach once on Tuesday, in the evening, wherever you please. Then twice on Wednesday, and twice on Thursday; but I must return the first thing on Friday morning. I thought I was coming over to serve the American Church; but, as the Committee prefer to give the collection for the chapel in London, I am content. Let me stay *in some quiet house*, where I shall not be overwhelmed with visitors. The lionizing is the worst part of my labours. I hope the visit will be blessed by God.

" Yours very heartily,

" C. H. SPURGEON."

Mr. Blood was especially impressed with the self-abnegation manifested by this note : and, writing after the services had been held, he thus referred to Mr. Spurgeon's disinterestedness in being willing " to serve the American Church " in Paris, when he had need of such a large amount to complete the Tabernacle :—

" He had no idea that the building of his chapel would be benefited by his visit. He expressed astonishment when he heard for the first time that it was proposed to be so. This ought at once to silence the slander of some evil-disposed correspondents of the London newspapers in their false reports of the collections made in the American Chapel. Had those collections been made *properly*,* as I suggested, either for the American Chapel or that in London, or for the poor of Paris, or had Mr. Spurgeon been in the least degree anxious on the subject, the collections might have been £600, instead of £60. But Mr. Spurgeon was not at all consulted, neither did he pass a thought upon the matter ; for he was invited *for one object*, and for that *alone* he came,—viz., to seek to lead souls to Christ ; and, thank God, this great result has been attained in several cases already known ! If it were prudent, many instances might be given as illustrations of this remark. One fact, may, however, be stated here. An English gentleman, occupying a high position in Paris, who had not entered any church for years, was led by curiosity, from the reports of the popularity of the preacher, to go and hear him. Some days after, a friend of the writer called to see him at his office, and was astonished to find him in a state of great excitement, weeping as if some great calamity had fallen upon his household. The Bible, which he had been reading, was open before him. His visitor enquired what was the matter with him ; and the gentleman replied that 'he had gone to hear that young man (Mr. Spurgeon) preach, his eyes had been opened to a consciousness of his real state before God, he had been led to see himself as a sinner of the vilest description, without God and without Christ in the world, and he was searching in the Holy Scriptures to try to find some ray of hope.' This and similar language described his state of mind, while it so excited the sympathy and emotion of his friend that they wept together, and joined in praying to God for mercy. His daughter, too, was similarly affected. She was a lady of fashion, though a religionist of the most formal kind. She had been scrupulous, like the apostle in his unconverted state, in attending to all the ceremonial of outward religion. She had been ' alive without the law once,' and even having the law she was blind as to its spiritual nature and convincing power ; but now, 'the commandment came,' applied to her conscience by the agency of the Holy Spirit, and she 'died' in despair as to any hope that the violated law could give her life, or even the promise of life. She saw her need of the vicarious sacrifice of the Son

* Mr Spurgeon dispensed with the collection from pew to pew, and simply had the plates held at the doors to receive the voluntary offerings of the worshippers.

of God ; she shut herself up in her room, and there, in agony of soul, sought the Saviour, gave up all dependence on her own righteousness, and submitted herself to ' the righteousness of Christ.' "

One specimen of the reports published in certain London newspapers will show that Mr. Blood did not write at all too strongly when he alluded to " the slander of some evil-disposed correspondents " concerning the collections at the services :—

" The unconquerable Spurgeon left Paris this morning, through which he passed, as it were, like a whirlwind. The Parisian public, however, seemed far less enchanted with him than he appeared to be with himself. Perhaps there might be good reason for this. Whatever may have been the moral result of Mr. Spurgeon's eloquence, it is certain that he has but little cause of complaint against the effect which he produced, for the extreme generosity of his congregations evinced itself in the well-filled plates, which, piled up with gold pieces, excited the astonishment of the few French listeners who had come, as usual, provided with their ten-sous-pieces, and who, on perceiving the magnificence displayed by the English portion of the audience, feeling ashamed of the contrast, passed by, and gave nothing at all. I have heard of a discontented individual, perhaps a rival French pastor, who left at the church a parcel of some weight and breadth, as his contribution to the erection of Mr. Spurgeon's Tabernacle. It was a tempting-looking packet, beautifully enveloped in silver paper, and carefully tied with rose-coloured ribbon. The chronicle speaks not of the varied emotions which must have agitated the heart of the person who opened it, but merely mentions that its contents consisted of a small brick from the factory of St. Germain, with a most polite note, in which the writer, regretting his inability to vie with the other contributors in money to that mighty work, begged to offer his *petit possible* in kind, expressing his opinion that, if every one of Mr. Spurgeon's legions of admirers were to do the same, not merely a church, but a city might be built with the materials thus collected. The friends of Lamartine, like those of ' Holloway,' ' Rowland,' and ' Day and Martin,' who never lose the opportunity of aiding their cause by the passing events of the day, have already made good use of the *rouleaux* of napoleons with which it was reported the plates of Spurgeon were well-nigh filled, and have pathetically compared the state of things they represent to that demonstrated by the miserable sum of five hundred thousand francs, subscribed by ' all France and foreign countries,' which poor Lamartine is obliged to pocket while waiting for the rest, which does not come.

" Mr. Spurgeon's egotism and arrogance have carried him so far as to advertise his sectarian chapel as ' THE *Metropolitan* Tabernacle,' thus ignoring all the other Dissenting chapels and ministers. The next step, doubtless, will be to call *himself*

the '*Metropolitan*' and his building the cathedral, thus ignoring also the Archbishop
of Canterbury ; but that humble and modest Christian will not dispute the point with
this upstart, even though he were ready to advertise his ready-cash shop as 'The
Metropolitan Tea Warehouse ! !'   But pride and avarice will soon be discovered,
especially when the holiest and most sacred subjects are used to fan the flame."

In vivid contrast to the above was the following article, written by. Dr.
Grandpierre, and published in the French religious paper, *L'Espérance :*—

"The eminent preacher officiated three times at the American Chapel, Rue de
Berri, and twice at the Church of the Oratoire.   The subject of his first discourse in
the American Chapel was, 'Salvation' (Acts xvi. 31) ; that of the second, 'The
Unfathomable Love of Christ' (Ephesians iii. 19) ; and the third, 'Jesus, the
Shepherd of the Faithful' (Psalm xxiii. 1).   At the Oratoire, he preached, the first
time, on 'Prayer' (Psalm lxxiii. 28), and the second, on 'The New Song of the
Redeemed' (Revelation xiv. 1—3).

"No one will feel inclined to contradict us when we declare that this celebrated
orator fully justified, or even surpassed, the high opinion which the generality of his
auditors had conceived of him.   Mr. Spurgeon appears of a strong constitution,
and nothing in his exterior betrays at first the excellence of the gifts which so
particularly distinguish him.   As a Christian, he is animated by the warmest piety ;
and, from his whole person, there seems to shine the sacred fire of the love of souls.
One feels that he preaches especially for the salvation of unconverted sinners, and
for the strengthening of the faith of those who are regenerate.   As a theologian, his
doctrine is clear, precise, square,—we might say ; he is Calvinistic, incontestably,—
but moderately so.   It was, with peculiar satisfaction, that we heard him proclaim,
from the pulpit of the Oratoire, with a vigour and a clearness equalled only by his
eloquence, the perfect Divinity of the Saviour, and redemption by the expiation of
His death, the eternal election of the children of God, and other essential points.

"As an orator, he is simple and powerful, clear and abundant.   The plans of
his sermons are easy to comprehend and to follow ; his developments are logical,
and his language, always flowing and elegant, never fatigues.   One would willingly
hear him for hours at a time.   Among the requisites to oratory which he possesses
in a remarkable degree, three particularly struck us,—a prodigious memory, which
furnishes him, on the instant, with the comparisons, facts, and images, best calculated
to throw light upon his ideas;—a full and harmonious voice, which he modulates with
peculiar ease, from the lowest to the highest tone,—and, lastly, a most fruitful
imagination, giving colour to all his thoughts, constantly varying their expression,
and painting to the eye of the mind the truths of Christ.

"Mr. Spurgeon is in reality a poet.   But without having heard him, an idea can scarcely be formed of the richness of his conceptions,—never, however, carrying him beyond the simplicity of the Christian pulpit, or the dignity of a minister of Christ. It is affirmed that Mr. Spurgeon has never been to College, and has been in the habit of preaching since the age of seventeen. He is not yet six-and-twenty; but once having heard him is enough to convince us that, in every respect, physically, morally, and spiritually, God has specially qualified him to be an orator,—and a Christian orator. He has left, in the hearts and minds of his auditory, the most pleasing, and, let us hope, the most salutary impression. Before and after his preaching, special meetings for private and public prayer took place, in order to beg of God to bless his proclamation of the gospel.

"We have no doubt that some souls have been converted. We are certain that all Christians must have felt their activity and inner life invigorated and reanimated. Our dear and honoured brother has received the most fraternal reception from the Christians of every Evangelical denomination in this capital, and he quitted us, apparently touched, grateful, and happy, promising to return, if possible, shortly, to visit us again. For our part, we bless God that the Council of our Reformed Church at Paris has considered it an honour and a privilege to respond to the request of his friend, in opening for him the doors of its great temple, which, during both services, was filled with a compact crowd. In the midst of this vast assemblage, the members of our own church were happily by no means in a minority. Our church has thus once more given proof that she possesses many families who value and appreciate the faithful and living exposition of the doctrine of our Lord and Saviour Jesus Christ."

Even more remarkable was the article in the *Journal des Débats*, from the pen of M. Prevost-Paradol, its principal leader-writer, and one of the most popular and distinguished of the Parisian *littérateurs ;* though a Romanist, he wrote in this appreciative strain of Mr. Spurgeon and his services :—

" Mr. Spurgeon has fulfilled his promise. The indefatigable apostle has spent three days among us, and during his visit he preached five times without our being able to detect the slightest weariness in this gifted man. Yet we do not think that any other orator could put more emphasis into his words, or give himself up more completely to his audience. Without posing, or getting too much excited, Mr. Spurgeon animates his discourse from beginning to end. The subject of his sermon is generally commonplace, and the end of it can be foreseen ; but what is neither commonplace nor foreseen, and which is incomprehensible without hearing Mr. Spurgeon, is the persuasive, familiar, and yet forcible way in which he compels his audience to follow him, without fatigue, through the long continuous recitals, full of vivid pictures, exhortations, timely warnings or entreaties, with which he, by so much art, makes up the rich and solid groundwork of his discourses. But why speak of art, when gifts are in question, or rather, we would say, the most inspired oratory we have ever had the pleasure of hearing? Never has a sermon been preached with less apparent preparation, or given to the hearer the idea of a studied discourse ; yet where is the audience that has noticed the least weakness, or the slightest hesitation, in his flowing and simple eloquence? One listens with pleasure to his powerful and sympathetic voice, which never rises or falls beyond proper limits, and yet fills the whole church with its sweet cadences.

" The man who possesses these gifts, and uses them so generously, is not yet twenty-six years of age. It is impossible to look upon his energetic and loyal face without reading there conviction, courage, and earnest desire to do the right. This orator, who is the most popular preacher in a country where liberty of speech and conscience exercises such potent influence, is not only the most modest, but also the most simple of men. It is true that he has the happiness to address a nation which does not think it necessary to be unjust in its public criticism ; but, after all, Mr. Spurgeon owes to himself alone the great and salutary influence which he has acquired, and yet no one could ever rightly accuse him of egotism. It is without affectation that he, unreservedly, ascribes all the glory to God. It seems to us that all disputes concerning religion ought to vanish before such an apostle ; and to recognize his power, is but just. As for us, who have seen in this youthful and eloquent preacher one of the most happy examples of what modern Christianity and liberty can produce, we feel that it is an honour to come into contact with such a man as Mr. Spurgeon, and to exchange with him the grasp of friendship."

Mrs. Spurgeon had the great joy of accompanying her dear husband on this visit. Deacon James Low, who was another of his Pastor's companions on this occasion, gave the following account of an extra service of considerable interest :—" By special invitation, Mr. Spurgeon visited the College at Passy, where there were several young men of great promise being educated for the mission field. Mr. Spurgeon received the students with much heartiness, and gave them a very touching and interesting address on the importance and duties of missionary work, especially urging them to preach Christ and Him crucified, as that doctrine would influence their hearers' hearts more than any other theme. The President translated the address into French, and the students appeared very grateful for the visit.

" Mr. Spurgeon was very much pressed by the various ministers and others to preach again in Paris as soon as possible. The results of the services were altogether most gratifying. To show the kindly feeling of the friends, collections were made, at the American Chapel, amounting to £64, towards the Tabernacle

Building Fund. Two collections were also made at the Oratoire for the poor of Paris ; they realized £40."

Mr. Blood wrote :—" It is gratifying to know that, not only in Paris was there a great wish to hear Mr. Spurgeon, but the same desire existed in different parts of France, in consequence of the articles which had been disseminated by the press. Several came hundreds of miles to attend the services ; and amongst others, the ministers of Marseilles and Lyons. After the last service at the Oratoire, Mr. Spurgeon was invited to meet the *Consistoire* at the house of the Pastors. There was a great number of Christian friends present ; in fact, the *salons* were crowded. Hymns of joy and praise were heartily sung, and fervent prayers were offered that God might bless the seed which had been sown, and cause it to take deep root in many a heart. Mr. Spurgeon was cordially thanked for his kind help to the Church in France, and he gave a brief farewell address. It was indeed a sweet and solemn time,—a little Pentecostal season, not soon to be forgotten. This service was entirely in French."

On his return home, Mr. Spurgeon wrote a loving letter of hearty greeting and thanks, from which the following extract may appropriately complete the records of that very memorable visit to Paris :—

" Mon Église a offert au Seigneur ses plus instantes supplications pour la prospérité et l'extension de l'Église de Christ en France. Nous vous porterons désormais sur nos cœurs, et nous espérons occuper aussi une place dans vos prières journalières . . . . Puis-je répondre toujours aux témoignages d'estime que vous avez bien voulu m'accorder ! Je m'incline jusqu'à terre sous le poids des miséricordes dont le Seigneur a daigné me favoriser, et les marques d'affection que me donnent Ses enfants pénètrent mon cœur de gratitude."

This chapter may fitly be closed with a brief reference to the week-day services at the Tabernacle, Moorfields, which were among the fixed engagements of each year. Dr. John Campbell, who had long stood forth as the friend and advocate of the young Pastor, thus spoke of this annual visit :—" Every 365 days, Mr. Spurgeon and his dear companion and the two little Princes Imperial honour my family with their presence for a whole day. We count on it ; it is a high day with us. By two sermons, on that occasion, Mr. Spurgeon almost entirely supports our City Mission at the Tabernacle." In the reminiscences, of which mention is made on page 82, Mr. Spurgeon referred to this happy compact in the following terms :—" It was always a great pleasure to me to have been associated with good old Dr. Campbell, the Editor of *The British Banner*. He was a very dear friend of mine. I used to preach for him every year, and it was understood that, when I went, I must take my dear wife and our two little boys with me. The day before we were to go, that great stern strong man, who had no mercy upon heretics, but would beat them black and blue,—I mean in a literary sense, not literally,—used to visit a toy-shop, and buy horses and carts or other playthings for the children. One time, when he sent the invitation for us all to go to his house, he wrote :—'Our cat has had some kittens on purpose that the boys may have something fresh to play with.' It showed what a kind heart the old man had when he took such pains to give pleasure to the little ones."

One of the most memorable of these annual visits was paid on Wednesday, March 14, 1860. There had been, near that time, a great many serious accidents and notable sudden deaths. A mill in America had fallen, and buried hundreds of persons in the ruins. A train had left the rails, and great numbers of the passengers were in consequence killed. The captain of the largest vessel then afloat, who had been brought safely through many a storm, had just said farewell to his family when he fell into the water, and was drowned. A judge, after delivering his charge to the grand jury with his usual wisdom, calmness, and deliberation, paused, fell back, and was carried away lifeless. Mr. Corderoy, a well-known generous Christian gentleman, was suddenly called away, leaving a whole denomination mourning for him. Mr. Spurgeon's sermon—"Memento Mori"—at Exeter Hall, the following Lord's-day morning, contained a reference to these occurrences, and also to another which more directly affected Dr. Campbell. Preaching from the words, "O that they were wise, that they understood this, that they would consider their latter end!" Mr. Spurgeon said :—

"It was but last Wednesday that I sat in the house of that mighty servant of God, that great defender of the faith, the Luther of his age,—Dr. Campbell ; we were talking then about these sudden deaths, little thinking that the like calamity would invade his very family ; but, alas ! we observed, in the next day's paper, that his second son had been swept overboard while returning from one of his voyages to America. A bold brave youth has found a liquid grave. So that here, there, everywhere, O Death ! I see thy doings. At home, abroad, on the sea, and across the sea, thou art at work. O thou mower ! how long ere thy scythe shall be quiet ? O thou destroyer of men, wilt thou never rest, wilt thou ne'er be still ? O Death ! must thy Juggernaut-car go crashing on for ever, and must the skulls and blood of human beings continue to mark thy track ? Yes, it must be so till He comes who is the King of life and immortality ; then the saints shall die no more, but be as the angels of God."

CHAPTER LIX.

Meeting in the Unfinished Tabernacle.

I hope I shall never, while I live, cease to have another project always in hand. When one thing is done, we will do something else. If we have tried to make ministers more diligent in preaching, we must try to make the churches more earnest in praying. When we have built our new chapel, we must build something else; we must always have something in hand. If I have preached the gospel in England, it must be my privilege to preach it beyond the sea; and when I have preached it there, I must solicit longer leave of absence that I may preach it in other countries, and act as a missionary throughout the nations.—C. H. S., *in sermon at the Music Hall, Royal Surrey Gardens, January 2, 1859.*

At a church-meeting, held in New Park Street Chapel, August 6, 1860, the following resolution was carried unanimously and enthusiastically :—

"We hereby record our sincere thankfulness to Almighty God for the gracious providence which has preserved our Pastor in foreign lands, and for the lovingkindness which has blest his travels to the restoration of his health. It is our earnest prayer that, for many years to come, our beloved Pastor may be spared to labour among us in the power of the Spirit and with the smile of our Heavenly Father. It is no small joy to us to hear of the great acceptance which the printed sermons of our dear Pastor have met with in France, Switzerland, Germany, Holland, Sweden, and the United States, and we equally rejoice that his personal presence among foreign churches has been attended with Divine blessing. Specially are we glad that our Pastor has been honoured to occupy the pulpit of John Calvin in the venerable city of Geneva, and we devoutly pray that on that city the love of the great Head of the Church may ever rest, and that all her ancient glory may be restored. Unto Father, Son, and Holy Ghost, be glory for the gracious success which has been with us even unto this day, and may it please our Covenant God to remember us for good even unto the end!"

HE first meeting in the Tabernacle was held on Tuesday afternoon, August 21, 1860, while the building was still unfinished. The object of the gathering was twofold ;—first, to give thanks to God for the success which had thus far attended the enterprise ; and, next, to raise as much as possible of the amount required to open the sanctuary free from debt. £22,196 19s. 8d. had been received up to that time, but more than £8,000 was still needed. Apsley Pellatt, Esq., presided, and heartily congratulated the congregation upon being present in the largest place of worship in Great Britain for the use of Nonconformist Christians. Several representative speakers delivered interesting and sympathetic addresses, and Mr. Spurgeon gave a detailed description of the main building in which the meeting was being held, and of the smaller rooms connected with it. After a few introductory sentences referring to his ministerial brethren who were about to speak, the Pastor said :—

"Now, my dear friends, you may perhaps guess the joy with which I stand before you to-day, but no man but myself can fathom its fulness, and I myself am quite unable to utter it. 'Bless the Lord, O my soul : and all that is within me, bless

His holy Name.' Much as I wish to express my gratitude, I must go at once to my business, and first say a few words about *the structure itself.* If the floor were to give way, our brethren, who are now upon the platform, would find themselves in the baptistery; and if, at any time, those of them who have never been baptized wish to be immersed in obedience to their Master's command, they will always find a willing servant in me. The baptistery will be usually uncovered, as we are not ashamed to confess our belief in believers' baptism.

THE BAPTISTERY AND PLATFORM, METROPOLITAN TABERNACLE.

"On the occasion of the administration of the Lord's supper, the table will also stand here; and there are steps on each side at the back of the platform by which the deacons will descend to distribute the memorials of the Saviour's death. You see, above us, the pulpit, or platform, which might hold a large number of persons. I cannot stand like a statue when I preach; I prefer a wide range both of thought and action.   The pulpit will also be convenient for public meetings, so that there will be no expense for erecting platforms.   Concerning this vast chapel, I believe it is the most perfect triumph of acoustics that has ever been achieved.   If it had been a failure at present, I should not have been at all disappointed, because the walls have yet to be covered with matched boarding, so that not a particle of brickwork is to be exposed,—it being my theory that soft substances are very much the best for hearing, having proved in a great number of buildings that stone walls are the main creators of an echo, and having seen hangings put up to break the reverberation, and to give the speaker a hope of being heard.

INTERIOR OF THE METROPOLITAN TABERNACLE, VIEWED FROM THE AREA.

"It has been remarked by a great many friends, as they entered, that the building was not so large as they expected ; and I was pleased to hear them say so, for it showed me that the structure did not appear huge and unsightly. To look very large, a building must be generally out of proportion, for when there is proportion, the idea of size is often lost. If you went down below, you would find the lecture-hall, about the same area as New Park Street Chapel, or rather larger; and the school-room, larger in its area than the venerable sanctuary in which my brother, Dr. Campbell, long preached the word,—I mean, the Tabernacle, Moorfields. I believe that four chapels like the one at Moorfields could be put into this building; two resting on the basement would only just fill up the same area, and then there would be room for two more on the top of them. Now, perhaps, you may get some idea of the size of the Tabernacle.

"With regard to the appearance of the structure, I have this much to say; I think it is highly creditable to the architect. The omission of the towers (see illustration on page 320,) has deprived him of much of the effect which he hoped to produce by his design, and is perhaps the reason why the roof seems to rise too much, but they will never be erected as long as I am here. I will have no ornament which has not a practical use, and I do not think those towers could have had any object except mere show. As for the front elevation, it is not surpassed by anything in London. The building has no extravagance about it, and yet, at the same time, it has no meanness. True, the roof rises to a very great height above the portico, and does not present a very architectural appearance from the Causeway, but we must recollect this,—those who only look at the Tabernacle from the outside have not subscribed anything towards its erection, and therefore cannot judge of its true beauty.

"The lecture-hall, beneath this platform, is for our church-meetings; it is rendered fully necessary, as we have now more than 1,500 members. The school-room will contain, I should think, 1,500 if not 2,000 children. There are large class-rooms which will be used on the Sabbath-day for classes, and on the week-days for my students. I have no doubt my friend, Mr. Rogers, who has so long been my excellent helper in that work,—and to whom very much credit is due,—will feel himself more comfortable when he has proper rooms in which all his young men can be taught in every branch necessary to give them a complete education for the ministry. There is a very fine room for the ladies' working meetings, which will also be available for a library,—a place where the works of all our former Pastors will be collected and preserved, for you must know that, of old, our church has ever been prolific of good works, in both senses of that term. We have the almost innumerable works of Keach,—they were so many that it was difficult to find them all. The chap-books, which used to be hawked about the country,—printed from worn type on bad brown paper, and adorned with quaint illustrations, yet containing good, sound theology,—I have no doubt interested the villagers, and greatly impressed the public mind at the time. Then we have the ponderous tomes of Gill, the tractates and hymns of Rippon, and the works of those who, since their day, have served us in the Lord. The pulpit of my glorious predecessor, Dr. Gill, will be brought here, and placed in the vestry below, that we may retain our ancient pedigree. It is said to have had a new bottom, and some of the four sides are new, yet I affirm it to be Dr. Gill's pulpit. I am as certain that it is so, as that I am the same man as I was seven years ago, though all the component parts of my body may have been changed in the meantime.

THE PASTOR'S VESTRY.

"Behind the upper platform, there are three spacious rooms : in the centre, is the minister's vestry ; to the right and left, are the rooms of the deacons and elders,—the officers of the army on either side of the captain, so that they may be ready to go forward at the word of command. Then above them, on the third story, there are three other excellent rooms, to be used for tract and Bible depositories, and for other schemes which we hope the church will undertake.

"I have thus tried to explain the structure of the building to you : I do not think that anything else remains to be said about it, except I draw your attention to the staircases by which you ascend to the galleries, each gallery having a distinct entrance and staircase, so that there is no fear of any overcrowding. I will only say that a design was never carried out with more fidelity by any builder than this has been. There have been improvements made as we have gone on, but they always have been improvements, to which, if they did not seem absolutely necessary, the builder has objected, lest he should have any extras ; and when we have compelled him to make them, he has done them as cheaply as possible. He is a man of whom I am proud that he is at once a member of the church, a member of the Building Committee, and the builder of th s house of God. Mr. Higgs, besides

THE DEACONS' ROOM.

being a most generous donor, gives us in solid brick and stone far more than he has done in cash. If I had ten thousand buildings to erect, I would never look to anybody else ; I would stick to my first love, for he has been faithful and true.

"I must pass on to another point, namely, *the present position of this project*. We have pushed beyond the era of objection to it. Now, those very wise friends (and they were very wise) who said the building ought not to be built, it would be too big, cannot undo it ; the only thing they can do is to help us through with it, for so much money has been spent already that we cannot propose to pull it down, however absurd the structure may be. Some of our brethren have asked, 'When Mr. Spurgeon dies, who will take his place?'—as if God could not raise up servants when He would, or as if we ought to neglect our present duty, because of something which may happen in fifty years' time. You say, perhaps, 'You give yourself a long lease,—fifty years.' I don't know why I should not have it; it may come to pass, and will, if the Lord has so ordained. Dr. Gill was chosen Pastor of this church when he was twenty-two, and he was more than fifty years its minister; Dr. Rippon was chosen at the age of twenty, and he was Pastor for

THE ELDERS' ROOM.

sixty-three years; I was nineteen when I was invited; and is it not possible that I also, by Divine grace, may serve my generation for a long period of time? At any rate, when I am proposing to commence a plan, I never think about whether I shall live to see it finished, for I am certain that, if it is God's plan, He will surely finish it, even if I should have to leave the work undone.

"I said, just now, that this project has gone beyond the era of objections; it has even passed beyond the realm of difficulties. We have had many difficulties, but far more providences. The ground was as much given to us by God as if He had sent an angel to clear it for us. The money, too, has been given, even beyond our hopes, and we have had it from quarters where we should least have expected it. All the Christian churches have contributed their portion, and almost all the ends of the earth have sent their offerings. From India, Australia, America, and everywhere, have we received something from God's people to help us in this work. We hope now we shall go on even to the end of it without feeling any diminution of our joy.

"Now I come to my closing remark, which is, *that we earnestly desire to open this place without a farthing of debt upon it.* You have heard that sentence again and again. Let me repeat it; and I pray that our brethren here, who have the command of the public press, will repeat it again and again for me. It is not because a small debt would weigh upon this church too much ; we are not afraid of that ; it is just this, we think it will tell well for the whole body of believers who rely upon the voluntary principle if this Tabernacle is completed without a loan or a debt. Our new place of worship has been spoken of in the House of Commons, it has been mentioned in the House of Lords ; and as everybody happens to know of it, since it stands so conspicuously, we want to do our utmost, and we ask our brethren to give us their help, that this forefront of Nonconformity, for the time being, may have about it no failure, no defeat to which anyone can point, and say, ' Your voluntaryism failed to carry the project through.' I believe in the might of the voluntary principle. I believe it to be perfectly irresistible in proportion to the power of God's Spirit in the hearts of those who exercise it. When the Spirit of God is absent, and the Church is at a low ebb, the voluntary principle has little or no power ; and then it becomes a question, with many carnal wise men, whether they shall not look to Egypt for help, and stay themselves on horses. But, when the Spirit of God is shed abroad, and men's hearts are in the right state, we find the voluntary principle equal to every need of the Church. Whenever I see members of any denomination turn aside, and begin to take so much as a single halfpenny from the hand of the State, I think they do not believe in their God as they ought, and that the Spirit of God is not with them in all His Divine power. Only give us a minister preaching Christ, and a people who will serve their God, and feel it to be their pleasure to devote themselves and their substance to His cause, and nothing is impossible.

"I ask you to prove this to all men ; and I appeal to you to help us in the effort to raise that remnant of £8,000. I believe we shall have a good and hearty response, and that, on the day of opening, we shall see this place filled with a vast multitude who will complete the work, and leave not a shilling unpaid. We pledge ourselves to the Christian public that they shall be no losers by us. While this building has been going on, we have done as much as any church for all other agencies,—as much as it was possible for us to do. We hope to help other places, by first giving to our young men an education when God has called them to the ministry, and afterwards helping them when they are settled. We wish our church to become a fruitful mother of children, and pray that God may make this Tabernacle a centre, from which rays of truth, and light, and glory, may radiate to dispel the darkness of the land. We will not be an idle church; we do not ask to have our load taken away, that we may eat, and drink, and play, but only that we may go straight on to do God's work. Of all things, I do abhor a debt. I shall feel like a guilty sneaking sinner if I come here with even a hundred pounds debt upon the building. 'Owe no man anything,' will stare me in the face whenever I try to address you. I do not believe that Scripture warrants any man in getting into debt. It may stimulate the people to raise more money; but, after all, attention to the simple Word of God is infinitely better than looking at the end which may be attained by the slightest deviation from it. Let us not owe a farthing to any living soul; and when we come here for the opening services, let us find that all has been paid."

In the course of the meeting, Mr. Spurgeon made other interesting remarks. After the address of the clergyman who had accepted his invitation to be present, and who had spoken with great heartiness of the Pastor and his work, Mr. Spurgeon said:—

"I thank my brother, the Rev. Hugh Allen, for coming here to-day. I know the opposition he has met with, and I believe he cares about as much for it as a bull does when a gnat settles on his horn. He shall have my pulpit at any time he likes,—I am quite sure he will commit no offence by preaching in it. I licensed Exeter Hall as a place of Dissenting worship, a few years ago, and the record stands on the book yet. If it is a sin for a clergyman to preach in a licensed place, there are one hundred clergymen who are great sinners, for about that number have since preached there."

Dr. Campbell having made some allusion to the name of the building, Mr. Spurgeon first stated that more than a million persons had contributed, chiefly in small sums, towards the erection of the Tabernacle, and then said:—"I am astonished at Dr. Campbell for not knowing that the word Tabernacle involves a religious doctrine, namely, that we have not come to the Temple-state here, we are now passing through the Tabernacle-state. We believe this building to be temporary, and only meant for the time that we are in the wilderness without a visible King. Our prayer is, 'Thy Kingdom come.' We do firmly believe in the real and personal reign of our Lord Jesus Christ, for which we devoutly wait. That is the reason why our new house of prayer is called a Tabernacle, not a Temple. We have not here the King in person, the Divine Solomon; till He come, we call it a Tabernacle still. Dr. Campbell and I will never quarrel for any precedence; his is a most mighty pen, he may have the kingdom of the pen if he will let me keep some part of the kingdom of the tongue. His pen is sharper and mightier than Ithuriel's spear; it has detected many of the toads of heresy, and transformed them to their right shape, and I have no doubt it will find out a great many more yet."

Mr. Spurgeon gave, at this meeting, a detailed and cheering account of the Continental tour which he had recently enjoyed, with Mrs. Spurgeon, Mr. Passmore, and another friend. The address was printed, shortly afterwards; but it contains so much interesting autobiographical information relating to the period, that at least a part of it must find a place here, to make the record as complete as possible. The Pastor said:—

"I have been requested by two well-known and deservedly eminent publishers to print some notes of my journey on the Continent; but I went there for rest and recreation, and I felt that this most sacred purpose could not be attained if I chained myself to the drudgery of book-writing. My congregation would have been disappointed if I had come home as tired as I went, and I could have had no solid excuse for ceasing my daily preaching if I had not really rested my weary brain. I believe, moreover, that the narrative of my journey will be far more valuable to me as a fountain of fresh illustrations and suggestions, than if I could pour it all out into a book. Will it not be better to retain my pearl, and let it glitter every now and then, than to melt it into one small draught, too shallow to satisfy the public thirst?

"I went from St. Katherine's Docks down the river, accompanied by my well-beloved deacons and several of my friends. At Gravesend, they left me and my party, with the kindest wishes, and with many a prayer to God for our safety. The journey was rendered abundantly pleasant by the evening which we spent together in prayer and fellowship before our departure. I never heard such kind words and such loving prayers uttered, concerning any human being, as I heard that night concerning myself. There was nothing like fulsome flattery, all the glory was given to God; but every brother invoked such choice blessings upon my head that I went away with a rich cargo of joy, knowing that a full wind of prayer was following behind.

"The captain of our vessel was from Essex, and as all Essex men have a high opinion of their countrymen, we soon found ourselves in full talk upon the excellences of our native county. Many were our anecdotes, and swiftly flew the time. Mine I have told so many times, I daresay you know them. Some of the captain's tales were new and original. I shall give you one, because it tends to illustrate the place in which we landed,—Antwerp. That city is so full of images of the Virgin Mary that you cannot turn the corner of a street without seeing them;

—sometimes under a canopy of many colours, arrayed in all manner of imitation jewellery, and at other times in neat little niches which seem to have been picked out of the wall for their special accommodation ; sometimes Mary is represented by an ugly black doll, and at other times by a decent respectable statue. So many of these objects are there, that the sailors may be excused for imagining every image which they see to be a Virgin Mary. One of them, who landed there, went to buy some tobacco ; and when he returned to the ship, his companions said, 'That is very good tobacco, Jack ; where did you get it ?' 'Oh !' he answered, 'you will know the shop, for there is a Virgin Mary sitting over the door, smoking a pipe.' I don't wonder at the man's blunder, for, among so many idols, one may easily mistake a Turk and his turban for the Virgin and her crown. I am sure they think vastly more of her than of our Lord Jesus Christ ; 'for, though we saw many crucifixes, and many representations of the Saviour, yet even in their image-work it seemed to me that the Virgin Mary was *cent per cent* beyond the Lord Jesus Christ.

" It happened, the very day we landed at Antwerp, that there was a grand procession just streaming in its full glory out of the cathedral, a fine and venerable building. There were priests in their robes, beadles resplendent in their livery, and a great number of men, whom I supposed to be penitents, carrying huge candles, certainly I should think two inches in diameter. These men walked two-and-two along the streets. Whether that burning of the candles typified the consumption of their sins, the melting of their church, or the illumination of soul which they so greatly needed, I do not know. There were also carried great lamps of silver, or electro-plate, very much like our own street lamps, only of course not quite so heavy ; and these, too, when the sun was shining brightly, and there was no need of the slightest artificial light. In all solemnity, the men marched along, not in the dark cathedral, but in the open streets, with these candles and lanterns blazing and shaming the sunlight. Someone told me they were taking 'the most blessed and comfortable sacrament' to some sick people ; but what the candles had to do with the sacrament, or the sacrament with the candles, or the people with the sacrament, I do not know. I noticed two little boys, very handsomely dressed, walking in the middle of the procession, and throwing flowers and oak leaves before the priests as they walked ; so that, as they went along, their holy feet scarcely needed to touch the soil, or to be hurt with the stones. The presence of those children, full of infantile joy, relieved the soul for a moment, and bade us pray that our own little ones might take part in a nobler celebration when the Lord Himself should come in the glory of His Father. Almost every house had, just before the window, a little place for holding a candle ; and as soon as the inmates heard the procession coming along, the candles were lighted. I noticed that, the moment it passed, the thrifty housewives blew out the lights, and so they saved their tallow if they did not save their souls. I enquired, and was informed—and I think on good authority,—that even some of the Protestants in Antwerp burn these candles in front of their houses lest their trade should be hindered if they did not conform to the customs of the rest of the people; it is an unutterable disgrace to them if they do so. I would like to have seen Martin Luther with a candle before his door when the priests were passing, unless, indeed, he had burned the Pope's Bull before their eyes. He would sooner have died than have paid respect to a baptized heathenism, a mass of idolatries and superstitions. Never did I feel my Protestant feelings boiling over so tremendously as in this city of idols, for I am not an outrageous Protestant generally, and I rejoice to confess that I feel sure there are some of God's people even in the Romish Church, as I shall have to show you by-and-by; but I did feel indignant when I saw the glory and worship, which belong to God alone, given to pictures, and images of wood and stone. When I saw the pulpits magnificently carved, the gems set in the shrines, the costly marbles, the rich and rare paintings upon which a man might gaze for a day, and see some new beauty in each face, I did not marvel that men were enchanted therewith; but when I saw the most flagrant violation of taste and of religion in their "Calvarys" and cheap prints, my spirit was stirred within me, for I saw a people wholly given unto idolatry. They seem as if they could not live without Mary the Virgin, and without continually paying reverence and adoration to her.

"We journeyed from Antwerp to Brussels. I cannot say that Brussels greatly interested me; I do not care much for places in which there is nothing but fine buildings and museums. I had much rather see an odd, old-fashioned city like Antwerp, with its sunny memories of Rubens, Quintin Matsys, and other princes in the realm of art. I think its singular houses, its quaint costumes, and its ancient streets, will never die out of my memory. In Brussels, I heard a good sermon in a Romish church. The place was crowded with people, many of them standing, though they might have had a seat for a halfpenny or a farthing; and I stood, too; and the good priest—for I believe he is a good man,—preached the Lord Jesus with all his might. He spoke of the love of Christ, so that I, a very poor hand at the French language, could fully understand him, and my heart kept beating within me as he told of the beauties of Christ, and the preciousness of His blood, and of His power to save the chief of sinners. He did not say, 'justification by faith,' but he did say, 'efficacy of the blood,' which comes to very much the same thing. He did not tell us we were saved by grace, and not by our works; but he did say that all the works of men were less than nothing when brought into competition with the blood of Christ, and that the blood of Jesus alone could save. True, there were objectionable sentences, as naturally there must be in a discourse delivered under such circumstances; but I could have gone to the preacher, and have said to him,

'Brother, you have spoken the truth;' and if I had been handling his text, I must have treated it in the same way that he did, if I could have done it as well. I was pleased to find my own opinion verified, in his case, that there are, even in the apostate church, some who cleave unto the Lord,—some sparks of Heavenly fire that flicker amidst the rubbish of old superstition, some lights that are not blown out, even by the strong wind of Popery, but still cast a feeble gleam across the waters sufficient to guide the soul to the rock Christ Jesus. I saw, in that church, a box for contributions for the Pope; he will never grow rich with what I put into it. I have seen money-boxes on the Continent for different saints,—Santa Clara, St. Francis, St. Dominic; another box for the Virgin, and another for the poor; but I never could make out how the money got to the Virgin, and to Dominic, and to the rest of them; but I have a notion that, if you were to discover how the money gets to the poor, you would find how it reaches the saints.

"After leaving Brussels, and getting a distant glimpse of the Lion Mound of Waterloo, we hurried down to Namur, and steamed along the Meuse,—that beautiful river, which is said to be an introduction to the Rhine, but which to my mind is a fair rival to it; it quite spoiled me for the Rhine. Everywhere, on each side, there were new phases of beauty, and sweet little pictures which shone in the sunshine like small but exquisite gems. It was not one vast Koh-i-noor diamond; it was not sublimity mingling its awe with loveliness such as you would see in Switzerland with its majestic mountains, but a succession of beautiful pearls, threaded on the silver string of that swiftly-flowing river. It is so narrow and shallow that, as the steamboat glides along, it drives up a great wave upon the banks on either side. In some parts, along the river, there were signs of mineral wealth, and the people were washing the ironstone at the water's edge to separate the ore from the earth.

"One thing which I saw here I must mention, as it is a type of a prevailing evil in Belgium. When there were barges of ironstone to be unloaded, *the women* bore the heavy baskets upon their backs. If there were coals or bricks to be carried, the women did it; they carried everything; and their lords and masters sat still, and seemed to enjoy seeing them at work, and hoped it might do them good, while they themselves were busily engaged in the important occupation of smoking their pipes. When we came to a landing-place, if the rope was to be thrown off so that the steam-boat might be secured, there was always a woman to run and seize it, and there stood a big, lazy fellow to give directions as to how she should do it. We joked with each other upon the possibility of getting our wives to do the like; but, indeed, it is scarcely a joking matter to see poor women compelled to work like slaves, as if they were only made to support their husbands in idleness. They were fagged and worn; but they looked more fully developed than the men, and seemed to be more masculine. If I had been one of those women, and I had got a little bit of a husband sitting there smoking his pipe, if there is a law in Belgium that gives a woman two months for beating her husband, I fear I should have earned the penalty. Anyhow, I would have said to him, 'I am very much obliged to you for doing me the honour of marrying me; but, at the same time, if I am to work and earn *your* living and my own, too, you will smoke your pipe somewhere else.' The fact is, my dear friends, to come to something that may be worth our thinking about, employment for women is greatly needed in our country, and the want of it is a very great evil; but it is not so much to be deplored as that barbarity which dooms women to sweep the streets, to till the fields, to carry heavy burdens, and to be the drudges of the family. We greatly need that watchmaking, printing, telegraphing, bookselling, and other indoor occupations should be more freely open to female industry, but may Heaven save our poor women from the position of their Continental sisters! The gospel puts woman where she should be, gives her an honourable position in the house and in the Church; but where women become the votaries of superstition, they will soon be made the burden-bearers of society. Our best feelings revolt at the idea of putting fond, faithful, and affectionate women to oppressive labour. Our mothers, our sisters, our wives, our daughters are much too honourable in our esteem to be treated otherwise than as dear companions, for whom it shall be our delight to live and labour.

"We went next to a sweet little village called Chaufontaine, surrounded with verdant hills, and so truly rural, that one could forget that there was such a place as a busy, noisy, distracting world. Here we found the villagers at work making gun-barrels with old-fashioned tilt-hammers. Here for the first time we saw industrious men. Talk about long hours in England! These blacksmiths rise at four o'clock in the morning, and I do not know when they leave off; only this I know, that we passed by them very late, and found them still hard at work at the blazing forge, hammering away at the gun-barrels, welding the iron into a tube, working almost without clothing, the sweat pouring down them, and mingling with the black and soot of their faces.

"The real workers on the Continent seem to be always toiling, and never appear to stop at all, except at dinner-time. Then you may go to the shop, and knock until your arm aches, but there is nobody to sell you anything; they are all having their dinner. That is a most important operation, and they do not like to come out even to wait upon a customer. I knocked a long time at a door in Zurich where I wanted to buy a print; but the man had gone to his dinner, so I had to wait till he had finished. That breaking up of the day, I have no doubt tends, after all, to shorten the hours of labour; but there is work to be done in the villages of the Continent by the Early Closing Association,—it will be well if they can persuade people that they can do quite as much if they work fewer hours. In the country villages, science appears to be very backward. My friend declared that he saw the linchpin of a waggon which weighed two pounds ; I never saw such a huge linchpin anywhere else. And as to the carts and waggons, they were like racks put on a couple of pairs of wheels, and in every case five times as heavy as they need be ; and thus the horses have a load to begin with before the cart is loaded. On the Continent, I think they have, in some towns and cities, made progress superior to our own ; but in the rural parts of any country you like to choose, you would find them far behind our village population. The intelligence of those countries is centered in the large towns, and it does not radiate and spread its healthy influence in the rural districts so swiftly as in our own beloved land. It is well to see progress even in these social matters, because, as men advance in arts and commerce, it often happens that they are brought into contact with other lands, and so the Word of God becomes more widely known. I believe every steam-engine, every railroad, every steamboat, and every threshing-machine, to be a deadly enemy to ignorance ; and what is ignorance but the corner-stone of superstition ?

"As everybody who goes on the Continent visits Cologne, so did we ; but I must say of Cologne that I have a more vivid recollection of what I smelt than of what I saw. The Cologne odour is more impressive than the Eau de Cologne. I had heard Albert Smith say he believed there were eighty-three distinct bad smells in Cologne, and in my opinion he understated the number, for every yard presented something more terrible than we had ever smelt before. Better to pay our heavy taxes for drainage than live in such odours. Our filthy friend, the Thames, is as sweet as rose-water when compared with Cologne or Frankfort. Hear this, ye grumblers, and be thankful that you are not worse off than you are ! We went down the Rhine ; and it was just a repetition of what we saw down the Meuse, with the addition of castles and legends. My want of taste is no doubt the cause of my disappointment upon seeing this river. The lakes of Westmoreland and Cumberland, and the lochs of Scotland, fairly rival the Rhine, and are of much the same character. Go and see for yourselves, and you will not repent it.

"We went across to Frankfort and Heidelberg, and then to Baden-Baden. Let me say a few words about Baden. I went to see the gaming-table there ; it was, without exception, the most mournful sight I ever looked upon. The Conversation House at Baden is a gorgeous building. Wealth could not make it more splendid than it is. All the luxuries that can be gathered from the very ends of the earth are lavished there. It is a fairy palace, more like the fantastic creation of a dream than sober substantial fact. You are freely admitted ; no charge is made, whilst the most beautiful music that can be found waits to charm your ear. Every place of amusement is free ; even the public library is free. You ask me how all this is supported. To the left of the building there are two rooms for gaming. There is a long table, and a great crowd standing round it ; the seats are all full, and there sit four men in the middle with long rakes, pulling money this way and that way, and shoving it here and there. I hardly ever saw such a mass of money, except upon a banker's counter. There are long piles of gold done up in marked quantities, and there are also heaps of silver money. You see a young man come in ; he does not seem like a gambler. He puts down a half-napoleon as a mere joke : in a minute it is shovelled away ; he has lost his money. He walks round again, and puts down another piece of gold ; this time he wins, and he has two. By-and-by he will play more deeply, and the day will probably come when he will stake his all, and lose it. You may see women sitting there all night playing for high stakes. Some people win, but everybody must lose sooner or later, for the chances are dreadfully against any man who plays. The bank clears an enormous sum every year ; I am afraid to mention the amount lest I should be thought to exaggerate. What staring eyes, what covetous looks, what fiery faces I saw there ! And what multitudes go into that place happy, and return to curse the day of their birth ! I had the sorrow of seeing some fools play. I saw young men, who lost so much that they had hardly enough to take them back to England. Such is the infatuation that I am not surprised when spectators are carried away by the torrent. There are some who defend the system ; I hold it to be fraught with more deadly evils than anything else that could be invented, even by Satan himself. I saw an old respectable-looking man put down ten pounds. He won, and he received twenty. He put down the twenty : he won again, and he had forty. He put down the forty, and received eighty. He put down the eighty, and took up one hundred and sixty pounds. Then he put it all in his pocket, and walked away as calmly as possible. The man would lose money by that transaction, because he would go back on the morrow, and probably play till he would sell the house that covers his children's heads, and pawn the very bed from under his wife. The worst thing that can happen to a man who gambles is to win. If you lose, it serves you right, and there is hope that you will repent of your folly ; if you win, the devil will have you in his net so thoroughly that escape will be well-nigh impossible. I charge every young man here, above all things never have anything to do with games of chance. If you desire to make your damnation doubly sure, and ruin both body and soul, go to the gaming-table ; but if not, avoid it, pass by it, look not at it, for it has a basilisk's eye, and may entice you ; and it has the sting of an adder, and will certainly destroy you if you come beneath its deadly influence.

"From Baden-Baden, we went to Freiburg, and afterwards to Schaffhausen. There, for the first time, we saw the Alps. It was a wonderful sight, though in the dim distance we hardly knew whether we saw clouds or mountains. We had to hold a sort of controversy with ourselves,—'Is that solid—that glittering whiteness, that sunny shimmering that we see there? Is it a bank of white mist? Is it cloud, or is it a mountain?' Soon you are assured that you are actually beholding the everlasting hills. If a man does not feel like praising God at such a moment, I do not think there is any grace in him; if there be anything like piety in a man's soul when he sees those glorious works of God, he will begin to praise the Lord, and magnify His holy Name. We went from Schaffhausen to Zurich. Everywhere there was something to delight us. The magnificent falls of the Rhine, the clear blue waters of the Zurich lake, the distant mountains, the ever-changing costumes of the people, —all kept us wide awake, and gratified our largest love of novelties. All nature presented us with a vast entertainment, and every turn of the head introduced us to something new and beautiful.

"At Zurich, I saw in the great fair what I also saw at Baden-Baden, a sight which gave me pleasure, namely, the little star of truth shining brightly amid the surrounding darkness. Opposite the house at Baden where Satan was ruining souls at the gaming-table, there was a stall at which an agent of the Bible Society was selling Bibles and Testaments. I went up and bought a Testament of him, and felt quite cheered to see the little battery erected right before the fortifications of Satan, for I felt in my soul it was mighty through God to the pulling down of the stronghold. Then, in the midst of the fair at Zurich, where the people were selling all manner of things, as at John Bunyan's Vanity Fair, there stood a humble-looking man with his stall, upon which there were Bibles, Testaments, and Mr. Ryle's tracts. It is always a great comfort to me to see my sermons, in French and other languages, sold at the same shops as the writings of that excellent man of God. There is the simple gospel in his tracts, and they are to my knowledge singularly owned of God. How sweet it is to see these dear brethren in other churches loving our Lord, and honoured by Him!

"At Lucerne, we spent our third Sabbath-day. Of all days in the year, Sabbath-days on the Continent are the most wretched, so far as the public means of grace are concerned; this one, however, was spent in quiet worship in our own room. Our first Sabbath was a dead waste, for the service at church was lifeless, spiritless, graceless, powerless. Even the grand old prayers were so badly read that it was impossible to be devout while hearing them, and the sermon upon 'the justice of God in destroying the Canaanites' was as much adapted to convert a sinner, or to edify a saint, as Burke's Peerage, or Walker's Dictionary; there was nothing, however, Puseyistical or heretical. Far worse was our second Sunday, in Baden, which effectually prevented my attending Episcopal service again until I can be sure of hearing truthful doctrine. The preacher was manifestly a downright Puseyite because, during one part of the service, he must needs go up to the Roman Catholic altar, and there bow himself with his back to us. The images and idols were not concealed in any way ; there they were in all their open harlotry, and I must say they were in full keeping with the sermon which was inflicted upon us. The preacher thought he would give us a smart hit, so he began with an attack upon all who did not subscribe to baptismal regeneration and sacramental efficacy. He did not care what we might say, he was certain that, when the holy drops fell from the fingers of God's ordained minister, regeneration there and then took place. I thought, ' Well, that is coming out, and the man is more honest than some of the wolves in sheep's clothing, who hold baptismal regeneration, but will not openly confess it.' The whole sermon through, he treated us to sacramental efficacy, and made some allusion to St. George's riots, saying that it was an awful thing that the servants of God were subjected to persecution, and then he told us we had not sufficient respect for our ministers, that the real ordained successors of the apostles were trodden down as mire in the streets. I abstained from going to church after that ; and if I were to continue for seven years without the public means of grace, unless I knew that a man of kindred spirit with Mr. Allen, Mr. Cadman, Mr. Ryle, and that holy brotherhood of Evangelicals, would occupy the pulpit, I never would enter an Anglican church again. These Puseyites make good Churchmen turn to the Dissenters, and we who already dissent, are driven further and further from the Establishment. In the name of our Protestant religion, I ask whether a minister of the Church of England is allowed to bow before the altar of a Popish church? Is there no rule or canon which restrains men from such an outrage upon our professed faith, such an insult to our Constitution? In the church at Lucerne, I think they had the head of John the Baptist, with some of the blood in a dish, and other relics innumerable ; yet I was expected to go on Sunday, and worship there! I could not do it, for I should have kept on thinking of John the Baptist's head in the corner. Though I have a great respect for that Baptist, and all other Baptists, I do not think I could have controlled myself sufficiently to worship God under such circumstances.

"We went up the Rigi, as everybody must do who visits the Alps, toiling up, up, up, ever so high, to see the sun go to bed ; and then we were awakened in the morning, with a dreadful blowing of horns, to get up and see the sun rise. Out we went, but his gracious majesty, the sun, would not condescend to show himself ; or, at least, he had been up half-an-hour before we knew it ; so we all went down again, and that was the end of our glorious trip. Yet it was worth while to go up to see the great mountains all around us, it was a sight which might make an angel stand and gaze, and gaze again ; the various sharp or rounded peaks and snowy summits, are all worthy of the toil which brings them into view. The circular panorama seen from the Rigi-Kulm is perhaps unrivalled. There is the lake of Zug, there the long arms of Lucerne, yonder Mount Pilatus, and further yet the Black Forest range. Just at your feet is the buried town of Goldau, sad tomb in which a multitude were crushed by a falling mountain. The height is dizzy to unaccustomed brains, but the air is bracing, and the prospect such as one might picture from the top of Pisgah, where the prophet of Horeb breathed out his soul to God.

"We went here, there, and everywhere, and saw everything that was to be seen; and, at last, after a long journey, we came to Geneva. I had received the kindest invitation from our esteemed and excellent brother, Dr. D'Aubigné. He came to meet me at the station, but he missed me. I met a gentleman in the street, and told him I was Mr. Spurgeon. He then said, 'Come to my house,—the very house where Calvin used to live.' I went home with him; and after we found Dr. D'Aubigné and Pastor Bard, I was taken to the house of Mr. Lombard, an eminent banker of the city, and a godly and gracious man. I think I never enjoyed a time more than I did with those real true-hearted brethren. There are, you know, two churches there,—the Established and the Free; and there has been some little bickering and some little jealousy, but I think it is all dying away; at any rate, I saw none of it, for brethren from both these churches came, and showed me every kindness and honour. I am not superstitious, but the first time I saw this medal, bearing the venerated likeness of John Calvin, I kissed it, imagining that no one saw the action. I was very greatly surprised when I received this magnificent present, which shall be passed round for your inspection. On the one side is John Calvin

FACSIMILE OF CALVIN MEDAL PRESENTED TO MR. SPURGEON AT GENEVA

with his visage worn by disease and deep thought, and on the other side is a verse fully applicable to him : 'He endured, as seeing Him who is invisible.' This sentence truly describes the character of that glorious man of God.   Among all those who have been born of women, there has not risen a greater than John Calvin ; no age before him ever produced his equal, and no age afterwards has seen his rival. In theology, he stands alone, shining like a bright fixed star, while other leaders and teachers can only circle round him, at a great distance,—as comets go streaming through space,—with nothing like his glory or his permanence.   Calvin's fame is eternal because of the truth he proclaimed ; and even in Heaven, although we shall lose the name of the system of doctrine which he taught, it shall be that truth which shall make us strike our golden harps, and sing, 'Unto Him that loved us, and washed us from our sins in His own blood, and hath made us kings and priests unto God and His Father ; to Him be glory and dominion for ever and ever ;' for the essence of Calvinism is that we are born again, 'not of blood, nor of the will of the flesh, nor of the will of man, but of God.'

"I preached in the cathedral at Geneva ; and I thought it a great honour to be allowed to stand in the pulpit of John Calvin.   I do not think half the people understood me ; but they were very glad to see and join *in heart* with the worship in which they could not join with the understanding.   I did not feel very happy when I came out in full canonicals, but the request was put to me in such a beautiful way that I could have worn the Pope's tiara, if by so doing I could have preached the gospel the more freely.   They said, 'Our dear brother comes to us from another country.   Now, when an ambassador comes from another land, he has the right to wear his own costume at Court ; but, as a mark of great esteem, he sometimes condescends to the manners of the people he is visiting, and wears their Court dress.' 'Well,' I said, 'yes, that I will, certainly, if you do not require it, but merely ask it as a token of my Christian love.   I shall feel like running in a sack, but it will be your fault.'   It was John Calvin's gown, and that reconciled me to it very much. I do love that man of God ; suffering all his life long, enduring not only persecutions from without but a complication of disorders from within, and yet serving his Master with all his heart.

"I ask your prayers for the Church at Geneva.   That little Republic stands now, like an island as it were, on each side shut in by France, and I can assure you there are no greater Anti-Gallicans in the whole world than the Genevese.   Without knowing that I trod upon tender ground, I frequently said, 'Why, you are almost French people!'   At last they hinted to me that they did not like me to say so, and I did not say it any more.   They are afraid of being Frenchified : they cannot endure the thought of it ; they know the sweets of liberty, and cannot bear that they should be absorbed into that huge monarchy.   Dr. D'Aubigné charged me with this message, 'Stir up the Christians of England to make Geneva a matter of special prayer.   We do not dread the arms of France, nor invasion ; but something worse than that, namely, the introduction of French principles.' There is a French population constantly crossing the border; they bring in infidelity, and neglect of the

THE PULPIT, ST. PETER'S CATHEDRAL, GENEVA.
(*Calvin's chair stands on the floor below the pulpit.*)

Sabbath-day, and Romanism is making very great advances. The brethren said, 'Ask the people to pray for us, that we may stand firm and true. As we have been the mother of many churches, desert us not in the hour of our need, but hold us up in your arms, and pray that the Lord may still make Geneva a praise throughout the earth.' After the service in the cathedral, it was arranged for me to meet the ministers ; D'Aubigné was there, of course, and Cæsar Malan, and most of the noted preachers of Switzerland. We spent a very delightful evening together, talking about our common Lord, and of the progress of His work in England and on the Continent ; and when they bade me 'Good-bye,' every one of those ministers—a hundred and fifty, or perhaps two hundred of them,—kissed me on both cheeks ! It was rather an ordeal for me, but it was meant to express their esteem and regard, and I accepted it in the spirit in which it was given. It was a peculiar pleasure to me to have the opportunity of visiting that great centre of earnest Protestantism, and of meeting so many of the godly and faithful men who had helped to keep the lamp of truth burning brightly. To my dying day, I shall remember those servants of Jesus Christ who greeted me in my Master's name, and loved me for my Master's sake. Hospitality unbounded, love unalloyed, and communion undisturbed, are precious pens with which the brethren in Geneva wrote their names upon my heart.

"At last we got away from Geneva, and went off to Chamouni. What a glorious place that Chamouni is ! My heart flies thither in recollection of her glories. The very journey from Geneva to Chamouni fires one's heart. The mind longs to climb the heavens as those mountains do. It seemed to sharpen my soul's desires and longings till, like the peaks of the Alps, I could pierce the skies. I cannot speak as I should if I had one of those mountains in view ; if I could point out of the window, and say, 'There! see its frosted brow! see its ancient hoary head!' and then speak to you of the avalanches that come rattling down the side, then I think I could give you some poetry. We went up the Mer de Glace on mules. I had the great satisfaction of hearing three or four avalanches come rolling down like thunder. In descending, I was in advance, and alone ; I sat down and mused, but I soon sprang up, for I thought the avalanche was coming right on me, there was such a tremendous noise. We crossed many places where the snow, in rushing down from the top, had swept away every tree and every stone, and left nothing but the stumps of the trees, and a kind of slide from the top of the mountain to the very valley. What extraordinary works of God there are to be seen there ! We have no idea of what God Himself is. As I went among those mountains and valleys, I felt like a little creeping insect. I sank lower and lower, and grew smaller and smaller, while my soul kept crying out,—

> "'Great God, how infinite art Thou!
> What worthless worms are we!'

"After leaving Chamouni, we came at last to what was to be the great treat of our journey, namely, the passage of the Simplon. The crossing of that mountain is an era in any man's life. That splendid road was carried over the Alps by Napoleon, not for the good of his species, but in order that he might transport his cannon to fight against Austria. Sir James Mackintosh described the Simplon road as 'the most wonderful of useful works.' There are other works which may contain more genius, and some which may seem to be more grand ; but this, in the midst of the rugged stern simplicity of nature, seemed to say, ' Man is little, but over God's greatest works man can find a pathway, and no dangers can confine his ambition.' Where the rock was so steep that the road could not be made by any other means, workmen were hung down from the top in cradles, and they chipped a groove, and thus carried the road along the precipitous face of the rock ; frequently, too, it was made to run through a huge tunnel cut in the solid rock. On and on we went up the enormous height until we came to the region of perpetual frost and snow. There one could make snowballs in the height of summer, and gather ice in abundance. On the top of the mountain stands the hospice ; there were some four or five monks, who came out and asked us to enter ; we did so, and would honour the religious feeling which dictates such constant hospitality. We were shown into a very nice room, where there was cake and wine ready, and if we had chosen to order it; meat, soup, and anything we liked to have, and nothing to pay. They entertain any traveller, and he is expected to pay nothing whatever for his refreshment ; of course, no one who could afford it would go away without putting something into the poor-box. It pleased me to find that they were Augustinian monks because, next to Calvin, I love Augustine. I feel that Augustine's works were the great mine out of which Calvin dug his mental wealth ; and the Augustinian monks, in their acts of charity, seemed to say, ' Our master was a teacher of grace, and we will practise it, and give to all comers whatsoever they shall need, without money and without price.' Those monks are worthy of great honour ; there they are, spending the best and noblest period of their lives on the top of a bleak and barren mountain, that they may minister to the necessities of the poor. They go out in the cold nights, and bring in those that are frostbitten ; they dig them out from under the snow, simply that they may serve God by helping their fellow-men. I pray God to bless the good works of these monks of the Augustinian Order, and may you and I carry out the spirit of Augustine, which is the true spirit of Christ, the spirit of love, the spirit of charity, the spirit which loves truth, and the spirit which loves man, and above all, loves the Man Christ Jesus ! We never need fear, with our strong doctrines, and the spirit of our Master in us, that we shall be carried away by the heresies which continually arise, and which would deceive, if it were possible, even the very elect.

" If any of you can save up money—after this Tabernacle is paid for,—to go to Switzerland, you will never regret it, and it need not be expensive to you. If you do not find your head grow on both sides, and have to put your hands up, and say, ' I feel as if my brains are straining with their growth, I do not think you have many brains to spare. As I have stood in the midst of those mountains and valleys, I have wished I could carry you all there. I cannot reproduce to you the thoughts that then passed through my mind; I cannot describe the storms we saw below us when we were on the top of the hill; I cannot tell you about the locusts that came in clouds, and devoured everything before them; time would utterly fail me to speak of all the wonders of God which we saw in nature and in providence. One more remark, and I have done. If you cannot travel, remember that our Lord Jesus Christ is more glorious than all else that you could ever see. Get a view of Christ, and you have seen more than mountains, and cascades, and valleys, and seas can ever show you. Thunders may bring their sublimest uproar, and lightnings their awful glory; earth may give its beauty, and stars their brightness; but all these put together can never rival HIM, of whom Dr. Watts so well sang,—

> "'Now to the Lord a noble song!
> Awake, my soul, awake, my tongue;
> Hosannah to th' Eternal Name,
> And all His boundless love proclaim.
>
> See where it shines in Jesus face,
> The brightest image of His grace;
> God, in the person of His Son,
> Has all His mightiest works outdone.
>
> The spacious earth and spreading flood
> Proclaim the wise and powerful God,
> And Thy rich glories from afar
> Sparkle in every rolling star.
>
> But in His looks a glory stands,
> The noblest labour of Thine hands;
> The pleasing lustre of His eyes
> Outshines the wonders of the skies.
>
> Grace! 'tis a sweet, a charming theme;
> My thoughts rejoice at Jesus' Name:
> Ye angels, dwell upon the sound,
> Ye heavens, reflect it to the ground!'"

In the course of the day, a total of £1,050 was added to the Tabernacle Building Fund. During the time that the great sanctuary was being completed, the remainder of the amount required was raised, so that the first Sabbath services in the new house of prayer were conducted in a building entirely free from debt.